CONTENTS

ACKNOWLEDGMENTS

A large percentage of the jokes, urban myths and illustrations in this book will be vaguely familiar to many readers because they all belong to that mysterious creative process we call *folklore*. Just as mysterious is their creative origin and ownership, with most jokes happily residing under the banner of 'anonymous'. This is both a joke book and a serious attempt to understand where jokes come from, how they are circulated and, most importantly, how we use humour in our lives. It is also a study of how the Internet has developed to become an important distributor of folklore, and humour in particular.

I am indebted to the many people who assisted me in collecting the examples cited in the book. In particular I thank Russell 'Big Russ' Hannah, Mike Salter, Stephen Wall, Morag White, Doug Ford, Richard Mills, Julian Ward, Keith McKenry, Stuart McCarthy, Tim Nicholas, Jim Leesses, Vincent Brophy, Rob Willis, Carol Higman, Stuart Coupe, Valda and Jim Law, Greg Bracketeer, Roger Holmes, Geoff Morgan, Bruce Cameron, Paul Hemphill, Geoff Francis, Peter Hicks, John Thompson, Gilly Darby, Greg Peacock, Garth Nix, Jeanette Wormold, Kate Andrews, Marcus Holden, David Gool, Stephen Elliott, Rebel Penfold-Russell, Paul Stewart, David Mulhallen, Mark Cavanagh and Rowan Webb. My mate Marita Blood gets a gong for the most prolific and eclectic joke sender in Australia. I also thank the anonymous creators and those who dutifully pass these jokes into cyberspace. Obviously there is absolutely no way to identify individual ownership of particular illustrations or jokes and I take this opportunity to thank anyone who has discovered their work in this collection. You should be flattered that your creation has tickled the fancy of folklore and found its own journey into cyberspace.

A word about censorship: don't. I do not believe in outright censorship of jokes, especially in a collection such as this. By all means censor what you send out in e-mails, definitely censor yourself if you are telling jokes live, and you probably shouldn't give this book to your great, great Aunty Fanny. Take the jokes in the spirit of humour and as an indication of what tickles the Australian funny bone.

Warren Fahey AM
Australian Folklore Unit
www.warrenfahey.com

INTRODUCTION: NO LAUGHING MATTER

No one really knows where jokes come from but we do know that they come in all shapes and sizes, and have a habit of returning just when you thought they had disappeared. Some say that there are only a dozen or so original jokes and all others are simply clever variants. I do not subscribe to this train of thought and believe human creativity extends a hell of a lot further than a baker's dozen. The same argument has been applied to traditional music, in that there are only a handful of basic tunes and all others are but variations. This is insensitive nonsense aimed at undervaluing traditional creativity and, more importantly, it doesn't stand the test of time. Traditional tunes are like pearls that have been honed in their shells with every new wave adding more polish to the gem. The same process applies to stories and, to some extent, jokes, in that they are continually changing depending on the whim and will of the person currently 'minding' that story.

I attempt to explain in my *Classic Bush Yarns* (HarperCollins, 2001) how the joke, or, in that particular case, the Australian tall story, was created and passed on in the tradition. I also suggested that because of the dramatic ways we have changed our entertainment patterns — being *entertained* rather than actually entertaining each other — the role of the joke-teller has changed. This book clearly shows how contemporary entertainment continues to change rapidly and especially the dominating role of the electronic media and the World Wide Web in particular.

The Internet has come to the forefront in disseminating jokes. We still tell jokes across the dinner table and at the club and pub but it is obvious from this recent study that the Internet has emerged as a major, if not *the* major, distribution vehicle. I would suggest that because e-mail now plays such an accepted and widespread role in most Australian offices, it stands to reason that it would also be used for non-office work, including entertainment. I also believe, because of the growing number of people working from home offices, the art of e-mail conversation has become an important diversion. Jokes are 'passed on' via e-mails in a conversational style reminiscent of the idle chatter one would find in the office coffee room.

There is also the growing army of 'recreational computer users', primarily younger and older people, who use the Internet as a means of communication between friends and for basic entertainment. It has been particularly interesting to see the large number of elderly Australians who are now 'wired' and see the passing on of humour as part of their daily routine.

Certain demographics prefer circulating jokes that are relevant to their circle of e-mail friends — their e-mail address lists. Young people prefer mobile text messages as a means of communication, probably viewing e-mails as too laborious and serious, and, as we know, they invent their own text languages in order to make these communications more personal. Teenagers, the high-tech generation, usually send a wide range of e-mails including humour related to their 'tribes' (surfer, skateboard, sport, music, school gang etc), and material related to youth popular culture, especially popular gossip snippets about celebrities. Once in the 'serious' workforce, and especially work entailing access to computers, and if they can get around company-enforced 'use of computer' regulations, this group appears to send millions of jokes on a daily basis. Their choice of humour is wide but certain subjects dominate; in particular, sport, sex, work, transport and, once again, celebrity gossip. Middle-aged folk seem to delight in humour about marriage, sex, children, dogs, sport and divorce. Older people, not surprisingly, send each other humour about aging, dealing with technology, sex, or lack of it, and death.

Without a doubt it is the office environment where the bulk of e-mail jokes originate. Remember when the folk circulated jokes on printed sheets? Many of these were work subject related and dealt with stress, sex and office management, and, as often as not, they would depict a worker in some unfathomable dilemma. They were usually funny and aimed at getting a shared laugh from the casual passer-by. They were small posters and stuck to walls, doors and filing cabinets. Sometimes they would mysteriously appear on the office notice board explaining 'new office regulations' or '10 reasons why the boss is a bastard'. Folklorists called these 'photocopy lore', and true to folklore's 'here today gone tomorrow' spirit, they seem to have almost disappeared, to be replaced by the same cartoons, sets of rules etc arriving on desks via the small screen. The beauty of e-mail is that it can blast the folklore to many screens in one push of the send key. Instant folklore!

The real wonder of the Internet is that it not only zips all around the office but it can also instantly send the message all over the country and all over the world. The jokes coming out of the September 11th 2001 terrorist attacks on America certainly showed the relevance and vitality of net transmission, arriving on Australian desks at the very same time as American desks. This particular collection of jokes started life the week after the attack on the Twin Towers and has provided a five-year survey of e-mail humour distribution. Obviously I had thousands of jokes to study and also the restriction of having to select a representative and entertaining collection. I then had to consider the restrictions of subject categories such as politics, travel, marriage etc in which to represent the jokes without becoming too bogged down in semantics. Above all, I hope to provide a good belly laugh and to show evidence of a particular Australian sense of humour. I have provided a short introduction to each section — so as to set the scene.

Folklore is a confusing word that carries a considerable amount of baggage. At the same time it has become an increasingly important tool in tracking our cultural roots, and especially how we cope with these stressful times. In a nutshell it is the lore we unconsciously create or pass on to our family and associated communities to distinguish ourselves as a people. We use folklore as an important part of our lives, passing on, among other things, traditional wisdom, values, custom, family history and, of course, humour. E-mail jokes are a very active part of the folklore process, usually being anonymous in origin and circulated in the same way we traditionally passed on spoken yarns. Many of the jokes are sent under the familiar guise of 'this is true and happened to a friend of a friend'.

Pundits now preach that we are rapidly headed for a global world where we have one currency, one language and one government. One assumes that they would also like to add the words 'one culture' to that scary list. Some say globalisation is tantamount to treason; however, the fact remains that we haven't been able to make the present systems work effectively and the world continues to sit under the gloomy clouds of terrorism, local war, poverty, greed, racial inequality and religious fanaticism. Because our lives have become so fractured we need to look at folklore to provide us with keys to some of the puzzles we face. Humour is an important tool in relieving our communal attitude to stressful situations and bad times.

One of the main showcase arguments of the global community is the promotion of world culture, and in many ways this has created an economic dilemma. When one considers the massive investments the popular culture machines of Hollywood, New York and London now make in their supposed blockbuster films, hit recordings and mass-marketed books, it is obvious that they need larger markets than their domestic one to recoup their investment. Australia, being an English-speaking nation, is a prime target for such cultural invasion and this needs to be stacked up against our Government's rulings on such things as Australian content levels on radio, television and in publishing. Personally I don't think we have been very successful in protecting or policing our cultural content levels; however, that is another argument for another platform.

Small nations, and Australia is a relatively small population, need to be aware of protecting their culture. It is inevitable that the blockbusters will keep coming and, to be brutally frank, who would want to be the spoilsport to stop them? What we do need is to accept that there is such a thing as an international culture and, at the same time, be aware that we also have our own 'home-grown' culture. Both can and should live in harmony, even if many nations appear unable to achieve such a relationship. In the case of Australia we are indeed fortunate in being an island floating in the Pacific Ocean and not a country surrounded by borders and other directly intrusive cultures.

Such physical isolation begs the question as to whether this is the key to our collective sense of humour. Australians have a reputation for possessing a laconic sense of humour best described as 'dry'. It has always seen the perverted comic side of misfortune, be it in the convict barracks, goldfields, shearing shed, or the pioneering family facing a seemingly never-ending cycle of flood, drought, bushfire and pestilence and commenting that things are 'as good as they get'.

It was during the pioneering 19th century that we really honed many areas of our national identity. The fact that the majority of our population lived in the bush rather than on the coast played a leading role in that identity, and also explains why so many urban-dwelling Australians still see themselves as bushwhackers complete with RM Williams clothing, Akubra hat and four-wheel drive. This overt Aussie-ism also shows itself in our attitude to humour; how we see ourselves identifying with the typical Australian bush stereotype.

Communities create and use folklore in many ways to record their history, celebrate success, express frustration, and to share despair and grief. It can be seen as a mechanism which allows us to look at our emotional sense. The epic poems and ballads composed centuries ago and passed on down through the years are folklore. The old bush songs of Australia that tell of our pioneering days are folklore. I use these two musical examples because most people associate folklore with folk song. The truth is that we all create and pass on lore and nowadays it is more likely to be an urban myth, yarn, word usage or some custom that seems to be a natural part of everyday life. Our lives abound in folklore and especially when we look at how we celebrate: for example, a death, birth or wedding. We take such customs and habits for granted even though much of the meaning behind the lore is symbolic and often long forgotten. Humour ranks high on these lists.

Jokes, be they spoken or transmitted electronically via the Internet, have become an important part of the folklore process and especially in these times of international uncertainty. Much has been spoken and written about the terrorist attack on America and most agree that this was indeed an unprecedented and horrific event in modern world history; however, this has not stopped us creating and passing on humour related to disaster and horror. The interesting aspect of this particular disaster is that we in Australia were intimately involved through the direct television coverage and the Internet. There was, of course, the fact that a number of Australians were working in the targeted buildings. This made us part of the story and, for that reason, closer to that particular horror. This closeness had a direct bearing on our need to eventually use humour as a de-stressing mechanism.

It is all very well to say that jokes trivialise the horror associated with disaster; however, folklorists know that as sure as night follows day, jokes will flow soon after such events. Of those who have seriously sought to understand jokes, most have explained that jokes are a form of aggression — a socially acceptable way of showing contempt and displaying superiority. We do this unconsciously, which is why when asked to explain the meaning of jokes we tend to dismiss them as meaningless and far too obvious to warrant explanation.

Of course, 'disaster' does not only relate to natural disasters and, for the sake of the joke, a similar response is felt when one experiences, and wants to share, one's disillusionment etc at failed marriage, infidelity, the frustration of travel, death and so many other aspects of modern life in the pits! As they say, 'You gotta laugh.'

I have collected thousands of disaster jokes circulated in Australia, including those concerning the Darwin cyclone, Port Arthur shootout, Bali bombings, Hoddle Street massacre, Granville rail disaster, Azaria and the dingo, tsunami, and more recently, the Beaconsfield mine collapse. Out of respect for families who lost loved ones in these tragic events, I have refrained from including them in this collection. They are available on my website *www.warrenfahey.com* (as an electronic book, *Shock Horror*) and a special Beaconsfield collection is also available on the site.

Ted Cohen in his *Philosophical Thoughts on Joking Matters* (University of Chicago Press, 1999) commented, 'It is a well known fact, and for many people a problematic and disturbing fact, that public topics for joking often and inevitably include misfortunes, sometimes horrible ones. There have been groups of jokes concerning earthquakes, hurricanes, plane crashes, space shuttle disasters, and, above and below all, death. These topics are as suitable as any others for cultivating the intimacy that goes with successful joking; but they have a special urgency all their own.' They are topics that are hard to confront, difficult to accept, and yet relentless in their insistence upon our attention. Humour in general and jokes in particular are among the most typical and reliable resources we have for meeting these devastating and incomprehensible matters. For example, no one understands death, no one can comprehend it and size it up without remainder, and no one can ignore it. Folklore helps us with closure.

As a folklorist I act as a 'recycling unit' gathering in folklore as it travels its ever-winding path. I attempt to make sense of the findings and then return them, suitably packaged, to the 'folk' as a way of showing how the collective process works. This book is an example of that process and dissemination. Folklore is a fascinating study because it knows absolutely no boundaries: be it the circulation of old bush yarns; locating remnants of long-forgotten songs; tracking traditional working skills; recording disappearing home crafts; or even the traditional singing of lullabies. Folklore makes our lives more interesting because of how we adopt and adapt and pass those creative items on to the next step. Most importantly it is a communal creativity that knows no master or ownership.

Joke-telling is considered 'an art' and because of changes brought about by technology, especially the penetration of e-mail, and the shift in entertainment patterns, many people are shy about public performance, including telling jokes. In times past nearly everyone was expected to have a 'party piece', a song, poem or yarn, which could be wheeled out as occasion demanded. Sometimes the same old chestnut would be presented, and often localised to include the names of friends. Nowadays the e-mail joke provides us with some of the warm fuzzy feeling we had as amateur entertainers. Sadly we are losing the real art along with the ability to hold an audience through twisting, lengthy yarn-telling, complete with character voices and wild emotive body movements. The e-mail joke, obviously, does not allow much room for emotional contact. Mind you, we do employ some tricks to convey emphasis: highlighted words or paragraphs in colours, different type size, italics and cute symbols. Many e-mail jokes are structured so that the reader is instructed to 'scroll down' and as they do they find messages like: '... wait for it' and 'it will be worth it'. Then, on completion of the punchline, they find a personalised message from the sender, along the lines of 'good, isn't it?'.

Some e-mail jokes encourage recipients to 'pass this on to your friends'. In the case of jokes about the role of the sexes you will often find a message specifically asking that the joke be 'sent to all your female friends' or 'male friends', as if the reader is automatically a member of a secret society sharing the one joke at the expense of everyone else.

A word on taboos in joke-telling and listening. In Australia we refer to jokes about sex as being either 'clean', 'dirty' or 'filthy'; however, we tend *not* to categorise jokes in other taboo areas such as racism. The jokes that any specific reader or listener will consider 'clean', dirty' or 'filthy' are almost entirely a matter of personal assessment based on that reader or listener's own experience or anxieties. The major advantage of the e-mailed joke is that one can become one's own censor by simply hitting the delete key. This censorship is far more difficult in a face-to-face situation. This option of deleting the joke most probably leads to the transmission of far more outrageous and insensitive material than the spoken-word tradition. Readers are more likely to be faced with racist material compared to a live situation where, hopefully, there would be cries protesting the teller's choice of subject.

Gershon Legman, in his groundbreaking study of the dirty joke (*The Rationale of the Dirty Joke*, 1975) argued there is a clear link between the joke-teller's choice of repertoire and also of the listener, in as much as they will search out particular subjects as teller and listener. Legman stated as axiomatic that 'a person's favourite joke is the key to that person's character'. He suggests that the artless directness of the joke-teller's 'favourite joke' is like the acting out of a charade of self-unveiling, or like the sending of a psycho-telegraphic SOS to the audience, whose sympathy and understanding are being unconsciously courted. I have found that certain people do send jokes of a particular category — for example, jokes about castration, homosexuality or impotence — but I am not sure how much I agree with Legman about pigeonholing their personality defects and neuroses.

Then there are the compulsive e-mail joke senders. I wonder what Legman would have had to say about the people who send out jokes on a daily basis, other than 'get a life'. The fact is that many people send out 50 or more jokes a day, which, in turn, encourages recipients to add them to their broadcast list, and that is why so many jokes are hurtling around in cyberspace. Is it a need to be 'in contact', albeit from a distance, is it a desire to be loved as if every joke transmitted carries a reminder that the person exists, or is it some sort of compulsive behaviour pattern? Many contributors to this collection told of archiving their received favourite jokes, and nearly all of these people told me that they rarely revisit these files. Why they have kept them is an interesting question. Possibly they feel they have some possession of these yarns and this too might be interpreted as a psychological need.

Different nationalities have different attitudes to humour. These styles are sometimes detected in the types of 'dirty' jokes they find funny. Whilst the following is only an indication, I suspect you will get the drift: French prefer jokes about sexual technique; Germans and Dutch seem fascinated by scatological humour, possibly connected to their supposedly strict Teutonic, anal-retentive upbringing; the English favour jokes about incest, mothers-in-law and homosexuality; Americans go for humour associated with oral–genital obsession (they had a field day with President Clinton's antics), and Asians, particularly Japanese, are not really amused by jokes. Of course, that all leads us to what Australians find funny. I think I can say here that we tend to find 'black humour' amusing, especially jokes that take tall poppies down. We are definitely laconic, something our contemporary humour shares with our colonial bush past where the typical bushman, hat pulled low on his noggin, fag hanging out of his mouth, had little to say, but when he did it was as dry as the Nullarbor.

In looking for the humour in most jokes, one needs to look at how we use humour in our everyday lives. Essentially it is how we make light of situations, react to particular events we observe as peculiar, and it is an intrinsic element in much of our entertainment. We 'laugh ourselves sick', 'laugh until it hurts', 'laugh so hard we think we will pee in our pants' and say 'I could have died laughing'. We talk of humour that is 'sick', 'cruel', 'biting' and 'black': Australian humour tends to embrace all of these elements.

Jokes are not the only form of e-mail humour and as computers and mobile telephones get more powerful, and more areas get high-speed cabling, the transmission of humorous video clips, MP3 sound files and other forms of communication are becoming more prevalent. The success of services like YouTube has resulted in easier transmission of favoured humour and some of these clips receive extraordinarily high strike rates. Software packages that allow sophisticated Photoshop treatment of images are also changing the face of humour. Just as face-to-face joke-telling has all but disappeared, replaced by e-mail, so too will written e-mailed jokes disappear, to be replaced by video clips, possibly of the very people who have been sending e-mail humour, 'live to camera' telling their jokes. The joke will have come full circle.

1 GOD'S OWN COUNTRY

ustralians believe that their country is especially blessed and 'God's own'. Maybe it has something to do with our isolation as an island continent, maybe it has to do with our natural wealth and beauty, and maybe it's simply the truth. Whatever the case, Australians love to spread this chest-beating *Cooee* far and wide through literature, song or, more likely than not, in the sporting arena.

I like to think that much of our mythical belief in ourselves was forged in colonial Australia, some 200 plus years ago. Even in our convict period we managed to turn hell into humour when ragged, pathetic convicts, sentenced to a flogging with the dreaded cat o' nine tails whip — a punishment that reduced a man's flesh to a quivering crimson jelly — sarcastically laughed it off by saying they were about 'to receive a new red shirt'. A similar brutal sentence of detention on the endless wheel of one of Sydney's treadmills was referred to as a visit to the 'Dancing Academy'.

In the early 19th century we saw the colonies move from penal settlements to boisterous cities, and the impenetrable bush conquered by determined explorers, farmers and gold diggers. We fought against the odds of drought, flood, bushfires, pestilence and faraway bureaucracy to survive and thrive. We felt pretty good about our colonial success and the way we had shaped the country. We felt proud how we had contributed to the wealth of Mother England as we shipped sheep, cattle, wheat and sugar back to the markets of London. We were fighters too as we responded to the call of the bugle to send troops to fight the Boers and, later, the Germans.

We were British but we were also independent and celebrated that fact when, in 1901, we were declared a federation of Australian states under one flag. Around the same time the bulk of the Australian population moved from the bush to the cities, where factory work was hopefully to be found.

WW1 saw us on Europe's frontline and our 'Diggers' gaining an international reputation for their particular 'sense of humour'. We were determined and fiercely loyal fighters but capable of idiosyncratic behaviour including a dislike of saluting. Australian soldiers typically referred to themselves as 'bloody windmills'. One yarn tells of a Digger in London 'on Blighty', i.e. on leave, who is walking up Oxford Street when he passes a general. The general, shocked that the soldier ambles past without saluting, yells at the man: 'Soldier! You are an Australian soldier, are you not?' 'Yeah,' comes the casual response. 'Well,' blusters the general, 'I am General Birdwood!' The Australian soldier looks at the general and says, 'Well why don't you pick those feathers off yer hat and shove 'em up yer arse and fly away like any other bird would!' The same man would have fought on the frontline until he dropped, and everyone, including the top brass, knew that as fact.

Our humour also came to the fore during the lean and bitter years of the Great Depression, in the 1930s, when one of the few things that kept up our pluck was an ability to laugh off our troubles. Humour came to the frontline again in WW2 and in many ways we have learnt that our national identity is one of laconic humour.

In this section you will find some 'raves', sent as humour, that can only be described as 'jingoistic', as they wave our flag and stab at concepts of being Australian. They are tongue-in-cheek, crude in style but probably sent with the best intent. They are only really humorous if we see them as such.

We have travelled quite a way down through the years and the Australian of the 21st century is still armed with an individual sense of humour that allows us to stand apart — we can laugh at most things, particularly ourselves.

Aussie study

The American government recently funded a study to see why the head of a man's penis was larger than the shaft. After one year and $180,000, they concluded that the reason was to give the man more pleasure during sex. After the US published the study, the French decided to do their own study. After $250,000 and three years of research, they concluded that the reason the head was larger than the shaft was to give the woman more pleasure during sex. Australians, dissatisfied with these findings, conducted their own study. After two weeks and a cost of around $75.46, and two cases of beer, they concluded that it was to keep a man's hand from flying off and hitting himself in the forehead.

Be alert (Australia needs more lerts)

The CIA, the FBI and the LAPD are each asked to prove their capability of apprehending terrorists. President Bush releases a white rabbit into a forest and tells each agency to catch it.

The FBI goes first. It sends animal informants into the forest. They question all plant and material witnesses. After three months of intensive investigations the FBI concludes rabbits do not exist.

The CIA goes in. After two weeks with no leads it bombs the forest, killing everything, including the rabbit. It makes no apologies; the rabbit had it coming, they insist.

The LAPD go in. They come out after just two hours with a badly beaten bear. The bear is sobbing, 'OK, OK, I'm a rabbit, I'm a rabbit!'

John Howard hears about his mate's idea and, deciding to try it here to test Australian law-enforcement agencies, he releases a white rabbit into Stromlo Forest Park, near Canberra.

The National Crime Authority can't catch it but promises that if it gets a budget increase it can recover $90 million in unpaid rabbit taxes and proceeds of crime.

The Victorian police go in. They're gone only 15 minutes, returning with a koala, a kangaroo and a tree fern, all three shot to pieces. 'They looked like dangerous rabbits and we acted in self-defence,' they explain.

The NSW police go in. Surveillance tapes later reveal top-ranking officers and rabbits dancing around a gum tree stoned out of their minds.

The Queensland police go in. They reappear driving a brand new Mercedes, with scantily clad rabbits draped all over them.

The WA police actually catch the white rabbit, but it inexplicably hangs itself when the attending officer 'slips out momentarily' for a cup of tea.

The SA and NT police join forces and beat the crap out of every rabbit in the forest, except the white one. They know it is the black ones who cause all the trouble.

The Australian Federal Police refuse to go in. They examine the issues, particularly cost, and decide that because of low priority, high overtime and the projected expense to the AFP as a whole, the matter should be returned to the referring authority for further analysis.

ASIO goes into the wrong forest.

Aussie etiquette

General rules
1. Never take a beer to a job interview.
2. Always identify people in your yard before shooting them.
3. It's tacky to take an Esky to church.
4. If you have to vacuum the bed, it's time to change the sheets.
5. Even if you're certain you're included in the will, it's rude to take the trailer to the funeral home.

Dining out
1. When decanting wine from the box, tilt the paper cup and pour slowly so as not to 'bruise' the wine.
2. If drinking directly from the bottle, hold it with both your hands.

Entertaining in your home
1. A centrepiece for the table should never be anything prepared by a taxidermist.
2. Don't allow the dog to eat at the table, no matter how good his manners.

Personal hygiene
1. While ears need to be cleaned regularly, this should be done in private, using one's OWN keys.
2. Even if you live alone, deodorant isn't a waste of money.
3. Use of toiletries can delay bathing for only a few days.

4. Dirt and grease under the fingernails is a no-no, as they detract from a woman's jewellery and alter the taste of finger foods.

Dating (outside the family)

1. Always offer to bait your date's hook, especially on the first date.
2. Be assertive. Let her know you're interested: 'I've been wanting to go out with you since I read that stuff on the men's bathroom wall two years ago.'
3. Establish with her parents what time she's expected back. Some will say 10 p.m., others might say 'Monday'. If the latter is the answer, it's the man's responsibility to get her to school on time.

Theatre etiquette

1. Crying babies should be taken to the lobby and picked up after the movie's ended.
2. Refrain from talking to characters on the screen. Tests have proven they can't hear you.

Weddings

1. Livestock is a poor choice for a wedding gift.
2. Kissing the bride for more than five seconds may get you shot.
3. For the groom, at least, rent a tux. A tracksuit with a cummerbund and a clean football jumper can create a tacky appearance.
4. Though uncomfortable, say 'yes' to socks and shoes for the occasion.

Driving etiquette

1. Dim your headlights for approaching vehicles, even if the gun's loaded and the pig's in sight.
2. When approaching a roundabout, the vehicle with the largest tyres doesn't always have the right of way.
3. Never tow another car using pantyhose and duct tape.
4. Don't burn rubber while travelling in a funeral procession.
5. When sending your wife down the road with a petrol can, it's impolite to ask her to bring back beer, too.

Life in the Australian army

Letter from a kid from Eromanga to Mum and Dad. (For those of you not in the know, Eromanga is a small town west of Quilpie in the far southwest of Queensland.)

Dear Mum and Dad,

I am doing fine. Hope youse are too. Tell me big brothers Doug and Phil that the army is better than workin' on the farm — tell them to get in bloody quick smart before the jobs are all gone! I wuz a bit slow in settling down at first, because ya don't hafta get outta bed until 6 a.m. Mind you, I like sleeping in now, cause all ya gotta do before brekky is make ya bed and shine ya boots and clean ya uniform. No bloody cows to milk, no calves to feed, no feed to stack — nothin'!!

Blokes haz gotta shave though, but it's not so bad, coz there's lotsa hot water and even a light to see what ya doing! At brekky ya get cereal, fruit and eggs but there's no kangaroo steaks or possum stew like wot Mum makes. You don't get fed again until noon, and by that time all the city boys are buggered because we've been on a 'route march' — geez, it's only just like walking to the windmill in the back paddock!!

This one will kill Doug and Phil with laughter. I keep getting medals for shootin' — dunno why. The bullseye is as big as a bloody possum's bum and it don't move and it's not firing back at ya like the Johnsons did when our big scrubber bull got into their prize cows before the Ekka last year! All ya gotta do is make yourself comfortable and hit the target — it's a piece of piss!! You don't even load your own cartridges — they come in little boxes and ya don't have to steady yourself against the rollbar of the truck when you reload!

Sometimes ya gotta wrestle with the city boys and I gotta be real careful coz they break! Easy — it's not like fighting with Doug and Phil and Jack and Boori and Steve and Muzza all at once like we do at home after the muster. Turns out I'm not a bad boxer either and it looks like I'm the best the platoon's got, and I've only been beaten by this one bloke from the Engineers. He's six foot five and 15 stone and three pick handles across the shoulders and as ya know I'm only five foot seven, and eight stone wringin' wet, but I fought him till the other blokes carried me off to the boozer.

I can't complain about the army — tell the boys to get in quick before the word gets around how bloody good it is.

Your loving daughter,

Jill

The Aussie BBQ – the way it should be

Australians love their barbecue; therefore, it is important to refresh your memory on the etiquette associated with outdoor cooking. Rightfully it is considered the only type of cooking a real man should do, probably because there is an element of danger involved.

When a man volunteers to do the barbecue the following chain of events is put into motion:

Stage one

The woman buys the food. The woman makes the salad, prepares the vegetables and makes dessert. The woman prepares the meat for cooking, places it on a tray along with the necessary cooking utensils and sauces and takes it to the man who is lounging beside the grill — beer in hand.

Stage two

At this stage the man places the meat on the grill. The woman goes inside to organise the plates and cutlery. The woman comes out to tell the man that the meat is burning. He thanks her and asks if she will bring another beer while he deals with the situation.

Stage three

The man now takes the meat off the grill and hands it to the woman. The woman prepares the plates, salad, bread, utensils, napkins, sauces, and brings them to the table. After eating, the woman clears the table and does the dishes.

Final stage

Everyone should praise the man and thank him for his outstanding cooking efforts.

Optional stage five

The man asks the woman how she enjoyed her night off. And, inevitably, upon seeing her annoyed reaction, concludes that there's just no pleasing some women …

The beer conference

The managing directors of Cascade Brewery (Tasmania), Toohey's (New South Wales), XXXX (Queensland) and Carlton (Victoria) were attending an international beer conference.

They decide to all go to lunch together and the waitress asks what they want to drink.

The boss of Toohey's says without hesitation, 'Make mine a Toohey's New.'

The head of Cascade Brewery smiles and says, 'I'll have a Cascade Draught, brewed from pure mountain water!'

Carlton's boss proudly says, 'I'll have a Carlton, the king of beers!'

The bloke from XXXX glances at his lunch mates and says, 'I'll have a Diet Coke.'

The others look at him like he has sprouted a new head.

The banana bender just shrugs and says, 'Well, if you blokes aren't drinking beer, then neither will I.'

(*They say there are only two states to be in: pissed and Queensland.*)

Letter from a Tasmanian mum to her Tasmanian son

Date: Fri, 31 May 2006 14:45:18

Dear son,

I'm writing this letter slow — because I know you can't read fast. We don't live where we did when you left home. When your dad read in the newspaper that most accidents happen within 20 kilometres from your home, we moved.

I won't be able to send you the address because the last Tasmanian family that lived here took the house numbers when they moved so that they wouldn't have to change their address. This place is really nice. It even has a washing machine. I'm not sure it works so well though: last week I put a load of clothes in and pulled the chain and haven't seen them since.

The weather isn't bad here. It only rained twice last week — the first time for three days and the second time for four days.

About that coat you wanted me to send you, your Uncle Stanley said it would be too heavy to send in the mail with the buttons on, so we cut them off and put them in the pockets. John locked his keys in the car yesterday. We were really worried because it took him two hours to get

*me and your father out. Your sister had a baby this morning; but I
haven't found out what it is yet so I don't know if you're an aunt or an
uncle. The baby looks just like your brother.*

*Uncle Ted fell in a whisky vat last week. Some men tried to pull him
out but he fought them off and drowned. We had him cremated and he
burned for three days. Three of your friends went off a bridge in a ute.
Ralph was driving. He rolled down the window and swam to safety.
Your other two friends were in the back. They drowned because they
couldn't get the tailgate down.*

There isn't much more news at this time. Nothing much has happened.

Love, Mum

*P.S. I was going to send you some money but I had already sealed the
envelope.*

The new widow

Three Aussies were working on a telephone tower — Steve, Bruce and Jed.
Steve falls off and is killed instantly. As the ambulance takes the body away,
Bruce says, 'Someone should go and tell his wife.'

Jed says, 'OK, I'm pretty good at that sensitive stuff — I'll do it.'

Two hours later, he comes back carrying a case of beer. Bruce says,
'Where did you get that, Jed?'

'Steve's wife gave it to me,' Jed replies.

'That's unbelievable! You told the lady her husband was dead and she
gave you beer?'

'Well, not exactly,' Jed says. 'When she answered the door, I said to her,
"You must be Steve's widow."'

'She said, "No, I'm not a widow!"'

'And I said, "I'll bet you a case of Foster's you are."'

Shipwrecked romance

An Aussie was washed up on a beach after a terrible shipwreck. Only a ratty
old sheep and a sheepdog were washed up with him. After looking around,
he realised that they were stranded on a deserted island.

After being there for a couple of months, he got into the habit of taking his two animal companions to the beach every evening to watch the sun set. One particular evening, the sky was a fiery red with beautiful cirrus clouds, the breeze was warm and gentle, the waves were lapping — a perfect night for romance. As they silently sat there, the sheep started looking better and better to the lonely Aussie. Soon, he leant over to the sheep and put his arm around it but the sheepdog, ever protective of the sheep, growled fiercely until the man took his arm away.

From that time on, the three of them continued to enjoy the sunsets together, but there was no more cuddling.

A few weeks passed by and, believe it or not, there was another shipwreck. The only survivor was a beautiful young woman, the most beautiful woman the man had ever seen. She was in a pretty bad way when he rescued her and he slowly nursed her back to health.

When the young girl was well enough, he introduced her to the evening beach ritual.

It was another beautiful evening — red sky, cirrus clouds, a warm and gentle breeze — perfect for a night of romance. Pretty soon, the Aussie started to get 'those feelings' again. He fought the urges as long as he could, but he finally gave in and leant over to the young woman, cautiously, and whispered in her ear, 'Would you mind taking the dog for a walk?'

Where the bloody hell are you?

These questions about Australia were supposedly posted on a Tourism Australia website. Helpful Australians suggested the responses.

Q: Does it ever get windy in Australia? I have never seen it rain on TV, so how do the plants grow? (UK)

A: We import all plants fully grown and then just sit around watching them die.

Q: Will I be able to see kangaroos in the street? (USA)

A: Depends how much you've been drinking.

Q: I want to walk from Perth to Sydney — can I follow the railroad tracks? (Sweden)

A: Sure, it's only 3000 miles; take lots of water.

Q: Are there any ATMs (cash machines) in Australia? Can you send me a list of them in Brisbane, Cairns, Townsville and Hervey Bay? (UK)

A: What did your last slave die of?

Q: Can you give me some information about hippo racing in Australia? (USA)

A: A-fri-ca is the big triangle-shaped continent south of Europe. Aus-tra-lia is that big island in the middle of the Pacific which does not … oh forget it. Sure, the hippo racing is every Tuesday night in Kings Cross. Come naked.

Q: Which direction is north in Australia? (USA)

A: Face south and then turn 90 degrees. Contact us when you get here and we'll send the rest of the directions.

Q: Can I bring cutlery into Australia? (UK)

A: Why? Just use your fingers like we do.

Q: Can you send me the Vienna Boys' Choir schedule? (USA)

A: Aus-tri-a is that quaint little country bordering Ger-man-y, which is … oh forget it. Sure, the Vienna Boys' Choir plays every Tuesday night in Kings Cross, straight after the hippo races. Come naked.

Q: Can I wear high heels in Australia? (UK)

A: You are a British politician, right?

Q: Can you tell me the regions in Tasmania where the female population is smaller than the male population? (Italy)

A: Yes, gay nightclubs.

Q: Do you celebrate Christmas in Australia? (France)

A: Only at Christmas.

Q: Are there killer bees in Australia? (Germany)

A: Not yet. But for you, we'll import them.

Q: Are there supermarkets in Sydney and is milk available all year round? (Germany)

A: No, we are a peaceful civilisation of vegan hunter-gatherers. Milk is illegal.

Q: Please send a list of all doctors in Australia who can dispense rattlesnake serum. (USA)

A: Rattlesnakes live in A-meri-ca, which is where *you* come from. All Australian snakes are perfectly harmless, can be safely handled and make good household pets.

Q: I have a question about a famous animal in Australia, but I forget its name. It's a kind of bear and lives in trees. (USA)

A: It's called a Drop Bear. They are so called because they drop out of gum trees and eat the brains of anyone walking underneath them. You can scare them off by spraying yourself with human urine before you go out walking.

Q: I was in Australia in 1969 on R&R, and I want to contact the girl I dated while I was staying in Kings Cross. Can you help? (USA)

A: Yes, and you will still have to pay her by the hour.

Q: Will I be able to speak English most places I go? (USA)

A: Yes, but you'll have to learn it first.

Aussie, Aussie, Aussie! Oi Oi Oi!

Being Australian is about driving in a German car to an Irish pub for Belgian beer, and then travelling home, grabbing an Indian curry or a Turkish kebab on the way, to sit on Swedish furniture and watch American shows on a Japanese TV. Oh and …

Only in Australia can a pizza get to your house faster than an ambulance.

Only in Australia do people order double cheeseburgers, large fries and a *Diet* Coke.

Only in Australia do banks leave both doors open and chain the pens to the counters.

Only in Australia do we leave cars worth thousands of dollars on the drive and lock our junk and cheap lawn mower in the garage.

Only in Australia do we use answering machines to screen calls and then have 'call waiting' so we won't miss a call from someone we didn't want to talk to in the first place.

Only in Australia are there disabled parking places in front of a skating rink.

Not to mention …

Three Aussies die each year testing if a 9v battery works on their tongue.

142 Aussies were injured in 1999 by not removing all pins from new shirts.

58 Aussies are injured each year by using sharp knives instead of screwdrivers.

31 Aussies have died since 1996 by watering their Christmas tree while the fairy lights were plugged in.

Eight Aussies had serious burns in 2000 trying on a new jumper with a lit cigarette in their mouth.

A massive 543 Aussies were admitted to Emergency in the last two years after opening bottles of beer with their teeth.

And finally …

In 2000 eight Aussies cracked their skull whilst throwing up into the toilet.

Job search

A major international company was looking to hire someone for a senior management position, so they interviewed dozens of applicants and narrowed their search down to three people from different parts of the world. In an attempt to pick one of them, they decided to give them all the same question to answer within 24 hours, and the one with the best answer would get the job.

The question was:

A man and a woman are in bed, nude. The woman is lying on her side with her back facing the man, and the man is lying on his side facing the woman's back. What is the man's name?

After the 24 hours was up, the three were brought in to give their answers.

The first, from Canada, said, 'My answer is: there *is* no answer.'

The second, from New Zealand, said, 'My answer is that there is no way to determine the answer with the information we were given.'

The third, from Australia, said, 'I'm not exactly sure, but I have it narrowed down to two names. It's either Willie Turner or Willie Nailer.'

The Australian got the job …

Big baby

A Queensland salesman is drinking in a South Australian hotel when he gets a call on his mobile phone. He hangs up, grinning from ear to ear, and excitedly yells, 'A round of drinks for everyone in the bar. My wife has just produced a bouncing baby boy weighing 25 pounds.'

Nobody can believe that any baby could weigh in at 25 pounds, but the Queenslander just shrugs, stating: 'That's about average in Queensland. Like I said, he's a typical Queensland baby boy.'

Congratulations shower him from every corner of the pub and many exclamations of 'Struth!' are heard.

Two weeks later the Queenslander returns to the bar. The bartender says, 'Aren't you the father of that Queensland baby that weighed 25 pounds at birth? Everybody's been having bets about how big he'd be at two weeks. So, how much does he weigh?'

The proud father answers, 'Seventeen pounds.'

The bartender, puzzled and concerned, says, 'What happened? He weighed 25 pounds the day he was born.'

The Queenslander takes a long, slow swig from his beer, wipes his lips on his shirt sleeve, leans onto the bar and proudly declares, 'Had the little blighter circumcised.'

Wet weather

In the year 2006, the Lord came unto Noah, who was now living in Australia, and said, 'Once again, the earth has become wicked and over-populated and I see the end of all flesh before me. Build another Ark and save two of every living thing along with a few good humans.'

He gave Noah the blueprints, saying, 'You have six months to build the Ark before I will start the unending rain for 40 days and 40 nights.'

Six months later, the Lord looked down and saw Noah weeping in his yard … but no Ark.

'Noah,' He roared, 'I'm about to start the rain! Where is the Ark?'

'Forgive me, Lord,' begged Noah. 'But things have changed. I needed a building permit. I've been arguing with the inspector about the need for a sprinkler system. My neighbours claim that I've violated the neighbourhood zoning laws by building the Ark in my yard and exceeding the height limitations. We had to go to the Development Appeal Board for a decision. Then the Transport Department and the energy companies demanded a bond be posted for the future costs of moving power, trolley and other overhead obstructions, to clear the passage for the Ark's move to the sea. I argued that the sea would be coming to us, but they would hear nothing of it.

'Getting the wood was another problem. There's a ban on cutting local trees in order to save the spotted owl and the koalas. I tried to convince the environmentalists that I needed the wood to save these little guys. But no go! When I started gathering the animals, an animal rights group sued me. They insisted that I was confining wild animals against their will. And they argued the accommodation was too restrictive and it was cruel and inhumane to put so many animals in a confined space. Then the Environment Department ruled that I couldn't build the Ark until they'd conducted an environmental impact study on your proposed flood. I'm still trying to resolve a complaint with the Human Rights Commission on how many minorities I'm supposed to hire for my building crew. Also, the trade unions say I can't use my sons. They insist I have to hire only union workers with Ark-building experience. To make matters worse, Customs and Excise seized all my assets, claiming I'm trying to leave the country illegally with endangered species. So, forgive me, Lord, but it's going to take at least 10 years to finish this Ark.'

Suddenly the skies cleared, the sun began to shine, and a rainbow stretched across the sky. Noah looked up in wonder and asked, 'You mean you're not going to destroy the world?'

'No,' said the Lord. 'Your government beat me to it.'

Tracking

An Australian tour guide was showing a group of American tourists the Top End. On their way to Kakadu he was describing the abilities of the Australian Aborigine to track man or beast over land, through the air, under the sea. The Americans were incredulous.

Later in the day, the tour rounded a bend on the highway and discovered, lying in the middle of the road, an Aborigine. He had one ear pressed to the white line while his left leg was held high in the air. The tour stopped and the guide and the tourists gathered around the prostrate Aborigine.

'Mate,' said the tour guide, 'what are you tracking and what are you listening for?'

The Aborigine replied, 'Down the road about 10 miles is a 1971 Valiant ute. It's red. The left front tyre is bald. The front end is out of whack and it has dents in every panel. There are nine blackfellas in the back, all drinking warm beer. There are three kangaroos on the roof rack and six dogs on the front seat.'

The American tourists moved forward, astounded by this precise and detailed knowledge.

'Goddammit, man, how do you know all that?' asked one.

The Aborigine replied, 'I just fell out of the fucking thing.'

God's own country

In the beginning God created day and night. He created day for footy matches, going to the beach and barbecues. He created night for going prawning, sleeping and barbecues. God saw that it was good.

Evening came and morning came and it was the Second Day.

On the Second Day God created water — for surfing, swimming and barbecues on the beach. God saw that it was good.

Evening came and morning came and it was the Third Day.

On the Third Day God created the earth to bring forth plants, to provide tobacco, malt and yeast for beer and wood for barbecues. God saw that it was good.

Evening came and morning came and it was the Fourth Day.

On the Fourth Day God created animals and crustaceans for chops, sausages, steak and prawns for barbecues. God saw that it was good.

Evening came and morning came and it was the Fifth Day.

On the Fifth Day God created a bloke — to go to the footy, enjoy the beach, drink the beer and eat the meat and prawns at barbecues. God saw that it was good.

Evening came and morning came and it was the Sixth Day.

On the Sixth Day God saw that this bloke was lonely and needed someone to go to the footy, surf, drink beer, eat and stand around the barbecue with. So God created mates, and God saw that they were good blokes. God saw that it was good.

Evening came and morning came and it was the Seventh Day.

On the Seventh Day God saw that the blokes were tired and needed a rest, so God created sheilas — to clean the house, carry children, wash, cook and clean the barbecue. And all was good.

Evening came and it was the end of the Seventh Day.

God sighed, looked around at the twinkling barbecue fires, heard the hiss of opening beer cans and the raucous laughter of all the blokes and sheilas, smelt the aroma of grilled chops and sizzling prawns, and God saw that it was not just good, it was better than that, it was bloody good.

It was Australia!

An Australian declaration

WE, the people of the broad brown land of Oz, wish to be recognised as a free nation of blokes and sheilas. We come from many lands (although a few too many of us come from New Zealand) and, although we live in the best country in the world, we reserve the right to bitch and moan about it, whenever we bloody like. We are one nation but we're divided into many states, descriptions of which follow: first, there's Victoria, named after a queen who didn't believe in lesbians. Victoria is the realm of turtleneck sweaters, cafe latte, grand final day and big horse races. Its capital is Melbourne, whose chief marketing pitch is that it's 'liveable'. At least that's what they think. The rest of us think it is too bloody cold and wet.

Next, there's NSW, the realm of pastel shorts, macchiato with sugar, thin books that can be read quickly and millions of dancing queens. Its capital, Sydney, has more queens than any other city in the world, and is proud of it and even celebrates it every year with a parade. Its mascots are Bondi lifesavers, who pull their Speedos up their cracks to keep the left and right sides of their brains separate.

Down south we have Tasmania, a state based on the notion that the family that bonks together stays together. In Tassie, everyone gets an extra chromosome at conception. Maps of Tasmania bring smiles to the sternest faces. It holds the world record for a single mass shooting, which the Yanks can't seem to beat, no matter how often they try.

South Australia is the province of half-decent reds, a festival of foreigners and bizarre axe murders. SA is the state of innovation — where else can you so effectively reuse country bank vaults and barrels as in

Snowtown? They had the Grand Prix, but lost it when the views of Adelaide sent the Formula One drivers to sleep at the wheel.

Western Australia is too far from anywhere to be relevant in this document. Its main claim to fame is that it doesn't have daylight saving because if it did all the men would get erections on the bus on the way to work. WA was the last state to stop importing convicts, and many of them still work there in the government and business.

The Northern Territory is the red heart of our land. Outback plains, sheep stations the size of Europe, kangaroos, jackaroos, emus, Ulurus and dusty kids with big smiles. It also has the highest beer consumption of anywhere on the planet, and its creek beds have the highest aluminium content of anywhere too. Although the Territory is the centrepiece of our national culture, few of us live there and the rest prefer to fly over it on our way to Bali.

And there's Queensland. While any mention of God seems silly in a document defining a nation of half-arsed agnostics, it is worth noting that God probably made Queensland. Why he filled it with dickheads remains a mystery.

Oh yes, and there's Canberra. The less said the better.

We, the citizens of Oz, are united by the Pacific Highway, whose treacherous twists and turns kill more of us each year than die by murder. We are united in our lust for international recognition, so desperate for praise we leap in joy when a ragtag gaggle of corrupt International Olympic Committee officials tells us Sydney is better than Beijing. We are united by a democracy so flawed that a political party, albeit a redneck gun-toting one, can get a million votes and still not win one seat in Federal Parliament while bloody Tasmanian Brian Harradine can get 24,000 votes and run the whole country. Not that we're whingeing — we leave that to our Pommy immigrants.

We want to make 'no worries, mate' our national phrase, 'she'll be right, mate' our national attitude, and 'Waltzing Matilda' our national anthem (so what if it's about a sheep-stealing criminal who commits suicide?).

We love sport so much our newsreaders can read the death toll from a sailing race and still tell us who's winning in the same breath. And we're the best in the world at all the sports that count, like cricket, netball, rugby, AFL, roo-shooting, two-up and horse racing.

We also have the biggest rock, the tastiest pies, and the worst-dressed Olympians in the known universe. We shoot, we root, we vote. We are girt by sea and pissed by lunchtime.

And even though we might seem a racist, closed-minded, sports-obsessed little people, at least we're better than the Kiwis.

An Australian job

Joe Bloggs started the day early having set his alarm clock (made in Japan) for 6 a.m. While his coffee pot (made in China) was perking, he shaved with his electronic razor (made in Hong Kong). He put on a dress shirt (made in Sri Lanka), designer jeans (made in Singapore) and tennis shoes (made in Korea). After cooking his breakfast in his new electric skillet (made in India), he sat down with his calculator (made in Mexico) to see how much he could spend today. After setting his watch (made in Taiwan) to the radio (made in India), he got in his car (made in Germany) and continued his search for a decent job.

At the end of yet another discouraging and fruitless day, Joe decided to relax for a while. He put on his sandals (made in Brazil), poured himself a glass of wine (made in France) and turned on his TV (made in Indonesia), and then wondered why he can't find a well-paid job in Australia.

Ain't it grand being an Aussie!

An American decided to write a book about famous churches around the world. For his first chapter he decided to write about American churches. So he bought a plane ticket and took a trip to Orlando, Florida, thinking that he would work his way across the country from south to north.

On his first day he was inside a church taking photographs when he noticed a golden telephone mounted on the wall that read '$10,000 per call'. The American, being intrigued, asked a priest who was strolling by what the telephone was used for. The priest replied that it was a direct line to heaven and that for $10,000 you could talk to God. The American thanked the priest and went along his way.

This continued throughout several continents and the traveller found the same scenario in each of the churches he visited — a phone that had a direct line to heaven which cost $10,000 a call.

Finally, the American decided to fly to Australia to see if Australians had the same direct phone. He arrived in Melbourne, and again there was the same golden telephone, but this time the sign under it read '40 cents per call'.

The American was surprised so he asked the priest about the sign. 'Father, I've travelled all over America, Canada, Europe and Asia and I've seen this same golden telephone in many churches. I'm told that it is a direct line to heaven, but in every place the price was $10,000 per call. Why is it so cheap here?'

The priest smiled and answered, 'You're in Australia now, mate. It's a local call.'

Plenty more where that came from

An Australian, a Kiwi and a South African are in a bar one night having a beer. All of a sudden the South African drinks his beer, throws his glass in the air, pulls out a gun and shoots the glass to pieces. He says, 'In Seth Efrika our glasses are so cheap that we don't need to drink from the same one twice.'

The Kiwi (obviously impressed by this) drinks his beer, throws his glass into the air, pulls out his gun and shoots the glass to pieces. He says: 'Wull, mate, in Niw Zulland we have so much sand to make the glasses that we don't need to drink out of the same glass twice either.'

The Australian, cool as a koala, picks up his beer and drinks it, throws his glass into the air, pulls out his gun and shoots the South African and the Kiwi. He says, 'In Australia we have so many South Africans and Kiwis that we don't need to drink with the same ones twice.'

Aussie culture – the definitive guide to being an Aussie
- The bigger the hat, the smaller the farm.
- The shorter the nickname, the more they like you.
- Whether it's the opening of Parliament, or the launch of a new art gallery, there is no Australian event that cannot be improved by a sausage sizzle.
- If the guy next to you is swearing like a wharfie he's probably a media billionaire. Or, on the other hand, he just might be a wharfie.
- There is no food that cannot be improved by the application of tomato sauce.

- On the beach, all Australians hide their keys and wallets by placing them inside their sandshoes. No thief has ever worked this out.
- Industrial design knows of no article more useful than the plastic milk crate.
- All our best heroes are losers.
- The alpha male in any group is he who takes the barbecue tongs from the hands of the host and blithely begins turning the snags.
- It's not summer until the steering wheel is too hot to hold.
- It is proper to refer to your best friend as 'a total bastard'. By contrast, your worst enemy is 'a bit of a bastard'.
- If it can't be fixed with pantyhose and fencing wire, it's not worth fixing.
- The most popular and widely praised family in any street is the one that has the swimming pool.
- It's considered better to be down on your luck than up yourself.
- The phrase 'we've got a great lifestyle' means everyone in the family drinks too much.
- If invited to a party, you should take cheap red wine and then spend all night drinking the host's beer. (Don't worry — he'll have catered for it.)
- The phrase 'a simple picnic' is not known. You should take everything you own. If you don't need to make three trips back to the car, you're not trying.
- Unless ethnic, you are not permitted to sit down in your front yard, or on your front porch. Pottering about, gardening or leaning on the fence is acceptable. Just don't sit. That's what backyards are for.
- On picnics, the Esky is always too small, creating a food vs. grog battle that can only ever be resolved by leaving the salad at home.
- When on a country holiday, the neon sign advertising the motel's pool will always be slightly larger than the pool itself.

2 MERE MALES

There are all sorts of stereotyped men, including he-men, she-men, macho-men, hen-pecked, the recently coined 'metrosexual' and, of course, real men who don't eat quiche. Humour addresses all these types and more, and one has to wonder why these yarns gain such wide circulation. Could it be a belittling campaign by hardened feminists? Possibly created by women who have not been able to penetrate the mysterious 'glass ceiling' of commerce? How about disgruntled wives sick of thankless household work? Whatever their origin, the jokes tend to be aimed at the 'mere male' in an attempt to render him harmless, be it in bed, at work or in a zillion other situations once considered a 'men's club'. To be fair, women get more than their fair share of jokes so it all ends up as — 'what's good for the goose is good for the gander'.

One aspect of the male joke, especially those with sexual references, is that they are so overtly anti-woman. In joke-telling days gone by there was a self-imposed censorship on how far jokes could go in female company, despite the fact that women have always told jokes amongst themselves. E-mail has lifted these censorship restrictions and the same jokes are sent to both sexes without fear or favour.

Can jokes help us understand the Australian male? Is he the rugged shearer, drover or timber-cutter of the 19th century? Is he the factory worker, city businessman or even the 21st century playboy, baby-boomer hippie, or above-mentioned metrosexual? Are our men like Bazza McKenzie, Norman Gunston, Crocodile Dundee or even Sir Les Patterson? This section of jokes, all about men, sees our heroes dissected, poked in the ribs, and, in good Australian style, put down.

Friendship bonds

Friendship between women
A woman didn't come home one night. The next day she told her husband that she had slept over at a friend's house. The man called his wife's 10 best friends. None of them knew about it.

Friendship between men
A man didn't come home one night. The next day he told his wife that he had slept over at a friend's house. The woman called her husband's 10 best friends. Eight of them confirmed that he had slept over, and two claimed that he was still there.

Brokeback Mountain weekly grocery list
For Ennis Del Mar and Jack Twist, summer, 1963

Week one
* Beans
* Bacon
* Coffee
* Whisky

Week two
* Beans
* Ham
* Coffee
* Whisky

Week three
* Beans al fresca
* Thin-sliced bacon
* Hazelnut coffee
* Skyy vodka and Tanqueray gin
* K-Y gel

Week four
* Beans en salade
* Pancetta
* Coffee (espresso grind)

* 5–6 bottles best Chardonnay
* 2 tubes K-Y gel

Week five

* Fresh fava beans
* Jasmine rice
* Prosciutto, approx. 8 ounces, thinly sliced
* Medallions of veal
* Porcini mushrooms
* 1/2 pint of heavy whipping cream
* 1 cub scout uniform, size 42 long
* 5–6 bottles Bordeaux (Estate Reserve)
* 1 extra large bottle Astroglide

Week six

* Yukon Gold potatoes
* Heavy whipping cream
* Asparagus (very thin)
* Organic eggs
* Spanish lemons
* Gruyere cheese (well aged)
* Crushed walnuts
* Arugula
* Clarified butter
* Extra virgin olive oil
* Pure balsamic vinegar
* 6 yards white silk organdie
* 6 yards pale ivory taffeta
* 3 cases of Dom Perignon Masters Reserve
* Large tin Crisco

Old western phrases we probably won't hear any more, thanks to *Brokeback Mountain*:

1. 'I'm gonna pump you fulla lead!'
2. 'Give me a stiff one, barkeep!'

3. 'Don't fret; I've been in tight spots before.'
4. 'Howdy, pardner.'
5. 'You stay here while I sneak around from behind.'
6. 'Two words: "saddle sore".'
7. 'Hold it right there! Now, move your hand, reeeal slow-like.'
8. 'Let's mount up!'
9. 'Nice spread ya got there!'
10. 'Ride 'em, cowboy!'
11. 'I reckon this might hurt a little.'

Men are like ...

Men are like laxatives: they irritate the shit out of you.

Men are like bananas: the older they get, the less firm they are.

Men are like holidays: they never seem to be long enough.

Men are like weather: nothing can be done to change them.

Men are like blenders: you need one, but you're not quite sure why.

Men are like chocolate bars: sweet, smooth, and they usually head right for your hips.

Men are like commercials: you can't believe a word they say.

Men are like department stores: their clothes are always half off.

Men are like government bonds: they take so long to mature.

Men are like mascara: they usually run at the first sign of emotion.

Men are like popcorn: they satisfy you, but only for a little while.

Men are like snowstorms: you never know when they're coming, how many inches you'll get or how long it will last.

Men are like lava lamps: fun to look at, but not very bright.

Men are like parking spots: all the good ones are taken, the rest are handicapped.

How many breasts?

A family is sitting around the supper table. The son asks his father, 'Dad, how many kinds of breasts are there?'

The father, surprised, answers, 'Well, son, there are three kinds of breasts. In her 20s, women's breasts are like melons, round and firm. In her 30s to 40s, they are like pears, still nice but hanging a bit. After 50, they are like onions.'

'Onions?'

'Yes, you see them and they make you cry.'

This infuriated the wife and daughter so the daughter said, 'Mum, how many kinds of willies are there?'

The mother, surprised, smiles and looks at her daughter and answers, 'Well, dear, a man goes through three phases. In a man's 20s, his willy is like an oak tree, mighty and hard. In his 30s and 40s, it is a birch, flexible but reliable. After his 50s, it is like a Christmas tree.'

'A Christmas tree?'

'Yep, dead from the root up and the balls are only for decoration.'

The National Gallery

A couple attending an art exhibition at the Australian National Gallery were staring at a portrait that had them completely confused. The painting depicted three black men totally naked sitting on a park bench. Two of the figures had black penises, but the one in the middle had a pink penis. The curator of the gallery realised that they were having trouble interpreting the painting and offered his assessment. He went on for nearly half an hour explaining how it depicted the sexual emasculation of African-Americans in a predominantly white, patriarchal society. 'In fact,' he pointed out, 'some serious critics believe that the pink penis also reflects the cultural and sociological oppression experienced by gay men in contemporary society.'

After the curator left, a Scottish man approached the couple and said, 'Would you like to know what the painting is really about?'

The couple politely queried, 'Now why would you claim to be more of an expert than the curator of the gallery?'

'Because I'm the guy who painted it,' he replied. 'In fact, there's no African-American depicted at all. They're just three Scottish coal miners. The guy in the middle went home for lunch.'

Zipper

A man walked into a Melbourne supermarket with his zipper down.

A lady cashier walked up to him and said, 'Your barracks door is open.'

This is not a phrase men normally use, so he went away looking a bit puzzled. When he was about done shopping, a man came up to him and said, 'Your fly is open.'

He zipped up and finished his shopping.

He then intentionally got in the checkout line being served by the lady who told him about his barracks door. He was planning to have a little fun with her. When he reached her counter he said, 'When you saw my barracks door open, did you see the soldier standing at attention?'

The lady (being smarter than a man) thought for a moment and said, 'No, I didn't. All I saw was a disabled veteran sitting on two duffel bags!'

A bottle of Merlot

A man entered his favourite restaurant and sat at his regular table.

After looking around, he noticed a gorgeous woman sitting at a table nearby and all alone. He motioned the waiter over and asked him to send their most expensive bottle of Merlot over to the woman, thinking that if she accepted the bottle, she would be his.

The waiter took the Merlot to the woman and said, 'This is from the gentleman seated over there,' indicating the sender.

She regarded the wine coolly for a second, not looking at the man, and decided to send a reply note to the man.

The waiter, who was lingering for a response, took the note from her and conveyed it to the gentleman. The note read: 'For me to accept this bottle, you need to have a Mercedes in your garage, a million dollars in the bank, and seven inches in your pants.'

After reading the note, the man decided to compose one of his own in return. He folded the note, handed it to the waiter and instructed him to return this to the woman. It read: 'For your information, I have a Ferrari Maranello, a BMW Z8, a Mercedes CL600 and a Porsche Turbo in my garage. There is over 20 million dollars in my bank account. But not even for a woman as beautiful as you would I cut three inches off. Just send the bottle back.'

Why do men pee standing up?

God was just about done creating man, but he had two things left over in his bag and He couldn't quite decide how to split them between Adam and Eve.

He thought He might just as well ask them.

He told them one of the things He had left was a thing that would allow the owner to pee while standing up. 'It's a very handy thing,' God said, 'and I was wondering if either one of you had a preference for it.'

Well, Adam jumped up and down and begged, 'Oh, please give that to me! I'd love to be able to do that! It seems like just the sort of thing a man should have. Please! Pleeease! Give it to me!' On and on he went in excitement.

Eve just smiled and told God that if Adam really wanted it so badly, he could have it. So God gave Adam the thing that allowed him to pee standing up.

Adam was so excited he just started whizzing all over the place — first on the side of a rock, then he wrote his name in the sand, and then he tried to see if he could hit a stump 10 feet away — laughing with delight all the while.

God and Eve watched him with amusement and then God said to Eve, 'Well, I guess you're kind of stuck with the last thing I have left.'

'What's it called?' asked Eve.

'Brains,' said God.

Shearer's boots

A lady went into a bar in Wagga Wagga and saw a shearer with his feet propped up on a table. He had the biggest boots she'd ever seen. The woman asked the shearer, 'Is it true what they say about men with big feet?'

The shearer grinned and said, 'Sure is, missus! Why don't yer come on out to the shed and let me prove it to you?'

The woman wanted to find out for herself, so she spent the night with him. The next morning she handed him a $100 bill. Blushing, he said, 'Well, thanks, ma'am. I'm really flattered. Ain't nobody ever paid me fer me services before.'

The woman replied, 'Don't be flattered … take the money and buy yourself some boots that fit.'

Fancy dress party

A countryman with a bald head and a wooden leg has been invited to a fancy dress party. He doesn't know what costume to wear to hide his head and his leg so he writes to a costume hire company in Sydney to explain the problem.

A few days later he receives a parcel with a note: 'Dear sir, please find enclosed a pirate's outfit. The spotted handkerchief will cover your bald head and, combined with your wooden leg, you will be just right as a pirate.'

The man thinks this is terrible because they have just emphasised his wooden leg and so he writes a really rude letter of complaint.

A week passes and he receives another parcel and a note which says, 'Dear sir, sorry about our previous suggestion — please find enclosed a monk's habit. The long robe will cover your wooden leg, and with your bald head you will really look the part.'

Now the man is really annoyed since they have gone from emphasising his wooden leg to emphasising his bald head and he writes the company a letter of complaint even angrier than the previous one.

The next day he receives a small parcel and a note. 'Dear sir, please find enclosed a tin of golden syrup. Why don't you pour the tin of golden syrup over your bald head, stick your wooden leg up your arse and go as a toffee apple!'

The marriage test

A man is dating three women and wants to work out which one to marry. He decides to give them a test. He gives each woman a present of $5000 and watches to see what they do with the money.

The first does a total makeover. She goes to a fancy beauty salon, gets her hair done, new make-up, and buys several new outfits and dresses up very nicely for the man. She tells him that she has done this to be more attractive for him because she loves him so much. The man is impressed.

The second goes shopping to buy the man gifts. She gets him a new set of golf clubs, some new gizmos for his computer, and some expensive clothes. As she presents these gifts, she tells him that she has spent all the money on him because she loves him so much. Again, the man is impressed.

The third invests the money in the stock market. She earns several times the $5000. She gives him back his $5000 and reinvests the remainder in a joint account. She tells him that she wants to save for their future because she loves him so much. Obviously, the man is impressed. He thinks for a long time about what each woman has done with the money he's given her.

Then he marries the one with the biggest tits. Men are like that, you know.

Good sons

Four friends, who hadn't seen each other in 30 years, reunited at a party. After several drinks, one of the men had to use the restroom. Those who remained talked about their kids.

The first guy said, 'My son is my pride and joy. He started working at a successful company at the bottom of the barrel. He studied Economics and Business Administration and soon began to climb the corporate ladder and now he's the president of the company. He became so rich that he gave his best friend a top of the line Mercedes for his birthday.'

The second guy said, 'Darn, that's terrific! My son is also my pride and joy. He started working for a big airline, and then went to flight school to become a pilot. Eventually, he became a partner in the company, where he owns the majority of its assets. He's so rich that he gave his best friend a brand new jet for his birthday.'

The third man said, 'Well, that's terrific! My son studied in the best universities and became an engineer. Then he started his own construction company and is now a multimillionaire. He also gave away something very nice and expensive to his best friend for his birthday: a 30,000 square foot mansion.'

The three friends congratulated each other just as the fourth returned from the restroom and asked: 'What are all the congratulations for?'

One of the three said: 'We were talking about the pride we feel for the successes of our sons. How's your boy doing?'

The fourth man replied: 'My son is gay and makes a living dancing as a stripper at a nightclub.'

The three friends said: 'What a shame ... what a disappointment.'

The fourth man replied: 'No, I'm not ashamed. He's my son and I love him. And he hasn't done too bad either. His birthday was two weeks ago, and he received a beautiful 30,000 square foot mansion, a brand new jet, and a top of the line Mercedes from his three boyfriends.'

Checkout

A man was standing next in line at a checkout, when the attractive blonde woman in front of him turned around and gave him a big smile.

'Hello,' she said, as she waited for her change.

'Er, I'm sorry. Do I know you?' the man said in some confusion.

'Oh, my mistake. I thought you were the father of one of my children,' she said apologetically, and picking up her shopping, she left the store.

The man was astonished. He thought, 'How amazing that a good-looking woman like that should have forgotten who fathered her children.'

Then he began to worry.

He had had an encounter in his youth that could have resulted in a child he didn't know about. She had been blonde, pretty, and about the same height.

On leaving the store, he saw the woman getting into her car. He ran over to her and said, 'Look, you couldn't have been the girl I met that night at a party in Vaucluse in 1980, could you? We shagged on the billiards table in front of everyone, things got really wild and I got so drunk that I didn't get your telephone number.'

The woman looked utterly outraged and said, 'No! I'm your son's English teacher.'

Bigger breasts

A flat-chested young lady went to Dr Smith for advice about breast enlargements. He told her, 'Every day when you get out of the shower, rub the top of your nipples and say, "Scooby dooby dooby, I want bigger boobs."'

She did this every day faithfully. After several months, it worked! She grew great boobs! One morning she was running late, and in her rush to leave for work, she realised she had forgotten her morning ritual. At this point she loved her boobs and didn't want to lose them, so she got up in the middle of the bus and said, 'Scooby dooby dooby, I want bigger boobs.'

A guy sitting nearby asked her, 'Do you go to Dr Smith by any chance?'

'Why yes, I do. How did you know?'

The man stood up and cupped his balls and said, 'Hickory dickory dock …'

Fly swatter

A woman walked into the kitchen to find her husband stalking around with a fly swatter.

'What are you doing?' she asked.

'Hunting flies,' he responded.

'Oh … killing any?' she asked.

'Yep: three males, two females,' he replied.

Intrigued, she asked, 'How can you tell?'

He responded, 'Three were on a beer can, two were on the phone.'

Good salesman

A little old lady answered a knock on the door one day, only to be confronted by a well-dressed young man carrying a vacuum cleaner.

'Good morning,' said the young man. 'If I could take a couple of minutes of your time, I would like to demonstrate the very latest in high-powered vacuum cleaners.'

'Shove off!' said the old lady. 'I haven't got any money.' And she proceeded to close the door.

Quick as a flash, the young man wedged his foot in the door and pushed it wide open. 'Don't be too hasty!' he said. 'Not until you have at least seen my demonstration.' And with that, he emptied a bucket of horseshit all over her hallway carpet. 'If this vacuum cleaner does not remove all traces of this horse manure from your carpet, madam, I will personally eat the remainder.'

'Well,' she said, 'I hope you've got a flamin' good appetite, because the electricity was cut off this morning.'

A question

A young boy went up to his father and asked, 'What's the difference between "potentially" and "realistically"?'

The father pondered for a while, then answered, 'Go ask your mother if she would sleep with Robert Redford for a million dollars. Also, ask your sister if she would sleep with Brad Pitt for a million dollars. Come back and tell me what you've learnt.'

So the boy went to his mother and asked, 'Would you sleep with Robert Redford for a million dollars?' The mother replied, 'Of course I would. I wouldn't pass up an opportunity like that.'

The boy then went to his sister and said, 'Would you sleep with Brad Pitt for a million dollars?' The girl replied, 'Oh gosh! I would just love to do that! I would be nuts to pass up that opportunity!'

The boy then thought about it for two or three days and went back to his dad. His father asked him, 'Did you find out the difference between "potentially" and "realistically"?'

The boy replied, 'Yes, potentially we're sitting on two million dollars, but realistically we're living with two slappers.'

Pest control

A woman was having a passionate affair with an inspector from a pest-control company. One afternoon they were carrying on in the bedroom together when her husband arrived home unexpectedly.

'Quick,' said the woman to her lover, 'into the closet!' and she pushed him in the closet, stark naked.

The husband, however, became suspicious and after a search of the bedroom discovered the man. 'Who are you?' he asked him.

'I'm an inspector from Bugs-B-Gone,' said the exterminator.

'What are you doing in there?' the husband asked.

'I'm investigating a complaint about an infestation of moths,' the man replied.

'And where are your clothes?' asked the husband.

The man looked down at himself and said, 'Those little bastards.'

Male blond

There were two blond blokes working for the Gosford City Council. One would dig a hole; the other would follow behind him and fill the hole in. They worked furiously all day without rest, one bloke digging a hole, the other filling it in again.

An onlooker was amazed at their hard work, but couldn't understand what they were doing. So he asked the hole digger, 'I appreciate the effort you are putting into your work, but what's the story? You dig a hole and your partner follows behind and fills it up again.'

The hole digger wiped his brow and sighed, 'Well, normally we are a three-man team, but the bloke who plants the trees is sick today.'

Male quickies

Q: What should you do when you see your ex-husband rolling around in pain on the ground?

A: Shoot him again.

Q: How many men does it take to open a beer?
A: None. It should be open when she brings it.

Q: Why is a laundromat a really bad place to pick up a woman?
A: Because a woman who can't even afford a washing machine will probably never be able to support you.

Q: Why do women have smaller feet than men?
A: It's one of those 'evolutionary things' that allows them to stand closer to the kitchen sink.

Q: How do you know when a woman is about to say something smart?
A: When she starts a sentence with 'A man once told me …'

Q: How do you fix a woman's watch?
A: You don't. There is a clock on the oven.

Q: Why do men fart more than women?
A: Because women can't shut up long enough to build up the required pressure.

Q: If your dog is barking at the back door and your wife is yelling at the front door, whom do you let in first?
A: The dog, of course. He'll shut up once you let him in.

Q: What's worse than a male chauvinist pig?
A: A woman who won't do what she's told.

Q: Why do men die before their wives?
A: They want to.

Q: Why do little boys whine?
A: They're practising to be men.

Q: How many men does it take to screw in a light bulb?
A: One — he just holds it up there and waits for the world to revolve around him.

Q: How many men does it take to screw in a light bulb?
A: Three — one to screw in the bulb, and two to listen to him brag about the screwing part.

Q: What do you call a handcuffed man?
A: Trustworthy.

Q: What does it mean when a man is in your bed gasping for breath and calling your name?
A: You didn't hold the pillow down long enough.

Q: Why does it take 100 million sperm to fertilise one egg?
A: Because not one will stop and ask for directions.

Q: What's the best way to kill a man?
A: Put a six-pack and a naked woman in front of him and ask him to choose just one.

Q: What do men and pantyhose have in common?
A: They either cling, run, or don't fit right in the crotch.

Q: Why do men whistle while they're on the toilet?
A: Because it helps them remember which end they need to wipe.

Q: What is the difference between men and women?
A: A woman wants one man to satisfy her every need. A man wants every woman to satisfy his one need.

Q: How does a man keep his youth?
A: By giving her money, diamonds and furs.

Q: How do you keep your husband from reading your e-mail?
A: Rename the mail folder 'instruction manuals'.

Scientists have discovered a food that diminishes a woman's sex drive by 90 per cent. It's called wedding cake.

Women will never be equal to men until they can walk down the street with a bald head and a beer gut and still think they are sexy.

In the beginning, God created the earth and rested. Then God created Man and rested. Then God created Woman. Neither God nor Man has rested since.

The big wheel

Two gay men at a fairground see the big wheel. One wants to go on but his boyfriend is too scared, so he just stays on the ground and watches. Shortly after the ride commences there is a huge creak, then the whole big wheel collapses and falls to the ground.

Scrambling through the twisted wreckage, the panic-stricken spectator eventually finds his boyfriend in the carnage. 'Are you hurt?' he shouts.

'Hurt? Hurt! Of course I'm fucking hurt! — I went round twice and you only waved once!'

Swapping places

A man was sick and tired of going to work every day while his wife stayed home. He wanted her to see what he went through so he prayed: 'Dear Lord: I go to work every day and put in eight hours while my wife merely stays at home. I want her to know what I go through, so please allow her body to switch with mine for a day. Amen.'

God, in his infinite wisdom, granted the man's wish. The next morning, sure enough, the man awoke as a woman.

He arose, cooked breakfast for his mate, awakened the kids, set out their school clothes, fed them breakfast, packed their lunches, drove them to school, came home and picked up the dry cleaning, took it to the cleaners and stopped at the bank to make a deposit, went grocery shopping, then drove home to put away the groceries, paid the bills and balanced the cheque book. He cleaned the cat's litter box and bathed the dog. Then it was already 1 p.m. and he hurried to make the beds, do the laundry, vacuum, dust, and sweep and mop the kitchen floor. Then he ran to the school to pick up the kids and got into an argument with them on the way home. He set out biscuits and milk and got the kids organised to do their homework, then set up the ironing board and watched TV while he did the ironing. At 4.30 he began peeling potatoes and washing vegetables for dinner, breaded the pork chops and snapped fresh beans. After dinner he cleaned the kitchen, ran the dishwasher, folded laundry, bathed the kids, and put them to bed. At 9 p.m. he was exhausted and, though his daily chores weren't finished, he went to bed where he was expected to make love, which he managed to get through without complaint.

The next morning he awoke and immediately knelt by the bed and said, 'Lord, I don't know what I was thinking. I was so wrong to envy my wife being able to stay home all day. Please, oh please, let us trade back.'

The Lord, in His infinite wisdom, replied, 'My son, I feel you have learnt your lesson and I will be happy to change things back to the way they were. You'll just have to wait nine months, though. You got pregnant last night.'

Terrible burns

A married couple were in a terrible accident where the woman's face was severely burned. The doctor told the husband that they couldn't graft any skin from her body because she was too skinny. So the husband offered to donate some of his own skin. However, the only skin that the doctor felt was suitable would have to come from his buttocks.

The husband and wife agreed that they would tell no one about where the skin came from, and requested that the doctor also honour their secret. After all, this was a very delicate matter.

When the surgery had been completed, everyone was astounded at the woman's new beauty. She looked more beautiful than she ever had before! All her friends and relatives just went on and on about her youthful beauty!

One day, she was alone with her husband, and she was overcome with emotion at his sacrifice. She said, 'Dear, I just want to thank you for everything you did for me. There is no way I could ever repay you.'

'My darling,' he replied, 'think nothing of it. I get all the thanks I need every time I see your mother kiss you on the cheek.'

Big embarrassment

A man goes to the doctor because he is very embarrassed about his 25-inch penis, and he is having difficulty trying to hide it. 'Doctor,' he asks, in total frustration, 'is there anything you can do for me?'

The doctor replies, 'Medically, son, there is nothing I can do. But I do know this witch doctor who may be able to help you.' So the doctor gives him directions to an African witch doctor.

The man calls upon the witch doctor and relays his story. 'Witch doctor, my penis is 25 inches long and I need help. Can anything be done to help me? You are my only hope.'

The witch doctor stares in amazement, scratches her head, and then replies, 'I think I may be able to help you with your problem. Do this. Go deep into the forest. You will find a pond. In this pond, you will find a frog sitting on a log. This frog has magic. You say to the frog, "Will you marry me?" When the frog says "No" you will find five inches less to your problem.'

The man's face lights up and he dashes off into the forest and finds the pond with the frog sitting on the other side. He calls out to the frog, 'Will you marry me?'

The frog looks at him dejectedly and replies, 'No.'

The man looks down and suddenly his penis is five inches shorter. '*Wow*,' he screams out, 'this is great! But it's still too long at 20 inches so I'll ask the frog to marry me again.'

'Frog, will you marry me?' the guy shouts.

The frog rolls its eyes back in its head and screams back, '*No!*'

The man feels another twitch in his penis, looks down, and it is another five inches shorter. The man laughs, 'This is fantastic.' He looks down at his penis again, 15 inches long, and reflects for a moment. Fifteen inches is still a monster; just a little less would be ideal.

Grinning, he looks across the pond and yells out, 'Frog, will you marry me?'

The frog looks back across the pond shaking its head. 'How many times do I have to tell you? *No, no, no!*'

Sexy days

A recent study found out which days men prefer to have sex. It was found that men preferred to engage in sexual activity on the days that start with the letter 'T'. Examples of those days are: Tuesday, Thursday, Thanksgiving, today, tomorrow, Thaturday and Thunday.

Why men get out of bed at night

A recent survey was conducted to discover why men get out of bed in the middle of the night: 5 per cent said it was to get a glass of water; 12 per cent said it was to go to the toilet; 83 per cent said it was to go home.

Active duty

One of our soldiers on duty in East Timor received a letter from his girlfriend recently. In the letter she explained that she had relations with two boys while he had been gone and she wanted to break up and she wanted the pictures of herself back.

So the Digger did what any switched-on Australian Infantry Digger would do. He went around to his mates and collected all the unwanted photos of women he could find. He then mailed about 25 pictures to his girlfriend with the following note: 'I'm sorry but I can't remember which one you are. Please take the one that belongs to you and send the rest back. Thank you.'

The bloke's prayer

Our beer
Which art in bottles
Hallowed be thy sport
Thy will be drunk
I will be drunk
At home as I am in the pub
Give us each day our daily schooners
And forgive us our spillage
As we forgive those who spillest against us
And lead us not into the practice of wine tasting
And deliver us from Tequila
For mine is the bitter
The chicks and the footy
Forever and ever
Barmen

A slight difference

A mechanic was removing the cylinder heads from the motor of a car when he spotted a world-famous Macquarie Street heart surgeon in his shop. The heart surgeon was standing off to the side, waiting for the service manager to come to take a look at his car. The mechanic shouted across the garage, 'Hello, Doctor, please come on over here for a minute.'

The famous surgeon, a bit surprised, walked over to where the mechanic stood. The mechanic straightened up, wiped his hands on a rag and asked, 'So, Doctor, look at this here. I also open hearts, take valves out, grind 'em, put in new parts, and when I finish this will work just like a new one. So how come you get the really big money when you and I are doing basically the same work?'

The doctor smiled, leant over and whispered to the mechanic, 'Try doing it with the engine running!'

Sunbathing

There was a man sunbathing in the nude on the beach. He saw a little girl coming towards him, so he covered himself with the newspaper he was reading.

The girl came up to him and asked, 'What do you have under the newspaper?'

Thinking quickly, the man replied, 'A bird.'

The girl walked away, and the guy fell asleep. When he woke up, he was in a hospital in tremendous pain. The police asked him what happened.

The man said, 'I don't know. I was lying on the beach, this little girl asked me a question, I guess I dozed off, and the next thing I know is I'm here.'

The police went to the beach, found the girl, and asked her, 'What did you do to that naked fellow?'

After a pause, the girl replied, 'To him? Nothing. I was playing with his bird and it spat on me, so I broke its neck, cracked its eggs, and set its nest on fire!'

Moral of the story — never lie to women.

3 WOMEN RULE!

The role of women in society continues to change although, according to most women, not fast enough. Inequality is a reality and so is the 'glass ceiling' preventing women from ascending to higher management because, yes you guessed it, they are female. Eve should never have taken that first bite of the forbidden apple!

It was not that long ago that women were seen as 'housewives' and/or sex objects. The 'Missus' traditionally stayed at home, cleaned the house, prepared the meals and raised the kids. When 'her man' came home she had to be at the front door with pipe, slippers and a cold beer. Times have changed. There are now plenty of women who are not inclined to marry and many who refuse to conform to the expectations of the stereotype. Jokes about women come in all shapes and disguises: some come from the stereotype male perspective of putting women down and in their supposed place, some are male support for feminism and many come from women themselves seeing humour as a useful tool to break down barriers.

It should be noted that whilst men see the female breast as the principal fetish of attraction, women in jokes appear not to be that focused on the penis. The size of a man's personality, wealth and sensitivity are more important as joke subjects.

Australians are fortunate to live in a progressive society and one that has played such an important role in championing women's rights. We were there with the suffragettes and we now have a healthy proportion of women in government. We recognise the role of strong bush women as portrayed in Australian classics like Tom Collins' *Such Is Life* and Henry Lawson's evocative story of *The Drover's Wife*. The pioneer women, in so many ways, were the backbone of colonial Australia and a far cry from Hollywood's 'Ma Kettle' and her kind. This does not prevent us laughing at ourselves, and why should it!

The majority of jokes in this section see women as strong and clever characters. They might appear as 'dumb blondes' but, in the majority of cases, they turn the tables to emerge as victors. Many of these jokes have had wide e-mail circulation and usually with a personal note: 'Send this to as many of your female friends as possible.' Or 'Women Rule!' Or, the most popular, 'Never underestimate a woman.'

Of course, there are 'put downs' alongside the successful trickster jokes. You'll learn about 'Women's English' as explained by men ('Yes' means 'No', 'No' means 'Yes' etc), how women describe themselves on the Internet, the 'geography' of women, and even visit the Melbourne Husband Shopping Centre.

10 things men understand about women

1.
2.
3.
4.
5.
6.
7.
8.
9.
10.

Buying a bra

A man walked into the ladies department of a Myer store, shyly walked up to the woman behind the counter and said, 'I'd like to buy a bra for my wife.'

'What type of bra?' asked the sales clerk.

'Type?' inquired the man. 'There's more than one type?'

'Look around,' said the saleslady, as she showed him a sea of bras in every shape, size, colour and material imaginable. 'Actually, even with all of this variety, there are really only four types of bras to choose from.'

Relieved, the man asked about the types.

The saleslady replied: 'There are the Catholic, the Salvation Army, the Presbyterian and the Baptist types. Which one would you prefer?'

Now totally befuddled, the man asked about the differences between them.

The saleslady responded, 'It is all really quite simple. The Catholic type supports the masses, the Salvation Army type lifts the fallen, the Presbyterian type keeps them staunch and upright, and the Baptist type makes mountains out of molehills.'

Bra sizes

Have you ever wondered why A, B, C, D, DD, E, F, G and H are the letters used to define bra sizes? Here is the chart used by most stores:

A = Almost boobs
B = Barely there

C = Can't complain!

D = Dang!

DD = Double dang!

E = Enormous!

F = Fake

G = Get a reduction

H = Help me, I've fallen and I can't get up!

Jump

Tom, a handsome fellow, walked into a sports bar around 9.58 p.m. He sat down next to a blonde at the bar and stared up at the TV. The 10 p.m. news was on. The news crew was covering a story of a man on a ledge of a large building preparing to jump.

The blonde looked at Tom and said, 'Do you think he'll jump?'

Tom said, 'You know, I bet he'll jump.'

The blonde replied, 'Well, I bet he won't.'

Tom placed a $20 bill on the bar and said, 'You're on!'

Just as the blonde placed her money on the bar, the guy on the ledge did a swan dive off the building, falling to his death.

The blonde was very upset, but willingly handed her $20 to Tom, saying, 'Fair's fair. Here's your money.'

Tom replied, 'I can't take your money. I saw this earlier on the five o'clock news and so I knew he would jump.'

The blonde replied, 'I did too; but I didn't think he'd do it again.'

Assassin

ASIO had an opening for an assassin. After all the background checks, interviews and testing were done, there were three finalists: two men and a woman.

For the final test, an ASIO agent took one of the men to a large metal door and handed him a gun. 'We must know that you will follow your instructions no matter what the circumstances. Inside the room you will find your wife sitting in a chair. Kill her!'

The man said, 'You can't be serious. I could never shoot my wife.'

The agent said, 'Then you're not the right man for this job. Take your wife and go home.'

The second man was given the same instructions. He took the gun and went into the room. All was quiet for about five minutes. The man came out with tears in his eyes. 'I tried, but I can't kill my wife.'

The agent said, 'You don't have what it takes. Take your wife and go home.'

Finally, it was the woman's turn. She was given the same instructions — to kill her husband. She took the gun and went into the room. Shots were heard, one after another. They heard screaming, crashing, banging on the walls. After a few minutes, all was quiet. The door opened slowly and there stood the woman. She wiped the sweat from her brow. 'This gun is loaded with blanks,' she said. 'So I had to beat him to death with the chair.'

Good Christian

A blonde cowgirl, who is visiting Texas from Arkansas, walks into a bar and orders three mugs of Bud. She sits in the back of the room, drinking a sip out of each one in turn. When she finishes them, she comes back to the bar and orders three more.

The bartender approaches and tells the cowgirl, 'You know, a mug goes flat after I draw it. It would taste better if you bought one at a time.'

The cowgirl replies, 'Well, you see, I have two sisters: one is in Australia, the other is in Ireland. When we all left our home in Arkansas, we promised that we'd drink this way to remember the days when we drank together. So I'm drinking one beer for each of my sisters and one for myself.'

The bartender admits that this is a nice custom, and leaves it there.

The cowgirl becomes a regular in the bar, and always drinks the same way. She orders three mugs and drinks them in turn.

One day, she comes in and only orders two mugs. All the regulars take notice and fall silent.

When she comes back to the bar for the second round, the bartender says, 'I don't want to intrude on your grief, but wanted to offer my condolences on your loss.'

The cowgirl looks quite puzzled for a moment, then the light dawns in her eyes and she laughs, 'Oh no, everybody's just fine,' she explains. 'It's just that my husband and I joined the Baptist Church and I had to quit drinking. Hasn't affected my sisters though.'

New drink

A woman and her boyfriend are out for New Year having a few drinks. While they're sitting there having a good time together she starts talking about this really great new drink. The more she talks about it the more excited she gets, and starts trying to talk her boyfriend into having one. After a while he gives in and lets her order the drink for him. The bartender brings the drink and puts the following on the bar — a saltshaker, a shot of Baileys and a shot of lime juice.

The boyfriend looks at the items quizzically and the woman explains: 'First you put a bit of the salt on your tongue, next you drink the shot of Baileys and hold it in your mouth, and finally you drink the lime juice.'

So, the boyfriend, trying to go along and please her, goes for it.

He puts the salt on his tongue — salty but OK. He drinks the shot of Baileys — smooth, rich, cool, and very pleasant. He thinks, this is OK. Finally he picks up the lime juice and drinks it — in one second the sharp lime taste hits ... at two seconds the Baileys curdles ... at three seconds the salty curdled bitter taste hits. This triggers his gag reflex but being manly, and not wanting to disappoint his girlfriend, he swallows the now nasty drink. When he finally chokes it down he turns to his girlfriend.

She smiles widely at him and says, 'So, how did you like it? It's called "Blow Job Revenge".'

Funeral procession

A woman was leaving a convenience store with her morning coffee when she noticed a most unusual funeral procession approaching the nearby cemetery. A long black hearse was followed by a second long black hearse about 50 feet behind the first one. Behind the second hearse was a solitary woman walking a pit bull on a leash. Behind her, a short distance back, were about 200 women walking single file.

The woman couldn't stand her curiosity. She respectfully approached the woman walking the dog and said, 'I am so sorry for your loss, and I know now is a bad time to disturb you, but I've never seen a funeral like this. Whose funeral is it?'

'My husband's.'

'What happened to him?'

The woman replied, 'My dog attacked and killed him.'

She inquired further, 'Well, who is in the second hearse?'

The woman answered, 'My mother-in-law. She was trying to help my husband when the dog turned on her.'

A poignant and thoughtful moment of silence passed between the two women.

'Can I borrow the dog?'

'Get in line.'

A woman's prayer

Dear Lord,

I pray for:

Wisdom, to understand a man,

Love, to forgive him, and

Patience, for his moods.

Because, Lord, if I pray for Strength

I'll just beat him to death.

Duties of wives

Three men were sitting together bragging about how they had given their new wives duties.

Terry had married a woman from America, and bragged that he had told his wife she needed to do all the dishes and housework. He said that it took a couple of days but on the third day he came home to a clean house and the dishes were all washed and put away.

Jimmie had married a woman from Canada. He bragged that he had given his wife orders that she was to do all the cleaning, dishes, and the cooking. He told them that the first day he didn't see any results, but the next day it was better. By the third day, his house was clean, the dishes were done, and he had a huge dinner on the table.

The third man had married an Australian girl. He boasted that he told her that her duties were to keep the house cleaned, dishes washed, laundry and ironing done twice a week, lawns mowed, windows cleaned and hot meals on the table, breakfast, lunch and dinner. He said the first day he didn't see anything, the second day he didn't see anything, but by the third day most of the swelling had gone down and he could see a little out of his left eye. Enough to fix himself a bite to eat, load the dishwasher, and call a handyman.

God bless Australian women.

A real cowboy

An old stockman from Queensland sat down at the bar and ordered a drink. As he sat sipping it, a young woman sat down next to him. She turned to the bushie and asked, 'Are you a real stockman?'

He replied, 'Well, I've spent my whole life breaking colts, working cows, going to rodeos, fixing fences, pulling calves, bailing hay, doctoring calves, cleaning barns, fixing flats, mending fences, working on tractors, and feeding my dogs, so I guess I am a stockman.'

She said, 'I'm a lesbian. I spend my whole day thinking about women. As soon as I get up in the morning, I think about women. When I shower, I think about women. When I watch TV, I think about women. I even think about women when I eat. It seems that everything makes me think of women.'

The two sat sipping their drinks in silence.

A little while later, a man sat down on the other side of the old stockman and asked, 'Are you a real stockman?'

The bushie replied, 'I always thought I was, but I just found out I'm a lesbian.'

Apples and wine

Women are like apples on trees. The best ones are at the top of the tree. Most men don't want to reach for the good ones because they are afraid of falling and getting hurt. Instead, they just take the rotten apples from the ground that aren't as good, but easy …

The apples at the top think something is wrong with them, when in reality, they're amazing. They just have to wait for the right man to come along, the one who's brave enough to climb all the way to the top of the tree.

Now men … Men are like a fine wine. They begin as grapes, and it's up to women to stomp the shit out of them until they turn into something acceptable to have dinner with.

Deodorant

A blonde walks into a pharmacy and asks for some rectum deodorant. The pharmacist, a little bemused, explains to the woman they don't sell rectum deodorant, and never have.

Unfazed, the blonde assures the pharmacist that she has been buying the stuff from this store on a regular basis and would like some more.

'I'm sorry,' says the pharmacist, 'we don't have any.'

'But I always buy it here,' says the blonde.

'Do you have the container that it came in?' asks the pharmacist.

'Yes,' said the blonde, 'I'll go home and get it.'

She returns with the container and hands it to the pharmacist, who looks at it and says to her, 'This is just a normal stick of underarm deodorant.'

Annoyed, the blonde snatches the container back and reads out loud: 'TO APPLY, PUSH UP BOTTOM.'

TGIF

A businessman got in a lift. When he entered, there was a blonde already inside who greeted him with a bright, 'T-G-I-F.'

He smiled at her and replied, 'S-H-I-T.'

She looked puzzled and repeated, 'T-G-I-F,' more slowly.

He again answered, 'S-H-I-T.'

The blonde was trying to keep it friendly, so she smiled her biggest smile, and said as sweetly as possible, 'T-G-I-F.'

The man smiled back at her and said once again, 'S-H-I-T.'

The exasperated blonde finally decided to explain. '"T-G-I-F" means "Thank Goodness It's Friday". Get it, duuhhh?'

The man answered, '"S-H-I-T" means "Sorry, Honey, It's Thursday".'

River walk

There's this blonde out for a walk. She comes to a river and sees another blonde on the opposite bank. 'Yoo-hoo!' she shouts. 'How can I get to the other side?'

The second blonde looks up the river then down the river and shouts back, 'You ARE on the other side.'

Knitting

A highway patrolman pulled alongside a speeding car on the Brisbane freeway. Glancing at the car, he was astounded to see that the blonde behind the wheel was knitting! Realising that she was oblivious to his flashing lights and siren, the trooper cranked down his window, turned on his bullhorn and yelled, 'PULL OVER!'

'NO!' the blonde yelled back. 'IT'S A SCARF!'

Bus trip

Two cheerleading teams, one of all blondes and one of all brunettes, chartered a double-decker bus for a weekend cheerleading competition in Brisbane. The brunette team rode on the bottom of the bus and the blonde team rode on the top level.

The brunette team down below were really whooping it up, having a great time, when one of them realised she hadn't heard anything from the blondes upstairs. She decided to go up and investigate. When the brunette reached the top, she found all the blondes frozen in fear, staring straight ahead at the road, clutching the seats in front of them with white knuckles.

The brunette asked, 'What the heck's going on up here? We're having a great time downstairs!'

One of the blondes looked up at her, swallowed hard and whispered, '*Yeah, but you've got a driver.*'

Tree hugging

Peg, the tree-hugging greenie, purchased a huge plot of timbered land in southwest Tasmania to save it from being clear-felled.

There was a very tall tree on the highest point of her property. She wanted to see all of her land so she began climbing the tree in a 'bear hug' fashion, but as she neared the top an angry possum attacked her. In a panic to escape, she let loose her grip with her arms and legs and slid down the trunk, at ever-increasing speed. Consequently she managed to get many splinters in the area of her private parts.

In considerable pain she hurried to the nearest doctor, who worked in the local logging camp nearby. He calmly listened to her story and then told her to go into the examination room where he would try to help her. She went into the room, sat down with much discomfort and waited for three hours before the doctor reappeared. Outraged, Peg demanded, 'What took you so long?'

The unperturbed doctor replied, 'Well, I had to get permits from the Environmental Protection Authority, the Forestry Commission and the Department of Land Management before I could remove old-growth timber from a recreational area.'

Cigarettes and tampons

A man walks into a Sydney pharmacy and wanders up and down the aisles. The salesgirl notices him and asks if she can help him. He answers that he is looking for a box of tampons for his wife.

She directs him down the correct aisle. A few minutes later, he deposits a huge bag of cotton balls and a ball of string on the counter.

She says, confused, 'Sir, I thought you were looking for some tampons for your wife?'

He answers, 'You see, it's like this: yesterday, I sent my wife to the store to get me a carton of cigarettes, and she came back with a packet of tobacco and some rolling papers, 'cause it's so much cheaper. So, I figure if I have to roll my own, so does she.'

Wife versus husband

A troubled couple drove down a country road for several miles, not saying a word. An earlier discussion had led to an argument and neither of them wanted to concede their position.

As they passed a barnyard of mules, goats and pigs, the husband asked sarcastically, 'Relatives of yours?'

'Yep,' the wife replied, 'in-laws.'

Genie

A woman was walking along the beach when she stumbled upon a genie's lamp. She picked it up, rubbed it and a genie appeared.

The amazed woman asked if she was entitled to three wishes.

The genie said, 'No. Due to inflation, constant downsizing, low wages in Third World countries and fierce global competition, I can only grant you one wish. So what'll it be?'

The woman didn't hesitate. She said, 'I want peace in the Middle East. See this map? I want these countries to stop fighting with each other.'

The genie looked at the map and exclaimed, 'Lady! These countries have been at war for thousands of years. I'm good, but I'm not *that* good! It can't be done. Make another wish.'

The woman thought for a minute and said, 'Well, I've never been able to find the right man. You know, one that's considerate and fun, likes to cook and helps with the housecleaning, is good in bed and gets along with my family, doesn't watch sports all the time … and is faithful. That's what I wish for … a good soul mate.'

The genie let out a long sigh and said, 'Let me see that map again.'

Go, girl, go

A blonde tries to go horseback riding even though she has had no lessons or prior experience. She mounts the horse unassisted and the horse immediately springs into action. It gallops along at a steady rhythmic pace, but the blonde begins to lose her grip and starts to slide in the saddle. In terror, she grabs for the mane but can't seem to get a firm grip. She tries to throw her arms around the horse's neck, but she slides down the side of the horse anyway. The horse gallops along, seemingly impervious to its slipping rider. Unfortunately, the blonde's foot has become entangled in the stirrup. She is now at the mercy of the hooves as her head is struck against the ground over and over again. As her head is battered against the ground she is moments away from losing consciousness when, to her great fortune, the Woolworths manager sees her and unplugs the horse.

Dictionary for women's personal advertisements

40-ish = 49

Adventurous = Slept with everyone

Athletic = No tits

Average-looking = Ugly

Beautiful = Pathological liar

Contagious smile = Does a lot of pills

Emotionally secure = On medication

Feminist = Fat

Free spirit = Junkie

Friendship first = Former slut

Fun = Annoying

New Age = Body hair in the wrong places

Old-fashioned = No BJs

Open-minded = Desperate

Outgoing = Loud and embarrassing

Passionate = Sloppy drunk

Professional = Bitch
Voluptuous = Very fat
Large frame = Hugely fat
Wants soul mate = Stalker

Women's English

Yes = No
No = Yes
Maybe = No
We need = I want
I'm sorry = You'll be sorry
We need to talk = I need to complain
Sure, go ahead = I don't want you to
Do what you want = You'll pay for this later
I'm not upset = Of course I'm upset, you moron!
Are you listening to me? = Too late, you're dead
You have to learn to communicate = Just agree with me
Be romantic, turn out the lights = I have flabby thighs
You're so … manly = You need a shave and you sweat a lot
Do you love me? = I'm going to ask for something expensive
It's your decision = The correct decision should be obvious by now
You're certainly attentive tonight = Is sex all you ever think about?
I'll be ready in a minute = Kick off your shoes and find a good game on TV
How much do you love me? = I did something today that you're not going
    to like

Men's English

I'm hungry = I'm hungry
I'm sleepy = I'm sleepy
I'm tired = I'm tired
Nice dress = Nice cleavage!
I love you = Let's have sex now
I'm bored = Do you want to have sex?
What's wrong? = I guess sex is out of the question
May I have this dance? = I'd like to have sex with you
Can I call you sometime? = I'd like to have sex with you

Do you want to go to a movie? = I'd like to have sex with you

Can I take you out to dinner? = I'd like to have sex with you

Will you marry me? = I want to make it illegal for you to have sex with other men

You look tense; let me give you a massage = I want to have sex with you within the next 10 minutes

Let's talk = I am trying to impress you by showing that I am a deep person and then I'd like to have sex with you

I don't think those shoes go with that outfit = I'm gay

The geography of women

Between 18 and 20, a woman is like Africa. Half-discovered, half-wild, naturally beautiful with fertile deltas.

Between 21 and 30, a woman is like America. Well-developed and open to trade, especially for someone with cash.

Between 31 and 35, she is like India. Very hot, relaxed and convinced of her own beauty.

Between 36 and 40, a woman is like France. Gently aging but still a warm and desirable place to visit.

Between 41 and 50, she is like parts of Eastern Europe. Ravaged by war, haunted by past mistakes. Massive reconstruction is now necessary.

Between 51 and 60, she is like Russia. Very wide and borders are unpatrolled. The frigid climate keeps people away.

Between 61 and 70, a woman is like Mongolia. A glorious and all-conquering past, but alas, no future.

After 70, they become like Afghanistan. Everyone knows where it is, but no one wants to go there.

The geography of man

Between 15 and 90, a man is like Australia. Ruled by a dick!

Intelligent lass

Eleven people were hanging onto a rope under a helicopter — 10 men and one woman.

The rope was not strong enough to carry them all, so they decided that one had to drop off; otherwise they all were going to fall.

They were not able to choose that person, but then the woman made a very touching speech. She said that she would voluntarily let go of the rope, because as a woman she was used to giving up everything for her husband and kids and for men in general without ever getting anything in return. As soon as she finished her speech, all the men applauded.

Fairy magic

A fairy suddenly appeared to a married couple celebrating 35 years of marriage. The fairy said: 'For being such an exemplary married couple for 35 years, I will give you each a wish.'

'I want to travel around the world with my dearest husband,' said the wife.

The fairy waved her magic stick, and *abracadabra*! Two first-class tickets appeared in her hands. The couple couldn't believe their eyes!

Now it was the husband's turn. He thought for a moment and said: 'Well, love, this moment is very romantic and all, but an opportunity like this only occurs once in a lifetime. So, I'm sorry, dearest, but my wish is to have a wife 30 years younger than me.'

The wife was deeply hurt and disappointed but a wish was a wish.

The fairy made a circle with her magic stick, and *abracadabra*! Suddenly the husband was 90 years old!

Men might be bastards, but fairies are females.

All the equipment

One morning the husband returns after several hours of fishing and decides to take a nap. Although not familiar with the lake, the wife decides to take the boat out. She motors out a short distance, anchors and continues to read her book.

Along comes a park ranger in his boat. He pulls up alongside the woman and says, 'Good morning, ma'am. What are you doing?'

'Reading a book,' she replies.

'You're in a restricted fishing area,' he informs her.

'I'm sorry, officer, but I'm not fishing; I'm reading.'

'Yes, but you have all the equipment. For all I know you could start at any moment. I'll have to take you in and write you an offence ticket.'

'If you do that, I'll have to charge you with sexual assault,' says the woman.

'But I haven't even touched you,' says the ranger.

'That's true, but you have all the equipment. For all I know you could start at any moment.'

'Have a nice day, ma'am.' And he leaves.

Nearly got caught

A brunette, a redhead and a blonde all worked in the same office with the same female boss. Every day, they noticed their boss left work early. One day, the girls decided that when the boss left, they'd leave right behind her. After all, she never called in or came back to the office when she left early, so how was she to know?

The next day, all three left the office right after the boss left. The brunette was thrilled to be home early. She did a little gardening and went to bed early. The redhead was elated to be able to get in a quick workout at the health club before meeting her dinner date.

The blonde was happy to be home, but when she got to the bedroom she heard a muffled noise from inside. Slowly, quietly, she cracked open the door and was mortified to see her husband in bed with *her boss*. Ever so gently, she closed the door and crept out of her house.

The next day at coffee break, the brunette and redhead decided they were leaving early again, and asked the blonde if she was coming with them. '*No way*,' she exclaimed, 'I almost got caught yesterday.'

A girl's prayer

Lord, before I lay me down to sleep,
I pray for a man who's not a creep,
One who's handsome, smart and strong,
One whose willy's thick and long.
One who thinks before he speaks,
When promises to call, he won't wait weeks.
I pray that he is gainfully employed,
And when I spend his cash, won't be annoyed.
Pulls out my chair and opens my door,
Massages my back and begs to do more.

Oh! Send me a man who will make love to my mind,
Knows just what to say, when I ask, 'How big's my behind?'
One who'll make love till my body's a twitchin',
In the hall, the loo, the garden and kitchen!
I pray that this man will love me no end,
And never attempt to shag my best friend.
And as I kneel and pray by my bed,
I look at the wanker you sent me instead.
Amen.

A boy's prayer

Lord, I pray for a lady with big tits.
Amen.

Young woman's diary

Monday: Went out with John tonight. We were in his car and he tried to get too friendly. I got out of the car and walked away. My legs are still my best friends.

Tuesday: Went out with Peter tonight. We were in his car and he tried to get too friendly also. I got out of the car and walked away. My legs are still my best friends.

Wednesday: Went out with Jock tonight. I like Jock. We were in his car and he tried to get too friendly. I didn't get out and walk away. Even the best of friends must part!

What women want in a man, original list

1. Handsome
2. Charming
3. Financially successful
4. A caring listener
5. Witty
6. In good shape
7. Dresses with style
8. Appreciates finer things
9. Full of thoughtful surprises
10. An imaginative, romantic lover

What women want in a man, revised list (age 32)

1. Nice looking
2. Opens car doors, holds chairs
3. Has enough money for a nice dinner
4. Listens more than talks
5. Laughs at my jokes
6. Carries bags of groceries with ease
7. Owns at least one tie
8. Appreciates a good home-cooked meal
9. Remembers birthdays and anniversaries
10. Seeks romance at least once a week

What women want in a man, revised list (age 42)

1. Not too ugly
2. Doesn't drive off until I'm in the car
3. Works steady — splurges on dinner out occasionally
4. Nods head when I'm talking
5. Usually remembers punchlines of jokes
6. Is in good-enough shape to rearrange the furniture
7. Wears a shirt that covers his stomach
8. Knows not to buy champagne with screw-top lids
9. Remembers to put the toilet seat down
10. Shaves most weekends

What women want in a man, revised list (age 52)

1. Keeps hair in nose and ears trimmed
2. Doesn't belch or scratch in public
3. Doesn't borrow money too often
4. Doesn't nod off to sleep when I'm talking
5. Doesn't retell the same joke too many times
6. Is in good-enough shape to get off couch on weekends
7. Usually wears matching socks and fresh underwear
8. Appreciates a good TV dinner
9. Remembers your name on occasion
10. Shaves some weekends

What women want in a man, revised list (age 62)

1. Doesn't scare small children
2. Remembers where bathroom is
3. Doesn't require much money for upkeep
4. Only snores lightly when asleep
5. Remembers why he's laughing
6. Is in good-enough shape to stand up by himself
7. Usually wears some clothes
8. Likes soft foods
9. Remembers where he left his teeth
10. Remembers that it's the weekend

What women want in a man, revised list (age 72)

1. Breathing
2. Doesn't miss the toilet

Respect

A reporter who did a story on gender roles in Kabul, Afghanistan, several years before the Afghan conflict, noted then that women customarily walked five paces behind their husbands.

She recently returned to Kabul and observed that women still walk behind their husbands.

She approached one of the Afghan women and asked: 'Why do you now seem happy with the old custom that you once tried so desperately to change?'

The woman looked her in the eyes and, without hesitation, said: 'Land mines!'

Moral of the story: behind every man is a damn smart woman!

Punctuation is important

An English professor wrote the words 'a woman without her man is nothing' on the blackboard and directed the students to punctuate it correctly.

The men wrote: 'A woman, without her man, is nothing.'
The women wrote: 'A woman: without her, man is nothing.'

Perspective is everything!

Dogs' names

A girl was visiting her blonde friend who had acquired two new dogs, and asked her what their names were. The blonde responded by saying that one was named Rolex and one was named Timex.

Her friend said, 'Whoever heard of someone naming dogs like that?'

'HelOOOooo,' answered the blonde. 'They're watch dogs!'

Girl's diary

Saturday, 16th August 2003

Saw John in the evening and he was acting really strangely. I went shopping with the girls and I did turn up a bit late in the afternoon so I thought it might be that. The bar was really crowded and loud so I suggested we go somewhere quieter to talk. He was still very subdued and distracted so I suggested we go somewhere nice to eat. All through dinner he just didn't seem himself; he hardly laughed, and didn't seem to be paying any attention to me or to what I was saying. I just knew that something was wrong. He dropped me back home and I wondered if he was going to come in; he hesitated, but followed. I asked him again if there was something the matter but he just half shook his head and turned the television on. After about 10 minutes of silence, I said I was going upstairs to bed. I put my arms around him and told him that I loved him deeply. He just gave a sigh, and a sad sort of smile. He didn't follow me up, but later he did, and I was surprised when we made love. He still seemed distant and a bit cold, and I started to think that he was going to leave me, and that he had found someone else. I cried myself to sleep.

Boy's diary

Saturday, 16th August 2003

Wallabies lost to New Zealand. Got a root.

Lesbian bar

A blind man enters a lesbian bar by mistake. He finds his way to a bar stool and orders a drink. After sitting there for a while, he yells to the bartender, 'Hey, you want to hear a blonde joke?'

The bar immediately falls absolutely quiet.

The woman next to him says, 'Before you tell that joke, sir, I think it's fair — given that you are blind — that you know five things: (1) the bartender is a blonde girl; (2) the bouncer is a blonde girl; (3) I'm a six-foot-tall blonde with a black belt in karate; (4) the woman sitting next to me is blonde and is a professional weightlifter; and (5) the lady to your right is a blonde and is a professional wrestler. Now, think about it seriously, mister. Do you still want to tell that joke?'

The blind man thinks for a second, shakes his head, and declares, 'Nah, not if I'm going to have to explain it five times.'

It's a girl thing

Q: What do you call a cupboard full of lesbians?
A: A licker cabinet.

Q: What do you call an Eskimo lesbian?
A: A Klondyke.

Q: What do you call 100 lesbians with guns?
A: Militia Etheridge.

Q: Why can't lesbians diet and wear make-up at the same time?
A: Because they can't eat Jenny Craig with Mary Kay on their face.

Q: What do you call two lesbians in a canoe?
A: Fur traders.

Q: What is a lesbian dinosaur called?
A: A Lickalotapus.

Q: What do you call a lesbian with long fingers?
A: Well hung.

Q: What's the difference between a Ritz cracker and a lesbian?
A: One's a snack cracker, the other's a crack smacker.

Q: What do lesbians call an open can of tuna?
A: Potpourri.

Q: What did the lesbian vampire say to her partner?
A: See you next month.

Q: Did you hear that Ellen DeGeneres drowned?
A: She was found face down in Ricki Lake.

Q: How can you tell a tough lesbian bar?
A: Even the pool table doesn't have balls.

Q: Do you know what drag is?
A: It's when a man wears everything a lesbian won't.

Q: What do you call lesbian twins?
A: Lick-a-likes.

Q: How can you tell if a lesbian is butch?
A: She kick-starts her vibrator and rolls her own tampons.

Q: What's the definition of confusion?
A: Twenty blind lesbians in a fish market.

Stranded

On a chain of beautiful deserted islands in the middle of nowhere, the following people are stranded:

- Two Italian men and one Italian woman
- Two French men and one French woman
- Two German men and one German woman
- Two Greek men and one Greek woman
- Two English men and one English woman
- Two Bulgarian men and one Bulgarian woman
- Two Japanese men and one Japanese woman
- Two Chinese men and one Chinese woman
- Two Irish men and one Irish woman
- Two American men and one American woman

One month later, the following things have occurred:

One Italian man killed the other Italian man for the Italian woman.

The two French men and the French woman are living happily together in a ménage à trois.

The two German men have a strict weekly schedule of alternating visits with the German woman.

The two Greek men are sleeping with each other and the Greek woman is cleaning and cooking for them.

The two English men are waiting for someone to introduce them to the English woman.

The two Bulgarian men took one look at the Bulgarian woman and started swimming to another island.

The two Japanese have faxed Tokyo and are awaiting instructions.

The two Chinese men have set up a restaurant, and have gotten the woman pregnant in order to supply employees for their store.

The two Irish men divided the island into North and South and set up a distillery. They do not remember if sex is in the picture because it gets somewhat foggy after a few litres of coconut whisky. However, they're satisfied because the English aren't having any fun.

The two American men are contemplating suicide, because the American woman will not shut up and complains relentlessly about her body, the true nature of feminism, what the sun is doing to her skin, how she can do anything they can do, the necessity of fulfilment, the equal division of household chores, how sand and palm trees make her look fat, how her last boyfriend respected her opinion and treated her better than they do, how her relationship with her mother is the root cause of all her problems, and why didn't they bring a damn cell phone so they could call 911 and get them all rescued off this godforsaken deserted island in the middle of frigging nowhere so she can get her nails done and go shopping …

Female fancy

In a recent Morgan online poll, 38,562 men across Australia were asked to identify a woman's ultimate fantasy — 97.8 per cent of the respondents said that a woman's ultimate fantasy is to have two men at once. While this has been verified by a recent sociological study, it appears that most men do not realise that in this fantasy, one man is cooking and the other is cleaning.

Blonde painter

This blonde decides one day that she is sick and tired of all these blonde jokes and how all blondes are perceived as stupid, so she decides to show her husband that blondes really are smart. While her husband is off at work, she decides that she is going to paint a couple of rooms in the house.

The next day, right after her husband leaves for work, she gets down to the task at hand.

Her husband arrives home at 5.30 and smells the distinctive smell of paint. He walks into the living room and finds his wife lying on the floor in a pool of sweat. He notices that she is wearing a ski jacket and a fur coat at the same time.

He goes over and asks her if she is OK. She replies yes. He asks what she is doing. She replies that she wanted to prove to him that not all blonde women are dumb and she wanted to do it by painting the house. He then asks her why she has a ski jacket over her fur coat. She replies that she was reading the directions on the paint can and they said: 'for best results, put on two coats.'

Melbourne's Husband Shopping Centre

Recently a 'Husband Shopping Centre' opened in Melbourne, where women could go to choose a husband. It was laid out in five floors, with the men increasing in positive attributes as you ascended. The only rule was, once you opened the door to any floor, you *had* to choose a man from that floor; if you went up a floor, you couldn't go back down, except to leave the place, never to return.

A couple of girlfriends went to the shopping centre to find husbands.

On the first floor the door had a sign saying: 'These men have jobs and love kids.' The women read the sign and said, 'Well, that's better than not having a job, or not loving kids, but I wonder what's further up?' So up they went.

At the second floor, the sign read: 'These men have high-paying jobs, love kids, and are extremely good looking.' 'Hmmm,' said the ladies. 'But I wonder what's further up?'

At the third floor the sign read, 'These men have high-paying jobs, are extremely good looking, love kids and help with the housework.'

'Wow!' said the women. 'Very tempting, *but* there's more further up!' And up they went. Fourth floor. This door had a sign saying, 'These men have high-paying jobs, love kids, are extremely good looking, help with the housework, and have a strong romantic streak.'

'Oh, mercy me, but just think! What must be awaiting us further on!' So up to the fifth floor they went. At the fifth floor the sign said, 'This floor is empty and exists only to prove that women are usually impossible to please.'

First-class ride

A plane is on its way to Melbourne when a blonde in Economy gets up and moves to the First Class section and sits down. The flight attendant watches her do this and asks to see her ticket. She then tells the blonde passenger that she paid for Economy and that she will have to go and sit in the back.

The blonde replies, 'I'm blonde, I'm beautiful, I'm going to Melbourne and I'm staying right here!'

The flight attendant goes into the cockpit and tells the pilot and co-pilot that there is some blonde bimbo sitting in First Class who belongs in Economy and won't move back to her seat.

The co-pilot goes back to the blonde and tries to explain that because she only paid for Economy she is only entitled to an Economy place and she will have to leave and return to her original seat.

The blonde replies, 'I'm blonde, I'm beautiful, I'm going to Melbourne and I'm staying right here!'

Exasperated, the co-pilot tells the pilot that it was no use and that he probably should have the police waiting when they land to arrest this blonde woman who won't listen to reason.

The pilot says, 'You say she's blonde? I'll handle this. I'm married to a blonde, and I speak fluent blonde!'

He goes back to the blonde, whispers in her ear, and she says, 'Oh, I'm sorry — I had no idea,' gets up and moves back to her seat in the Economy section.

The flight attendant and co-pilot are amazed and ask him what he said to make her move without any fuss.

The pilot replies, 'I told her First Class isn't going to Melbourne.'

Computer signs

Perfect breasts: (o)(o)
Fake silicone breasts: (+)(+)
Perky breasts: (*)(*)
Big nipple breasts: (@)(@)

A cups: o o

D cups: (O)(O)

Wonderbra breasts: (oYo)

Cold breasts: (^)(^)

Lopsided breasts: (o)(O)

Pierced breasts: (Q)(O)

Hanging tassels breasts: (p)(q)

Grandma's breasts: \ o /\ o /

Against-the-shower-door breasts: ( )( )

Android breasts: o   o

Dolly Parton's breasts: ($)($)

Three men and a river

One day, three men were hiking and unexpectedly came upon a large, raging, violent river. They needed to get to the other side, but had no idea how to do so. The first man prayed to God, saying, 'Please, God, give me the strength to cross this river.'

Poof! God gave him big arms and strong legs, and he was able to swim across the river in about two hours, after almost drowning a couple of times.

Seeing this, the second man prayed to God, saying, 'Please, God, give me the strength and the tools to cross this river.'

Poof! God gave him a rowboat and he was able to row across the river in about an hour, after almost capsizing the boat a couple of times.

The third man had seen how this worked out for the other two, so he also prayed to God, saying, 'Please, God, give me the strength and the tools — and the intelligence — to cross this river.'

And *poof!* God turned him into a woman. She looked at the map, hiked upstream a couple of hundred yards then walked across the bridge.

Barbecue

A woman was standing before the bedroom mirror, admiring herself in her expensive new outfit. She posed this way and that. Her husband, looking on with disinterest, remarked, 'Your bum is the size of a three-burner barbecue!'

Later that evening, tucked up cosy in bed, he leant over, tapped her on the shoulder, and asked hopefully, 'How about it?'

She replied, 'It's hardly worth lighting the barbie for half a sausage, now, is it?'

WomenSpeak

MENtal illness, MENstrual cramps, MENtal breakdown, MENopause. Ever notice how all of women's problems start with men?

And when we have real problems, it's HISterectomy! with the GUYnecologist!

Male understanding of words women use

Fine: This is the word women use to end an argument when they feel they are right and you need to shut up. Never use 'fine' to describe how a woman looks — this will cause you to have One of Those Arguments.

Five minutes: This is half an hour. It is equivalent to the five minutes that your football game is going to last before you take out the garbage, so it's an even trade.

Nothing: This means 'something', and you should be on your toes. 'Nothing' is usually used to describe the feeling a woman has of wanting to turn you inside out, upside down, and backwards. 'Nothing' usually signifies an argument that will last 'five minutes' and end with 'fine'.

Go ahead (with raised eyebrows): This is a dare. One that will result in a woman getting upset over 'nothing' and will end with the word 'fine'.

Go ahead (normal eyebrows): This means: 'I give up' or 'do what you want because I don't care'. You will get a raised-eyebrow 'go ahead' in just a few minutes, followed by 'nothing' and 'fine' and she will talk to you in about 'five minutes' when she cools off.

Loud sigh: This is not actually a word, but is a non-verbal statement often misunderstood by men. A 'loud sigh' means she thinks you are an idiot at that moment, and wonders why she is wasting her time standing here and arguing with you over 'nothing'.

Soft sighs: Again, not a word, but a non-verbal statement. 'Soft sighs' mean that she is content. Your best bet is to not move or breathe, and she will stay content.

That's OK: This is one of the most dangerous statements that a woman can make to a man. 'That's OK' means that she wants to think long and hard before paying you back for whatever it is that you have done. 'That's OK' is often used with the word 'fine' and in conjunction with a 'raised eyebrow'.

Go ahead: At some point in the near future, you are going to be in some mighty big trouble.

Please do: This is not a statement, it is an offer. A woman is giving you the chance to come up with whatever excuse or reason you have for doing whatever it is that you have done. You have a fair chance with the truth, so be careful and you shouldn't get a 'That's OK'.

Thanks: A woman is thanking you. Do not faint. Just say 'you're welcome'.

Thanks a lot: This is very different from 'thanks'. A woman will say 'thanks a lot' when she is really ticked off at you. It signifies that you have offended her in some callous way, and it will be followed by the 'loud sigh'. Be careful not to ask what is wrong after the 'loud sigh', as she will only tell you 'nothing'.

Course for men

Proposed schedule and course descriptions. (Note: due to the complexity and level of difficulty involved in acquiring an understanding of these concepts, each course can accept a maximum of six participants.)

Topic 1: How to fill up the ice-cube trays
Step-by-step instructions with slide presentation, followed by hands-on exercises in the lab.

Topic 2: Toilet-paper rolls – do they grow on the holders?
Round-table discussion.

Topic 3: Target practice – is it possible to urinate using the technique of lifting the seat and avoiding the floor/walls and nearby bathtub?
Field trip to nearby bathroom and group session.

Topic 4: Fundamental differences between the laundry hamper and the floor
Pictures and explanatory graphics.

Topic 5: Dishes and silverware – can they levitate and fly into the kitchen sink after dinner?
Secret camera video presentations of dining tables after meals.

Topic 6: Loss of identity – dealing with those times when the remote is in the hands of your significant other
Helpline contacts given for support groups.

Topic 7: Learning how to find things – starting with looking in the right place instead of turning the house upside down while shouting
Open forum.

Topic 8: Health watch – can bringing her flowers ever be harmful?
Graphics and audiotape.

Topic 9: Can men ask for directions when lost?
Some real-life testimonials.

Topic 10: Men as co-pilots – is it genetically possible to control the impulse to back-seat drive?
Driving simulation exercises, including sitting quietly without wincing as she parallel parks.

Topic 11: Learning to live – so what exactly are the basic differences between mother and wife?
Class discussions and role-playing.

Topic 12: How to be her ideal shopping companion
Relaxation exercises, meditation and breathing techniques.

Topic 13: Fighting cerebral atrophy – you can remember birthdays, anniversaries, and other important dates (plus, calling when you're going to be late)
Shock therapy sessions and full lobotomies offered.

Feminist slogans

SO MANY MEN, SO FEW WHO CAN AFFORD ME.

GOD MADE US SISTERS, PROZAC MADE US FRIENDS.

COFFEE, CHOCOLATE, MEN … SOME THINGS ARE JUST BETTER RICH.

DON'T TREAT ME ANY DIFFERENTLY THAN YOU WOULD THE QUEEN.

I'M OUT OF OESTROGEN AND I HAVE A GUN.

WARNING: I HAVE AN ATTITUDE AND I KNOW HOW TO USE IT.

OF COURSE I DON'T LOOK BUSY … I DID IT RIGHT THE FIRST TIME.

DO NOT START WITH ME. YOU WILL NOT WIN.

ALL STRESSED OUT AND NO ONE TO CHOKE.

HOW CAN I MISS YOU IF YOU WON'T GO AWAY?

DON'T UPSET ME! I'M RUNNING OUT OF PLACES TO HIDE THE BODIES.

IF YOU WANT BREAKFAST IN BED, SLEEP IN THE KITCHEN.

Good girl

A blonde girl comes home from school one evening. She runs to her mum and says: 'Mummy, today at school we learnt how to count. Well, all the other girls only counted to five, but listen to me: 1, 2, 3, 4, 5, 6, 7, 8, 9, 10. That's good, innit?'

'Yes, darling, very good.'

'Is that because I'm blonde?'

'Yes, darling, it's because you're blonde.'

Next day, the girl comes back from school and says: 'Mummy, today at school we learnt the alphabet. All the other girls only went as far as D, but listen to me: A, B, C, D, E, F, G, H, I, J, K! That's good, innit?'

'Yes, darling, very good.'

'Is that because I'm blonde, Mummy?'

'Yes, darling, it's because you're blonde.'

Next day, she returns from school and cries: 'Mummy, today we went swimming, and well, all the other girls have no breasts, but look at me!' She proceeds to flash her impressive 36Ds at her mum. 'Is that because I'm blonde, Mummy?'

'No, darling, it's because you're 25.'

Brain transplant

The relatives gathered in the waiting room of the hospital where their family member lay gravely ill.

Finally, the doctor came in looking sad and sombre. 'I'm afraid I'm the bearer of bad news,' he said as he surveyed the worried relatives. 'The only hope left for your loved one at this time is a brain transplant. It's an experimental procedure, very risky, but it is the only chance. However, no insurance will cover the procedure, so you will have to pay for the brain yourselves.'

The family members sat silent as they absorbed the news. After a great length of time, someone asked, 'Well, how much does a brain cost?'

The doctor quickly responded, '$5000 for a male brain, and $200 for a female brain.'

The moment turned awkward. Men in the room tried not to smile, avoiding eye contact with the women, but some actually smirked. A man, unable to control his curiosity, blurted out the question everyone wanted to ask, 'Why is the male brain so much more?'

The doctor smiled at the childlike innocence and explained to the entire group, 'It's just standard pricing procedure. We have to mark down the price of the female brains because they've actually been used.'

Hard

A man is in a hotel lobby. He wants to ask the clerk a question. As he turns to go to the front desk, he accidentally bumps into a woman beside him and, as he does, his elbow goes into her breast. They are both quite startled.

The man turns to her and says, 'Ma'am, if your heart is as soft as your breast, I know you'll forgive me.'

She replies, 'If your penis is as hard as your elbow, I'm in room 221.'

4 COURTSHIP

The jokes in this section are as old as Moses. Well, at least they seem to be one of the most enduring joke categories, and one common to all cultures. Somehow we find this particular endeavour a favourite for all manner of story-telling from nursery stories to smutty jokes. Some can be interpreted as traditional learning, where wisdom is gleaned from cautionary tales, while others are pure amusement. They come in all shapes and sizes with travelling salesmen being one of the most popular categories. Maybe it is a comment on the vast size of Australia where visitors knocking on outback station doors were few and far between, and viewed as curiosities. More likely, they are popular characters because they arrive and disappear mysteriously. It appears that in most rural jokes the young girl is often dim-witted whilst in the city it is the young man who is likely to be the one to learn a lesson.

Australian courtship, of the 'Dave and Mabel' variety ('Get off the table, Mabel, the money's for the beer.') is rough and ready and full of gawky bush characters who, one is led to believe, have never seen a member of the opposite sex, at least of the human variety. There's quite a lot of the Barry Humphries character 'Bazza McKenzie' in the bush male when it comes to courting and it is easy to imagine the common ground of the country wedding or dance, where the girls are up one end, hankies in hand, and the fellows the other, eyeing the keg. Sex seems a long way away from either side's minds.

You will learn here the 'five secrets of a perfect relationship', what happens to travelling salesmen, what happened to the farmer's four daughters, and some keen insights from kids on how courtship works.

Mateship

A bloke stops to visit his mate who has a broken leg.

His friend says, 'My feet are cold, mate; can you go and get my slippers from upstairs, please?'

He goes upstairs, and there are his mate's gorgeous twin 20-year-old daughters. Thinking quickly he says, 'Hi, girls. Your dad sent me up here to shag you.'

The first daughter says, 'I don't believe that's true.'

He says, 'I'll prove it,' and yells down the stairs, 'Both of them?'

His mate yells back, 'Of course, both of them.'

Manners

During class, an elderly teacher trying to teach good manners asks the students:

'Michael, if you were on a date, having supper with a nice young lady, how would you tell her that you had to go to the bathroom?'

Michael replied, 'Just a minute, I have to go pee.'

The teacher scolds him, 'That would be rude and impolite! What about you, Peter, how would you say it?'

Peter offers, 'I am sorry, but I really need to go to the bathroom. I'll be right back.'

'That's better,' says the teacher, 'but it's still not very nice to say the word "bathroom" at the dinner table.'

She continues, 'And you, little Johnny, are you able to use your intelligence for once and show us your good manners?'

Johnny stood up and announced, 'I would say: "Darling, may I please be excused for a moment? I have to shake hands with a very dear friend of mine, whom I hope you'll get to meet after supper."'

The teacher fainted.

Just flatmates

A young man called Dale invited his mother for dinner. During the course of the meal, his mother couldn't help but notice how handsome Dale's flatmate was. She had long been suspicious of a relationship between the two boys, and this only made her more curious.

Over the course of the evening, while watching the two interact, she started to wonder if there was more between Dale and his flatmate than met the eye. Reading his mother's thoughts, Dale volunteered, 'I know what you must be thinking, but I assure you, Simon and I are just flatmates.'

About a week later, Simon approached Dale, saying, 'Ever since your mother came to dinner, I've been unable to find the frying pan. You don't suppose she took it, do you?'

Dale thought, 'Well, I doubt it, but I'll e-mail her just to be sure.'

Here is the letter he wrote:

Dear Mother,
I'm not saying that you 'did' take the frying pan from my apartment, I'm not saying that you 'did not' take the frying pan, but the fact remains that it has been missing ever since you were here for dinner.
Love, Dale

Several days later, Dale received this e-mail from his mother:

Dear son,
I'm not saying that you 'do' sleep with Simon, and I'm not saying that you 'do not' sleep with Simon, but the fact remains that if he was sleeping in his own bed, he would have found the frying pan by now.
Love, Mum

Black Bob's holiday

Black Bob and his mate Will were having a few Cascades in the Launceston pub. 'Ya know, I reckon I'm 'bout ready for a holiday. Only this year I reckon I'm gonna do it a little different. The last few years, I've taken your advice about where to go. Three years ago when you said to go to Hawaii I went to Hawaii and Earlene got pregnant.'

Will nodded as he sipped his beer.

'Then two years ago, you told me to go to San Francisco, and Earlene got pregnant again.'

Will nodded again.

'Last year you suggested Bali and darned if Earlene didn't get pregnant again.'

'So, what you gonna do this year that's different?' inquired Will.

Black Bob knowingly said, 'This year I'm taking Earlene with me!'

Marital dues

On their wedding night, the young bride approached her new husband and asked for $20 for their first lovemaking encounter. In his highly aroused state he readily agreed. This scenario was repeated each time they made love, for the next 30 years, with him thinking that it was a cute way for her to afford new clothes and other incidentals that she needed.

Arriving home around noon one day, she was surprised to find her husband in a very drunken state. During the next few minutes, he explained that his employer was going through a process of corporate downsizing, and he had been fired. It was unlikely that, at the age of 55, he'd be able to find another position that paid anywhere near what he'd been earning, and therefore they were financially ruined.

Calmly, his wife handed him her bankbook, which showed 30 years of deposits with interest, totalling nearly one million dollars. Then she showed him certificates of deposits issued by the bank, worth over two million dollars, and informed him that they were one of the largest depositors in the bank. She then explained that for the 30 years she had charged him for sex, these holdings had multiplied and these were the results of her savings and investments.

Faced with evidence of cash and investments worth over three million dollars, her husband was so astounded he could barely speak, but finally he found his voice and blurted out, 'If I'd had any idea what you were doing, I would have given you all my business!'

That's when she shot him.

Booze business

Tom had been in the liquor business for 25 years. Finally sick of the stress he quit his job and bought 50 acres of land in Alaska, as far from humanity as possible. He saw the postman once a week and got groceries once a month. Otherwise it was total peace and quiet.

After six months or so of almost total isolation, someone knocked on his door. He opened it and a huge, bearded man was standing there.

'Name's Lars, your neighbour from 40 miles up the road,' the man said. 'Having a Christmas party Friday night. Thought you might like to come.'

'Great,' said Tom, 'after six months out here I'm ready to meet some local folks. Thank you.'

As Lars was leaving, he stopped. 'Gotta warn you, there'll be some drinkin'.'

'Not a problem,' said Tom. 'After 25 years in the business, I can drink with the best of 'em.'

Again, the big man started to leave and stopped. 'More'n likely gonna be some fightin' too.'

'Well, I get along with people, I'll be all right. I'll be there. Thanks again.'

'More'n likely be some wild sex, too.'

'Now, that's really not a problem,' said Tom, warming to the idea. 'I've been all alone for six months! I'll definitely be there. By the way, what should I wear?'

'Don't much matter. Just gonna be the two of us.'

Maximum security

A prisoner escapes from his maximum-security prison where he has been detained for 15 years. As he runs away, he finds a house and breaks into it. He finds a young couple in bed. He gets the guy out of bed, ties him up on a chair, ties up the woman to the bed, climbs on top of her, kisses her on the neck, then gets up and goes to the bathroom. While he's there, the husband whispers to his wife: 'Listen, this guy is a prisoner; look at his clothes! He probably spent a lot of time in prison and hasn't seen a woman in years. I saw the way he kissed your neck. If he wants sex, don't resist, don't complain, just do what he tells you, give him satisfaction. This guy is probably dangerous: if he gets angry, he'll kill us both. Be strong, honey, and remember, I love you.'

To which the wife responds, 'He wasn't kissing my neck. He was whispering in my ear. He told me that he found you very sexy, and asked if we kept any Vaseline in the bathroom. Be strong, honey, and remember, I love you too.'

Two new elements added to the Periodic Table of the Elements

1. Element Name: WOMANIUM
Symbol: WO

Atomic Weight: (Don't even go there)

Physical Properties: Generally soft and round in form. Boils at nothing and may freeze at any time. Melts when treated properly. Very bitter if not used well.

Chemical Properties: Very active. Highly unstable. Possesses strong affinity with gold, silver, platinum and precious stones. Violent when left alone. Able to absorb great amounts of exotic food. Turns slightly green when placed next to a better specimen.

Usage: Highly ornamental. An extremely good catalyst for dispersion of wealth. Probably the most powerful income-reducing agent known.

Caution: Highly explosive in inexperienced hands.

2. Element Name: MANIUM

Symbol: XY

Atomic Weight: (180 +/- 50)

Physical Properties: Solid at room temperature, but gets bent out of shape easily. Fairly dense and sometimes flaky. Difficult to find a pure sample. Due to rust, aging samples are unable to create electricity.

Chemical Properties: Attempts to bond with any WO any chance it can get. Also tends to form strong bonds with itself. Becomes explosive when mixed with KD (Element: CHILDIUM) for prolonged periods of time. Neutralise by saturating with alcohol.

Usage: None known. Possibly good methane source. Good samples are able to produce large quantities on command.

Caution: In the absence of WO, this element rapidly decomposes and begins to smell.

The five secrets of the perfect relationship ...

1. It is important that a man helps you around the house and has a job.
2. It is important that a man makes you laugh.
3. It is important to find a man you can count on and who doesn't lie to you.
4. It is important that a man is good in bed and loves making love to you.
5. It is important that these four men don't know each other.

Doin' The Twist

It's the spring of 1957 and Bobby goes to pick up his date. Bobby's a pretty hip guy with cool clothes and his own car. When he gets to the front door, the girl's father answers and invites him in.

'Carrie's not ready yet, so why don't you have a seat?'

'That's cool,' says Bobby.

Carrie's father asks Bobby what they're planning to do.

Bobby replies politely that they will probably just go to a milk bar or a film.

Carrie's father responds, 'Why don't you two go out and screw? I hear all the kids are doing it.'

Naturally, this comes as quite a surprise to Bobby, so he asks Carrie's dad to repeat it. 'Yeah,' says Carrie's father, 'Carrie really likes to screw — she'll screw all night if we let her!'

Well, this just makes Bobby's eyes light up, and he immediately revises his plans for the evening.

A few minutes later, Carrie comes downstairs in her little poodle skirt and announces that she's ready to go. Almost breathless with anticipation, Bobby escorts his date out the front door.

About 20 minutes later, a thoroughly dishevelled Carrie rushes back into the house, slams the door behind her, and screams at her father: *'Dammit, Daddy! The Twist! It's called The Twist!!'*

Fire alarm

Two girlfriends went out one Saturday night without their husbands, and they had such a good time they got somewhat inebriated. Staggering on their way home, they both desperately needed a wee. With no public toilets in sight, the nearest venue was a cemetery, so they both ducked behind the fence to relieve themselves. After they'd finished, the first woman took off her knickers to wipe herself and then threw them away. The other woman, realising she was wearing some very expensive knickers, didn't want to throw hers away, so she looked around for something else before deciding to use the ribbon off a nearby wreath. So now, both feeling a lot better, they carried on with their stagger home.

The following morning the two husbands were talking to each other on the phone. One commented, 'I think we need to start keeping a closer eye on our wives, you know. I reckon they're up to no good. My wife came home last night without any knickers on!'

The other one replied, 'Tell me about it! If you think that's bad, my wife came home with a card stuck to her arse. It read "All the members at the Rural Fire Brigade will never forget you."'

Guilt money

A man met a beautiful girl and she agreed to spend the night with him for $400. So they spent the night together. In the morning, before he left, he told the girl that he did not have any cash with him, but that he would have his secretary write a cheque and mail it to her, calling the payment 'Rent for Apartment'. On the way to the office, he regretted what he had done, realising that the whole event was not worth the price. So, he sent a cheque for $200 and enclosed a note:

> Dear Madam,
>
> Enclosed find a cheque in the amount of $200 for rent of your apartment. I am not sending the amount agreed upon because when I rented the apartment, I was under the impression that:
>
> 1. It had never been occupied.
>
> 2. There was plenty of heat.
>
> 3. It was small enough to make me cosy and at home.
>
> Last night, however, I found out that it had been previously occupied, that there wasn't any heat, and that it was entirely too large.

Upon receipt of the note, the girl immediately sent back the following reply:

Dear Sir,
First of all, I cannot understand how you expect such a beautiful apartment to remain unoccupied indefinitely. As for the heat, there is plenty of it if you know how to turn it on. Regarding the space, the apartment is indeed of regular size, but if you don't have enough furniture to fill it, please don't blame the landlord. I will expect full payment due immediately or I will be forced to hire someone to remove your furniture.

Meet the parents

A girl asks her boyfriend to come over Friday night and have dinner with her parents. Since this is such a big event, the girl announces to her boyfriend that, after dinner, she would like to go out and make love for the first time.

Well, the boy is ecstatic, but he has never had sex before, so he takes a trip to the pharmacist to get some condoms. The pharmacist helps the boy for about an hour. He tells the boy everything there is to know about condoms and sex. At the register, the pharmacist asks the boy how many condoms he'd like to buy: a three-pack, 10-pack, or family pack. The boy insists on the family pack because he thinks he will be rather busy, it being his first time and all.

That night, the boy shows up at the girl's parents' house and meets his girlfriend at the door.

'Oh, I'm so excited for you to meet my parents,' she says. 'Come on in!'

The boy goes inside and is taken to the dinner table, where the girl's parents are seated.

The boy quickly offers to say grace and bows his head. A minute passes, and the boy is still deep in prayer, with his head down. Ten minutes pass, and still no movement from the boy.

Finally, after 20 minutes with his head down, the girlfriend leans over and whispers to the boyfriend, 'I had no idea you were this religious.'

The boy turns, and whispers back, 'I had no idea your father was a pharmacist.'

Chinese torture

A young man was lost wandering in a forest, when he came upon a small house. He knocked on the door and was greeted by an ancient Chinese man with a long, grey beard.

'I'm lost,' said the young man. 'Can you put me up for the night?'

'Certainly,' the old man said, 'but on one condition. If you so much as lay a finger on my daughter, I will inflict upon you the three worst Chinese tortures known to man.'

'OK,' said the young man, thinking that the daughter must be pretty old as well, and entered the house. Before dinner, the daughter came down the stairs. She was young, beautiful, and had a fantastic figure. She was obviously attracted to the young man since she couldn't keep her eyes off him during the meal. Remembering the old man's warning, he ignored her and went up to bed alone.

During the night, he could bear it no longer, and sneaked into her room for a night of passion. He was careful to keep everything quiet so the old man wouldn't hear. Near dawn he crept back to his room, exhausted, but happy. He woke to feel a pressure on his chest. Opening his eyes he saw a large rock on his chest with a note on it that read: 'Chinese Torture 1: Large rock on chest.'

'Well, that's pretty crappy,' he thought. 'If that's the best the old man can do then I don't have much to worry about.' He picked the boulder up, walked over to the window and threw the boulder out. As he did so he noticed another note on it that read: 'Chinese Torture 2: Rock tied to left testicle.'

In a panic he glanced down and saw that the rope was already getting close to the end. Figuring that a few broken bones were better than castration, he jumped out of the window after the boulder. As he plummeted downward he saw a large sign on the ground that read: 'Chinese Torture 3: Right testicle tied to bedpost.'

The farmer's four daughters

There was a farmer who had four daughters. One night, he heard a knock at the door and found a young man standing there.

The young man said, 'My name is Freddy. I've come to pick up Betty. We're going out for spaghetti. I hope she's ready.'

The farmer thought that this was cute, so he let them go out.

Pretty soon there was another knock at the door and another young man was there. He said, 'My name is Vance. I've come for Nance. We're going to a dance. Is she ready by chance?'

Again, the farmer thought this was cute and let them go.

Soon, another knock on the door with yet another young man standing there. He said, 'My name is Moe. I'm here to get Flo. We're going to a show. Is she ready to go?'

Again, the farmer was amused and let them go.

Once again there was a knock on the door and a young man was standing there. He began, 'My name is Chuck …'

The farmer shot him.

The glass eye

A man is dining in a fancy restaurant and there is a gorgeous redhead sitting at the next table. He has been checking her out since he sat down, but lacks the nerve to talk with her. Suddenly, she sneezes and her glass eye comes flying out of its socket towards the man. He reflexively reaches out, grabs it out of the air, and hands it back.

'Oh my, I am so sorry,' the woman says as she pops her eye back in place. 'Let me buy you dinner to make it up to you.'

They enjoy a wonderful dinner together, and afterwards go to the theatre followed by drinks. They talk, they laugh, she shares her deepest dreams and he shares his. After paying for everything, she asks him if he would like to come to her place for a nightcap ... and stay for breakfast.

The next morning, she cooks a gourmet meal with all the trimmings. The guy is amazed! Everything has been SO incredible! 'You know,' he says, 'you are the perfect woman. Are you this nice to every guy you meet?'

'No,' she replies. 'You just happened to have caught my eye.'

A recent survey revealed ...

10 per cent of the women had sex within the first hour of their first date.

20 per cent of the men had sex in a non-traditional place.

36 per cent of the women favour nudity.

45 per cent of the women prefer dark men with blue eyes.

46 per cent of the women experienced anal sex.

70 per cent of the women prefer sex in the morning.

80 per cent of the men have never experienced homosexual relations.

90 per cent of the women would like to have sex in the forest.

99 per cent of the women have never experienced sex in the office.

Conclusion: Statistically speaking, you have a better chance of having anal sex in the morning with a strange woman in the forest than to have sex in the office at the end of the day.

Moral: Do not stay late in the office. Nothing good will ever come of it.

Baby, it's cold

A countrywoman and her daughter were riding in an old buggy one cold, blustery day. The daughter said to her mother, 'My hands are so cold.'

The mother replied, 'Put them between your legs; your body heat will warm them up.'

So the daughter did and her hands warmed up.

The next day the daughter was riding with her boyfriend and he said, 'My hands are freezing cold.'

The girl said, 'Put them between my legs. The warmth of my body will warm them up.'

So he did and warmed his hands.

The next day the boyfriend was again in the buggy with the daughter. He said, 'My nose is cold.'

The girl replied, 'Put it between my legs. The warmth of my body will warm it up.'

So he did and warmed his nose.

The next day the boyfriend was smiling when he got into the buggy with the daughter, and said, 'My penis is frozen solid.'

The following day the daughter was riding in the buggy with her mother, and she said, 'Have you ever heard of a "penis"?'

Slightly concerned, the mother said, 'Why yes. Why do you ask?'

The daughter replied, 'Well they make one hell of a mess when they defrost, don't they?'

Worth the money

A man is walking along the strip in Las Vegas and a knockout hooker catches his eye. He strikes up a conversation and eventually asks her, 'How much?'

The hooker replies, 'It starts at $500 for a hand job.'

The guy says, '$500! For a hand job! No hand job is worth that kind of money!'

The hooker says, 'Do you see that Denny's on the corner?'

'Yes.'

'Do you see the Denny's about a block further down?'

'Yes.'

And beyond that, do you see that third Denny's?'

'Yes.'

'Well,' says the hooker, smiling invitingly, 'I own those. And, I own them because I give a hand job that's worth $500.'

The guy says, 'What the hell? I'll give it a try.'

They retire to a nearby motel. Shortly afterwards, the guy is sitting on the bed realising that he just experienced the hand job of a lifetime, worth every bit of $500.

He is so amazed, he says, 'I suppose a blowjob is $1000?'

The hooker replies, '$1500.'

'$1500? No blow job could be worth that.'

The hooker replies, 'Step over here to the window, big boy. Do you see that casino just across the street? I own that casino outright. And I own it because I give a blowjob that's worth every cent of $1500.'

The guy, basking in the afterglow of that terrific hand job, says, 'Sign me up!'

Later that evening, he is sitting on the bed more amazed than before. He can't believe it, but he feels he truly got his money's worth. He decides to dip into the retirement savings for one glorious and unforgettable experience.

He asks the hooker, 'How much for some pussy?'

The hooker says, 'Come over here to the window. Do you see how the whole city of Las Vegas is laid out before us, all those beautiful lights, gambling palaces, and showplaces?'

'Damn!' the guy says, in awe. 'You own the whole city?'

'No,' the hooker replies, 'but I would if I had a pussy.'

Ear infection

A girl goes to see the doctor about an ear infection and he asks her to take off her shirt so he can examine her.

On her chest she has a huge blue 'K'. The doctor asks, 'How did you get that blue "K" on your chest?'

She replies, 'My boyfriend goes to Kings and he's so proud of his school that he never takes off his sweatshirt, even when we're making love.'

So the next day the doctor has to examine another girl. She takes off her shirt and has a huge pink 'J' on her chest. The doctor asks, 'How did you get that pink "J" on your chest?'

The girl replies, 'My boyfriend goes to Joey's and he's so proud of his school that he never takes off his sweatshirt, even when we're making love.'

The next day the doctor has to examine another girl. She takes off her shirt and she has a huge blue 'M' on her chest.

The doctor asks, 'Do you have a boyfriend who goes to Mosman High?'

And the girl replies, 'No, but I have a girlfriend who goes to Wenona.'

5 MARRIAGE VOWS AND BLOWS

Songwriters often have a knack for summing up our feelings, and especially that songwriter who boldly declared that love and matrimony are as inextricably linked as a horse and carriage. However, if humour is to be believed, the horse is more likely to bolt and the wheels fall off the carriage. Love may be blind but humour is brutally forthright in its tendency to attack the institution, from courtship through to death and divorce. Nothing is sacred, not even the marriage ceremony itself, as jokes take the mickey out of every aspect of 'till death do they part'.

There was a time, say 50 years ago, when marriage was held in higher esteem and the humour associated with it was mainly about inexperienced, and often embarrassingly incapable, brides, feet-shuffling husbands, often wedded with a shotgun in their back, and never-ending jokes about meddling mothers-in-law. Television humour appears to have played a role in developing marriage as 'black humour' and one would have to point the bone at a long line of happily/unhappily married couples manufactured by Hollywood & co, including *I Love Lucy*'s Lucy and Desi, Fred and Ethel, George Burns and Gracie Allen, and Archie Bunker and his long-suffering wife, and then there's the classic on-stage, off-stage squabbles of couples like Sonny and Cher. There were Australian productions too and who could forget the couples in *Number 96*? Next came a string of Hollywood feature films that centred on deceitful, conniving, sometimes murderous, husbands and wives. Then, with the increased popularity of television, including cable, the institution was subjected to marriages of all types from the weird to the downright ridiculous.

We have developed acute insensitivity towards marriage, punctuated by hysterical canned laughter whenever the dim-witted wife or dumb-arsed husband enters the room. Then there's the public romps of the British royal family, an American president's philandering and the much-publicised engagements, marriages, divorces etc of every third-rate film or television celebrity that fuel the pages of the trash press and electronic media. There are also countless reality television programs ranging from *The Dating Game* through to *Divorce Court* and *Wife Swap*, where marriage, and its breakdown, is the central issue.

Sex in and out of marriage is a prime humour target and anything and everything can and will go wrong. Sex is considered ridiculous and humour interprets this in every possible way, be it embarrassment, deceit, deviance, dysfunction, divorce or whatever. The more exaggerated and preposterous the better, and nobody is spared as a target.

Happy anniversary

Who says Australian men don't remember anniversaries?

A woman awakens during the night to find that her husband is not in their bed. She puts on her robe and goes downstairs to look for him and finds him sitting at the kitchen table with a hot cup of coffee. He appears to be in deep thought, just staring at the wall. She watches as he wipes a tear from his eye and takes a sip of his coffee.

'What's the matter, dear?' she whispers as she steps into the room. 'Why are you down here at this time of night?'

The husband looks up from his coffee. 'Do you remember 20 years ago when we were dating, and you were only 16?' he asks solemnly.

The wife is touched to tears thinking that her husband is so caring and sensitive. 'Yes, I do,' she replies.

The husband pauses. The words are not coming easily. 'Do you remember when your father caught us in the back seat of my car?'

'Yes, I remember,' says the wife, lowering herself into a chair beside him.

The husband continues. 'Do you remember when he shoved the shotgun in my face and said, "Either you marry my daughter, or I will send you to jail for 20 years"?'

'I remember that too,' she replies softly.

He wipes another tear from his cheek and says, 'I would have gotten out today.'

Headaches

A woman comes home and tells her husband, 'Remember those headaches I've been having all these years? Well, they're gone.'

'No more headaches?' the husband asks. 'What happened?'

His wife replies, 'Margie referred me to a hypnotist. He told me to stand in front of a mirror, stare at myself and repeat, "I do not have a headache, I do not have a headache, I do not have a headache." It worked! The headaches are all gone.'

The husband replies, 'Well, that is wonderful.'

His wife then says, 'You know, you haven't been exactly a ball of fire in the bedroom these last few years. Why don't you go see the hypnotist and see if he can do anything for that?'

The husband agrees to try it.

Following his appointment, the husband comes home, rips off his clothes, picks up his wife and carries her into the bedroom. He puts her on the bed and says, 'Don't move, I'll be right back.'

He goes into the bathroom, comes back a few minutes later, jumps into bed and makes passionate love to his wife like never before.

His wife says, 'Boy, that was wonderful!'

The husband says, 'Don't move! I will be right back.'

He goes back into the bathroom, comes back and round two is even better than the first time. The wife sits up and her head is spinning.

Her husband again says, 'Don't move, I'll be right back.'

With that, he goes back in the bathroom. This time, his wife quietly follows him and there, in the bathroom, she sees him standing at the mirror and saying, 'She's not my wife. She's not my wife. She's not my wife!'

His funeral service will be held on Monday.

Dear husband

Dear husband,

I'm writing you this letter to tell you that I'm leaving you for good.

I've been a good woman to you for seven years and I have nothing to show for it. These last two weeks have been hell. Your boss called to tell me you had quit your job today, and that was the last straw.

Last week you came home and didn't notice that I had gotten my hair and nails done, cooked your favourite meal and even wore a brand new negligee. You came home and ate in two minutes, and went straight to sleep after watching the game. You don't tell me you love me any more, you don't touch me, or anything. You are either cheating or you don't love me any more. Whatever the case is, I'm gone.

Your ex-wife

P.S. If you're trying to find me, don't. Your brother and I are moving away to New Zealand together! Have a great life!

Dear ex-wife,

Nothing has made my day more than receiving your letter. It's true that you and I have been married for seven years, although a good woman is a far cry from what you've been. I watch sports so much to try to drown out your constant nagging. Too bad that doesn't work. I did notice when you cut off all of your hair last week — the first thing that came to mind was: 'You look just like a man!' My mother raised me to not say anything if you can't say anything nice. When you cooked my favourite meal, you must have gotten me confused with my brother, because I stopped eating pork seven years ago. I went to sleep on you when you had on that new negligee because the price tag was still on it. I prayed that it was a coincidence that my brother had just borrowed $50 from me that morning and your negligee was $49.99. After all of this, I still loved you and felt that we could work it out. So when I discovered that I had hit the lotto for 10 million dollars, I quit my job and bought us two tickets to Jamaica. But when I got home you were gone. Everything happens for a reason, I guess. I hope you have the fulfilling life you always wanted. My lawyer said with the letter that you wrote you wouldn't get a dollar from me. So take care.

Signed, Rich as Hell and Free!

P.S. I don't know if I ever told you this but Carl, my brother, was born Carla. I hope that's not a problem.

The perfect dress

Jennifer's wedding day was fast approaching. Nothing could dampen her excitement — not even her parents' nasty divorce. Her mother had found the perfect dress to wear and would be the best-dressed mother-of-the-bride ever!

A week later, Jennifer was horrified to learn that her father's new young wife had bought the exact same dress! Jennifer asked her to exchange it, but she refused, saying: 'Absolutely not! I look a million dollars in this dress, and I'm wearing it.'

Jennifer told her mother, who graciously said, 'Never mind, sweetheart. I'll get another dress. After all, it's your special day.' A few days later, they went shopping and found another gorgeous dress. When they stopped for lunch, Jennifer asked her mother, 'Aren't you going to return the other dress? You really don't have another occasion where you could wear it.' Her mother just smiled and replied, 'Of course I do, dear. I'm wearing it to the rehearsal dinner the night before the wedding!'

(Now I ask you: is there a woman out there, anywhere, who wouldn't enjoy this story?)

Voices

A man was walking down a street when he heard a voice from behind: 'If you take one more step, a brick will fall on your head and kill you.'

The man stopped and a big brick fell right in front of him. The man was astonished.

He went on, and after a while he was about to cross the road when once again the voice shouted: 'Stop! Stand still! If you take one more step a car will run over you and you will die.'

The man did as he was instructed, just as a car came flying around the corner, barely missing him.

'Where are you? Who are you?' the man asked.

'I am your guardian angel,' the voice answered.

'And where were you when I got married??'

Home early

The wife comes home early and finds her husband in their master bedroom making love to a beautiful, sexy, young girl!

'You unfaithful, disrespectful pig! What are you doing? How dare you do this to me, your faithful wife, the mother of your children! I'm leaving this house, I want a divorce!'

The husband replies, 'Wait! Wait a minute! Before you leave, at least listen to what happened.'

'Hmmm, I don't know. Well, it'll be the last thing I'll hear from you. But make it fast, you unfaithful pig, you.'

The husband begins to tell his story ...

'While I was driving home, this young lady asked for a lift. She looked so defenceless that I went ahead and decided to help. I noticed that she was very thin, badly dressed and very dirty. She mentioned that she had not eaten for three days. With great compassion, I brought her home and warmed up the pasta bake that I made for you last night that you wouldn't eat because you're afraid you'll gain weight. The poor thing practically devoured the lot. Since she was very dirty I asked her to take a shower.

'While she was showering, I noticed her clothes were dirty and full of holes so I threw her clothes away. Since she needed clothes, I gave her the pair of jeans that you have had for a few years, but which you can no longer wear because they are too tight on you. I also gave her the blouse that I gave you on our anniversary and you don't wear because I "don't have good taste". I gave her the pullover that my sister gave you for Christmas that you will not wear just to bother my sister, and I also gave her the boots that you bought at the expensive boutique that you never wore again after you saw your co-worker wearing the same pair.'

The husband continues his story. 'The young woman was very grateful to me and I walked her to the door. When we got to the door she turned around and with tears coming out of her eyes she asked me: "Sir, do you have anything else that your wife does not use?"'

Lay-off time

The vice-president of a local company had quite a problem. He was told by his boss to lay off one of his employees, either Mary or Jack.

His choice was a tough one because Mary had been a devoted employee for 10 years and Jack was a fine worker who had a family to support.

That night, the VP tossed and turned in his sleep trying to decide which of his employees he would lay off. Finally he decided the first one to come to work tomorrow would be the one.

Morning finally came and the VP waited at the office for one of the two employees to arrive.

At 8.55 Mary walked into the office. 'I've got a difficult decision,' the VP said. 'I either have to lay you or Jack off.'

'Oh? Jack off,' Mary said. 'I've got a headache.'

How often?

An elderly couple had been dating for some time. Eventually they decided it was time for marriage.

Before the wedding, they went out to dinner and had a long conversation regarding how their marriage might work. They discussed finances, living arrangements and so on.

Finally the old gentleman decided it was time to broach the subject of their physical relationship. 'How often do you like sex?' he asked, rather hopefully.

'Well,' she said, responding very carefully, 'I like it infrequently.'

The old gentleman responded: 'Was that one word or two?'

Golf

A couple was golfing one day on a very, very exclusive golf course, lined with million-dollar houses. On the third tee the husband said, 'Honey, be very careful when you drive the ball. Don't knock out any windows — it'd cost us a fortune to fix.'

The wife teed up and shanked it right through the window of the biggest house on the course. The husband cringed and said, 'I told you to watch out for the houses. All right, let's go up there, apologise and see how much this is going to cost.'

They walked up, knocked on the door, and heard a voice say, 'Come on in.' They opened the door and saw glass all over the floor and a broken bottle lying on its side in the foyer. A man on the couch said, 'Are you the people that broke my window?'

'Uh, yeah. Sorry about that,' the husband replied.

'No, actually I want to thank you. I'm a genie that was trapped for a thousand years in that bottle. You've released me. I'm allowed to grant three wishes — I'll give you each one wish, and I'll keep the last one for myself.'

'OK, great!' the husband said. 'I want a million dollars a year for the rest of my life.'

'No problem — it's the least I could do. And you, what do you want?' the genie said, looking at the wife.

'I want a house in every country of the world,' she said.

'Consider it done,' the genie replied.

'And what's your wish, genie?' the husband said.

'Well, since I've been trapped in that bottle, I haven't had sex with a woman in a thousand years. My wish is to sleep with your wife.'

The husband looked at the wife and said, 'Well, we did get a lot of money and all those houses, honey. I guess I don't care.'

The genie took the wife upstairs and ravished her for two hours. After they were finished, the genie rolled over, looked at the wife, and said, 'How old is your husband, anyway?'

'Thirty-five,' she replied.

'And he still believes in genies? That's amazing.'

Indigenous wisdom

The old Aboriginal chief sat in his hut by the river, smoking his pipe, eyeing the government officials sent to interview him.

'Chief Billy,' one official began, 'you have observed the white man for 90 years. You have observed his wars and his material wealth. You have seen his progress and the damage he has done.'

The chief nodded that it was so. The official continued, 'Considering all these events, in your opinion, where did the white man go wrong?'

The chief stared at the government officials for over a minute, and then calmly replied, 'When white man came to this land, the Aborigines were running it. No taxes. No debt. Plenty kangaroo. Plenty wallaby. Women did all the work. Medicine grew on tree. Aboriginal man he spends all day hunting and fishing, all night screwing women.'

The chief leant back and smiled, adding, 'White man dumb enough to think he could improve system like that.'

True story

The finals of the national poetry contest last year came down to two finalists. One was a Melbourne University law school graduate from an upper-crust family. He was well bred and well connected. The other finalist was a Westie 'bogan' from Broadmeadows TAFE. The rules of the contest required each finalist to compose a four-line poem in one minute or less, and the poem had to contain the word 'Timbuktu'.

The Melbourne University graduate went first. About 30 seconds after the clock started he jumped up and recited the following:

'Slowly across the desert sand,
Trekked the dusty caravan,
Men on camels, two by two,
Destination — Timbuktu.'

The audience went wild. How, they wondered, could the Broadmeadows 'bogan' top that? The clock started again and the second contestant sat in silent thought. Finally in the last few seconds, our man jumped up and recited:
'Tim and me, a-huntin' went,
Met three sluts in a pop-up tent,
They was three, we was two,
So I bucked one and Timbuktu.'

An idiot's sex quiz

A condom is a large apartment complex. True or False
Spread eagle is an extinct bird. True or False
A menstrual cycle has three wheels. True or False
A G-string is part of a fiddle. True or False
Anus is a Latin term for yearly. True or False
Testicles are found on an octopus. True or False
Asphalt describes rectal problems. True or False
Masturbate is used to catch large fish. True or False
Fetus is a character on *Gunsmoke*. True or False
An umbilical cord is part of a parachute. True or False
A pubic hair is a wild rabbit. True or False
An orgasm is a person who accompanies a church choir. True or False
A diaphragm is a drawing in geometry. True or False
An erection is when Japanese people vote. True or False
A lesbian is a person from the Middle East. True or False
Pornography is the business of making records. True or False
Genitals are people of non-Jewish origin. True or False

First blow job

A young man walks up and sits down at the bar.
'What can I get you?' the bartender inquires.
'I want six shots of Jagermeister,' responds the young man.
'Six shots? Are you celebrating something?'

'Yeah, my first blow job.'

'Well, in that case, let me give you a seventh on the house.'

'No offence, sir. But if six shots won't get rid of the taste, nothing will.'

Flight statistics

A businessman boards a flight and is lucky enough to be seated next to an absolutely gorgeous woman.

They exchange brief hellos and he notices she is reading a manual about sexual statistics. He asks her about it and she replies, 'This is a very interesting book about sexual statistics. It identifies that Arabs have the longest average penis and Polish men have the biggest average diameter. By the way, my name is Jill. What's yours?'

He coolly replies, 'Mohammad Kowalski, nice to meet you.'

Appointments

One night, as a couple is lying in bed, the husband gently taps his wife on the shoulder and starts rubbing her arm.

The wife turns over and says: 'I'm sorry, honey, I've got a gynaecologist appointment tomorrow and I want to stay fresh.'

The husband, rejected, turns over and tries to sleep. A few minutes later, he rolls back over and taps his wife again. This time he whispers in her ear: 'Do you have a dentist appointment tomorrow too?'

A pickle

Bill worked in a pickle factory. He had been employed there for a number of years when he came home one day to confess to his wife that he had a terrible compulsion. He had an urge to stick his penis into the pickle slicer. His wife suggested that he should see a sex therapist to talk about it, but Bill indicated that he'd be too embarrassed. He vowed to overcome the compulsion on his own.

One day a few weeks later, Bill came home absolutely ashen. His wife could see at once that something was seriously wrong. 'What's wrong, Bill?' she asked.

'Do you remember that I told you how I had this tremendous urge to put my penis into the pickle slicer?'

'Oh, Bill, you didn't.'

'Yes, I did.'

'My God, Bill, what happened?'

'I got fired.'

'No, Bill. I mean, what happened with the pickle slicer?'

'Oh … she got fired too.'

Comatose

A man is visiting his wife in hospital where she has been in a coma for several years. On this visit he decides to rub her left breast instead of just talking to her. On doing this she lets out a sigh. The man runs out and tells the doctor, who says this is a good sign and suggests he should try rubbing her right breast to see if there is any reaction. The man rubs her right breast and this brings a moan too. From this, the doctor suggests that the man should go in and try oral sex, saying he will wait outside as it is a personal act and he doesn't want the man to be embarrassed. The man goes in then comes out about five minutes later, white as a sheet, and tells the doctor his wife is dead. The doctor asks what happened, to which the man replies: 'She choked.'

Big bloke

A small white guy goes into an elevator and when he gets in he notices a huge black dude standing next to him. The big black dude looks down upon the small white guy and says: 'seven foot tall, 350 pounds, 15 inch dick, three pound left ball, three pound right ball, Turner Brown.'

The small white guy faints! The big black dude picks up the small white guy and brings him round by slapping his face and shaking him, and then asks the small white guy, 'What's wrong?'

The small white guy says, 'Excuse me, but what did you say?'

The big black dude looks down and says, 'Seven foot tall, 350 pounds, 15 inch dick, three pound left ball, three pound right ball, my name is Turner Brown.'

The small white guy says: 'Thank God! I thought you said "Turn around".'

Anniversary bells

There was this couple who had been married for 50 years.

They were sitting at the breakfast table one morning when the old gentleman said to his wife, 'Just think, honey, we've been married for 50 years.'

'Yeah,' she replied. 'Just think, 50 years ago we were sitting here at this breakfast table together.'

'I know,' the old man said, 'we were probably sitting here naked as jaybirds 50 years ago.'

'Well,' the granny snickered, 'what do you say … should we get naked?'

Whereupon the two stripped to the buff and sat back down at the table.

'You know, honey,' the little old lady breathlessly replied, 'my nipples are as hot for you today as they were 50 years ago.'

'I wouldn't be surprised,' replied gramps. 'One's in your coffee and the other is in your porridge!'

Don't fart in bed

This is a story about a couple that had been happily married for years. The only friction in their marriage was the husband's habit of farting loudly every morning when he awoke. The noise would wake his wife and the smell would make her eyes water and make her gasp for air. Every morning she would plead with him to stop ripping them off because it was making her sick. He told her he couldn't stop it and that it was perfectly natural. She told him to see a doctor; she was concerned that one day he would blow his guts out.

The years went by and he continued to rip them out. Then one Christmas morning as she was preparing the turkey for dinner and he was upstairs sound asleep, she looked at the bowl where she had put the turkey innards, neck, gizzard, liver and all the spare parts, and a malicious thought came to her. She took the bowl and went upstairs where her husband was sound asleep and, gently pulling back the bed covers, she held back the elastic waistband of his underpants and emptied the bowl of turkey guts into his shorts. Some time later she heard her husband waken with his usual trumpeting, which was followed by a blood curdling scream and the sound of frantic footsteps as he ran into the bathroom.

The wife could hardly control herself as she rolled on the floor laughing, tears in her eyes! After years of torture she reckoned she had got him back.

About 20 minutes later, her husband came downstairs in his bloodstained underpants with a look of horror on his face. She bit her lip as she asked him what was the matter.

He said, 'Honey, you were right. All these years you have warned me and I didn't listen to you.'

'What do you mean?' asked his wife.

'Well, you always told me that one day I would end up farting my guts out, and today it finally happened. But by the grace of God, some Vaseline, and these two fingers, I think I got most of them back in!'

A small step for mankind

On 20 July 1969, as commander of the Apollo 11 lunar module, Neil Armstrong was the first person to set foot on the moon. His first words after stepping on the moon, 'That's one small step for a man, one giant leap for mankind,' were televised to earth and heard by millions. Folklore has it that just before he re-entered Apollo, he made the enigmatic remark: 'Good luck, Mr Gorsky.'

According to the story, many people at NASA thought it was a casual remark concerning some rival Soviet cosmonaut; however, upon checking, there was no Gorsky in either the Russian or American space programs. Over the years many people questioned Armstrong as to what the 'Good luck, Mr Gorsky' statement meant, but Armstrong always just smiled.

On 5 July 1995, in Tampa Bay, Florida, while answering questions following a speech, a reporter brought up the 26-year-old question to Armstrong. This time he finally responded. Mr Gorsky had died, so Neil Armstrong felt he could answer the question.

In 1938 when he was a kid in a small Midwest town, he was playing baseball with a friend in the backyard. His friend hit the ball, which landed in his neighbour's yard by the bedroom windows. His neighbours were Mr and Mrs Gorsky. As he leant down to pick up the ball, young Armstrong heard Mrs Gorsky shouting at Mr Gorsky: 'Oral sex! You want oral sex? You'll get oral sex when the kid next door walks on the moon!'

Terror firmer

One morning while making breakfast, a man walked up to his wife, pinched her on the bum and said, 'If you firmed this up, we could get rid of your control top pantyhose.' While this was on the edge of intolerable, she kept silent. The next morning, the man woke his wife with a pinch on each of her breasts and said, 'You know, if you firmed these up, we could get rid of your bra.' Without a word, she rolled over and grabbed him by his penis. With a death grip in place, she said, 'You know, if you firmed this up, we could get rid of the gardener, the postman, the pool man and your brother.'

Masked fancy dress party

A couple were invited to a swanky masked fancy dress Halloween party. The wife got a terrible headache and told her husband to go to the party alone. He, being a devoted husband, protested, but she argued and said she was going to take some aspirin and go to bed, and there was no need for his good time to be spoiled by not going. So he took his costume and away he went. The wife, after sleeping soundly for about an hour, awakened without pain, and, as it was still early, decided to go to the party. As her husband did not know what her costume was, she thought she would have some fun by watching him to see how he acted when she was not with him. So she joined the party and soon spotted her husband cavorting around on the dance floor, dancing with every nice girl he could, and copping a little feel here, and a little kiss there.

His wife went up to him and, being rather seductive herself, he left his partner high and dry and devoted his time to the new woman who had just arrived. She let him go as far as he wished, naturally, since he was her husband.

After some more to drink he finally whispered a little proposition in her ear and she agreed, so off they went to one of the cars and had a quickie in the back seat.

Just before unmasking at midnight, she slipped away home, put the costume away and got into bed, wondering what kind of explanation he would make up for his outrageous behaviour.

She was sitting up reading when he came in, so she asked what kind of time he had had. He said, 'Oh, the same old thing. You know I never have a good time when you're not there.'

Then she asked, 'Did you dance much?'

He replied, 'I'll tell you, I never even danced one dance. When I got there I met Pete, Bill Brown and some other guys, so we went into the spare room and played poker all evening.'

Then she said with unashamed sarcasm, 'You must have looked really silly wearing that costume playing poker all night!'

The husband responded, 'Actually, I gave my costume to your dad. Apparently he had a whale of a time.'

Pretend marriage

A man and a woman, who have never met before, find themselves assigned to the same sleeping room on a transcontinental train. Though initially embarrassed and uneasy over sharing the room, the two are tired and fall asleep quickly … he in the upper bunk and she in the lower.

At 1 a.m., he leans over and gently wakes the woman, saying, 'Ma'am, I'm sorry to bother you, but would you be willing to reach into the closet to get me a second blanket? I'm awfully cold.'

'I have a better idea,' she replies. 'Just for tonight, let's pretend that we're married.'

'Wow! That's a great idea!' he exclaims.

'Good,' she replies. 'Get your own fucking blanket!'

Loud sex

A wife went in to see a therapist and said, 'I've got a big problem, Doctor. Every time we're in bed and my husband climaxes, he lets out this ear-splitting yell.'

'My dear,' the shrink said, 'that's completely natural. I don't see what the problem is.'

'The problem is,' she complained, 'it wakes me up!'

Quiet sex

Tired of a listless sex life, the man came right out and asked his wife during a recent lovemaking session, 'How come you never tell me when you have an orgasm?'

She glanced at him casually and replied, 'You're never home!'

Confounded sex

A man was in a terrible accident, and his 'manhood' was mangled and torn from his body. His doctor assured him that modern medicine could give him back his manhood, but that his insurance wouldn't cover the surgery, since it was considered cosmetic.

The doctor said the cost would be $3500 for 'small', $6500 for 'medium' and $14,000 for 'large'.

The man was sure he would want a medium or large, but the doctor urged him to talk it over with his wife before he made any decision.

The man called his wife on the phone and explained their options.

The doctor came back into the room, and found the man looking dejected.

'Well, what have the two of you decided?' asked the doctor.

The man answered, 'She'd rather have a new kitchen.'

Wedding anniversary sex

A husband and his wife had a bitter quarrel on the day of their 40th wedding anniversary.

The husband yelled, 'When you die, I'm getting you a headstone that reads: "Here Lies My Wife — Cold As Ever."'

'Yeah,' she replied, 'and when you die, I'm getting you a headstone that reads: "Here Lies My Husband — Stiff At Last."'

Happy sex

A couple is lying in bed. The man says, 'I am going to make you the happiest woman in the world.'

The woman says … 'I'll miss you.'

Bye bye

A married couple is driving along a highway doing a steady 40 miles per hour. The wife is behind the wheel.

Her husband suddenly looks across at her and speaks in a clear voice: 'I know we've been married for 20 years, but I want a divorce.'

The wife says nothing, keeps looking at the road ahead but slowly increases her speed to 45 mph.

The husband speaks again. 'I don't want you to try and talk me out of it,' he says, 'because I've been having an affair with your best friend, and she's a far better lover than you are.'

Again the wife stays quiet, but grips the steering wheel more tightly and slowly increases the speed to 55.

He pushes his luck. 'I want the house,' he says insistently.

The car revs up to 60.

'I want the car, too,' he continues.

65 mph.

'And,' he says, 'I'll have the bank accounts, all the credit cards and the boat.'

The car slowly starts veering towards a massive concrete bridge. This makes him a wee bit nervous, so he asks her, 'Isn't there anything you want?'

The wife at last replies in a quiet and controlled voice. 'No, I've got everything I need,' she says.

'Oh, really?' he inquires. 'So what have you got?'

Just before they slam into the wall at 75 mph, the wife turns to him and smiles. 'The airbag.'

Next *Survivor* series

Six married men will be dropped on an island with one car and four kids each for six weeks. Each kid will play two sports and either take music or dance classes.

There is no fast food.

Each man must take care of his four kids, keep his assigned house clean, correct all homework, complete science projects, cook, do laundry, and pay a list of 'pretend' bills with not enough money.

In addition, each man will have to budget for groceries each week. Each man must also take each child to a doctor's appointment, a dentist appointment, and an appointment for a haircut. He must also make a cake or biscuits for a social function.

Each man will be responsible for decorating his own assigned house, planting flowers outside and keeping it presentable at all times.

The men will only have access to television when the kids are asleep and all chores are done.

There is only one TV between them.

Each father will be required to know all of the words to every stupid song that comes on TV and the name of each and every repulsive character in cartoons.

The men must shave their legs and wear make-up daily, which they will apply themselves either while driving or making four lunches.

They must adorn themselves with jewellery, wear uncomfortable yet stylish shoes, and keep their nails polished and eyebrows groomed.

During one of the six weeks, they will have to endure severe stomach cramps, back aches, and have extreme, unexplained mood swings, but never once complain or slow down from other duties.

They must attend weekly school meetings and find time at least once to spend the afternoon at the park or a similar setting.

He will need to bathe the children each night, dress them, brush their teeth and comb their hair each morning by 7 a.m.

A test will be given at the end of the six weeks, and each father will be required to know all of the following information: each child's birthday, height, weight, shoe size, clothes size and doctor's name. Also the child's weight at birth, length, time of birth, and length of labour.

They must clean up after a sick child at 3 a.m. and then spend the remainder of the day tending to that child and waiting on them hand and foot until they are better.

Each man will have to make an Indian hut model with six toothpicks and a tortilla; and get a four-year-old to eat a serving of peas.

The kids vote them off the island based on performance.

The last man wins only if ... he still has enough energy to be intimate with his spouse at a moment's notice.

If the last man does win, he can play the game over and over and over again for the next 18–25 years ... eventually earning the right to be called Mother!

Number 69

A Chinese couple gets married. She's a virgin and, truth be told, he is none too experienced either. On the wedding night, she cowers naked under the bed sheets as her husband undresses.

He climbs in next to her and tries to be reassuring. 'My daring,' he says, 'I know dis yo firs time and you berry frighten. I pomise you, I give you anyting you want, I do anyting — jus anyting you want. Whatchou want?' he asks, trying to sound experienced. He hopes this will impress his virgin bride.

A thoughtful silence follows and he waits patiently (and eagerly) for her request. She eventually replies shyly and unsurely, 'I want … a 69.'

Now he is caught up in thoughtful silence. Eventually, in a puzzled tone he asks, 'You want … beef wif broccori?'

Divorce court

A man and his wife were in court getting a divorce.

The problem was who should get custody of the child.

The wife jumped up and said: 'Your Honour. I brought the child into the world with pain and labour. She should be in my custody.'

The judge turned to the husband and said: 'Do you have anything to say?'

The man sat for a while contemplating. Then he slowly rose. 'Your Honour, if I put a dollar in a vending machine and a Coke comes out, whose Coke is it, the machine's or mine?'

My husband doesn't understand me

A judge was interviewing a woman regarding her pending divorce, and asked, 'What are the grounds for your divorce?'

She replied, 'About four acres and a nice little home in the middle of the property with a stream running by.'

'No,' he said, 'I mean, what is the foundation of this case?'

'It is made of concrete, brick and mortar,' she responded.

'I mean,' he continued, 'what are your relations like?'

'I have an aunt and uncle living here in town, and so do my husband's parents.'

He said, 'Do you have a real grudge?'

'No,' she replied, 'we have a two-car carport and have never really needed one.'

'Please,' he tried again, 'is there any infidelity in your marriage?'

'Yes, both my son and daughter have stereo sets. We don't necessarily like the music, but the answer to your question is yes.'

'Ma'am, does your husband ever beat you up?'

'Yes,' she responded, 'about twice a week he gets up earlier than I do.'

Finally, in frustration, the judge asked, 'Lady, why do you want a divorce?'

'Oh, I don't want a divorce,' she replied. 'I've never wanted a divorce. My husband does. He says he can't communicate with me!'

An Irish toast

John O'Reilly hoisted his beer and said, 'Here's to spending the rest of me life, between the legs of me wife!'

That won him the top prize for the best toast of the night!

He went home and told his wife Mary, 'I won the prize toast of the night.'

She said, 'Aye, what was your toast?'

John said, 'Here's to spending the rest of me life, sitting in church beside me wife.'

'Oh that is very nice indeed, John!' Mary said.

The next day, Mary ran into one of John's toasting buddies on the street corner. The man chuckled leeringly and said, 'John won the prize the other night with a toast about you, Mary.'

She said, 'Aye and I was a bit surprised meself! You know, he's only been there twice! Once he fell asleep, and the other time I had to pull him by the ears to make him come.'

The mistress

A husband and wife are having dinner at a very fine restaurant when this absolutely stunning young woman comes over to their table, gives the husband a big open-mouthed kiss, then says she'll see him later and walks away.

The wife glares at her husband and says, 'Who the hell was that?'

'Oh,' replies the husband, 'she's my mistress.'

'Well, that's the last straw,' says the wife. 'I've had enough. I want a divorce!'

'I can understand that,' replies her husband, 'but remember, if we get a divorce it will mean no more shopping trips to Paris, no more wintering in Barbados, no more summers in Tuscany, no more Mercedes or Lexus in the garage and no more yacht club. But the decision is yours.'

Just then, a mutual friend enters the restaurant with a gorgeous babe on his arm.

'Who's that woman with Jim?' asks the wife.

'That's his mistress,' says her husband.

'Ours is prettier,' she replies.

Wedded bliss quickies

- At a cocktail party, one woman said to another, 'Aren't you wearing your wedding ring on the wrong finger?' The other woman replied, 'Yes I am — I married the wrong man.'
- A lady inserted an ad in the classifieds: 'Husband wanted'. Next day she received a hundred letters. They all said the same thing: 'You can have mine.'
- When a woman steals your husband, there is no better revenge than to let her keep him.
- A woman is incomplete until she is married. Then she is finished.
- A little boy asked his father, 'Daddy, how much does it cost to get married?' And the father replied, 'I don't know, son, I'm still paying.'
- Then there was a woman who said, 'I never knew what real happiness was until I got married; and by then it was too late.'
- Marriage is the triumph of imagination over intelligence.
- If you want your spouse to listen and pay strict attention to every word you say, talk in your sleep.
- First man: 'My wife's an angel!' Second man: 'You're lucky, mine's still alive.'
- Women will never be equal to men until they can walk down the street with a bald head and a beer gut, and still think they are attractive to the opposite sex.

Marriage from hell

A few minutes before the church service started, the townspeople were sitting in their pews and talking. Suddenly, Satan appeared at the front of the church. Everyone started screaming and running for the front entrance, trampling each other in a frantic effort to get away from evil incarnate.

Soon everyone had exited the church except for one elderly gentleman who sat calmly in his pew without moving, seemingly oblivious to the fact that God's ultimate enemy was in his presence.

So Satan walked up to the old man and said, 'Don't you know who I am?'

The man replied, 'Yep, sure do.'

'Aren't you afraid of me?' Satan asked.

'Nope, sure ain't,' said the man.

'Don't you realise I can kill you with a word?' asked Satan.

'Don't doubt it for a minute,' returned the old man, in an even tone.

'Did you know that I could cause you profound, horrifying, physical pain for all eternity?' persisted Satan.

'Yep,' was the calm reply.

'And you're still not afraid?' asked Satan.

'Nope.'

More than a little perturbed, Satan asked, 'Well, why aren't you afraid of me?'

The man calmly replied, 'Been married to your sister for over 48 years.'

Little Sally

Little Sally came home from school with more than five dollars in small change. 'Where did this money come from?' her mother asked. Sally explained that she had been doing handstands for the boys, for which they paid her 40 cents a time. Her mum was furious and told her that it was not ladylike to show her knickers to the boys. The following day Sally came home with over 10 dollars. 'I hope you have not been doing handstands and letting the boys see your knickers,' her mum said. 'No, Mummy,' replied Sally. 'I took my knickers off first.'

Why condoms come in boxes of three, six or 12

A man walks into a chemist with his 13-year-old son. They happen to walk by the condom display, and the boy asks, 'What are these, Dad?'

To which the father matter-of-factly replies, 'Those are called condoms, son. Men use them to have safe sex.'

'Oh I see,' replies the boy pensively. 'Yes, I've heard of that in health class at school.' He looks over the display and picks up a package of three and asks, 'Why are there three in this package?'

The father replies, 'Those are for high-school boys. One for Friday, one for Saturday, and one for Sunday.'

'Cool!' says the boy. He notices a six pack and asks, 'Then who are these for?'

'Those are for college boys,' the father answers. 'Two for Friday, two for Saturday, and two for Sunday.'

'*Wow!*' exclaims the boy. 'Then who uses *these?*' he asks, picking up a 12-pack.

With a sigh, the father replies, 'Those are for married men. One for January, one for February, one for March ...'

6 WORK STATION

A bus station is where a bus stops.
A train station is where a train stops.
Many of us have a work station …

The modern office is a far cry from the pen-pushing, ledger-keeping, file-posting, nine-to-five days of the last century. Most factories and offices are dependent on computers and exist in environments that are usually impersonal, insensitive and frustrating. Buzz words fly around like blowflies at a barbecue. Stress is everywhere. Workers attempt to cope by personalising their 'space' — especially with humour. They stick photocopied signs on their partitions, especially words of wisdom like 'work hard and you will be rewarded', which appears under a cartoon of a man or woman skewered by a screw. Many of these paper 'jokes' are cartoons, and many are about computers showing our 'love–hate' relationship with technology. We also personalise our work spaces with small toys, keepsakes, and photographs of family and friends. Because much of today's business is based on individual effort, even if part of a team, we feel isolated and that is most probably why jokes transmitted via e-mails are such an important aspect of our daily lives. These jokes also waste a hell of a lot of time and management often attempts to combat such illegal fun by sending regular 'Please refrain' memos, which, in turn, usually end up being sarcastically rewritten and circulated, thus adding to the problem.

Human Resource Officers, or HRO if you're savvy to the new terminology, are the people hired to hire and fire in the new business world. They cop a fair whack in humour and are seen as heartless individuals who do the company dirty work, regardless of the fact they may have been the very person who employed you. The boss, of course, also comes in for a poke in the eye but the biggest target, by far, is the actual place of work and the methods we all work by.

One of the largest areas of jokes about work and business relates to lawyers. If a profession could be judged by the amount of humour it attracts, one would have to put the legal eagles at the top of the list. Lawyers and the law are key figures of ridicule, much of it quite vicious. Obviously many people have suffered at their hands.

These jokes are aimed at making us smile, to get through the week and to stop us entering the 'stress zone'. Pass them on.

You didn't get the job

Human Resources Managers were asked to describe their most unusual experience interviewing prospective employees.

1. A job applicant challenged the interviewer to an arm wrestle.
2. Interviewee wore a Walkman, explaining that she could listen to the interviewer and the music at the same time.
3. Candidate fell and broke arm during interview.
4. Candidate announced she hadn't had lunch and proceeded to eat a hamburger and French fries in the interviewer's office.
5. Candidate explained that her long-term goal was to replace the interviewer.
6. Candidate said he never finished high school because he was kidnapped and kept in a closet in Mexico.
7. Balding candidate excused himself and returned to the office a few minutes later wearing a hairpiece.
8. Applicant said if he were hired he would demonstrate his loyalty by having the corporate logo tattooed on his forearm.
9. Applicant interrupted interview to phone her therapist for advice on how to answer specific interview questions.
10. Candidate brought large dog to interview.
11. Applicant refused to sit down and insisted on being interviewed standing up.
12. Candidate dozed off during interview.

Post Xmas

There was a man who worked for the Melbourne Post Office whose job it was to process all the mail that had illegible addresses.

One day just before Christmas, a letter landed on his desk, simply addressed in shaky handwriting to 'God'. With no other clue on the envelope, he opened the letter and read:

Dear God,
I am an 85-year-old war widow living on the pension. Yesterday someone stole my purse. It had $160 in it, which was all the money I had in the world and no pension due until after Christmas. Next week is Christmas and I had invited two of my dear friends over for Xmas dinner. Without that money, I have

nothing to buy food with. I have no family to turn to, and you are my only hope. God, can you please help me?

The postal worker was really moved, and put a copy of the letter up on the staff notice board at the main sorting office where he worked.

The letter touched the other postal workers and they all dug into their pockets and had a whip round.

Between them they raised $130. Using an official franked post office envelope, they sent the cash on to the old lady, and for the rest of the day all the workers felt a warm glow thinking of the nice thing they had done.

Christmas came and went. A few days later, another letter simply addressed to 'God' landed in the sorting office. Many of the postal workers gathered around while the letter was opened. It read:

Dear God,
How can I ever thank you enough for what you did for me? Because of your generosity, I was able to provide a lovely dinner for my friends. We had a very nice day, and I told my friends of your wonderful gift — in fact we haven't got over it and our Vicar is beside himself with joy.
By the way, there was $30 missing. I think it must have been those thieving bastards at the post office.

How to recruit the right person for the job

Put about 100 bricks in some particular order in a closed room with an open window. Then send two or three candidates into the room and close the door. Leave them alone, come back after four hours and then analyse the situation.

- If they are counting the bricks — put them in the Accounts Department.
- If they are recounting them — put them in Auditing.
- If they have messed up the whole place with the bricks — put them in Engineering.
- If they are arranging the bricks in some strange order — put them in Planning.
- If they are throwing the bricks at each other — put them in Operations.

- If they are sleeping — put them in Security.
- If they have broken the bricks into pieces — put them in Information Technology.
- If they are sitting idle — put them in Human Resources.
- If they say they have tried different combinations, yet not a brick has been moved — put them in Sales.
- If they have already left for the day — put them in Marketing.
- If they are staring out of the window — put them in Strategic Planning.
- And then last but not least, if they are talking to each other and not a single brick has been moved — congratulate them and put them into Senior Management.

Signs of the time

- 'Remember, it's not "How high are you?", it's "Hi, how are you?"' — Nimbin health centre
- 'Fighting for peace is like screwing for virginity' — graffiti
- 'No matter how good she looks, some other guy is sick and tired of putting up with her shit' — men's room, Gold Coast
- 'At the feast of ego everyone leaves hungry' — Sizzler steakhouse, Mt Gravatt
- 'It's hard to make a comeback when you haven't been anywhere' — written in the dust on the back of a bus, Alice Springs
- 'Make love, not war — Hell, do both, GET MARRIED!' — women's restroom, Garden City, Brisbane
- 'If voting could really change things, it would be illegal' — bookshop, Garden City
- 'If pro is the opposite of con, then what is the opposite of progress? Congress!' — men's restroom, House of Representatives, Canberra
- 'Arts degree: please take one' — written on toilet-sheet dispenser, Sydney University
- 'This has got to be the worst chewing gum I have ever eaten' — written on condom dispenser, Kings Cross Hotel
- 'Express lane: five beers or less' — sign over one of the urinals, The London Tavern, Paddington, NSW

- 'You're too good for him' — sign over mirror in women's restroom, The Chancellor, Melbourne
- 'No wonder you always go home alone' — sign over mirror in men's restroom, The Chancellor
- 'A Woman's Rule of Thumb: if it has tyres or testicles, you're going to have trouble with it' — women's restroom, Inala, Brisbane

Notes left for the milkman

Dear Milkman …

- 'Dear Milkman, I've just had a baby, please leave another one.'
- 'Please leave an extra pint of paralysed milk.'
- 'Please don't leave any more milk. All they do is drink it.'
- 'Milkman, please close the gate behind you because the birds keep pecking the tops off the milk.'
- 'Sorry not to have paid your bill before, but my wife had a baby and I've been carrying it around in my pocket for weeks.'
- 'Sorry about yesterday's note. I didn't mean one egg and a dozen pints, but the other way round.'
- 'When you leave my milk, knock on my bedroom window and wake me because I want you to give me a hand to turn the mattress.'
- 'My daughter says she wants a milkshake. Do you do it before you deliver or do I have to shake the bottle?'
- 'Please send me a form for cheap milk, for I have a baby two months old and did not know about it until a neighbour told me.'
- 'Milk is needed for the baby. Father is unable to supply it.'
- 'From now on please leave two pints every other day and one pint on the days in between, except Wednesdays and Saturdays when I don't want any milk.'
- 'My back door is open. Please put milk in fridge, get money out of cup in drawer and leave change on kitchen table, because we want to play bingo tonight.'
- 'Please leave no milk today. When I say today, I mean tomorrow, for I wrote this note yesterday or is it today?'
- 'When you come with the milk, please put the coal on the boiler, let dog out and put newspaper inside the screen door. P.S. Don't leave any milk.'

- 'No milk. Please do not leave milk at No. 14 either as he is dead until further notice.'

The rabbit and the snake

Once upon a time, in a nice little forest, there lived a blind little bunny and a blind little snake.

One day, the bunny was hopping through the forest, and the snake was slithering through the forest, when the bunny tripped over the snake and fell down. This, of course, knocked the snake about quite a bit.

'Oh my,' said the bunny, 'I'm terribly sorry. I didn't mean to hurt you. I've been blind since birth, so I can't see where I'm going. In fact, I don't even know what I am.'

'It's quite OK,' replied the snake. 'Actually, my story is much the same as yours. I, too, have been blind since birth. Tell you what, maybe I could kinda slither over you, and figure out what you are, so at least you'll have that going for you.'

'Oh, that would be wonderful,' replied the bunny.

So the snake slithered all over the bunny, and said, 'Well, you're covered with soft fur; you have really long ears; your nose twitches; and you have a soft cottony tail. I'd say that you must be a bunny.'

'Oh, thank you, thank you,' cried the bunny in obvious excitement.

The bunny then suggested to the snake, 'Maybe I could feel you with my paw, and help you the same way you've helped me.'

So the bunny felt the snake all over, and remarked, 'Well, you're scaly and smooth, and you have a forked tongue, no backbone and no balls. I'd say you must be either a politician, a lawyer, or possibly someone in upper management.'

Wise words

1. I can only please one person per day. Today is not your day. Tomorrow is not looking good either.
2. I love deadlines. I especially like the whooshing sound they make as they go flying by.
3. Tell me what you need, and I'll tell you how to get along without it.
4. Needing someone is like needing a parachute. If they aren't there the first time, chances are you won't be needing them again.

5. I don't have an attitude problem — you have a perception problem.
6. On the keyboard of life, always keep one finger on the escape key.
7. I don't suffer from stress. I am a carrier.
8. Everybody is somebody else's weirdo.
9. Never argue with an idiot. They drag you down to their level, and then beat you with experience.
10. A pat on the back is only a few centimetres from a kick up the arse.
11. Don't be irreplaceable — if you can't be replaced, you can't be promoted.
12. After any salary raise, you will have less money at the end of the month than you did before.
13. The more crap you put up with, the more crap you are going to get.
14. You can go anywhere you want if you look serious and carry a clipboard.
15. If it weren't for the last minute, nothing would get done.
16. When you don't know what to do, walk fast and look worried.
17. Following the rules will not get the job done.

Returned soldier?

A man goes to the post office to interview for a job.

The interviewer asks him, 'Are you a returned serviceman?'

The guy says, 'Why yes. In fact, I served two stints in Vietnam.'

'Good,' says the interviewer. 'That counts in your favour. Do you have any service-related disabilities?'

The man says, 'In fact I am 100 per cent disabled. During a battle, an explosion removed my private parts, so they declared me disabled. It doesn't affect my ability to work, though.'

'Sorry to hear about the damage, but I have some good news for you — I can hire you right now! Our working hours are eight to four. Come on in about 10, and we'll get you started.'

The fellow says, 'If working hours are from eight to four, why do you want me to come at 10?'

'Well, here at the post office, we don't do anything but sit round and scratch our balls for the first two hours. No point you coming in for that.'

Hard time

- In prison, you spend the majority of your time in an 8 x 10 cell. At work, you spend most of your time in a 6 x 8 cubicle.
- In prison, you get three meals a day. At work, you get a break for one meal and you have to pay for it.
- In prison, you get time off for good behaviour. At work, you get rewarded for good behaviour with more work.
- In prison, a guard locks and unlocks all the doors for you. At work, you must carry around a security card and unlock and open all the doors yourself.
- In prison, you can watch TV and play games. At work, you get fired for watching TV and playing games.
- In prison, you get your own toilet. At work, you have to share.
- In prison, they allow your family and friends to visit. At work, you can't even speak to your family and friends.
- In prison, you spend most of your life looking through bars from inside wanting to get out. At work, you spend most of your time wanting to get out and go inside bars.
- In prison, there are wardens who are often sadistic. At work, they are called supervisors.

Now get back to work!

Work rules

1. Rome did not create a great empire by having meetings; they did it by killing all people who opposed them.
2. If you can stay calm, while all around you is chaos … then you probably haven't completely understood the seriousness of the situation.
3. Doing a job *right* the first time gets the job done. Doing the job *wrong* 14 times gives you job security.
4. Eagles may soar, but weasels don't get sucked into jet engines.
5. Artificial Intelligence is no match for Natural Stupidity.
6. A person who smiles in the face of adversity probably has a scapegoat.
7. Plagiarism saves time.
8. If at first you don't succeed, try management.

9. Never put off until tomorrow what you can avoid altogether.
10. 'Teamwork' means never having to take all the blame yourself.
11. The beatings will continue until morale improves.
12. Never underestimate the power of very stupid people in large groups.
13. We waste time, so you don't have to.
14. Hang in there; retirement is only 50 years away!
15. Go the extra mile. It makes your boss look like an incompetent slacker.
16. A snooze button is a poor substitute for no alarm clock at all.
17. When the going gets tough, the tough take a coffee break.
18. Indecision is the key to Flexibility.
19. Succeed in spite of management.
20. Aim Low, Reach Your Goals, Avoid Disappointment.

I hate my job day

When you have an 'I hate my job' day, try this: on your way home from work, stop at your pharmacy and go to the thermometer section. You will need to purchase a rectal thermometer made by Johnson & Johnson. Be very sure you get this brand.

When you get home, lock your doors, draw the drapes and disconnect the phone so you will not be disturbed during your therapy.

Change to very comfortable clothing, such as a tracksuit, and lie down on your bed. Open the package and remove the thermometer. Carefully place it on the bedside table so that it will not become chipped or broken. Take out the material that comes with the thermometer and read it. You will notice that in small print there is a statement: 'Every rectal thermometer made by Johnson & Johnson is personally tested.'

Now close your eyes and repeat out loud five times: 'I am so glad I do not work for quality control at the Johnson & Johnson company.'

Have a nice day, and remember there is always someone with a worse job than yours.

Corporate condoms

Imagine if major companies from all around the world started producing or sponsoring condoms. They would become fashionable and companies would probably advertise more openly.

Nike Condoms: Just do it

Toyota Condoms: Oh, what a feeling

Ford Condoms: The ride of your life

Microsoft Condoms: Where do you want to go today?

Optus Condoms: Yes!

KFC Condoms: Finger lickin' good

M&Ms Condoms: Melt in your mouth, not in your hands

Duracell Condoms: Keep going and going and going

Pringles Condoms: Once you pop you can't stop

Sydney Olympic Condoms: Share the spirit

Hyundai Condoms: All day, every day

Tip Top Condoms: Good onya, Mum (available in Tasmania only)

Panasonic Condoms: Even more than you expected

VB Condoms: As a matter of fact, I've got one now

Swan Lager Condoms: They said you'd never make it …

Vegemite Condoms: Puts a rose in every cheek (target gay market)

Levi Condoms: Do you fit the legend?

Nescafe Condoms: It brings you together

Quicken Condoms: Quicken. Easy.

McDonald's Condoms: Things that make you go hmm …

Horse sense

Bush wisdom says that when you discover you are riding a dead horse, the best strategy is to dismount. In business, however, it seems that we often try other strategies with dead horses, including the following:

1. Buying a stronger whip.
2. Changing riders.
3. Saying things like 'This is the way we have always ridden this horse.'
4. Appointing a committee to study the horse.
5. Arranging to visit other sites to see how they ride dead horses.
6. Increasing the standards to ride dead horses.
7. Appointing a focus team to revive the dead horse.
8. Creating a training session to increase our riding ability.
9. Comparing the state of dead horses in today's environment.
10. Changing the requirements, declaring, 'This horse is not dead.'

11. Hiring contractors to ride the dead horse.

12. Harnessing several dead horses together for increased speed.

13. Declaring 'No horse is too dead to beat.'

14. Providing additional funding to increase the horse's performance.

15. Doing a case study to see if contractors can ride it cheaper.

16. Purchasing a product to make dead horses run faster.

17. Declaring the horse is 'better, faster and cheaper' dead.

18. Forming a quality circle to find uses for dead horses.

19. Revisiting the performance requirements for horses.

20. Saying this horse was procured with cost as an independent variable.

21. Promoting the dead horse to a supervisory position.

You don't know Jack Schitt!

Many people are at a loss for a response when someone says to them, 'You don't know Jack Schitt.' Now you can handle this problem properly.

Jack Schitt is the only son of Awe Schitt and O. Schitt. Awe Schitt, the fertiliser magnate, married O. Schitt, a partner of Kneedeep & Schitt Inc.

In turn, Jack Schitt married Noe Schitt, and the deeply religious couple produced six children: Holie Schitt, Fulla Schitt, Giva Schitt, Bull Schitt and the twins: Deep Schitt and Dip Schitt.

After being married for only 15 years, Jack and Noe Schitt divorced. Noe Schitt later married Mr Sherlock, and because her kids were living with them, she wanted to keep her previous name. She was known as Noe Schitt-Sherlock.

Despite her parents' objections, Deep Schitt married Dumb Schitt, a high-school dropout. Dip Schitt married Loda Schitt and they produced a nervous son, Chicken Schitt.

Fulla Schitt and Giva Schitt were inseparable throughout childhood and subsequently married the Happens brothers in a dual ceremony. The wedding announcement in the newspaper highlighted the Schitt-Happens wedding.

The Schitt-Happens children were Dawg, Byrd and Hoarse.

Bull Schitt, the prodigal son of Jack Schitt and Noe Schitt-Sherlock, left home to tour the world. He returned from Italy with his new bride, Pisa Schitt.

Most Schitts are happy, law-abiding people like you and me, and treasure the family unit. As such they come together from all over the countryside for all sorts of Schitt. Funerals are popular, as there is nothing better than seeing off a dead Schitt in style.

So now if someone says, 'You don't know Jack Schitt,' you can correct them. Not only do you know Jack, you know the whole Schitt family!

New words for the Australian workforce

Essential additions to the workplace vocabulary:

ADMINISPHERE: The rarefied organisational layers beginning just above the rank and file. Decisions that fall from the adminisphere are often profoundly inappropriate or irrelevant to the problems they were designed to solve.

ARSEMOSIS: The process by which some people seem to absorb success and advancement by kissing up to the boss rather than working hard.

BLAMESTORMING: Sitting around in a group, discussing why a deadline was missed or a project failed, and who was responsible.

CUBE FARM: An office filled with cubicles.

404: Someone who's clueless. From the World Wide Web error message '404 Not Found', meaning that the requested document could not be located.

GENERICA: Features of the landscape that are exactly the same no matter where one is, such as fast food joints, shopping malls, subdivisions.

IRRITAINMENT: Entertainment and media spectacles that are annoying but you find yourself unable to stop watching them.

MOUSE POTATO: The online, wired generation's answer to the couch potato.

OHNOSECOND: That minuscule fraction of time in which you realise that you've just made a *big* mistake.

PERCUSSIVE MAINTENANCE: The fine art of whacking the crap out of an electronic device to get it to work again.

SCRUB DOGGING: When someone yells or drops something loudly in a cube farm, and people's heads pop up over the walls to see what's going on.

SEAGULL MANAGER: A manager who flies in, makes a lot of noise, craps on everything, and then leaves.

SITCOMs: Single Income, Two Children, Oppressive Mortgage. What yuppies turn into when they have children and one of them stops working to stay home with the kids.

STRESS PUPPY: A person who seems to thrive on being stressed out and whiney.

SWIPEOUT: An ATM or credit card that has been rendered useless because the magnetic strip is worn away from extensive use.

XEROX SUBSIDY: Euphemism for swiping free photocopies from one's workplace.

Special high intensity training

In order to assure the highest levels of quality work and productivity from employees, it is our policy to keep all employees well trained through our program of Special High Intensity Training (SHIT). We are trying to give employees more SHIT than anyone else. If you feel you do not receive your share of SHIT on the job, please see your manager. You will be immediately placed at the top of the SHIT list, and our managers are especially skilled at seeing that you get all the SHIT you can handle.

Employees who don't take their SHIT will be placed in Departmental Employee Evaluation Programs (DEEPSHIT). Those who fail to take DEEPSHIT seriously will have to go to Employee Attitude Training (EATSHIT). Since our managers took SHIT before they were promoted, they don't have to do SHIT any more, and are full of SHIT already.

If you are full of SHIT you may be interested in training others. We can add your name to our Basic Understanding Lecture List (BULLSHIT). Those who are full of BULLSHIT will get the SHIT jobs, and can apply for promotion to Director of Intensity Programming (DIPSHIT). If you have further questions, please direct them to our Head Of Training, Special High Intensity Training (HOTSHIT).

Thank you,

Boss In General

Special High Intensity Training

(BIGSHIT)

Sexual Harassment

A man told a co-worker that her hair smelt nice. The woman immediately stormed into her supervisor's office to file a sexual harassment suit. The supervisor was puzzled and told her, 'I don't understand. What's wrong with a co-worker telling you that your hair smells nice?'

The woman replied, 'Because he's a midget!'

New employee handbook

SICK DAYS. We will no longer accept a doctor's statement as proof of sickness. If you are able to go to the doctor, you are able to come to work.

SURGERY. Operations are now banned. As long as you are an employee here, you need all your organs. You should not consider removing anything. We hired you intact. To have something removed constitutes a breach of employment.

PERSONAL DAYS. Each employee will receive 104 personal days each year. They are called 'Saturday' and 'Sunday'.

HOLIDAYS. All employees will take their holidays at the same time every year. The vacation days are as follows: 1 January, 25 April and 25 December.

BEREAVEMENT LEAVE. Bereavement is no excuse for missing work. There is nothing you can do for your dead friends, relatives or co-workers. Every effort should be made to have non-employees attend to the arrangements. In rare cases where employee involvement is necessary, the funeral should be scheduled in the late afternoon. We will be glad to allow you to work through your lunch hour and subsequently leave one hour early, provided your share of the work is done.

ABSENCE DUE TO YOUR OWN DEATH. This will be accepted as an excuse. However, we require at least two weeks' notice, as it is your duty to train your own replacement.

RESTROOM USE. Entirely too much time is being spent in the restroom. In future, we will follow the practice of going in alphabetical order. For instance, all employees whose names begin with 'A' will go from 8.00 to 8.20; employees whose names begin with 'B' will go from 8.20 to 8.40 and so on. If you are unable to go at your allotted time, it will be necessary to wait until the next day when your turn comes again. In extreme emergencies, employees may swap their time with a co-worker. Both employees' supervisors must approve this exchange in writing. In addition, there is now a strict, three-minute time limit inside the stalls. At the end of three minutes, an alarm will sound, the toilet-paper roll will retract, and the stall door will open.

LUNCH BREAK. (a) Skinny people get one hour for lunch, as they need to eat more so they can look healthy. (b) Middle-weight people get 30 minutes for lunch, so they can get a balanced meal to maintain their average figures. (c) Fat people get five minutes for lunch, because that's all the time they need to drink a Slim Fast and take a diet pill.

DRESS CODE. It is advised that you come to work dressed according to your salary. If we see you wearing a pair of $350 Prada running shoes and carrying a $600 Gucci bag, we will assume that you are doing well financially and therefore do not need a raise.

THANK YOU. Thank you for your loyalty to our company. We are here to provide a positive employment experience. Therefore all questions, comments, concerns, complaints, frustrations, irritations, aggravations, insinuations, allegations, accusations, contemplations, consternations, or input should be directed elsewhere.

Have a nice week.

Management

The future is now

A fishing boat docked in a tiny Mexican village. An American tourist complimented the young fisherman on the quality of his catch and asked how long it took him.

'Not very long,' answered the Mexican.

'Well, why didn't you stay out longer and catch more?' asked the American.

The Mexican explained that his small catch was sufficient to meet his needs and those of his family.

'But what do you do with the rest of your time?' asked the tourist.

'I sleep late, fish a little, play with my children, and take a siesta with my wife. In the evenings I go into the village to see my friends, have a few drinks, play the guitar, and sing a few songs … I have a full life.'

The American interrupted. 'I have an MBA from Harvard and I can help you. You should start by fishing longer every day, and sell the extra fish you catch. With the extra revenue you can buy a bigger boat. With the extra money the larger boat will bring, you can buy a second one and a third one, and so on until you have an entire fleet of trawlers. Instead of selling your fish to a middle man, you can negotiate directly with the processing plants and maybe even open your own plant. Then you can leave this little village and move to Mexico City, Los Angeles … even New York, and direct your huge enterprise.'

'How long would that take?' asked the Mexican.

'Twenty, maybe 25 years,' replied the American.

'And after that?'

'That's when it gets really interesting,' laughed the American. 'When your business gets really big, you can start selling stocks and make millions!'

'Millions? Really? And after that?'

'After that you'll be able to retire, live in a tiny village near the coast, sleep late, play with your children, catch a few fish, take siestas with your wife, and spend your evenings drinking and enjoying your friends!'

Ring at the door

Bazza is getting into the shower just as his wife is finishing up her shower, when the doorbell rings. After a few seconds of arguing over which one should go and answer the doorbell, the wife gives up, quickly wraps herself up in a towel and runs downstairs. When she opens the door, there stands Bob, the next-door neighbour. Before she says a word, Bob says, 'I'll give you $800 to drop that towel that you have on.' After thinking for a moment, the woman drops her towel and stands naked in front of him. After a few seconds, Bob hands her $800 and leaves.

Confused, but excited about her good fortune, the woman wraps up in the towel and goes back upstairs. When she gets back to the bathroom, Bazza asks from the shower, 'Who was that?'

'It was Bob, the next-door neighbour,' she replies.

'Great,' the husband says, 'did he say anything about the $800 he owes me?'

The manager and the genie

A sales rep, an administration clerk and their manager are walking to lunch when they find an antique oil lamp. They rub it and a genie comes out in a puff of smoke. The genie says, 'I usually only grant three wishes, so I'll give each of you just one.'

'Me first! Me first!' says the administration clerk. 'I want to be in the Bahamas, driving a speedboat, without a care in the world.' *Poof!* She's gone.

In astonishment the sales representative says, 'Me next! Me next! I want to be in Hawaii, relaxing on the beach with my personal masseuse, an endless supply of pina coladas and the love of my life.' *Poof!* He's gone.

'OK, you're up,' the genie says to the manager. The manager says, 'I want those two back in the office after lunch.'

Moral of the story: Always let your boss have the first say.

Water torture

A water bearer in China had two large pots, each hung on the ends of a pole that he carried across his neck. One of the pots had a crack in it while the other pot was perfect and always delivered a full portion of water.

At the end of the long walk from the stream to the house, the cracked pot arrived only half full. For two years this went on daily, with the bearer delivering only one and a half pots of water to his house.

Of course, the perfect pot was proud of its accomplishments, for which it was made. But the poor cracked pot was ashamed of its own imperfection, and miserable that it was able to accomplish only half of what it had been made to do.

After these two years of what it perceived to be bitter failure, it spoke to the water bearer one day by the stream: 'I am ashamed of myself, because this crack in my side causes me to leak out all the way back to your house.'

The bearer said to the pot, 'Did you notice that there are flowers on your side of the path, but not on the other pot's side? That's because I have always known about your flaw, so I planted flower seeds on your side of the path, and every day while we walk back, you water them. For two years I have been able to pick these beautiful flowers to decorate the table. Without you being just the way you are, there would not be this beauty to grace the house.'

Each of us has our own unique flaw. But it's the cracks and flaws we each have that make our lives together so very interesting and rewarding. You've just got to take each person for what they are and look for the good in them.

To all of my crackpot friends, and there are many, have a great day and remember to smell the flowers.

Centrelink client

A tattooed, pierced guy walks into his local Centrelink office, marches straight up to the counter and says, 'Hey, bro. Hate being on the dole. I'd really rather have a job, man.'

The clerk behind the Centrelink desk says, 'Your timing is excellent, sir, we've just got a job opening from a very wealthy old man who wants a chauffeur/bodyguard for his nymphomaniac daughter. You'll have to drive around in his Mercedes, but he'll supply all of your clothes, and because of the long hours, meals will be provided. You'll be expected to escort the daughter on her overseas holiday trips. You'll have a two-bedroom apartment above the garage. The starting salary is $200,000 a year.'

The guy says, 'You're bullshitting me!'

The Centrelink officer says, 'Yeah, well, you started it.'

The new Lord's Prayer

Our cash
Which art on plastic
Hallowed be thy name
Thy Cartier watch
Thy Prada bag
In Myer
As it is in David Jones
Give us each day our Platinum Visa
And forgive us our overdraft
As we forgive those who stop our MasterCard
Lead us not into Macy's
And deliver us from Harrods
For thine is the D&G, the Miu Miu and the Armani
For Chanel No 5 and Eternity
Amex

Deaf bookkeeper

A Mafia godfather finds out that his bookkeeper has screwed him for 10 million bucks.

This bookkeeper is deaf. It was considered an occupational benefit, and why he landed the job in the first place, since it was assumed that a deaf bookkeeper would not be able to hear anything he'd ever have to testify about in court.

When the godfather goes to shake down the bookkeeper about his missing 10 million bucks, he takes his attorney, who knows sign language.

The godfather asks the bookkeeper: 'Where is the 10 million bucks you embezzled from me?'

The attorney, using sign language, asks the bookkeeper where the 10 million dollars is hidden.

The bookkeeper signs back: 'I don't know what you are talking about.'

The attorney tells the godfather: 'He says he doesn't know what you're talking about.'

That's when the godfather pulls out a 9mm pistol, puts it to the bookkeeper's temple, cocks it, and says: 'Ask him again!'

The attorney signs to the underling: 'He'll kill you for sure if you don't tell him!'

The bookkeeper signs back: 'OK! You win! The money is in a brown briefcase, buried behind the shed in my cousin Enzo's backyard.'

The godfather asks the attorney: 'Well, what'd he say?'

The attorney replies: 'He says you don't have the balls to pull the trigger.'

No ears

Sadly, Dave was born without ears. And although he proved to be successful in business, his lack of ears annoyed him greatly. One day he needed to hire a new manager for his company, so he set up three interviews.

The first guy was great. He knew everything he needed to know and was very interesting. At the end of the interview Dave asked, 'Do you notice anything different about me?'

'Why yes, I couldn't help but notice that you have no ears,' came the reply. Dave did not appreciate the guy's candour and threw him out of the office.

The second interview was with a woman, and she was even better than the first applicant. He asked her the same question: 'Do you notice anything different about me?'

'Well,' she said, stammering, 'you have no ears.' Dave again got upset and chucked her out in a rage.

The third and final interviewee was the best of the bunch; he was a young man who had recently earned his MBA. He was smart, he was handsome, and he seemed to be a better businessman than the first two put together.

Dave was anxious, but went ahead and asked the young man the same question: 'Do you notice anything different about me?'

Much to Dave's surprise, the young man answered, 'Yes, you wear contact lenses, don't you?'

Dave was shocked and realised this was an incredibly observant person. 'How in the world did you know that?' he asked.

The young man then fell off his chair laughing hysterically and replied, 'Well, it's pretty hard to wear glasses with no fucking ears.'

Amazing technology

One day in line at the company cafeteria, Jack says to Mike, 'My elbow hurts like hell. I guess I better see a doctor.'

'Listen, you don't have to spend that kind of money,' Mike replies. 'There's a diagnostic computer at the chemist. Just give it a urine sample and the computer will tell you what's wrong and what to do about it. It only takes 10 seconds and costs $10.'

So Jack deposits a urine sample in a small jar and takes it to the store. He deposits $10, and the computer lights up and asks for the urine sample. He pours the sample into the slot and waits. Ten seconds later, the computer ejects a printout:

You have tennis elbow. Soak your arm in warm water and avoid heavy lifting. It will improve in about two weeks.

That night while thinking how amazing this new technology was, Jack begins wondering if the computer could be fooled. He mixes some tap water, a stool sample from his dog, urine samples from his wife and daughter, and masturbates into the mixture. Jack hurries back to the chemist, eager to check the results. He deposits $10, pours in the concoction, and waits for the results.

The computer ejects a printout:

1. Your tap water is too hard. Get a softener.
2. Your dog has ringworm. Bathe him with anti-fungal shampoo.
3. Your daughter has a cocaine habit. Get her into rehab.
4. Your wife is pregnant … twin girls. They're not yours. Get a lawyer.
5. If you don't stop playing with yourself, your elbow will never get better.

The Lord's Prayer

The CEO of Ingham's manages to arrange a meeting with the Pope. After receiving the Papal blessing, he whispers, 'Your Holiness, we have an offer for you. Ingham's is prepared to donate $100 million to the church if you change the Lord's Prayer from "Give us this day our daily bread" to "Give us this day our daily chicken".'

The Pope responds, 'That is impossible. The prayer is the word of the Lord; it must not be changed.'

'Well,' says the CEO, 'we anticipated your reluctance. For this reason, we will increase our offer to $300 million. All we require is that you change the Lord's Prayer from "Give us this day our daily bread" to "Give us this day our daily chicken".'

Again, the Pope replies, 'That, my son, is impossible. For the prayer is the word of the Lord and it must not be changed.'

Finally, the CEO says, 'Your Holiness, we at Ingham's respect your adherence to your faith, but we do have one final offer. We will donate $500 million — that's half a billion dollars — to the great Catholic Church if you would only change the Lord's Prayer from "Give us this day our daily bread" to "Give us this day our daily chicken". Please consider it.' And he leaves.

The next day the Pope convenes the College of Cardinals. 'There is some good news,' he announces, 'and some bad news. The good news is that the Church will come into $500 million.'

'And the bad news, your Holiness?' asks a cardinal.

'We're losing the Tip Top account.'

Perception – it all depends

A man walks into a bar. He sees a beautiful, well-dressed woman sitting on a bar stool alone. He walks up to her and says, 'Hello there, how's it going tonight?'

She turns to him, looks him straight in the eyes, and says, 'I'll screw anybody, any time, anywhere, any place. It doesn't matter to me.'

The guy raises his eyebrows and says, 'No kidding? Me too! What law firm are you with?'

A classic tale

A frog goes into a bank and approaches the teller. He can see from her nameplate that her name is Pattie Whack. 'Miss Whack, I'd like to get a $30,000 loan to take a holiday.'

Pattie looks at the frog in disbelief and asks his name. The frog says his name is Kermit Jagger, his dad is Mick Jagger, and that it's OK, he knows the bank manager. Pattie explains that he will need to secure the loan with some collateral.

The frog says, 'Sure, I have this,' and produces a tiny porcelain elephant, about half an inch tall — bright pink and perfectly formed.

Very confused, Pattie explains that she'll have to consult with the bank manager and disappears into a back office. She finds the manager and says, 'There's a frog called Kermit Jagger out there who claims to know you and wants to borrow $30,000, and he wants to use this as collateral.' She holds up the tiny pink elephant. 'I mean, what in the world is this?'

The bank manager looks back at her and says, 'It's a knick-knack, Pattie Whack. Give the frog a loan. His old man's a Rolling Stone.'

Career advisor

ARCHITECT: Someone who was neither macho enough to become an engineer nor gay enough to become a designer.

BANKER: Someone who lends you his umbrella when the sun is shining and takes it back when it starts to rain.

CONSULTANT: Someone who uses your wife's watch, tells you the time, and then charges you for it.

DIPLOMAT: Someone who tells you to go to hell in a way that makes you eager to start the journey.

ECONOMIST: An expert who will know tomorrow why that which he predicted yesterday didn't happen today.

PESSIMIST: Optimist with experience.

PROGRAMMER: Someone who fixes a problem you didn't know you had in a way you don't understand.

PSYCHOLOGIST: Someone who looks at everyone else when an attractive woman enters the room.

STATISTICIAN: Someone who is good with numbers but lacks the
    personality to be an engineer.
PRIEST: Someone addressed by everyone as 'Father' except his children
    who call him 'Uncle'.

Your turn

A blonde and a lawyer are seated next to each other on a flight from Sydney to Perth. The lawyer asks the blonde if she would like to play a fun game. The blonde, tired, just wants to take a nap, so she politely declines and rolls over to the window to catch a few winks. The lawyer persists and explains that the game is easy and a lot of fun.

He says, 'I ask you a question, and if you don't know the answer, you pay me five dollars, and vice versa.'

Again, she declines and tries to get some sleep.

The lawyer, now agitated, says, 'OK, if you don't know the answer, you pay me $5, and if I don't know the answer, I will pay you $500.'

This catches the blonde's attention and, figuring there will be no end to this torment, agrees to the game.

The lawyer asks the first question: 'What's the distance from the earth to the moon?'

The blonde doesn't say a word, reaches into her purse, pulls out a five dollar note, and hands it to the lawyer.

'OK,' says the lawyer, 'your turn.'

She asks, 'What goes up a hill with three legs and comes down with four legs?'

The lawyer, puzzled, takes out his laptop computer and searches all his references ... no answer. He taps into the air phone with his modem and searches the Internet ... no answer. Frustrated, he sends e-mails to all his friends and co-workers but to no avail. After an hour, he wakes the blonde and hands her $500.

The blonde thanks him and turns back to get some more sleep.

The lawyer, who is more than a little miffed, stirs the blonde and asks, 'Well, what's the answer?'

Without a word, the blonde reaches into her purse, hands the lawyer $5, and goes back to sleep.

Generous lawyer

One afternoon, a wealthy lawyer was riding in the back of his limousine when he saw two men eating grass by the roadside. He ordered his driver to stop and he got out to investigate. 'Why are you eating grass?' he asked one man. 'We don't have any money for food,' the poor man replied.

'Oh, well, you can come with me to my house,' said the lawyer.

'But, sir, I have a wife and two children with me!'

'Bring them along!' replied the lawyer. He turned to the other man and said: 'You come with us, too.'

'But, sir, I have a wife and six children!' the second man answered.

'Bring them as well!' answered the lawyer as he headed for his limo.

They all climbed into the car, which was no easy task, even for a car as large as the limousine.

Once under way, one of the poor fellows said: 'Sir, you are too kind. Thank you for taking all of us with you.'

The lawyer replied: 'Glad to do it. You'll love my place; the grass is almost a foot tall.'

Legally married

A lawyer married a woman who had previously divorced 10 husbands.

On their wedding night, she told her new husband, 'Please be gentle, I'm still a virgin.'

'What?' said the puzzled groom. 'How can that be if you've been married 10 times?'

'Well, Husband number 1 was a sales representative; he kept telling me how great it was going to be. Husband number 2 was in software services; he was never really sure how it was supposed to function, but he said he'd look into it and get back to me. Husband number 3 was from field services; he said everything checked out diagnostically but he just couldn't get the system up. Husband number 4 was in telemarketing; even though he knew he had the order, he didn't know when he would be able to deliver. Husband number 5 was an engineer; he understood the basic process but wanted three years to research, implement and design a new state-of-the-art method. Husband number 6 was from finance and administration; he thought he knew how, but he wasn't sure whether it was his job or not.

Husband number 7 was in marketing; although he had a nice product, he was never sure how to position it. Husband number 8 was a psychologist; all he ever did was talk about it. Husband number 9 was a gynaecologist; all he did was look at it. Husband number 10 was a stamp collector; all he ever did was … God! I miss him! But now that I've married you, I'm really excited!'

'Good,' said the new husband, 'but why?'

'You're a lawyer. This time I know I'm going to get screwed!'

Lawyers' seasonal greeting

From us ('the wishor') to you ('hereinafter called the wishee'). Please accept without obligation, implied or implicit, our best wishes for an environmentally conscious, socially responsible, politically correct, low stress, non-addictive, gender neutral, celebration of the summer solstice holiday, practised within the most enjoyable traditions of the religious persuasion of your choice, or secular practices of your choice, with respect for the religious/secular persuasions and/or traditions of others, or their choice not to practise religious or secular traditions at all … and a financially successful, personally fulfilling and medically uncomplicated recognition of the onset of the generally accepted calendar year, but with due respect for the calendars of choice of other cultures or sects, and having regard to the race, creed, colour, age, physical ability, religious faith, choice of computer platform or dietary preference of the wishee.

By accepting this greeting you are bound by these terms; that:

This greeting is subject to further clarification or withdrawal.

This greeting is freely transferable provided that no alteration shall be made to the original greeting and that the proprietary rights of the wishor are acknowledged.

This greeting implies no promise by the wishor to actually implement any of the wishes.

This greeting may not be enforceable in certain jurisdictions and/or the restrictions herein may not be binding upon certain wishees in certain jurisdictions and is revocable at the sole discretion of the wishor.

This greeting is warranted to perform as reasonably may be expected within the usual application of good tidings, for a period of one year or until the issuance of a subsequent holiday greeting, whichever comes first.

The wishor warrants this greeting only for the limited replacement of this wish or issuance of a new wish at the sole discretion of the wishor.

Any references in this greeting to 'the Lord', 'Father Christmas', 'Our Saviour', or any other festive figures, whether actual or fictitious, dead or alive, shall not imply any endorsement by or from them in respect of this greeting, and all proprietary rights in any referenced third party names and images are hereby acknowledged.

Shares and stock

As you know, the stock market has not been in the greatest shape lately. It seems that, because of current economic conditions, many companies are contemplating mergers and acquisitions. Here are a few to keep an eye on:

1. XEROX and WURLITZER (They're going to make reproductive organs)
2. FAIRCHILD ELECTRONICS and HONEYWELL COMPUTERS (The new company will be called Fairwell Honeychild)
3. POLYGRAM RECORDS, WARNER BROTHERS and ARNOTT'S (The new company will be called Poly-Warner-Cracker)
4. WR GRACE CO, FULLER BRUSH CO, MARY KAY COSMETICS, and HALE BUSINESS SYSTEMS (The new company will be called Hale, Mary, Fuller, Grace)
5. 3M and GOODYEAR (The new company will be called Mmm Good)
6. JOHN DEERE and ABITIBI-PRICE (The new company will be called Deere Abi)
7. HONEYWELL, IMASCO and HOME OIL (The new company will be called Honey Im Home)
8. DENISON MINES, ALLIANCE and METAL MINING (The new company will be called Mine All Mine)
9. GREY POUPON and DOCKERS PANTS (The new company will be called Poupon Pants)
10. KNOTT'S BERRY FARM and THE NATIONAL ORGANISATION FOR WOMEN (The new company will be called Knott NOW)
11. ZIPPO MANUFACTURING, AUDI, DOFASCO and DAKOTA MINING (The new company will be called Zip Audi Do-Da)

Cheese

A man goes into his bank to tell them of his plans for a new business: 'I'm thinking of starting up in the cheese business,' he says.

'Yes?' says the bank manager. 'What are you thinking of calling the cheese?'

'Don't know,' says the man.

'Try the name of a place.'

After a long thought, the businessman says, 'Cheddar!'

'Nope,' replies the bank manager. 'There's already a cheese from that place. Try again.'

The man goes away. Three months later, he's back: 'I've thought of a name.'

'What is it?'

'Bega.'

'No, there's already a cheese from there too.'

The man goes away. Six months later, he's back again: 'Leinster.'

'Sorry. There's one from there too. Try another place.'

The man goes away. Nine months later, he's back. More adventurous this time. 'Edam,' he says.

'Sorry. Much better, but there's one from there, too. Try further afield.'

The man goes away. A year later, he's back again. 'Nazareth,' he says.

'Excellent,' says the bank manager. 'It's a place name. And it hasn't been used by anybody else in the industry. Brilliant, that's the product sorted out. Now what are you going to call the company?'

And the man replies, 'Cheeses of Nazareth.'

A healthy deposit

A man goes into a bank and walks up to the cashier's desk. 'Nice tits, love. I want to open a fucking bank account,' he says.

She looks in horror, saying, 'You can't talk to me like that, sir.'

'Listen, you dumb bitch,' he says, 'I want to open a fucking bank account!'

'I'm sorry, sir,' she says, bottom lip starting to quiver. 'I can't help you if you're going to talk to me like that.' And with that she leaves her window, walks over to the bank manager and whispers in his ear.

The two return to the window and the manager asks stiffly, 'What seems to be the problem here?'

'There's no fucking problem,' the man insists. 'I just won 10 million dollars in the fucking lottery and I want to open a fucking bank account!'

'I see, sir,' the manager quickly replies. 'And this slut's giving you a hard time, is she?'

7 MY COMPUTER IS DRIVING ME NUTS

Love them or hate them, it has become almost impossible to avoid computers. They help us run our work schedule, plan our leisure time, provide us with information at the push of a Google or Yahoo search, and have emerged as a major form of entertainment, both individually and with friends. The computer has all but replaced the traditional secretary as we now compose our own correspondence, with computerised spell checks (even if this produces some strange variations), shop online, pay accounts online, do our own filing, and send e-mails instead of letters. Computers also work behind the scenes — everywhere we go — be it closing theatre curtains, projecting films, monitoring traffic lights and even writing us 'personalised junk mail letters'.

We have learnt to live with computers; however, most people harbour a deep distrust of computer technology. We all remember HAL 9000 in the film *2001: A Space Odyssey*. Could they turn on us? Ask a geek!

One of the few ways we can get our revenge on technology is through the circulation of e-mails. They express our hidden fears and, more often, our frustration at having to deal with computer 'crashes', faulty software packages, outdated technology, confusing technological jargon, recorded telephone messages and so-called 'helplines' which are no help at all.

Computer gender

A French teacher was explaining to her college class that in French, unlike English, nouns are designated as either masculine or feminine. House is feminine: *la maison*. Pencil is masculine: *le crayon*. A student asked, 'What gender is *computer*?'

Instead of giving the answer, the teacher split the class into two groups — male and female — and asked them to decide for themselves whether *computer* should be a masculine or a feminine noun. Each group was asked to give four reasons for their recommendation.

The men's group decided that *computer* should definitely be the feminine gender (*la computer*) because:

1. No one but their creator understands their internal logic;
2. The native language they use to communicate with other computers is incomprehensible to everyone else;
3. Even the smallest mistakes are stored in long-term memory for possible later review; and
4. As soon as you make a commitment to one, you find yourself spending half your pay packet on accessories for it.

The women's group, however, concluded that *computer* should be masculine (*le computer*) because:

1. In order to do anything with them, you have to turn them on;
2. They have a lot of data but still can't think for themselves;
3. They are supposed to help you solve problems, but half the time they *are* the problem; and
4. As soon as you commit to one, you realise that if you had waited a little longer, you could have gotten a better model.

The women won.

Spellcheck: why is English so hard to learn?
1. The bandage was wound around the wound.
2. The farm was used to produce produce.
3. The dump was so full that it had to refuse more refuse.
4. We must polish the Polish furniture.
5. He could lead if he would get the lead out.

6. The soldier decided to desert his dessert in the desert.
7. Since there is no time like the present, it was time to present the present.
8. I did not object to the object.
9. There was a row among the oarsmen about how to row.
10. They were too close to the door to close it.
11. Upon seeing the tear in the painting I shed a tear.
12. How can I intimate this to my most intimate friend?
13. I shed my clothes in the shed.

Let's face it — English is sometimes a ridiculous language.

There is no egg in eggplant, nor ham in a hamburger; neither apple nor pine in a pineapple. English muffins weren't invented in England, nor French fries in France. Sweetmeats are lollies while sweetbreads are neither bread nor sweet, but meat.

We take English for granted. But if we explore its paradoxes, we find that quicksand can work slowly, boxing rings are square and a guinea pig is neither from Guinea nor is it a pig. And why is it that bakers bake, but grocers don't groce? If the plural of tooth is teeth, why isn't the plural of booth beeth? One goose, two geese. So one moose, two meese? If teachers taught, why didn't preachers praught? If a vegetarian eats vegetables, what does a humanitarian eat? We ship by truck and send cargo by ship?

We have noses that run and feet that smell? How can a slim chance and a fat chance be the same, while a wise man and a wise guy are opposites?

You have to marvel at the unique lunacy of a language in which your house can burn up as it burns down, in which you fill in a form by filling it out, and in which an alarm goes off by going on.

English was invented by people, not computers, and it reflects the creativity of the human race (which, of course, isn't a race at all). That is why, when the stars are out, they are visible, but when the lights are out, they are invisible.

And finally, how about when you want to shut down your computer you have to hit 'start'.

Connecting your Internet

Customer: I'm trying to connect to the Internet with your CD, but it just doesn't work. What am I doing wrong?

Tech support: OK, you've got the CD in the CD drive, right?

Customer: Yeah …

Tech support: And what sort of computer are you using?

Customer: Computer? Oh no, I haven't got a computer. It's in the CD player, and all I get is weird noises. Listen …

Tech support: Aaaarrrrgggghhhh!

Tech support: What kind of computer do you have?

Customer: A white one …

Tech support: Click on the 'my computer' icon on the left of the screen.

Customer: Your left or my left?

Tech support: Good day. How may I help you?

Male customer: Hello … I can't print.

Tech support: Would you click on 'start' for me and …

Customer: Listen, pal, don't start getting technical on me! I'm not Bill Gates, damn it!

Customer: Hi, good afternoon, this is Martha, I can't print. Every time I try, it says 'Can't find printer'. I've even lifted the printer and placed it in front of the monitor, but the computer still says he can't find it.

Customer: I have problems printing in red …

Tech support: Do you have a colour printer?

Customer: Aaaah … thank you.

Tech support: What's on your monitor now, ma'am?

Customer: A teddy bear my boyfriend bought for me in the supermarket.

Customer: My keyboard is not working any more.

Tech support: Are you sure it's plugged into the computer?

Customer: No. I can't get behind the computer.

Tech support: Pick up your keyboard and walk 10 paces back.

Customer: OK.

Tech support: Did the keyboard come with you?

Customer: Yes.

Tech support: That means the keyboard is not plugged in. Is there another keyboard?

Customer: Yes, there's another one here. Ah … that one does work.

Tech support: Your password is the small letter 'a' as in apple, a capital letter 'V' as in Victor, the number 7.

Customer: Is that 7 in capital letters?

Customer: I can't get on the Internet.

Tech support: Are you sure you used the right password?

Customer: Yes, I'm sure. I saw my colleague do it.

Tech support: Can you tell me what the password was?

Customer: Five stars.

Tech support: What anti-virus program do you use?

Customer: Netscape.

Tech support: That's not an anti-virus program.

Customer: Oh, sorry … Internet Explorer.

Customer: I have a huge problem. A friend has placed a screen saver on my computer but every time I move the mouse, it disappears.

Tech support: How may I help you?

Customer: I'm writing my first e-mail.

Tech support: OK, and what seems to be the problem?

Customer: Well, I have the letter 'a' in the address, but how do I get the circle around it?

A woman customer called the Canon help desk with a problem with her printer.

Tech support: Are you running it under Windows?

Customer: No, my desk is next to the door, but that is a good point. The man sitting in the cubicle next to me is under a window, and his printer is working fine.

Tech support: OK, Bob, let's press the control and escape keys at the same time. That brings up a task list in the middle of the screen. Now type the letter 'P' to bring up the Program Manager.

Customer: I don't have a 'P'.

Tech support: On your keyboard, Bob.

Customer: What do you mean?

Tech support: 'P' on your keyboard, Bob.

Customer: *I'm not going to do that!*

Oops! My website!

All of these are legitimate companies that didn't spend quite enough time considering how their online names might appear … and be misread. These are not made up. Check them out yourself!

1. Who Represents is where you can find the name of the agent that represents any celebrity. Their website is *www.whorepresents.com*
2. Experts Exchange is a knowledge base where programmers can exchange advice and views at *www.expertsexchange.com*
3. Looking for a pen? Look no further than Pen Island at *www.penisland.net*
4. Need a therapist? Try Therapist Finder at *www.therapistfinder.com*
5. There's the Italian Power Generator Company, *www.powergenitalia.com*
6. And don't forget the Mole Station Native Nursery in New South Wales, *www.molestationnursery.com*
7. If you're looking for IP computer software, there's always *www.ipanywhere.com*
8. The First Cumming Methodist Church website is *www.cummingfirst.com*
9. And the designers at Speed of Art await you at their wacky website, *www.speedofart.com*

Woman's work

An ambitious yuppie finally decides to take a vacation. He books himself on a Caribbean cruise and proceeds to have the time of his life. Until the boat sinks.

The man finds himself swept up on the shore of an island with no other people, no supplies — nothing — only bananas and coconuts.

After about four months, he is lying on the beach one day when the most gorgeous woman he has ever seen rows up to him. In disbelief, he asks her, 'Where did you come from? How did you get here?'

'I rowed from the other side of the island,' she says. 'I landed here when my cruise ship sank.'

'Amazing,' he says. 'You were really lucky to have a rowboat wash up with you.'

'Oh, this?' replies the woman. 'I made the rowboat out of raw material I found on the island; the oars were whittled from gum tree branches; I wove the bottom from palm branches; and the sides and stern came from a eucalyptus tree.'

'But … but … that's impossible,' stutters the man. 'You had no tools or hardware. How did you manage?'

'Oh, that was no problem,' replies the woman. 'On the south side of the island, there is a very unusual stratum of alluvial rock exposed. I found if I fired it to a certain temperature in my kiln, it melted into forgeable ductile iron. I used that for tools and used the tools to make the hardware.'

The guy is stunned.

'Let's row over to my place,' she says. After a few minutes of rowing, she docks the boat at a small wharf. As the man looks onto shore, he nearly falls out of the boat. Before him is a stone walk leading to an exquisite bungalow painted in blue and white. While the woman ties up the rowboat with an expertly woven hemp rope, the man can only stare ahead, dumbstruck.

As they walk into the house, she says casually, 'It's not much but I call it home. Sit down please; would you like to have a drink?'

'No, no thank you,' he says, still dazed. 'Can't take any more coconut juice.'

'It's not coconut juice,' the woman replies. 'I have a still. How about a pina colada?'

Trying to hide his continued amazement, the man accepts, and they sit down on her couch to talk. After they have exchanged their stories, the woman announces, 'I'm going to slip into something more comfortable. Would you like to take a shower and shave? There is a razor upstairs in the bathroom cabinet.'

No longer questioning anything, the man goes into the bathroom. There, in the cabinet, is a razor made from a bone handle. Two shells honed to a hollow ground edge are fastened onto its end inside of a swivel mechanism. 'This woman is amazing,' he muses. 'What next?'

When he returns, she greets him wearing nothing but vines — strategically positioned — and smelling faintly of gardenias. She beckons for him to sit down next to her. 'Tell me,' she begins suggestively, slithering closer to him, 'we've been out here for a really long time. You've been lonely. There's something I'm sure you really feel like doing right now, something you've been longing for all these months? You know.' She stares into his eyes.

He can't believe what he's hearing. 'You mean,' he swallows excitedly, 'I can check my e-mail from here?'

Bill Gates at the conference

For all of us who feel only the deepest love and affection for the way computers have enhanced our lives, read on. At a recent computer expo Bill Gates reportedly compared the computer industry with the auto industry and stated, 'If GM [General Motors] had kept up with technology like the computer industry has, we would all be driving $25 cars that got 1000 miles to the gallon.'

In response to Bill's comments, General Motors issued a press release stating: If GM had developed technology like Microsoft, we would all be driving cars with the following characteristics:

1.   For no reason whatsoever, your car would crash twice a day.
2.   Every time they repainted the lines in the road, you would have to buy a new car.
3.   Occasionally, your car would die on the freeway for no reason. You would have to pull over to the side of the road, close all of the windows, shut off the car, restart it, and reopen the windows before you could continue. For some reason you would simply accept this.
4.   Occasionally, executing a manoeuvre such as a left turn would cause your car to shut down and refuse to restart, in which case you would have to reinstall the engine.
5.   Macintosh would make a car that was powered by the sun, was reliable, five times as fast and twice as easy to drive — but would run on only five per cent of the roads.

6. The oil, water temperature, and alternator warning lights would all be replaced by a single 'This Car Has Performed An Illegal Operation' warning light.
7. The airbag system would ask, 'Are you sure?' before deploying.
8. Occasionally, for no reason whatsoever, your car would lock you out and refuse to let you in until you simultaneously lifted the door handle, turned the key and grabbed hold of the radio antenna.
9. Every time a new car was introduced car buyers would have to learn how to drive all over again because none of the controls would operate in the same manner as the old car.
10. You'd have to press the 'Start' button to turn the engine off.

Please share this with your friends who love — but sometimes hate — their computer.

Memo to computer field engineers

Re: Replacement of mouse balls

If a mouse fails to operate or should it perform erratically, it may need a ball replacement. Mouse balls are now available as FRU (Field Replacement Units). Because of the delicate nature of this procedure, only properly trained personnel should attempt replacement of mouse balls.

Before proceeding, determine the type of mouse balls by examining the underside of the mouse. Domestic balls will be larger and harder than foreign balls.

Ball removal procedures differ depending upon the manufacturer of the mouse. Foreign balls can be replaced using the pop-off method. Domestic balls are replaced by using the twist-off method. Mouse balls are not usually static sensitive. However, excessive handling can result in sudden discharge.

Upon completion of ball replacement, the mouse may be used immediately. It is recommended that each person have a pair of spare balls for maintaining optimum customer satisfaction.

Any customer missing his balls should contact the local personnel in charge of removing and replacing these necessary items.

Please keep in mind that a customer without properly working balls is an unhappy customer.

It started in a chat room

SON: Daddy, how was I born?

DAD: Well, my son, one day Mum and Dad got together in a chat room on MSN. Dad set up a date via e-mail with your mum and we met at a cyber cafe. We snuck into a secluded room, and then your mother downloaded from dad's memory stick. As soon as dad was ready for an upload, it was discovered that neither one of us had used a firewall. Since it was too late to hit the delete button, nine months later the blessed virus appeared. And that's the story.

Australian population base

The population of this country is 20.1 million, of which 10.4 million are retired or unemployed.

That leaves 9.7 million to do the work.

There are 3.4 million in school, which leaves 6.3 million to do the work. Of this, there are 4.1 million employed by the federal government, leaving 2.2 million to do the work.

Some 0.4 million are in the armed forces, which leaves 1.8 million to do the work.

Take from the total the 1,650,000 people who work for state and city governments, and that leaves 150,000 to do the work.

At any given time there are 102,000 people in hospitals, leaving 48,000 to do the work.

Now, there are 47,998 people in prisons.

That leaves just two people to do the work.

You and me.

And you're sitting at your computer reading jokes ...

Windows

A blonde woman goes into a department store and tells the salesman she wants a pair of pink curtains. He assures her they have a good selection of pink curtains. He shows her many textures, prints and hues of pink fabrics.

Once she has finally picked out a pink floral pattern, the salesman asks her, 'What size do you need?'

She replies, 'Just 15 inches.'

He exclaims, '*15 inches?!* What room are they for?'

She says, 'I only need one, and it's not for a room. It's for my computer monitor.'

The surprised salesman exclaims, 'Miss, computers do not have curtains.'

The blonde says, 'HELLOOoooooo ... I've got windows!'

Helpline

WordPerfect helpline (transcribed from a recording monitoring the customer care department)

Operator: 'Rigby Hall, computer assistance — may I help you?'

Caller: 'Yes, well, I'm having trouble with WordPerfect.'

Operator: 'What sort of trouble?'

Caller: 'Well, I was just typing along, and all of a sudden the words went away.'

Operator: 'Went away?'

Caller: 'They disappeared.'

Operator: 'Hmm. So what does your screen look like now?'

Caller: 'Nothing.'

Operator: 'Nothing?'

Caller: 'It's blank; it won't accept anything when I type.'

Operator: 'Are you still in WordPerfect, or did you get out?'

Caller: 'How do I tell?'

Operator: 'Can you see the C: prompt on the screen?'

Caller: 'What's a sea-prompt?'

Operator: 'Never mind. Can you move your cursor around the screen?'

Caller: 'There isn't any cursor: I told you, it won't accept anything I type.'

Operator: 'Does your monitor have a power indicator?'

Caller: 'What's a monitor?'

Operator: 'It's the thing with the screen on it that looks like a TV. Does it have a little light that tells you when it's on?'

Caller: 'I don't know.'

Operator: 'Well, then look on the back of the monitor and find where the power cord goes into it. Can you see that?'

Caller: 'Yes, I think so.'

Operator: 'Great. Follow the cord to the plug, and tell me if it's plugged into the wall.'

Caller: 'Yes, it is.'

Operator: 'When you were behind the monitor, did you notice that there were two cables plugged into the back of it, not just one?'

Caller: 'No.'

Operator: 'Well, there are. I need you to look back there again and find the other cable.'

Caller: 'OK, here it is.'

Operator: 'Follow it for me, and tell me if it's plugged securely into the back of your computer.'

Caller: 'I can't reach.'

Operator: 'Uh huh. Well, can you see if it is?'

Caller: 'No.'

Operator: 'Even if you maybe put your knee on something and lean way over?'

Caller: 'Oh, it's not because I don't have the right angle — it's because it's dark.'

Operator: 'Dark?'

Caller: 'Yes — the office light is off, and the only light I have is coming in from the window.'

Operator: 'Well, turn on the office light then.'

Caller: 'I can't.'

Operator: 'No? Why not?'

Caller: 'Because there's a power failure.'

Operator: 'A power ... a power failure? Aha, OK, we've got it licked now. Do you still have the boxes and manuals and packing stuff your computer came in?'

Caller: 'Well, yes, I keep them in the closet.'

Operator: 'Good. Go get them, and unplug your system and pack it up just like it was when you got it. Then take it back to the store you bought it from.'

Caller: 'Really? Is it that bad?'

Operator: 'Yes, I'm afraid it is.'

Caller: 'Well, all right then, I suppose. What do I tell them?'

Operator: 'Tell them you're too stupid to own a computer.'

Signs of the times

We all know those cute little computer symbols called 'emoticons', where :) or :-) means a smile and :(or :-(is a frown.

Well, how about some 'ASSICONS'? Here goes:

(_!_) a regular ass

(__!__) a fat ass

(!) a tight ass

(_*_) a sore ass

(_!_) a swishy ass

(_o_) an ass that's been around

(_x_) kiss my ass

(_X_) leave my ass alone

(_zzz_) a tired ass

(_E=mc2_) a smart ass

(_$_) money coming out of his ass

(_?_) dumb ass

How many Internet mail list subscribers does it take to change a light bulb?

- one to change the light bulb and to post that the light bulb has been changed.
- 14 to share similar experiences of changing light bulbs, and discuss how the light bulb could have been changed differently.
- seven to caution about the dangers of changing light bulbs.
- one to move the discussion to the Lighting list.
- two to argue then move it to the Electricals list.
- seven to point out spelling and grammar errors in posts about changing light bulbs.
- five to flame the spellcheckers.
- three to correct the spelling and grammar flames.
- two industry professionals to inform the group that the proper term is 'lamp'.
- 15 know-it-alls who claim that they were in the industry too, and that 'light bulb' is perfectly correct.
- 19 to post that this forum is not about light bulbs, and people should please take this discussion to a light bulb forum.

- 11 to defend the posting to this forum, saying that we all use light bulbs, and therefore the posts are relevant to this forum.
- 36 to debate which method of changing light bulbs is superior, where to buy the best light bulbs, what brand of light bulbs works best for this technique, and what brands are faulty.
- seven to post URLs where one can see examples of various light bulbs.
- four to post that the URLs were posted incorrectly, and then to post the corrected URLs.
- three to post about links they found from those URLs that are relevant to this group, which makes light bulbs relevant to this group.
- 13 to link all posts to date, quote them in their entirety, including all headers and signatures, and add 'Me too'.
- five to post to the group that they will no longer post because they cannot handle the light-bulb controversy.
- four to say, 'Didn't we go through this already, a short time ago?'
- 13 to say, 'Do a Google search on light bulbs before posting questions about light bulbs.'
- one forum lurker to respond to the original post six months from now and start it all over again.

'Quoth the server 404'

Once upon a midnight dreary, while I porn-surfed, weak and weary,
Over many a strange and spurious porn-site of 'hot chicks galore',
While I clicked my favourite bookmark, suddenly there came a warning,
And my heart was filled with mourning, mourning for my dear amour,
'Tis not possible,' I muttered. 'Give me back my free hardcore!'
Quoth the server, '404.'

Another version:
Once upon a midnight dreary, while I porn-surfed, weak and weary,
For many a quaint and curious website of X-rated lore,
Found the server nearly napping, http replies a-slacking,
Though my loins were filled with burning,
yearning for a teenage whore,
And as I paused awhile in hope that service be restored —
Quoth the server, '404.'

Another version:

Once upon a night-time dreary, as I web-surfed, red-eyed, weary,

I resisted strange and lurid websites of hot sex galore,

But my curiosity grew stronger; hesitating then no longer,

I gave in and clicked the link to see what waited there in store.

And with the clicking, came the ticking, of the page that was no more.

Quoth the server, '404.'

Another version:

Once upon a porn-site dreary, where I lingered, red-eyed, bleary,

O'er many a strangely grammared page of Russian girls galore,

Closing pop-ups then cascading, spyware programs now pervading,

Came a sight that set me thinking, linking to hot chicks galore.

'Fetch the URL,' I muttered, but browser stuttered as before —

Quoth the server, '404.'

How to start your day with a positive outlook

1. Open a new file in your PC
2. Name it 'Housework'
3. Send it to the RECYCLE BIN
4. Empty the RECYCLE BIN
5. Your PC will ask you, 'Are you sure you want to delete housework permanently?'
6. Answer calmly, 'Yes,' and press the mouse button firmly ...
7. Feel better?

Hired cannibals

A big corporation recently hired several cannibals. 'You are all part of our team now,' said the HR rep during the welcoming briefing. 'You get all the usual benefits and you can go to the cafeteria for something to eat, but please don't eat any of the other employees.'

The cannibals promised they would not.

Four weeks later their boss remarked, 'You're all working very hard, and I'm quite satisfied with you. However, one of our secretaries has disappeared. Do any of you know what happened to her?'

The cannibals all shook their heads implying no.

After the boss had left, the leader of the cannibals said to the others, 'Which one of you idiots ate the secretary?'

A hand rose hesitantly, to which the leader of the cannibals continued, 'You fool! For four weeks we've been eating managers and no one noticed anything, but noooooo, you had to go and eat someone important!'

New virus

I thought you would want to know about this e-mail virus. Even the most advanced programs from Norton or McAfee cannot take care of this one. It appears to affect those people who were born prior to 1960. Symptoms:

1. Causes you to send the same e-mail twice.
2. Causes you to send a blank e-mail.
3. Causes you to send e-mail to the wrong person.
4. Causes you to send it back to the person who sent it to you.
5. Causes you to forget to attach the attachment.
6. Causes you to hit 'SEND' before you've finished.
7. Causes you to hit 'DELETE' instead of 'SEND'.
8. Causes you to hit 'SEND' when you should 'DELETE'.

It is called the 'C-Nile Virus'.

World's easiest quiz – circulated by e-mail

(Passing requires four correct answers)

1. How long did the Hundred Years War last?
2. Which country makes Panama hats?
3. From which animal do we get catgut?
4. In which month do Russians celebrate the October Revolution?
5. What is a camel's hair brush made of?
6. The Canary Islands in the Pacific are named after what animal?
7. What was King George VI's first name?
8. What colour is a purple finch?
9. Where are Chinese gooseberries from?
10. What is the colour of the black box in a commercial airplane?

All done? Check your answers below!

Answers to the quiz

1) How long did the Hundred Years War last?
   *116 years
2) Which country makes Panama hats?
   *Ecuador
3) From which animal do we get catgut?
   *Sheep and horses
4) In which month do Russians celebrate the October Revolution?
   *November
5) What is a camel's hair brush made of?
   *Squirrel fur
6) The Canary Islands in the Pacific are named after what animal?
   *Dogs
7) What was King George VI's first name?
   *Albert
8) What colour is a purple finch?
   *Crimson
9) Where are Chinese gooseberries from?
   *New Zealand
10) What is the colour of the black box in a commercial airplane?
   *Orange, of course.

What do you mean you failed?

Pass this on to some other brilliant friends.

Rejected password

A woman was helping her computer-illiterate husband set up his computer, and at the appropriate point in the process, she told him that he would need to now choose and enter a password — something he would need to use to log on. The husband was in a rather amorous mood and figured he would try for the shock effect to bring this to his wife's attention. So, when the computer asked him for his password, he made it plainly obvious to his wife that he was keying in the word:

P E N I S

His wife fell off her chair laughing when the computer replied:

PASSWORD REJECTED — NOT LONG ENOUGH

Dear Tech Support:

Last year I upgraded from Boyfriend 5.0 to Husband 1.0 and noticed a slowdown in the overall performance, particularly in the Flower and Jewellery applications that had operated flawlessly under Boyfriend 5.0.

In addition, Husband 1.0 uninstalled many of the valuable programs, such as Romance 9.5 and Personal Attention 6.5, but installed undesirable programs such as AFL 5.0 and Cricket 3.0 and now Conversation 8.0 no longer runs and House Cleaning 2.6 simply crashes the system.

I've tried running Nagging 5.3 to fix the problems, but to no avail. What can I do?

Signed,
Desperate

And the reply:

Dear Desperate:

First, keep in mind Boyfriend 5.0 is an entertainment package, while Husband 1.0 is an operating system. Try entering the command C: I THOUGHT YOU LOVED ME and download Tears 6.2 to install Guilt 3.0.

If all works as designed, Husband 1.0 should then automatically run the applications Jewellery 2.0 and Flowers 3.5. But remember, overuse can cause Husband 1.0 to default to Grumpy Silence 2.5, Happy Hour 7.0 or Beer 6.1. Beer 6.1 is a very bad program that will create snoring loudly. wav files.

Whatever you do, DO NOT install Mother-in-Law 1.0 or reinstall another Boyfriend program. These are not supported applications and will crash Husband 1.0.

In summary, Husband 1.0 is a great program, but it does have a limited memory and cannot learn new applications quickly. You might consider additional software to improve memory and performance. I personally recommend Hot Food 3.0 and Lingerie 6.9.

Good luck,
Tech Support

IT Marketing

Over the years, people have often asked me to explain the various concepts of Marketing Communications. The following analogies might help clarify the 'tools of the trade'.

You see a handsome guy at a party. You go up to him and say, 'I'm fantastic in bed.' — That's Direct Marketing.

You're at a party with a bunch of friends and see a handsome guy. One of your friends goes up to him and, pointing at you, says, 'She's fantastic in bed.' — That's Advertising.

You see a handsome guy at a party. You go up to him and get his telephone number. The next day you call and say, 'Hi, I'm fantastic in bed.' — That's Telemarketing.

You're at a party and see a handsome guy. You get up and straighten your dress. You walk up to him and pour him a drink. You say, 'May I?' and reach up to straighten his tie, brushing your breast lightly against his arm, and then say, 'By the way, I'm fantastic in bed.' — That's Public Relations.

You're at a party and see a handsome guy. He walks up to you and says, 'I hear you're fantastic in bed.' — That's Brand Recognition.

You're at a party and see a handsome guy. You talk him into going home with your friend. — That's a Sales Representation.

Your friend can't satisfy him so he calls you. — That's Tech Support.

You're on your way to a party when you realise that there could be handsome men in all these houses you're passing. So you scream out at the top of your lungs, 'I'm fantastic in bed!' — That's Spam.

New-tech money

A shepherd was looking after his sheep on the side of a deserted Queensland road. Suddenly a brand new Porsche screeches to a halt. The driver, a young man dressed in an Armani suit, Ray-Bans, TAG Heuer watch, Cerutti shoes, tailor-made mauve shirt, with a Boss tie, gets out and asks the shepherd, 'If I can guess how many sheep you have, can I keep one?'

The shepherd looks at the large flock of sheep and says, 'OK.'

The young man connects his laptop to his mobile phone-fax, enters the NASA website, scans the field using his GPS, opens the database linked to 60 Excel tables, filled with logarithms and pivot tables, then prints out a 150 page report on his high-tech mini printer. He studies the reports and says to the shepherd, 'You have 1586 sheep.'

The shepherd replies, 'That's correct. You can have the pick of my flock.'

The young man packs away his equipment, looks at the flock and puts one into the boot of the Porsche.

As he is about to leave, the shepherd says, 'If I can guess what your profession is, will you return the animal to me?'

The young man thinks for a minute and says, 'OK.'

The shepherd says, 'You are a management consultant.'

The young man says, 'Correct. How did you know?'

The shepherd replies, 'Simple. First, you came here without being invited. Second, you charge me a fee for something I already knew. Third, you don't understand anything about my business. Now can I have my dog back?'

Mail

A man was in his front yard mowing grass when the attractive blonde female neighbour came out of the house and went straight to the mailbox. She opened it then slammed it shut and stormed back in the house. A little later she came out of her house again, went to the mailbox, and again opened it and slammed it shut. Angrily, back into the house she went.

As the man was getting ready to edge the lawn, she came out again, marched to the mailbox, opened it and then slammed it closed harder than ever.

Puzzled by her actions the man asked her, 'Is something wrong?'

To which she replied, 'There certainly is! My stupid computer keeps saying, "YOU'VE GOT MAIL."'

New chemical element

The heaviest element known to science was recently discovered by investigators at a major research university. The element, which has been named Administratium, has no protons or electrons and thus has an atomic number of 0. However, it does have one neutron, 125 assistant neutrons, 75 vice neutrons and 111 assistant vice neutrons, which gives it an atomic mass of 312. These 312 particles are held together by a force that involves the continuous exchange of meson-like particles called morons. It is surrounded by vast quantities of lepton-like particles called peons. Since it has no electrons, Administratium is inert. However, it can be detected chemically as it impedes every reaction it comes in contact with. According to the discoverers, a minute amount of Administratium causes one reaction to take over four days to complete, when it would normally have occurred in less than a second. Administratium has a normal half-life of approximately three years, at which time it does not decay, but instead undergoes a reorganisation in which a portion of the assistant neutrons, vice neutrons and assistant vice neutrons exchange places. In fact, an Administratium sample's mass actually *increases* over time, since with each reorganisation some of the morons inevitably become neutrons, forming new isotopes. This characteristic of moron promotion leads some scientists to speculate that perhaps Administratium is spontaneously formed whenever morons reach a certain quantity in concentration. This hypothetical quantity is referred to as 'critical morass'.

Comprehending engineers

Two engineering students were riding their bikes across the campus when one said, 'Where did you get such a great bike?'

The second engineer replied, 'Well, I was walking along yesterday minding my own business when a beautiful woman rode up on this bike. She threw the bike to the ground, took off all her clothes and said, "Take what you want."'

The second engineer nodded approvingly, 'Good choice; the clothes probably wouldn't have fitted.'

Don't mess with the computer guys

Letter of resignation from an employee at a major computer firm to his boss.

Dear Mr Baker,

As an employee of an institution of higher education, I have a few very basic expectations. Chief among these is that my direct superiors have an intellect that ranges above the common ground squirrel. After your consistent and annoying harassment of my co-workers and myself during the commission of our duties, I can only surmise that you are one of the few true genetic wastes of our time. Asking me, a network administrator, to explain every little nuance of everything I do each time you happen to stroll into my office is not only a waste of time, but also a waste of precious oxygen.

I was hired because I know how to network computer systems, and you were apparently hired to provide amusement to myself and other employees, who watch you vainly attempt to understand the concept of 'cut and paste' for the hundredth time. You will never understand computers. Something as incredibly simple as binary still gives you too many options. You will also never understand why people hate you, but I am going to try and explain it to you, even though I am sure this will be just as effective as telling you what an IP is. Your shiny new iMac has more personality than you ever will. You walk around the building all day, shiftlessly looking for fault in others. You have a sharp-dressed useless look about you that may have worked for your interview, but now that you actually have responsibility, you pawn it off on overworked staff, hoping their talent will cover for your glaring ineptitude. In a world of managerial evolution, you are the blue-green algae that everyone else eats and laughs at. Managers like you are a sad proof of the Dilbert principle.

Seeing as this situation is unlikely to change without you getting a full frontal lobotomy reversal, I am forced to tender my resignation; however, I have a few parting thoughts.

1. When someone calls you in reference to employment, it is illegal to give me a bad recommendation. The most you can say to hurt me is 'I prefer not to comment.' I will have friends randomly call you over the next couple of years to keep you honest, because I know you would be unable to do it on your own.

2. I have all the passwords to every account on the system, and I know every password you have used for the last five years. If you decide to get cute, I am going to publish your 'favourites list', which I conveniently saved when you made me 'back up' your useless files. I do believe that terms like 'Lolita' are not usually viewed favourably by the administration.

3. When you borrowed the digital camera to 'take pictures of your mother's birthday', you neglected to mention that you were going to take pictures of yourself in the mirror nude. Then you forgot to erase them like the techno-moron you really are. Suffice it to say I have never seen such odd acts with a ketchup bottle, but I assure you that those have been copied and kept in safe places pending the authoring of a glowing letter of recommendation. (Try to use a spellcheck please; I hate having to correct your mistakes.)

Thank you for your time, and I expect the letter of recommendation on my desk by 8 a.m. tomorrow. One word of this to anybody, and all of your little twisted repugnant obsessions will be open to the public. Never fuck with your systems administrator. Why? Because they know what you do with all that free time!

Down on the new-tech farm

A farmer ordered a high-tech milking machine. It happened that the equipment arrived when his wife was away. So, he decided to test it on himself first. He inserted his penis into the equipment, turned the switch on and … voila, everything else was automatic! He really had a good time as the equipment provided him with as much pleasure as his wife did. However, when the fun was over, he found that he could not take the instrument off. He read the manual, but did not find any useful information. He tried every button on the instrument — some made the equipment squeeze, shake, or suck harder or less, but still without success. Panicking, he called the supplier's Customer Service Hotline.

The farmer: 'Hello, I just bought a milking machine from your company. It worked fantastic. But how can I take it off from the cow's udder?'

Customer service: 'Don't worry. The machine was programmed such that it will release automatically after collecting about two litres of milk.'

Technically correct

A man in a hot air balloon realised he was lost. He reduced altitude and spotted a woman below. He descended a bit more and shouted, 'Excuse me, can you help me? I promised a friend I would meet him an hour ago, but I don't know where I am.'

The woman below replied, 'You are in a hot air balloon hovering approximately 30 feet above the ground. You are between 40 and 41 degrees north latitude and between 59 and 60 degrees west longitude.'

'You must be an engineer,' said the balloonist.

'I am,' replied the woman, 'how did you know?'

'Well,' answered the balloonist, 'everything you told me is technically correct, but I have no idea what to make of your information, and the fact is I am still lost. Frankly, you've not been much help so far.'

The woman below responded, 'You must be in senior management.'

'I am,' replied the balloonist, 'but how did you know?'

'Well,' said the woman, 'you don't know where you are or where you are going. You have risen to where you are due to a large quantity of hot air. You made a promise which you have no idea how to keep, and you expect people beneath you to solve your problems. The fact is you are in exactly the same position you were in before we met, but somehow, it's now my fault.'

8 SPORTING LIFE AND STRIFE

Australians have an international reputation as being 'sports crazy'. It is true we have given the world some mighty sportsmen and women, and have brought home various trophies in rowing, cricket, tennis, swimming and netball. We have also brought home and passed around a hell of a lot of humour associated with games, players and scandals. The Internet plays an ever-increasing role in distributing such stories and is also used to circulate stories about players, sometimes grossly unfair stories. E-mails are also used to cut down 'tall poppies' in sport — a particularly Australian pastime where success is sometimes seen as big noting and therefore that person should be 'cut down to size'. Mind you, considering the obsessional media coverage of sport on television, newspapers, magazines, radio, trash magazines and blogs, and the massive amount of weekly editorial they demand, it is small wonder every last story is squeezed out of every event and sportsperson. I have strolled down a cautious path in this section, avoiding scandalous jokes that pry into sports celebrities' lives. Some would say that celebrities deserve everything they receive because they usually play the celebrity game. I believe jokes about real people engaging in seemingly unsavoury behaviour is an integral part of humour but not necessary for this collection. I suspect we already know enough about Shane Warne's sex life. Nonetheless, for the sake of balance, I have included one widely distributed Shane Warne yarn. Wayne Carey, David Beckham, Tiger Woods, the All Blacks, Canterbury Bulldogs and some of our other renowned players and teams also get a run. The facts usually fly out the window when it comes to such jokes. The folk never let the truth get in the way of a good story!

What you will find here are funny stories about golf, cricket, rugby etc. As with the jokes about personalities, there is no real way of verifying what is fact and fable. The particular point in publishing them here is to record that these supposed insults have been so widely circulated as part of the folklore process.

Little Johnny

Little Johnny was in his primary school class when the teacher asked the children what their fathers did for a living.

All the typical answers came up — fireman, policeman, salesman.

Johnny was being uncharacteristically quiet, and so the teacher asked him about his father.

'My father's an exotic dancer in a gay cabaret and takes off all his clothes in front of other men.'

The teacher hurriedly set the other children to work on some colouring in and took little Johnny aside to ask him, 'Is that really true about your father working in a gay strip club?'

'No,' said Johnny, 'he really plays Test cricket for England but I was too embarrassed to say.'

Flying Doctor Service

Two hunters are out in the bush when one of them collapses. He doesn't seem to be breathing and his eyes are glazed.

The other man whips out his phone and calls the emergency Flying Doctor Service. He gasps: 'My friend is dead! What can I do?'

The operator says: 'Calm down, I can help. First, let's make sure he's dead.'

There is a silence, then a shot is heard.

Back on the phone, the guy says: 'OK, now what?'

Lost golf ball

A man staggers into an emergency room with concussion, multiple bruises, two black eyes and a five-iron wrapped tightly around his throat. Naturally, the doctor asks him what happened.

'Well,' says the man, 'I was having a quiet round of golf with my wife when, at a difficult hole, we both sliced our balls into a field of cows. We went to look for them. After a while I noticed one of the cows had something white at its rear end, so I walked over and lifted up the cow's tail. Sure enough, there was a golf ball, and it had my wife's monogram on it.'

'What did you do?' asks the doctor.

'Well, I don't remember too much,' says the man. 'I lifted the cow's tail, yelled to my wife, "Hey, this looks like yours!" and right after that everything went dark.'

Fishing

A man came home and was greeted by his wife, who was dressed only in very sexy underwear and holding a couple of short velvet ropes.

'Tie me up,' she purred, 'and you can do anything you want.'

So, he tied her up and went fishing.

News report from the Children's Court

A seven-year-old boy was at the centre of a Parramatta, NSW courtroom drama yesterday when he challenged a court ruling over who should have custody of him. The boy has a history of being beaten by his parents and the judge initially awarded custody to his aunt, in keeping with child custody law and regulations requiring that family unity be maintained to the degree possible.

The boy surprised the court when he proclaimed that his aunt beat him more than his parents and he adamantly refused to live with her. When the judge then suggested that he live with his grandparents, the boy cried out that they also beat him.

After considering the remainder of the immediate family and learning that domestic violence was apparently a way of life among them, the judge took the unprecedented step of allowing the boy to propose who should have custody of him. After two recesses to check legal references and confer with child welfare officials, the judge granted temporary custody to the English cricket team, whom the boy firmly believes are not capable of beating anyone.

Golfing

Two old friends were just about to tee off at the first hole of their local golf course when a guy carrying a golf bag called out to them, 'Do you mind if I join you? My partner didn't turn up.'

'Sure,' they said, 'you're welcome.'

So they started playing and enjoyed the game and the company of the newcomer. Part way around the course, one of the friends asked him, 'What do you do for a living?'

'I'm a hitman,' was the reply.

'You're joking!' was the response.

'No, I'm not!' he said, reaching into his golf bag, and pulling out a beautiful Martini sniper's rifle with a large telescopic sight. 'Here are my tools.'

'That's a beautiful telescopic sight,' said the other friend. 'Can I take a look? I think I might be able to see my house from here.'

So he picked up the rifle and looked through the sight in the direction of his house. 'Yeah, I can see my house all right. This sight is fantastic. I can see right in the window ... Wow, I can see my wife in the bedroom. Ha ha, I can see she's naked! Wait a minute, that's my neighbour in there with her ... He's naked, too!! The bitch!'

He turned to the hitman, 'How much do you charge for a hit?'

'I'll do a flat rate for you: $1000 every time I pull the trigger.'

'Can you do two for me now?'

'Sure, what do you want?'

'First, shoot my wife — she's always been mouthy, so shoot her in the mouth — then the neighbour. He's a friend of mine, so just shoot his dick off to teach him a lesson.'

The hitman took the rifle and took aim, standing perfectly still for a few minutes.

'Are you going to do it or not?' said the friend impatiently.

'Just be patient,' said the hitman calmly. 'I think I can save you a grand here ...'

Primary teacher

A primary teacher started a new job at a school in Bankstown and, trying to make a good impression on her first day, explained to her class that she was a Canterbury Bulldogs fan.

She asked her students to raise their hands if they, too, were Bulldogs fans. Everyone in the class raised their hand except one little girl.

The teacher looked at the girl with surprise and said: 'Mary, why didn't you raise your hand?'

'Because I'm not a Bulldogs fan,' she replied.

The teacher, still shocked, asked: 'Well, if you're not a Bulldogs fan, then who are you a fan of?'

'I'm a Roosters fan, and proud of it,' Mary replied.

The teacher could not believe her ears. 'Mary, why are you a Roosters fan?'

'Because my mum and dad are from Bondi, and my mum is a Roosters fan and my dad is a Roosters fan, so I'm a Roosters fan too!'

'Well,' said the teacher, in an obviously annoyed tone, 'that's no reason for you to be a Roosters fan. You don't have to be just like your parents all of the time. What if your mum was a prostitute, your dad was a drug addict, and your brother was a car thief — what would you be then?'

'Then,' Mary said, 'I'd be a Bulldogs fan.'

Summer Olympics

Here are the top seven 'blooper' comments supposedly made by sports commentators during the summer Olympics:

1. Weightlifting commentator: 'This is Gregoriava from Bulgaria. I saw her snatch this morning during her warm-up and it was amazing.'
2. Dressage commentator: 'This is really a lovely horse and I speak from personal experience since I once mounted her mother.'
3. Paul Hamm, gymnast: 'I owe a lot to my parents, especially my mother and father.'
4. Boxing analyst: 'Sure there have been injuries, and even some deaths in boxing, but none of them really that serious.'
5. Softball announcer: 'If history repeats itself, I should think we can expect the same thing again.'
6. Basketball analyst: 'He dribbles a lot and the opposition doesn't like it. In fact, you can see it all over their faces.'
7. At the rowing medal ceremony: 'Ah, isn't that nice, the wife of the IOC president is hugging the cox of the British crew.'

The quiz

Colin is on *Who Wants To Be A Millionaire* and has reached the million-dollar question.

Eddie McGuire says, 'Right, Colin, this is for one million dollars. And remember, you still have two lifelines left, so please take your time. Here's your question:

'What type of animal lives in a sett? Is it: (a) a badger; (b) a ferret; (c) a mole; or (d) a cuckoo?'

Colin ponders for a while and says, 'No, I'm sorry, Eddie, I'm not too sure. I'll have to go 50–50.'

'Right, Colin, let's take away two wrong answers and see what you're left with. Badger and cuckoo are the two remaining answers.'

Colin has a long think, then scratches his head and says, 'No, Eddie, I'm still not sure, I'm going to have to phone a friend.'

'So who are you going to call, Colin?' says Eddie.

'Hmmm … I think I'll call David Beckham.'

So he phones David Beckham. 'David, this is Colin, a fan from Australia, on *Who Wants To Be A Millionaire*, and with your help I might win one million dollars.

'David,' he adds. 'What type of animal lives in a sett? Is it a badger or a cuckoo?'

'It's a badger, mate,' says Becks without hesitation.

'You sure, son?' says Colin.

'Definitely. One hundred per cent. It's a badger. Definitely.'

'Right, Eddie,' says Colin, 'I'll go with David. The answer's a badger.'

'Final answer, Colin?' says Eddie. 'That's the correct answer. You've won one million dollars!'

The next morning Colin calls Beckham. 'Son, that was brilliant last night. I thought I might be taking a gamble giving you a call, but you played a blinder! But how the hell did you know that a badger lives in a sett?'

'Oh, I didn't,' replies Beckham. 'But everybody knows a cuckoo lives in a clock.'

Rules for bedroom golf

1. Each player shall furnish his own equipment for play, normally one club and two balls.
2. Play on a course must be approved by the owner of the hole.
3. Unlike outdoor golf, the object is to get the club in the hole and keep the balls out of the hole.
4. For most effective play, the club should have a firm shaft. Course owners are permitted to check the shaft for firmness before play begins.
5. Course owners reserve the right to restrict the length of the club to avoid damage to the hole.
6. The object of the game is to take as many strokes as necessary until the course owner is satisfied that play is complete. Failure to do so may result in being denied permission to play on the course again.

7. It is considered bad form to begin playing the hole immediately upon arrival at the course. The experienced player will normally take time to admire the entire course with special attention to the well-formed bunkers.

8. Players are cautioned not to mention other courses they have played or are currently playing to the owner of the course being played. Upset course owners have been known to damage a player's equipment for this reason.

9. Players are encouraged to have proper rain gear along, just in case.

10. Players should assure themselves that their match has been properly scheduled, particularly when a new course is being played for the first time. Previous players have been known to become irate if they discover someone else is playing what they consider to be a private course.

11. Players should not assume a course is in shape for play at all times. Some players may be embarrassed if they find the course is temporarily under repair. Players are advised to be extremely tactful in this situation. More advanced players will find alternate means of play when this is the case.

12. Players are advised to obtain the course owner's permission before attempting to play the back nine.

13. Slow play is encouraged; however, players should be prepared to proceed at quicker pace, at least temporarily, at the course owner's request.

14. It is considered outstanding performance, time permitting, to play the same hole several times in one match.

15. The course owner will be the sole judge of who is the best player.

Golf balls

A man entered the bus, with both of his front pant pockets full of golf balls, and sat down next to a blonde. The blonde kept looking quizzically at him and his bulging pockets. Finally, after many such glances from her, he said, 'It's golf balls.'

The blonde continued to look at him thoughtfully and finally asked, 'Does it hurt as much as tennis elbow?'

The marathon runner

A woman was having a daytime affair while her husband was at work.

One wet and lusty day she was in bed with her boyfriend when, to her horror, she heard her husband's car pull into the driveway.

'Oh, my God, hurry! Grab your clothes and jump out the window. My husband's home early!'

'I can't jump out the window — it's raining out there!'

'If my husband catches us in here, he'll kill us both!' she replied. 'He's got a hot temper and a gun, so the rain is the least of your problems!'

So the boyfriend scooted out of bed, grabbed his clothes and jumped out the window.

As he ran down the street in the pouring rain, he quickly discovered he had run right into the middle of the town's annual marathon, so he started running along beside the others, about 300 of them.

Being naked, with his clothes tucked under his arm, he tried to blend in as best he could. After a little while a small group of runners, who had been watching him with some curiosity, jogged closer. 'Do you always run in the nude?' one asked.

'Oh yes!' he replied, gasping in air. 'It feels so wonderfully free!'

Another runner moved alongside. 'Do you always run while carrying your clothes under your arm?'

'Oh, yes,' our friend answered breathlessly. 'That way I can get dressed right at the end of the run and get in my car to go home!'

Then a third runner cast his eyes a little lower and queried, 'Do you always wear a condom when you run?'

'Nope … just when it's raining.'

Shane's panties

Shane Warne's teammates were perplexed one morning to see Shane walk into the change rooms with a pair of women's panties on his arm. Somewhat used to Shane's tendencies, they let it go and went about getting ready. The day wore on, Shane bowled a few overs and the batsmen came and went with puzzled expressions on their faces — but no one dared ask about the panties.

Finally, Ricky Ponting walked up to Shane between overs and gently whispered to him. 'Er, Shane,' he said, 'we've come to expect many unusual things from you, but we're a bit worried that you seem to be wearing a pair of women's panties on your arm. Please tell me this doesn't mean more trouble.'

'Oh no,' Shane grinned. 'It's the patch. I'm trying to quit.'

Golfer's transplant

A pro golfer was involved in a terrible car crash and was rushed to hospital. Just before he was put under, the surgeon popped in to see him. 'I have some good news and some bad news,' said the surgeon. 'The bad news is that I have to remove your right arm!'

'Oh, God, no!' cried the man. 'My career is over! Please, Doc, tell me the good news.'

'The good news is I have another one to replace it with, but it's a woman's arm! I'll need your permission before I go ahead with the transplant.'

'Go for it, Doc,' said the golfer. 'As long as I can play golf again.'

The operation went well and six months later the man was out on the golf course when he bumped into the surgeon.

'Hi, how's the new arm?' asked the surgeon.

'Just great,' replied the golfer. 'I'm playing the best golf of my life. My new arm has a much finer touch and my putting has really improved.'

'That's great,' said the surgeon.

'Not only that,' continued the golfer, 'my handwriting has improved, I've learnt how to sew my own clothes and I've even taken up painting landscapes in watercolours.'

'Unbelievable!' said the surgeon. 'I'm so glad to hear the transplant was such a success.'

'Well, there is one problem,' said the golfer. 'Every time I try to jerk off I get a headache!'

Locker-room talk

Several men are in the locker room of a golf club. A cell phone on a bench rings and a man engages the hands-free speaker function and begins to talk.

Man: 'Hello.'
Woman: 'Honey, it's me. Are you at the club?'

Man: 'Yes.'

Woman: 'I am at the mall now and I found this beautiful leather coat. It's only $1000. Is it OK if I buy it?'

Man: 'Sure … go ahead, if you like it that much.'

Woman: 'I also stopped by the Mercedes dealership and saw the new model. I saw one I really liked.'

Man: 'How much?'

Woman: '$60,000.'

Man: 'OK, but for that price I want it with all the options.'

Woman: 'Great! Oh, and one more thing … the house we wanted last year is back on the market. They're asking $950,000.'

Man: 'Well, then go ahead and give them an offer, but just offer $900,000.'

Woman: 'OK. I'll see you later! I love you!'

Man: 'Bye … I love you, too.'

The man hangs up. The other men in the locker room are looking at him in astonishment. Then he asks: 'Anyone know who this phone belongs to?'

Rugby World Cup

A man has tickets for the Rugby World Cup final. As he sits down, another man comes and asks if anyone is sitting in the seat next to him. He replies, 'The seat is empty.'

'This is incredible,' says the man. 'Who in their right mind would have a seat like this for the World Cup final, one of the biggest sporting events in the world, and not use it?'

He says, 'Well, actually, the seat belongs to me. I was supposed to come with my wife, but she passed away. This is the first time we haven't been together at a World Cup final since we got married in 1987.'

'Oh … I'm sorry to hear that. That's terrible. But couldn't you find someone else — a friend or relative, or even a neighbour — to take the seat?'

The man shakes his head. 'No. They're all at the funeral.'

Dog's life

A man walks into a Paddington hotel bar with a dachshund under his arm. The dog is wearing an England rugby jersey and is festooned with English colours and pom-poms.

The bartender says, 'Hey! No pets are allowed! You'll have to leave.'

The man begs him, 'Look, I'm desperate! We're both big rugby fans, the TV's broken at home, and this is the only place around where we can see the final game.'

After securing a promise that the dog will behave, and warning him that he and the dog will be thrown out if there's any trouble, the bartender relents and allows them to stay in the bar and watch the game. The big match begins with the Poms receiving the kick-off. They march down field, get stopped at the 22, and kick a penalty goal.

Suddenly, the dog jumps up on the bar and begins walking up and down the bar giving high-fives to everyone. The bartender says, 'Wow, that is the most amazing thing I've seen! What does the dog do if they score a try?'

The owner replies, 'I don't know — I've only had him for three years.'

Rugby quickies

Q: What do you do for a drowning New Zealand rugby player?
A: Nothing. You could drag him to the top, but he'll choke anyway.

Q: What's the difference between the All Blacks and an arsonist?
A: An arsonist wouldn't waste five matches.

The All Blacks are bringing out a new bra! Plenty of support, soft and *no cup*!

Did you hear about the Kiwi politician who was found dead in an All Black jersey?

The police had to dress him up in women's underwear in order to save his family from the embarrassment.

Anthem

A Kiwi bloke was out in his yard practising doing the Haka. Somewhere in space, aliens were watching this unusual dance.

'Kamate, kamate, ka-ora, ka-ora ... Kamate, kamate, ka-ora, ka ora ...'

The aliens were very interested by this ritual and wanted to see what effect it would have on this human if they removed a part of his brain.

So, using their alien technology, they shot down a laser beam — it hit the Kiwi's head and immediately vaporised a part of his brain. The aliens then sat back and watched ...

'Ka-mate, ka-mate, ka-ora, ka-ora …'

The aliens were amazed at what they saw. There seemed no discernible change in the Kiwi, yet he now had less than a full brain. The aliens decided to vaporise another part of his brain, then they watched with interest.

'Ka-mate, ka-mate, ka-ora, ka-ora …'

'*What!*' the aliens exclaimed to each other. 'This Kiwi shows no change in behaviour after the removal of half of his brain. Let's see what happens if we take the rest of it away and leave him with no brain at all.'

With a push of a button the aliens shot down another beam down and took away the final part of the Kiwi's brain. 'Now surely we should see some change!'

And sure enough, with no brain, no knowledge of anything, the aliens watched, and then they heard it …

'Waltzing Matilda … Waltzing Matilda …'

Handicapped

An Englishman, an Irishman and a Scotsman are all playing golf with their wives. The Englishman's wife steps up to the tee and, as she bends over to place her ball, a gust of wind blows her skirt up and reveals her lack of underwear.

'Good God, woman! Why aren't you wearing any knickers?' her husband demanded.

'Well, you don't give me enough housekeeping money to afford to buy any.'

The Englishman immediately reaches into his pocket and says, 'For the sake of decency, here's $50. Go and buy yourself some underwear.'

Next the Irishman's wife bends over to set her ball on the tee. Her skirt blows up to show that she is also wearing no undies. 'Blessed Virgin Mary, woman! You've no knickers — why not?'

She replies, 'I can't afford any on the money you give me.'

He reaches into his pocket and says, 'For the sake of decency, here's $20. Go and buy some underwear!'

Lastly, the Scotsman's wife bends over. The wind also takes her skirt over her head to reveal that she, too, is naked under it. 'Hoot, mon, woman! Why are ye not wearing knickers?'

She too explains, 'You dinna give me enough housekeepin' money ta be able ta afford any.'

The Scot reaches into his pocket and says, 'Well, fer the sake of decency, here's a comb. Tidy yurrrself up a bit.'

Steroids

On the subject of drugs in tennis, the Williams sisters were recently discussing this in the warm-up room before a doubles match. 'I think Dad might be slipping us steroids,' whispered Serena.

'What makes you say that?' replied a stunned Venus.

'Well,' started Serena, looking embarrassed, 'I've started to grow hair on parts of my body that have never had hair before!'

'Shit … like where?' asked Venus.

'Like … my balls!' replied Serena.

Tiger in Ireland

On a golf tour in Ireland, Tiger Woods drives his BMW into a petrol station in a remote part of the Irish countryside.

The attendant at the pump greets him in a typical Irish manner, completely unaware of whom the golfing pro is.

'Top of the mornin' to yerz, sir,' says the attendant. Tiger nods a quick 'hello' and bends forward to pick up the nozzle. As he does so, two tees fall out of his shirt pocket onto the ground.

'What are dey den, son?' asks the attendant.

'They're called tees,' replies Tiger.

'Well, what on de good earth are dey for?' inquires the Irishman.

'They're for resting my balls on when I'm driving,' says Tiger.

'Feckin Jaysus,' says the Irishman. 'Dem boys at BMW tink of everything!'

Oh Wayne

Wayne Carey wakes up one morning, showers and puts on his best tracksuit, ready for another hard day's work of being an overpaid footballer. Catching sight of himself in the mirror he thinks, 'By God, Wayne, you're looking good this morning.' He admires the fine cut of his outfit and the neat trim of his hair, and flexes his biceps.

'Feeling good too,' he notes proudly at the firm swell of muscle underneath the tight tracksuit.

He enters the kitchen downstairs, where his girlfriend hands him a bowl of cornflakes. 'You're looking fit this morning, Wayne.'

'You don't have to tell me,' says Wayne appreciatively.

'But you're not smelling so good, mind you,' comments his beloved.

Wayne takes a sniff. 'You're right there,' he says, worriedly. 'I am smelling a bit rough.'

He eats his cereal, downs his coffee, and sets off for Arden Street. 'Good morning, Denis,' he grins at Denis Pagan.

'It's a fine morning, Wayne,' says Denis, 'and you're looking really good.'

'Why thank you. I look good and I feel pretty good as well,' says Wayne, flexing both arms for his benefit.

'Oh, Wayne!' winces Denis in disgust. 'You smell awful!'

Worried, Wayne visits his doctor. 'Doc, I've got a problem. I look good, I feel great, but I smell awful.'

The doc reaches down for his medical dictionary. 'You look good,' he scans down the page, 'you feel great … but … smell awful. Hmmm yes … It's quite simple, Wayne,' the doctor says. 'You're a c**t.'

Footie fan

Two boys are playing kick-to-kick in a park in Sydney's eastern suburbs, when one lad is attacked by a vicious Rottweiler. Thinking quickly, the other boy grabs a branch and manages to wedge it down the dog's collar and twist, luckily breaking the dog's neck and stopping its attack.

A reporter who is strolling by sees the incident and rushes over to interview the boy. 'Young Rooster Fan Saves Friend From Vicious Animal,' he starts writing in his notebook.

'But I'm not a Rooster fan,' the little hero replies.

'Sorry, since we are in the eastern suburbs, I just assumed you were,' says the reporter and starts again. 'Young Rabbits Fan Rescues Friend From Horrific Attack,' he continues writing in his notebook.

'I'm not a Rabbits fan either!' the boy says.

'I assumed everyone in the eastern suburbs was either for the Roosters or the Rabbits, so what team *do* you barrack for?' the reporter asks.

'I'm a Canterbury fan!' the child beams.

The reporter starts a new sheet in his notebook and writes: 'Little Prick From Lakemba Kills Beloved Family Pet.'

Give it all

A man on his way home from work comes to a dead halt in traffic and thinks to himself, this traffic seems worse than usual. He notices a police officer walking back and forth between the lines of cars, so he rolls down his window. 'Officer, what's the hold-up?'

The officer replies: 'It's a French football fan. He's so depressed about losing to the Danish, being knocked out of the World Cup, finishing behind England, and the prospect of winning nothing after bragging all year, he's threatening to douse himself in petrol and set himself on fire. He says his family hates him and his friends are all laughing at him. I'm walking around taking a collection for him.'

'Really?' says the executive. 'How much have you collected?'

'So far,' replies the policeman, 'only half a gallon, but a lot of people are still siphoning.'

Sign language

A young bloke, out on the town with his mates, spies the girl of his dreams, across the dance floor. Having admired her from afar he finally gets up the courage to talk to her. Everything goes better than expected and she agrees to accompany him on a date the following Saturday evening. On Saturday night the man arrives at her house with flowers and chocolates.

To his surprise, she answers the door in nothing but a towel. 'I'm sorry,' she exclaims, 'I am running a bit late. Please come in and I'll introduce you to my parents, who will entertain you while I finish getting dressed. I should warn you, though, they are both deaf mutes.' She ushers him into the living room, introduces him to her parents and promptly disappears.

As you can imagine, this is a little uncomfortable as both of the parents are completely silent. Dad is sitting in his armchair watching golf on TV, and Mum is busy knitting. After about 10 minutes of complete silence, Mum jumps from her chair, pulls up her skirt, pulls down her knickers, and pours a glass of water over her backside. Just as suddenly, Dad launches himself across the room, bends her over the couch, and takes her from behind. He then sits back down in his chair and balances a matchstick in front of his eye. The room is plunged back into eerie silence and the young man is shocked into disbelief.

After a further 10 minutes, the daughter returns fully dressed and ready for the evening.

The date is a disaster with the young man completely distracted by the goings on earlier in the living room. At the end of the night, the girl asks, 'What's the matter? Have I done something wrong?'

'No, it's not you,' he replies, 'it's just that the strangest thing happened while I was waiting for you, and I am still a bit shocked. Well, first your mother jumps from her chair, lifts up her skirt, pulls down her panties, and throws a glass of water over her behind. Then, as if that weren't enough, your father races from his chair, leans her over the couch and does her from behind. He then sits back down and places a matchstick by his eye.'

'Oh, is that all?' replies the girl.

The man can't believe her casual response.

'Mum was simply saying, "Are you going to get this arsehole a drink?" and Dad was replying, "No, fuck him — I'm watching the match."'

David Beckham's sperm donation

David Beckham walks into a sperm donor bank. 'I'd like to donate some sperm,' he says to the receptionist.

'Certainly, sir,' she replies. 'Have you donated before?'

'Yes,' replies Beckham, 'you should have my details on your computer.'

'Oh, yes, I've found your details,' says the receptionist, 'but I see you're going to need help. Shall I call Posh Spice for you?'

'Why do I need help to donate sperm?' asks Beckham.

'Well,' the receptionist replies, 'it says on your record that you're a useless wanker.'

9 PLANES, TRAINS AND AUTOMOBILES

This section explores our fascination in circulating humour associated with travel, be it international air travel or the Holden or Ford in the garage at home. Travel has become a frustrating aspect of 21st century life. Terrorism has made air travel a nightmare of queues, searches, questionnaires, delays and more delays. Domestically, especially in the big cities, car travel has also become nightmarish as our cars snake their way down expressways, petrol prices go up and down, mostly up, at a horrifying pace, and meters guzzle down our coins wherever we park.

Of course, we have always found the idea of moving from one place to another humorous: horse wagons and coaches produced their fair share of jokes in colonial Australia, as did the introduction of the railways.

A man entered a railway refreshment room at Werris Creek.

The hard-faced waitress was obviously having a bad day. 'What d'ya want!' she demanded.

'I'll have a pie and sauce, and a couple of kind words,' the man said.

She turned around, slapped the pie and sauce down with a whack. 'Two shillings!' she demanded.

He looked at her and whispered, 'And the few kind words?'

She glared back. 'Don't eat the pie!'

The introduction of the motor vehicle produced an endless string of cartoons, monologues, songs, poems and jokes. We were absolutely fascinated by these old jalopies, and the stories about the people who rode in them. Part of our desire to create humour about the motor car was the fear we held for our safety. We held a bigger fear of flying.

One old bush tale concerns two drovers who were watching Sir Charles Kingsford Smith doing circles up in the sky:

'You wouldn't get me up there in one of those,' offered one of the men. The other drover thought about this for a good hour and then remarked, looking up to the heavens, 'Yer wouldn't get me up there without one.'

As with many aspects of contemporary society we tend to accept the downside of travel as a necessary evil. This provides the ideal grounds for jokes as revenge. Humour allows us to look at the ridiculous side of travel, especially the frustrations, high costs and safety issues, and share them with our community, albeit anonymously. This is why so many e-mail travel jokes are accompanied by personal notes allowing the joke sender to 'endorse' the sentiments expressed: 'Hear, hear' or 'Ain't it so.'

Air disaster

Abe and Esther are flying to Australia for a two-week vacation to celebrate their 40th anniversary. Suddenly, over the public address system, the captain announces, 'Ladies and gentlemen, I am afraid I have some very bad news. Our engines have ceased functioning and we will attempt an emergency landing. Luckily, I see an uncharted island below us and we should be able to land on the beach. However, the odds are that we may never be rescued and will have to live on the island for the rest of our lives!'

Thanks to the skill of the flight crew, the plane lands safely on the island. An hour later Abe turns to his wife and asks, 'Esther, did we pay that $5000 charity pledge yet?'

'No, sweetheart,' she responds.

Abe, still shaken from the crash landing, then asks, 'Esther, did we pay our American Express card yet?'

'Oh, no! I'm sorry. I forgot to send the cheque,' she says.

'One last thing, Esther. Did you remember to send cheques for the Visa and MasterCard this month?' he asks.

'Oy, forgive me, Abe,' begs Esther. 'I didn't send that one, either.'

Abe grabs her and gives her the biggest kiss in 40 years. Esther pulls away and asks him, 'What was that for?'

Abe answers, 'They'll find us!'

Hitching a ride

Two fleas from Detroit have an agreement to meet every winter in Miami for a vacation.

Last year when one flea gets to Miami, he's all blue, shivering and shaking, damn near frozen to death!

The other flea asks him, 'What the hell happened to you?'

The first flea says, 'I rode down here from New York in the moustache of a guy on a Harley.'

The other flea responds, saying, 'That's the worst way to travel. Try what I do. Go to the Metro airport bar. Have a few drinks. While you are there, look for a nice stewardess. Crawl up her leg and nestle in where it's warm and cosy. It's the best way to travel that I can think of.'

The first flea thanks the second flea and says he will give it a try next winter. A year goes by ... when the first flea shows up in Miami he is all blue, and shivering and shaking again. Damn near frozen to death.

The second flea says, 'Didn't you try what I told you?'

'Yes,' says the first flea, 'I did exactly as you said ... I went to the Metro airport bar. I had a few drinks. Finally, this nice young stewardess came in. I crawled right up to her warm cosy spot. It was so nice and warm that I fell asleep immediately. When I woke up, I was back in the moustache of the guy on the Harley.'

Upgrade

The following scene took place on a BA flight between Johannesburg and London. A white woman, about 50 years old, was seated next to a black man. Obviously disturbed by this, she called the air hostess.

'Madam, what is the matter?' the hostess asked.

'You obviously do not see it then?' the white woman responded. 'You placed me next to a black man. I do not agree to sit next to someone from such a repugnant group. Give me an alternative seat.'

'Be calm, please,' the hostess replied. 'Almost all the places on this flight are taken. I will go to see if another place is available.'

The hostess went away and then came back a few minutes later. 'Madam, just as I thought, there is no other available seat in the economy class. I spoke to the captain and he informed me that there is also no seat in the business class. All the same, we still have one place in the first class.'

Before the woman could say anything, the hostess continued: 'It is not usual for our company to permit someone from the economy class to sit in the first class. However, given the circumstances, the captain feels that it would be scandalous to make someone sit next to someone so disgusting.'

She turned to the black man, and said, 'Therefore please, sir, if you would like to collect your hand luggage, a seat awaits you in first class.'

At that moment, the other passengers who were shocked by what they had just witnessed stood up and applauded.

Good excuse

A fellow bought a new Mercedes and was trying it out on the Sydney to Newcastle freeway. The top was down, the breeze was blowing through what was left of his hair, and he decided to 'let her rip'.

As the speedo jumped up to 120 kilometres per hour he suddenly saw flashing red and blue lights behind him. There's no way they can catch a Mercedes, he thought to himself, and opened her up further. The needle hit 130.

Then the reality of the situation hit him. 'What am I doing?' he thought, and pulled over.

The cop came up to him, took his licence without a word and examined it and the car. The cop then offered, 'It's been a long day and this is the end of my shift, and it's Friday the 13th. I don't feel like more paperwork, so if you can give me an excuse for your driving that I haven't heard before, you can go.'

The man thought for a second and said, 'Last week my wife ran off with a cop. I was afraid you were trying to give her back!'

'Have a nice weekend,' said the officer.

Divorce imminent

A police officer pulls over a speeding car.

The officer says, 'I clocked you at 80 miles per hour, sir.'

The driver says, 'Gee, officer, I had it on cruise control at 60; perhaps your radar gun needs calibrating.'

Not looking up from her knitting the wife says: 'Now, don't be silly, dear, you know that this car doesn't have cruise control.'

As the officer writes out the ticket, the driver looks over at his wife and growls, 'Can't you please keep your mouth shut for once?'

The wife smiles demurely and says, 'You should be thankful your radar detector went off when it did.'

As the officer makes out the second ticket for the illegal radar detector unit, the man glowers at his wife and says through clenched teeth, 'Darn it, woman, can't you keep your mouth shut?'

The officer frowns and says, 'And I notice that you're not wearing your seat belt, sir. That's an automatic $75 fine.'

The driver says, 'Yeah, well, you see, officer, I had it on, but took it off when you pulled me over so that I could get my licence out of my back pocket.'

The wife says, 'Now, dear, you know very well that you didn't have your seat belt on. You never wear your seat belt when you're driving.'

And as the police officer is writing out the third ticket the driver turns to his wife and barks, '*Why don't you please shut up?*'

The officer looks over at the woman and asks, 'Does your husband always talk to you this way, ma'am?'

'Only when he's been drinking.'

Shocking Porsche accident in Melbourne

A Melbourne lawyer parks his brand new Porsche in front of the Collins Street office, to show it off to his colleagues. As he's getting out of the car, a semi-trailer comes flying along too close to the kerb and takes off the door before speeding off. Distraught, the lawyer grabs his mobile and calls the cops. Five minutes later, the police arrive. Before the cop has a chance to ask any questions, the lawyer starts screaming hysterically: 'My Porsche, my beautiful silver Porsche is ruined. No matter how long it's with the panel beater it'll simply never be the same again!'

After the lawyer finally finishes his rant, the policeman shakes his head in disgust. 'I can't believe how materialistic you bloody lawyers are,' he says. 'You lot are so focused on your possessions that you don't notice anything else in your life.'

'How can you say such a thing at a time like this?' snaps the lawyer.

The policeman replies, 'Didn't you realise that your right arm was torn off when the truck hit you?'

The lawyer looks down in absolute horror. 'Fucking hell!' he screams. 'Where's my Rolex?'

Selecting the right airline

A fellow sitting at an airport bar in New York noticed a beautiful woman sitting next to him. He thought, 'Wow, she's so gorgeous she must be a flight attendant. But which airline does she work for?'

Hoping to gain her attention, he leant towards her and uttered the Delta Air Lines slogan, 'Love to fly and it shows?' She gave him a blank, confused stare, and he immediately thought to himself, 'Nope, not Delta.'

A moment later, another slogan popped into his head. He leant towards her again, 'Something special in the air?' She gave him the same confused look. He mentally kicked himself, and scratched American Airlines off the list.

Next he tried the United slogan, 'I would really love to fly your friendly skies?' This time the woman savagely turned on him, 'What the fuck do you want?'

The man smiled, then slumped back in his chair, and said, 'Ahhh, Qantas!'

Drinking on the job

Bert and Mal are a couple of drinking buddies who work as airplane mechanics at Mascot airport. One day the airport is fogged in and they're stuck in the hangar with nothing to do. Mal says, 'Man, I wish we had something to drink.' Bert says, 'Me, too. Y'know, I heard you can drink jet fuel and get a buzz. You wanna try it?' So they pour themselves a couple of glasses of high-octane hooch and get completely smashed. The next morning Bert wakes up and is surprised at how good he feels. In fact, he feels great. No hangover. No bad side effects. Nothing. Then the phone rings. It's Mal.

Mal: 'Hey, how do you feel this morning?'

Bert: 'Great!'

Mal: 'I feel great, too. You don't have a hangover?'

Bert: 'No, that jet fuel is great stuff! No hangover, nothing. We oughta do this more often.'

Mal: 'Yeah. Well, there's just one thing …'

Bert: 'What's that?'

Mal: 'Have you farted yet?'

Bert: 'No.'

Mal: 'Well, don't, 'cause I'm in Adelaide.'

Not so silly

A blonde walks into a bank in New York City and asks for the loan officer. She says she's going to Australia on business for two weeks and needs to borrow $5000. The bank officer says the bank will need some kind of security for the loan, so the blonde hands over the keys to a new Rolls-Royce. The car is parked on the street in front of the bank; she has the rego papers, and everything checks out. The bank agrees to accept the car as collateral for the loan. The bank's president and its officers all enjoy a good laugh at the blonde for using a brand new Rolls as collateral against a $5000 loan. An employee of the bank then drives the Rolls into the bank's underground garage and parks it there.

Two weeks later, the blonde returns and repays the $5000 and the interest, which comes to $15.41. The loan officer says, 'Miss, we are very happy to have had your business, and this transaction has worked out very nicely; but we are a little puzzled. We checked you out and found that you are a multimillionaire. What puzzles us is — why would you bother to borrow $5000?'

The blonde replies: 'Where else in New York City can I park my car for two weeks for only $15.41 and expect it to be there when I return?'

Airline quotes

All too rarely, airline attendants make an effort to make the in-flight 'safety lecture' and announcements a bit more entertaining. Here are some real examples that have been heard or reported:

1. On a Southwest Airlines flight (Southwest has no assigned seating; you just sit where you want) passengers were apparently having a hard time choosing, when a flight attendant announced, 'People, people, we're not picking out furniture here — find a seat and get in it!'
2. On a Continental flight with a very 'senior' flight attendant crew, the pilot said, 'Ladies and gentlemen, we've reached cruising altitude and will be turning down the cabin lights. This is for your comfort and to enhance the appearance of your flight attendants.'
3. On landing, the stewardess said, 'Please be sure to take all of your belongings. If you're going to leave anything, please make sure it's something we'd like to have.'
4. 'There may be 50 ways to leave your lover, but there are only four ways out of this airplane.'
5. 'Thank you for flying Delta Business Express. We hope you enjoyed giving us the business as much as we enjoyed taking you for a ride.'
6. As a plane landed and was coming to a stop at Ronald Reagan Airport in Washington, a lone voice came over the loudspeaker: 'Whoa, big fella. *Whoa!*'

7. After a particularly rough landing during thunderstorms in Memphis, a flight attendant on a Northwest flight announced, 'Please take care when opening the overhead compartments because, after a landing like that, sure as hell everything has shifted.'

8. From a Southwest Airlines employee: 'Welcome aboard Southwest flight 245 to Tampa. To operate your seat belt, insert the metal tab into the buckle, and pull tight. It works just like every other seat belt; and, if you don't know how to operate one, you probably shouldn't be out in public unsupervised.'

9. 'In the event of a sudden loss of cabin pressure, masks will descend from the ceiling. Stop screaming, grab the mask, and pull it over your face. If you have a small child travelling with you, secure your mask before assisting with theirs. If you are travelling with more than one small child, pick your favourite.'

10. 'Weather at our destination is 10 degrees with some broken clouds, but we'll try to have them fixed before we arrive. Thank you, and remember, nobody loves you or your money more than Southwest Airlines.'

A day's outing

A blonde was about two hours from Surfers Paradise when she was flagged down by a man whose truck had broken down.

The man walked up to the car and asked, 'Are you going to Surfers?'

'Sure,' answered the blonde, 'do you need a lift?'

'Not for me. I'll be spending the next three hours fixing my truck. My problem is I've got two chimpanzees in the back, which have to be taken to Movie World. They're a bit stressed already so I don't want to keep them on the road all day. Could you possibly take them to Movie World for me? I'll give you $300 for your trouble.'

'I'd be happy to,' said the blonde. So the two chimpanzees were ushered into the back seat of the blonde's car and carefully strapped into their seat belts. Off they went.

Six hours later, the truckie was driving through the heart of Surfers Paradise when suddenly he saw the blonde walking down the main street, holding hands with the two chimps, much to the amusement of a big crowd.

With a screech of brakes he pulled off the road, horrified, and ran over to the blonde. 'What the heck are you doing here?' he demanded. 'I gave you $300 to take these chimpanzees to Movie World.'

'Yes, I know you did,' said the blonde, 'but we had money left over — so now we're going to Sea World!'

There's a body in the boot

Woman: Is there a problem, officer?

Officer: Ma'am, you were speeding.

Woman: Oh, I see.

Officer: Can I see your licence, please?

Woman: I'd give it to you but I don't have one.

Officer: Don't have one?

Woman: Lost it four times for drunk driving.

Officer: I see … Can I see your vehicle registration papers, please?

Woman: I can't do that.

Officer: Why not?

Woman: I stole this car.

Officer: Stole it?

Woman: Yes, and I killed and hacked up the owner.

Officer: You what?

Woman: His body parts are in plastic bags in the trunk, if you want to see.

The officer looks at the woman and slowly backs away to his car and calls for back-up. Within minutes five police cars circle the woman and a senior officer slowly approaches the car, clasping his half-drawn gun.

Officer 2: Ma'am, could you step out of your vehicle, please!

Woman: Is there a problem, sir?

Officer 2: The officer told me that you stole this car and murdered the owner.

Woman: Murdered the owner?

Officer 2: Yes, could you open the boot of your car, please?

The woman opens the boot, revealing nothing but an empty trunk.

Officer 2: Is this your car, ma'am?

Woman: Yes, here are the registration papers.

The officer is quite stunned.

Officer 2: The officer claims that you do not have a driver's licence.

The woman digs into her handbag, pulls out a clutch purse and hands it to the officer. The officer snaps open the clutch purse and examines the licence. He looks quite puzzled.

Officer 2: I must admit, ma'am, that I'm confused; the officer told me you didn't have a licence, that you stole this car, and that you murdered the owner.

Woman: I suppose the lying bastard told you I was speeding, too.

Sign of the times

A mother was working in the kitchen, listening to her five-year-old son playing with his new electric train in the living room. She heard the train stop and her son saying, 'All of you fucking bastards who want off, get the hell off now, 'cause this is the last stop! And all of you bastards who are getting on, get your arse in the train, 'cause we are going down the tracks to Sydney Central — *now*!'

The horrified mother went in and told her son, 'We don't use that kind of language in this house. Now I want you to go to your room and you are to stay there for *two hours*. When you come out, you may play with your train, but I want you to use nice language.'

Two hours later, the son came out of the bedroom and resumed playing with his train. Soon the train stopped and the mother heard her son say, 'All passengers who are disembarking the train at Sydney Central, please remember to take all of your belongings with you. We thank you for travelling with us today and hope your trip was a pleasant one.'

She then hears the little boy continue, 'For those of you just boarding, we ask you to stow all of your hand luggage under your seat. Remember, there is no smoking on the train. We hope you will have a pleasant and relaxing journey with us today.'

As the mother began to smile, the child added, 'For those of you who are pissed off about the *two-hour* delay, please see the bitch in the kitchen.'

Bad sneeze

A man and a woman were sitting beside each other in the Qantas first-class section of the plane. The woman sneezed, took a tissue, gently wiped her nose and then shuddered quite violently in her seat. The man went back to his reading. A few minutes passed. The woman sneezed again, took a tissue, gently wiped her nose and shuddered quite violently in her seat. The man was becoming more and more curious about the shuddering. A few more minutes passed and the woman sneezed one more time. Again she took a tissue, gently wiped her nose and shuddered violently.

The man had finally had all he could handle. He turned to the woman and said, 'You've sneezed three times, you've taken a tissue and wiped your nose, and then shuddered violently. Are you all right?'

The woman replied, 'I'm sorry if I disturbed you. I have a rare condition and when I sneeze, I have an orgasm.'

The man was feeling a little embarrassed but even more curious and said, 'I've never heard of that before. What are you taking for it?'

The woman looked at him and said, 'Pepper.'

Qantas flight announcements

Part of a flight attendant's announcement:

'We'd like to thank you folks for flying with us today. And, the next time you get the insane urge to go blasting through the skies in a pressurised metal tube, we hope you'll think of Qantas.'

'Your Jetstar seat cushions can be used for flotation; and, in the event of an emergency water landing, please paddle to shore and take them with our compliments.'

'As you exit the plane, make sure to gather all of your belongings. Anything left behind will be distributed evenly among the flight attendants. Please do not leave children or spouses.'

From the pilot during his welcome message: 'Jetstar is pleased to have some of the best flight attendants in the industry. Unfortunately, none of them are on this flight!'

An airline pilot wrote that on this particular flight he had hammered his ship into the runway really hard. The airline had a policy which required the first officer to stand at the door while the passengers exited, smile, and give them a 'Thanks for flying our airline.' He said that, in light of his bad landing, he had a hard time looking the passengers in the eye, thinking that someone would have a smart comment. Finally, everyone had gotten off except for a little old lady walking with a cane. She said, 'Sir, do you mind if I ask you a question?' 'Why, no, ma'am,' said the pilot. 'What is it?' The little old lady said, 'Did we land, or were we shot down?'

Part of a flight attendant's arrival announcement:

'Ladies and gentlemen, if you wish to smoke, the smoking section on this airplane is on the wing and if you can light 'em, you can smoke 'em.'

A plane was taking off from Mascot airport. After it reached a comfortable cruising altitude, the captain made an announcement over the intercom, 'Ladies and gentlemen, this is your captain speaking. Welcome to Flight Number XYZ, non-stop from Sydney to Auckland. The weather ahead is good and, therefore, we should have a smooth and uneventful flight. Now sit back and relax — *oh, my God*!'

Silence followed and after a few minutes, the captain came back on the intercom and said, 'Ladies and gentlemen, I am so sorry if I scared you earlier; but, while I was talking, the flight attendant brought me a cup of coffee and spilled the hot coffee in my lap. You should see the front of my pants!'

A passenger in economy said, 'That's nothing. He should see the back of mine!'

Make me feel like a woman

On a Qantas transatlantic flight, a plane passes through a severe storm. The turbulence is awful, and things go from bad to worse when a wing is struck by lightning. One woman in particular loses it.

Screaming, she stands up in the front of the plane. 'I'm too young to die,' she wails. Then she yells, 'Well, if I'm going to die, I want my last minutes on earth to be memorable! Is there *anyone* on this plane who can make me feel like a *woman*?'

For a moment there is silence. Everyone has forgotten his or her own peril. They all stare at the desperate woman. Then a man stands up in the rear of the plane. He is tall, handsome, well built, with reddish-blond hair and hazel eyes. He starts to walk slowly up the aisle, unbuttoning his shirt …

… one button at a time.

No one moves.

He removes his shirt …

… muscles ripple across his chest as he whispers: 'Iron this.'

Ice cream

A vacationing penguin from King Island is driving across the Nullarbor in his Jaguar XJS convertible when he notices the oil-pressure light is on. He gets out to look and sees oil dripping out of the motor. He drives to the nearest town and stops at the first petrol station. After dropping the car off, the penguin goes for a walk around town. He sees an ice cream shop and, being a penguin in the desert, decides that something cold would really hit the spot. So he gets a big dish of vanilla ice cream and sits down to eat. Having no hands, he makes a real mess trying to eat with his little flippers.

After finishing his ice cream, he goes back to the gas station and asks the mechanic if he's found the problem.

The mechanic looks up from the engine and says, 'It looks like you've blown a seal.'

'No, no,' the penguin replies, wiping his mouth. 'It's just ice cream.'

Expensive car

A lady walks into a Lexus dealership. She browses around, then spots the perfect car and walks over to inspect it. As she bends to feel the fine leather upholstery, a loud fart escapes her. Very embarrassed, she looks around nervously to see if anyone has noticed her little accident and hopes a salesperson doesn't pop up right now. But he does.

'Good day, madam. How may we help you today?'

Uncomfortably she asks, 'Sir, what is the price of this lovely vehicle?'

He answers, 'Madam, if you farted just touching it, you are going to shit yourself when you hear the price.'

10 POLITICS — IT'S A JOKE

Political satire is about the only sure way the average person can 'get back at' political leaders and the system. Voting simply doesn't work because the old maxim remains true: *whomever you vote for — a politician gets in.*

This is a no-holds-barred arena where any politician — local, state, federal or international; minor or major ratbag — is an open target for the jokester. Some jokes start life as one-liners delivered by talk-show hosts like Jay Leno or Conan O'Brien, whilst others are the product of the usual anonymous creator. Many are simply recycled from another era, or country, and changed to suit the current situation.

E-mail distribution has brought an immediacy that adds a level of believability despite the usual preposterous situations. One wrong step and the politician is liable to be ridiculed on a level never before possible. Some can be cartoon images; however, because of download limitations, e-mail jokes are the preferred weapon. The political Left cop it just as much as the Right, and it is not unusual to have the sender add a personal endorsement along the lines of 'This will make you laugh' or 'The bastard had it coming'.

Not surprisingly, much recent material has lampooned George W. Bush, Saddam Hussein, Osama bin Laden and, locally, Prime Minister Howard. Some are incident based and, with such humour, it has a 'use-by date', after which it is not so funny. In many ways the jokes concerning bin Laden and Hussein are typical of the jokes created and distributed to belittle these leaders and make them the face of the enemy. The same can be said of past jokes about Hitler, Mussolini and so many other tyrants. Possibly, by putting a face to the enemy or demonising them, we can alleviate the tension that we feel. It allows us to let off some steam. For many people jokes also act as a national or even international rallying point, reinforcing that we are right and they, whoever they may be, are wrong.

Moses and President Bush

Recently, while going through an airport during one of his many trips, President Bush encountered a man with long grey hair, wearing a white robe and sandals, holding a staff.

President Bush went up to the man and said, 'Has anyone told you that you look like Moses?'

The man didn't answer. He just kept staring straight ahead.

The President said, 'Moses!' in a loud voice.

The man just stared ahead, never acknowledging the president. The president pulled a Secret Service agent aside and, pointing to the robed man, asked him, 'Am I crazy or does that man not look like Moses to you?'

The Secret Service agent looked at the man and agreed.

'Well,' said the president, 'every time I say his name, he ignores me and stares straight ahead, refusing to speak. Watch!' Again the president yelled, 'Moses!' and again the man ignored him.

The Secret Service agent went up to the man in the white robe and whispered, 'You look just like Moses. Are you Moses?'

The man leant over and whispered back, 'Yes, I am Moses. However, the last time I talked to a bush, I spent 40 years wandering in the desert and ended up leading my people to the only spot in the entire Middle East where there was no oil.'

Gonorrhea Lectim

The Centre for Disease Control has issued a warning about a new virulent strain of sexually transmitted disease. The disease is contracted through dangerous and high-risk behaviour. The disease is called Gonorrhea Lectim and pronounced 'gonna re-elect him'. Many victims contracted it in the US in 2004, after having been screwed for the past four years.

Cognitive characteristics of individuals infected include: anti-social personality disorders, delusions of grandeur with messianic overtones, extreme cognitive dissonance, inability to incorporate new information, pronounced xenophobia and paranoia, inability to accept responsibility for own actions, cowardice masked by misplaced bravado, uncontrolled facial smirking, ignorance of geography and history, tendencies towards evangelical theocracy, categorical all-or-nothing behaviour.

Naturalists and epidemiologists are amazed at how this destructive disease originated only a few years ago from a bush found in Texas.

Important test

This test only has one question, but it's a very important one. By giving an honest answer, you will discover where you stand morally. The test features an unlikely, completely fictional situation in which you will have to make a decision. Remember that your answer needs to be honest, yet spontaneous.

You are in Darwin, NT. There is chaos all around you caused by a cyclone with severe flooding. This is a flood of biblical proportions. You are a photojournalist working for a major newspaper, and you're caught in the middle of this epic disaster. The situation is nearly hopeless. You're trying to shoot career-making photos. There are houses and people swirling around you, some disappearing under the water. Nature is unleashing all of its destructive fury.

Suddenly you see a man floundering in the water. He is fighting for his life, trying not to be taken down with the debris. You move closer; somehow the man looks familiar. You suddenly realise who it is. It's John Howard. At the same time you notice that the raging waters are about to pull him under. You have two options — you can save the life of 'Little Johnny' or you can shoot a dramatic Pulitzer Prize-winning photo, documenting the death of the Australian prime minister.

So here's the question, and please give an honest answer:

Would you select high-contrast colour film, or would you go with the classic simplicity of black and white?

The Bush line

Iranian president Mahmoud Ahmadinejad calls President Bush and tells him, 'George, I had a wonderful dream last night. I could see America, the whole beautiful country, and on each house I saw a banner.'

'What did it say on the banners?' Bush asks.

Mahmoud replies, 'ALLAH IS GOD, GOD IS ALLAH.'

Bush says, 'You know, Mahmoud, I am really happy you called. Last night I had a similar dream. I could see all of Tehran, and it was more beautiful than ever. It had been rebuilt completely, and on each house flew an enormous banner.'

'What could you see on the banners?' Mahmoud asks.

Bush replies, 'I don't know, I can't read Hebrew.'

Naval conference

A US navy admiral was attending a naval conference that included admirals from the US, English, Canadian, Australian and French navies. At a cocktail reception, he found himself standing with a group of half a dozen or so officers that included personnel from most of the countries.

Everyone was chatting away in English as they sipped their drinks but a French admiral suddenly complained that, whereas Europeans learn many languages, Americans learn only English. He then asked: 'Why is it that we always have to speak English in these conferences rather than speaking French?'

Without hesitating, the American admiral replied: 'Maybe it's because the Brits, Canadians, Aussies and Americans went to great trouble and arranged it so you wouldn't have to speak German!'

The red carpet

At Heathrow airport in England, a 300-foot red carpet was stretched out to Air Force One and President Bush strode out to a warm but dignified handshake from Queen Elizabeth II. They rode in a silver 1934 Bentley to the edge of central London, where they boarded an open 17th-century coach hitched to six magnificent white horses. As they travelled towards Buckingham Palace, each looking to their side and waving to the thousands of cheering Brits lining the streets, all was going well. This was indeed a glorious display of pageantry and dignity.

Suddenly the scene was shattered when the right rear horse let rip the most horrendous, earth-shattering, eye-smarting blast of flatulence, and the coach immediately filled with noxious fumes.

Uncomfortable, but maintaining control, the two dignitaries did their best to ignore the whole incident, but then the Queen decided that was a ridiculous manner with which to handle a most embarrassing situation.

She turned to Mr Bush and explained, 'Mr President, please accept my regrets. I'm sure you understand that there are some things even a queen cannot control.'

George W., ever the Texas gentleman, replied, 'Your Majesty, please don't give the matter another thought. You know, if you hadn't said something, I would have assumed it was one of the horses.'

Osama still kicking?

After numerous rounds of 'We don't even know if Osama is still alive', Osama himself decided to send George Bush a letter in his own handwriting to let him know he was still in the game.

Bush opened the letter and it appeared to contain a single line of coded message: 370HSSV–0773H.

Bush was baffled, so he e-mailed it to Condi Rice. Condi and her aides had not a clue either, so they sent it to the FBI. No one could solve it at the FBI so it went to the CIA, then to the National Security Agency.

Eventually they asked Britain's MI-6 for help — same result.

In despair they sent it to ASIO. ASIO found it most confusing. However, one agent took it home and discussed it with his family. His eight-year-old daughter solved it immediately. 'Dad,' she said, 'it's easy. It's just written upside down.'

Camilla walks the aisle

As Camilla was making last-minute preparations to walk down the aisle, she found that her shoes were missing. She was forced to borrow her sister's, which were a bit on the small side.

When the day's festivities were finally over, Charles and Camilla retired to their room, right next door to the Queen's and Prince Philip's.

As soon as Charles and Camilla were inside their room, Camilla flopped on the bed and said, 'Darling, please get these shoes off. My feet are killing me.'

The ever-obedient Prince of Wales attacked the right shoe with vigour, but it was stuck fast. 'Harder!' Camilla yelled. 'Harder!' 'I'm trying, darling!' the Prince yelled back. 'It's just so bloody tight!' 'Come on! Give it all you've got!'

There was a big groan from the prince, and then Camilla exclaimed, 'There! That's it! Oh, that feels good! Oh, that feels *sooo* good!'

In the bedroom next door, the Queen turned to Prince Philip and said, 'See, I told you, with a face like that she was still a virgin.'

Bush-isms

- 'The vast majority of our imports come from outside the country.'
  — George W. Bush
- 'If we don't succeed, we run the risk of failure.' — George W. Bush
- 'One word sums up probably the responsibility of any Governor, and that one word is "to be prepared".' — George W. Bush
- 'I have made good judgments in the past. I have made good judgments in the future.' — George W. Bush
- 'The future will be better tomorrow.' — George W. Bush
- 'We're going to have the best educated American people in the world.'
  — George W. Bush
- 'I stand by all the misstatements that I've made.' — George W. Bush
- 'We have a firm commitment to NATO; we are a part of NATO. We have a firm commitment to Europe; we are a part of Europe.'
  — George W. Bush
- 'Public speaking is very easy.' — George W. Bush
- 'A low voter turnout is an indication of fewer people going to the polls.' — George W. Bush
- 'We are ready for any unforeseen event that may or may not occur.'
  — George W. Bush
- 'For NASA, space is still a high priority.' — George W. Bush
- 'Quite frankly, teachers are the only profession that teach our children.' — George W. Bush
- 'It isn't pollution that's harming the environment. It's the impurities in our air and water that are doing it.' — George W. Bush
- 'It's time for the human race to enter the solar system.'
  — George W. Bush

Robot bartender

A man enters a bar and orders a drink. The bar has a robot bartender. The robot serves him a perfectly prepared cocktail, and then asks him, 'What's your IQ?'

The man replies '150' and the robot proceeds to make conversation about global warming factors, quantum physics and spirituality, bio-mimicry, environmental interconnectedness, string theory, nanotechnology, and sexual proclivities. The customer is very impressed and thinks, 'This is really cool.'

He decides to test the robot. He walks out of the bar, turns around, and comes back in for another drink. Again, the robot serves him the perfectly prepared drink and asks him, 'What's your IQ?'

The man responds, 'About 100.'

Immediately the robot starts talking, but this time about league, Holdens, racing, the new Big Mac, tattoos, Paris Hilton and women's tits in general.

Really impressed, the man leaves the bar and decides to give the robot one more test. He heads out and returns. The robot serves him and asks, 'What's your IQ?'

The man replies, 'Err, 50, I think.'

And the robot says, real slowly, 'So, ya gonna vote for John Howard?'

Politics made easy

Democrat
You have two cows. Your neighbour has none. You feel guilty for being successful.

Republican
You have two cows. Your neighbour has none.

Socialist
You have two cows. The government takes one and gives it to your neighbour. You form a cooperative to tell him how to manage his cow.

Communist
You have two cows. The government seizes both and provides you with milk. You wait in line for hours to get it. It is expensive and sour.

Capitalist, American style
You have two cows. You sell one, buy a bull, and build a herd of cows.

Bureaucrat, American style
You have two cows. Under the new farm program the government pays you to shoot one, milk the other, and then pours the milk down the drain.

American corporation
You have two cows. You sell one, lease it back to yourself and do an initial public offering on the second one. You force the two cows to produce the

milk of four cows. You are surprised when one cow drops dead. You spin an announcement to the analysts stating you have downsized and are reducing expenses. Your stock goes up.

French corporation

You have two cows. You go on strike because you want three cows. You go to lunch and drink wine. Life is good.

Japanese corporation

You have two cows. You redesign them so they are one-tenth the size of an ordinary cow and produce 20 times the milk. They learn to travel on unbelievably crowded trains. Most are at the top of their class at cow school.

German corporation

You have two cows. You engineer them so they are all blonde, drink lots of beer, give excellent quality milk, and run a hundred miles an hour. Unfortunately they also demand 13 weeks of vacation per year.

Italian corporation

You have two cows but you don't know where they are. While ambling around, you see a beautiful woman. You break for lunch. Life is good.

Russian corporation

You have two cows. You have some vodka. You count them and learn you have five cows. You have some more vodka.

You count them again and learn you have 42 cows. The mafia shows up and takes over, however many cows you really have.

Belgian corporation

You have one schizophrenic cow that thinks she's two cows. Sometimes the cow thinks she's French, other times she's Flemish. The Flemish cow won't share with the French cow. The French cow wants control of the Flemish cow's milk. The cow asks permission to be cut in half. The cow dies happy.

Florida corporation

You have a black cow and a brown cow. Everyone votes for the best-looking one. Some of the people who actually like the brown one best accidentally vote for the black one. Some people vote for both. Some people vote for neither. Some people can't figure out how to vote at all. Finally, a bunch of guys from out-of-state tell you which one you think is the best-looking cow.

California corporation
You have millions of cows. They make real California cheese. Only five speak English. Most are illegal. Governor Arnold Schwarzenegger likes the ones with the big udders.

How about a quickie?
George Bush and Dick Cheney are enjoying a celebration lunch at a fancy Washington restaurant. A waitress approaches their table to take their order; she is young and very attractive. She asks Cheney what he wants, and he replies, 'I'll have the heart-healthy salad.'

'Very good, sir,' she replies, and turning to Bush she asks, 'And what do you want, Mr President?'

Bush answers, 'How about a quickie?'

Taken aback, the waitress slaps him and says, 'I'm shocked and disappointed in you. I thought you were committed to high principles and morality. I'm sorry I voted for you.' With that, the waitress departs in a huff.

Cheney leans over to Bush, and says, 'Mr President, I believe that's pronounced "quiche".'

Heaven or hell?
While walking down the street, a well-known politician is hit by a dunny truck and dies. His soul arrives in heaven, and he is met by St Peter at the entrance. 'Welcome to heaven,' says St Peter. 'Before you settle in, it seems there is a problem … We seldom see such politicians up here, you see, and so we're not sure what to do with you.'

'Just let me in,' says the politician.

'Well, I'd like to, but I have orders from "on high". What we do is have you spend a day in hell, and a day in heaven. Then you can choose where to spend eternity.'

'OK, I've made up my mind. I want to be in heaven,' says the politician.

'I'm sorry, but we have our rules,' insists St Peter. And, with that, St Peter escorts him to the escalator and he goes down to hell.

The doors open and the politician finds himself in the middle of a green golf course. In the distance is a clubhouse, and standing in front of it are all his friends and other politicians who'd worked with him.

Everyone is happy and they run to greet him, shake his hand, and reminisce about the good times.

They play a great game of golf and then dine on crayfish, caviar and champagne. Also present is the devil, who's really a very friendly guy; dancing and telling jokes. They're all having such a good time that, before he realises, it is time to go.

Everyone gives him a hearty farewell and waves while the escalator starts on its upward journey …

The escalator goes all the way up to heaven, where St Peter is waiting.

'Now it's time for you to visit heaven.'

So the pollie joins a group of contented souls, moving from cloud to cloud, playing the harp and, before he realises it, the 24 hours have gone by.

St Peter returns. 'Well, you've spent a day in hell and a day in heaven. Now choose for eternity.'

The politician reflects for a minute, then answers: 'Well, I never would have said it before — I mean, heaven has been delightful — but I think I'd be better off in hell.'

So, St Peter escorts him to the escalator and he goes down, down, down to hell …

The doors of the elevator open, and the politician finds himself in the middle of a barren land covered with waste and debris. He sees all of his friends, dressed in rags, picking up the trash, and putting it in bags.

The devil comes over to him and puts his arm around his shoulder.

'I don't understand,' stammers the pollie. 'Yesterday there was a golf course and a clubhouse, we ate crayfish and caviar, drank champagne, danced, and had a great time. Now there's nothing but a wasteland full of garbage, and my friends look miserable. What happened?'

The devil looks at him, smiles, and says, 'Yesterday we were campaigning … today you voted.'

What is politics?

A little boy goes to his dad and asks, 'What is "politics"?'

Dad says, 'Well, son, let me try to explain it this way: I'm the head of the family, so call me the President.

'Your mother is the administrator of the money, so we call her the Government. We're here to take care of your needs, so we'll call you the People.

'The nanny, we'll consider her the Working Class.

'And your baby brother, we'll call him the Future. Now think about that and see if it makes sense.'

So the little boy goes off to bed thinking about what his dad has said.

Later that night, he hears his baby brother crying, so he gets up to check on him. He finds that the baby has severely soiled his diaper. So the little boy goes to his parents' room and finds his mother sound asleep. Not wanting to wake her, he goes to the nanny's room. Finding the door locked, he peeks in the keyhole and sees his father in bed with the nanny. He gives up and goes back to bed.

The next morning, the little boy says to his father, 'Dad, I think I understand the concept of politics now.'

The father says, 'Good, son, tell me in your own words what you think politics is all about.'

The little boy replies, 'The President is screwing the Working Class while the Government is sound asleep. The People are being ignored and the Future is in deep shit.'

First Jewish woman president

The year is 2012 and the United States of America has recently elected the first woman, as well as the first Jewish, president, Susan Goldfarb.

She calls up her mother a few weeks after election day and says, 'So, Mom, I assume you will be coming to my inauguration?'

'I don't think so. It's a 10 hour drive, your father isn't as young as he used to be, and my leg is acting up again.'

'Don't worry about it, Mom. I'll send Air Force One to pick you up and take you home. And a limousine will pick you up at your door.'

'I don't know. Everybody will be so fancy-schmantzy; what on earth would I wear?'

'Oh, Mom,' replies Susan, 'I'll make sure you have a wonderful gown custom-made by the best designer in New York.'

'Honey,' Mom complains, 'you know I can't eat those rich foods you and your friends like to eat.'

The President-to-be responds, 'Don't worry, Mom. The entire affair is going to be handled by the best caterer in New York, kosher all the way. Mom, I really want you to come.'

So Mom reluctantly agrees and on 21 January 2013, Susan Goldfarb is being sworn in as President of the United States of America. In the front row sits the new president's mother, who leans over to a senator sitting next to her.

'You see that woman over there with her hand on the Bible, becoming President of the United States?'

The senator whispers back, 'Yes, I do.'

Says Mom proudly, 'Her brother's a doctor.'

British courtesy

An American tourist in London found himself desperately needing to go to the toilet. After a long search he just couldn't find any public toilet to relieve himself. So he went down one of the side streets to take care of business. Just as he was unzipping, a London police officer showed up.

'Look here, sir, what are you doing?' the officer asked.

'I'm sorry,' the American replied, 'but I really gotta go.'

'You can't do that here, sir,' the officer told him. 'Please, follow me.'

The police officer led him to a beautiful garden with lots of grass, pretty flowers, and manicured hedges. 'Here,' said the policeman, 'whiz away, sir.'

The American tourist shrugged, turned, unzipped, and started urinating on the flowers. 'Ahhh,' he said in relief. Then turning towards the officer, he said, 'This is very nice of you. Is this British courtesy?'

'No, sir,' retorted the policeman. 'It's the French Embassy.'

Terrorists

A group of terrorists burst into the conference room of a hotel, where the American Bar Association was holding its Annual Convention. More than 500 lawyers were taken as hostages.

The terrorist leader announced that, unless their demands were met, they would release one lawyer every hour.

The Queen and Dolly Parton

Queen Elizabeth and Dolly Parton die on the same day, and they both go before the angel to find out if they'll be admitted to heaven.

Unfortunately, there's only one space left that day, so the angel must decide which of them gets in.

The angel asks Dolly if there is some particular reason why she should go to heaven, whereupon Dolly takes off her top and says, 'Look at these. They're the most perfect breasts God ever created, and I'm sure it will please God to be able to see them every day for eternity.'

The angel thanks Dolly, and asks Her Majesty the same question.

The Queen drops her skirt and panties and takes a bottle of Perrier out of her purse, shakes it up and douches with it.

The angel says, 'OK, Your Majesty, you may go in.'

Dolly is outraged. 'What is that all about? I show you two of God's own perfect creations and you turn me down. She performs a rude act of hygiene and she gets in. Can you explain that to me?'

'Sorry, Dolly,' says the angel, 'but even in heaven, a royal flush beats two of a kind.'

George Bush and the Queen

George Bush meets the Queen, and says to her: 'As I'm the President, I'm thinking of changing how my country is referred to, and I'm thinking that it should be a kingdom.'

The Queen replies, 'I'm sorry, Mr Bush, but to be a kingdom you have to have a king in charge — and you're not a king.'

George Bush thinks for a while and then says: 'How about a principality then?'

To which the Queen replies, 'Again, to be a principality you have to be a prince — and you're not a prince.'

Bush thinks long and hard and comes up with: 'How about an empire then?'

The Queen, getting a little annoyed by now, replies, 'Look, Bush, to be an empire you must have an emperor in charge — and you are not an emperor.'

Before George Bush can utter another word, the Queen says: 'I think you're doing quite nicely as a country.'

My son, the martyr

Two Palestinians are chatting. One of them has his wallet out and is flipping through pictures.

'Yeah, this is my eldest. He's a martyr. And this is my second son. He's a martyr, too.'

There's a pause and the second Palestinian says wistfully, 'Ah, they blow up so fast, don't they?'

What would you do?

You are the President of the United States.

Scientists have discovered that a meteor is headed towards the earth. They have calculated that it will strike France in two days, at approximately 2.30 a.m. The meteor is large enough to completely wipe France from the face of the earth forever.

France and the United Nations have requested that the United States sends all available ships and aircraft to help evacuate the country. Among the ships and planes you could be sending are many that are being used to fight the war on terror overseas. As the president, you must decide.

Do you:

(a) Stay up late on the night of the impact to watch the coverage live?

(b) Tape it and watch it in the morning?

American presidents

Look what happens when a president gets elected in a year with a '0' at the end. Also notice it goes in increments of 20 years.

1840: William Henry Harrison (died in office)
1860: Abraham Lincoln (assassinated)
1880: James A. Garfield (assassinated)
1900: William McKinley (assassinated)
1920: Warren G. Harding (died in office)
1940: Franklin D. Roosevelt (died in office)
1960: John F. Kennedy (assassinated)
1980: Ronald Reagan (survived assassination attempt)
2000: George W. Bush?

And to think that the US had two guys fighting it out in the courts to be the one elected in 2000.

Have a history teacher explain this – if they can

Abraham Lincoln was elected to Congress in 1846. John F. Kennedy was elected to Congress in 1946.

Abraham Lincoln was elected president in 1860. John F. Kennedy was elected president in 1960.

Both were particularly concerned with civil rights. Both wives lost children while living in the White House.

Both presidents were shot on a Friday. Both presidents were shot in the head.

Now it gets really weird …

Lincoln's secretary was named Kennedy. Kennedy's secretary was named Lincoln.

Southerners assassinated both.

Southerners named Johnson succeeded both.

Andrew Johnson, who succeeded Lincoln, was born in 1808. Lyndon Johnson, who succeeded Kennedy, was born in 1908.

John Wilkes Booth, who assassinated Lincoln, was born in 1839. Lee Harvey Oswald, who assassinated Kennedy, was born in 1939.

Both assassins were known by their three names. Both names are composed of the same number of letters.

Now hang on to your seat …

Lincoln was shot at a theatre named Ford. Kennedy was shot in a car called Lincoln made by Ford.

Booth and Oswald were assassinated before their trials.

And here's the kicker …

A week before Lincoln was shot, he was in Monroe, Maryland. A week before Kennedy was shot, he was with (in?) Marilyn Monroe.

Afghanistan TV guide

SUNDAY

0800 — My 33 Sons

0830 — Osama Knows Best

0900 — I Dream of Mohammed

0930 — Let's Mecca Deal

1000 — The Kabul Hillbillies

MONDAY

0800 — Husseinfeld

0900 — Mad About Everything

0930 — Monday Night Stoning

1000 — Win Bin Laden's Money

1030 — Allah McBeal

TUESDAY

0800 — Wheel of Poverty

0830 — The Price is Right if Osama Says it's Right

0900 — Children are Forbidden from Saying the Darndest Things

0930 — Taliban's Wackiest Public Execution Bloopers

1000 — Buffy the Yankee Imperialist Dog Slayer

WEDNESDAY

0800 — Beat the Press

0830 — Two Guys, a Girl, and Pita Bread

0900 — Just Shoot Everyone

0930 — Veilwatch

THURSDAY

0800 — Fatima Loves Chachi

0830 — M*U*S*T*A*S*H

0900 — Veronica's Closet Full of Long, Black, Shapeless Dresses and Veils

0930 — Married with 139 Children

1000 — Eye for an Eye Witness News

FRIDAY

0800 — Judge Bin Laden

0830 — Suddenly Sanctions

0900 — Who Wants to Marry a Terrorist Millionaire?

0930 — Cave and Garden Television

1000 — No-Witness News

SATURDAY

0800 — Spongebob Squareturban

0830 — Who's Koran Is It Anyway?

0900 — Teletalibans

Noblesse oblige

One morning on his walk to school along a tree-lined, busy street of an inner-city suburb, a boy saw a puffing and panting middle-aged jogger bobbing and weaving towards him on the footpath. As the two approached each other the jogger tripped and stumbled off the footpath, onto the roadway and into the path of an oncoming taxi.

The boy, both quick-witted and nimble, stepped onto the road, took hold of the jogger's tracksuit and, in the nick of time, pulled him out of danger.

When he regained his composure, the jogger thanked the boy profusely. 'You have done your country a great service,' he exclaimed. 'I am John Winston Howard, your prime minister, and I want to reward you for your bravery. I will give you anything that is in my power to give.'

The boy thought for a moment and then asked, 'Can I have a state funeral, please?'

'A state funeral?' responded Howard in surprise. 'But you're only 12 years old. Why on earth do you want a state funeral?'

'Because,' retorted the boy, 'when I get home and tell my dad what I've done, he'll kill me.'

A real tragedy

President George W. Bush is visiting an elementary school one day, and he visits one of the classes. They are in the middle of a discussion related to words and their meanings. The teacher asks the president if he would like to lead the class in the discussion of the word 'tragedy'. So the illustrious leader asks the class for an example of a tragedy.

One little boy stands up and offers, 'If my best friend, who lives next door, is playing in the street and a car comes along and runs him over, that would be a tragedy.'

'No,' says Bush, 'that would be an *accident*.'

A little girl raises her hand. 'If a school bus carrying 50 children drove off a cliff, killing everyone involved, that would be a tragedy.'

'I'm afraid not,' explains Mr President. 'That's what we would call a *great loss*.'

The room goes silent. No other children volunteer. President Bush searches the room. 'Isn't there someone here who can give me an example of a tragedy?'

Finally, way in the back of the room, a small boy raises his hand. In a quiet voice he says, 'If Air Force One, carrying Mr and Mrs Bush, were struck by a missile and blown up to smithereens, by a terrorist like Osama bin Laden, that would be a tragedy.'

'Fantastic!' exclaims Bush. 'That's right. And can you tell me *why* that would be a tragedy?'

'Well,' says the boy, 'because it wouldn't be an accident, and it certainly wouldn't be a great loss.'

George Washington's ghost

One night, in the White House, George Washington's ghost awakens George W. Bush.

Bush asks: 'George, what is the best thing I could do to help the country?'

'Set an honest and honourable example, just as I did,' Washington advises.

The next night, the ghost of Thomas Jefferson moves through the dark bedroom. 'Tom,' Bush asks, 'what is the best thing I could do to help the country?'

'Cut taxes and reduce the size of government,' Jefferson advises.

Bush still isn't sleeping well and the next night sees another figure moving in the shadows. It's Abraham Lincoln's ghost. 'Abe, what is the best thing I could do to help the country?' Bush asks.

Abe answers: 'Go see a play.'

A matter of security

The Australian government's $15 million fridge magnet campaign to educate Australians about terrorism scooped an international award as one of the most stupid security measures introduced since September 11. The competition, run by Privacy International, which is best known for its annual Big Brother awards for intrusive practices, received almost 5000 nominations from 35 countries.

The government took out the Most Egregiously Stupid Award for the kit, which urged Australians to report anything suspicious while asking them to be 'alert but not alarmed'.

The Delta Terminal at JFK Airport in New York won the Most Flagrantly Intrusive Award for forcing a mother travelling with a four-month-old baby to drink three bottles of her own breast milk, for fear that the bottles contained explosives or chemical agents.

Heathrow Airport also picked up an award for quarantining a quantity of Gunpowder (green) tea. The tea was eventually allowed but the packaging bearing the Gunpowder label was confiscated and destroyed.

Another airport, Philadelphia International, received the Most Inexplicably Stupid Award for issuing a code-red hazardous materials alert that closed a hospital emergency ward and two local shops because of a bottle of suspect cologne.

'There is a serious issue of respect for people's rights being eroded by stupid security measures,' said Tim Dixon, a judge on the Stupid Security competition panel and a spokesman for the Australian Privacy Foundation. 'Many of these measures do not make us any safer.'

Mr Dixon said the Australian government-backed public education scheme stood out because of its scale, cost and its 'meaningless nature'.

Newsflash (from 2003)

All K-Mart stores in Iraq will be closing on or before 28 March. After that, they will all become Targets.

Greetings From Osama

To — All Al Qaeda Fighters
From — Bin Laden, Osama
Subject — The Cave

Hi, guys,

We've all been putting in long hours recently but we've really come together as a group and I love that! However, while we are fighting a jihad, we can't forget to take care of the cave, and frankly I have a few concerns:

First of all, while it's good to be concerned about cruise missiles, we should be even more concerned about the dust in our cave. We want to avoid excessive dust inhalation (a health and safety issue) so we need to sweep the cave daily. I've done my bit on the cleaning roster

… have you? I've posted a sign-up sheet near the cave reception area (next to the halal toaster).

Second, it's not often I make a video address but when I do, I'm trying to scare the shit out of most of the world's population, OK? That means that while we're taping, please do not ride your scooter in the background or keep doing the 'Wassup' thing. Thanks.

Third, food. I bought a box of Dairy Milk chocolates recently, clearly wrote 'Ossy' on the front, and put it on the top shelf. Today, two of my chocolates were gone. Consideration. That's all I'm saying.

Fourth, I'm not against team spirit and all that, but we must distance ourselves from the infidels' bat and ball games. Please do not chant 'Ossy Ossy Ossy, Oy Oy Oy' when I ride past on the donkey. Thanks.

Five, graffiti. To whoever wrote 'OSAMA SH*GS DONKEYS' on the group toilet wall, it's a lie. The donkey backed into me, whilst I was relieving myself at the edge of the mountain.

Six, the use of chickens is strictly for food. Assam, the old excuse that the 'chicken backed into me, whilst I was relieving myself at the edge of the mountain' will not be accepted in future. (With donkeys, there is a grey area.)

Finally, we've heard that there may be Western soldiers in disguise trying to infiltrate our ranks. I want to set up patrols to look for them. First patrol will be Omar, Muhammad, Abdul, Akbar and Dave.

Love you lots, Group Hug.
Os

PS — I'm sick of having 'Osama's Bed Linen' scribbled on my laundry bag. Cut it out, it's not funny any more.

George Bush in hell

George Bush had a heart attack and died. He went to hell, where the devil was waiting for him. 'I don't know what to do here,' said the devil. 'You are on my list but I have no room for you. You definitely have to stay here, so I'll tell you what I'm going to do. I've got three folks here who weren't quite as bad as you. I'll let one of them go, but you have to take their place. I'll even let *you* decide who leaves.'

George thought that sounded pretty good, so he agreed. The devil opened the first room: in it was Richard Nixon and a large pool of water. He kept diving in and surfacing empty-handed over and over and over. Such was his fate in hell. 'No!' George said. 'I don't think so. I'm not a good swimmer and I don't think I could do that all day long.'

The devil led him to the next room: in it was Tony Blair with a sledgehammer and a room full of rocks. All he did was swing the hammer, time after time after time. 'No, I've got this problem with my shoulder. I would be in constant agony if all I could do was break rocks all day!' commented George.

The devil opened a third door. In it, George saw Bill Clinton, lying on the floor with his arms staked over his head, and his legs staked in spread eagle pose. Bent over him was Monica Lewinsky, doing what she does best. George Bush looked at this in disbelief for a while and finally said, 'Yeah, I can handle this.'

The devil smiled and said, 'OK, Monica, you're free to go!'

Bush and Powell and the blonde

President Bush and Colin Powell are sitting in a bar.

A guy walks in and asks the barman, 'Isn't that Bush and Powell sitting over there?'

The barman says, 'Yep, that's them.'

So the guy walks over and says, 'Wow, this is a real honour. What are you guys doing in here?'

Bush says, 'We're planning WWIII.'

And the guy says, 'Really? What's going to happen?'

Bush says, 'Well, we're going to kill 140 million Arabs and one blonde with big tits.'

The guy exclaimed, 'A blonde with big tits? Why kill a blonde with big tits?'

Bush turns to Powell, punches him on the shoulder and says, 'See, smart ass? I told you no one would worry about 140 million Arabs!'

Muslim suicide

Everyone seems to be wondering why Muslim terrorists are so quick to commit suicide.

No beer.

No bars.

No television.

No *Playboy* or *Penthouse*.

No cricket.

No baseball.

No football.

No rugby.

No basketball.

No hockey.

No golf.

No bikinis on the beach.

No nude beaches.

No summer mini skirts and braless beauties.

No hot dogs.

No burgers.

No lobster, shellfish, or even frozen fish sticks.

No chocolate-chip cookies.

No Christmas.

Rags for clothes and towels for hats.

Constant wailing from the guy next door because he's sick and there are no doctors.

Constant wailing from the guy in the tower.

You can't shave, your wife can't shave, and you can't shave your wife.

Sand is everywhere, sand gets into everything.

You wipe your backside with your left hand without toilet paper.

You can't shower to wash off the smell of donkey cooked over burning camel dung.

The women have to wear baggy dresses and veils at all times.

Your bride is picked by someone else.

Then your leaders tell you that when you die, you get 27 virgins and it all gets better!

Get acquainted

Before his presidential inauguration, George Bush was invited to a get-acquainted tour of the White House. After drinking several glasses of iced tea, he asked Bill Clinton if he could use his personal bathroom. George was astonished to see that the president had a solid gold urinal.

That afternoon, George told his wife, Laura, about the urinal. 'Just think,' he said, 'when I am president, I'll get to have a gold urinal!'

Later, when Laura had lunch with Hillary at her tour of the White House, she told Hillary how impressed George had been with his discovery that in the president's private bathroom, there was a gold urinal.

That evening, Bill and Hillary were getting ready for bed. Hillary turned to Bill and said, 'Well, I found out who pissed in your saxophone!'

Party faithfuls

John Howard goes to Washington for a meeting with then-president Bill Clinton. After dinner, Bill says to John: 'Well, John, I don't know what you think of the members of your Cabinet, but mine are all bright and brilliant.'

'How do you know?' asks John.

'Oh well, it's simple,' says Bill. 'They all have to take special tests before they can be a minister. Wait a second.'

He calls Madeleine Albright over and says to her, 'Tell me, Madeleine, who is the child of your father and of your mother who is not your brother and is not your sister?'

'Ah, that's simple, Mr President,' says Madeleine, 'it is me!'

'Well done, Madeleine,' says Clinton, and John Howard is very impressed.

John Howard returns to Canberra and wonders about the intelligence of the members of his Cabinet. He calls in Tim Fischer and says: 'Tim, tell me, who is the child of your father and of your mother who is not your brother and is not your sister?'

Tim thinks and thinks and doesn't know the answer. 'Can I think about it a bit further, John? May I let you know tomorrow?'

'Of course,' says Howard, 'you've got 24 hours.' Tim Fischer goes away, thinks as hard as he can, calls in his team but no one knows the answer. Twenty hours later, Tim is very worried — still no answer and only four hours to go.

Eventually he says, 'I'll ask Peter Costello — he's clever, he'll know the answer.'

He calls Costello. 'Peter, he says, tell me who is the child of your father and of your mother who is not your brother and is not your sister?'

'Very simple,' says Peter, 'it's me!'

'Of course,' says Tim, and rings John Howard.

'John,' says Tim, 'I've got the answer: it's Peter Costello.'

'No, you idiot,' says Howard, 'it's Madeleine Albright.'

The big boys

It is 1999, and Boris Yeltsin, Bill Clinton, and Bill Gates are invited to have dinner with God.

During dinner God says, 'I invited you to dinner because I needed three important people to send out my message — tomorrow I will destroy the earth!'

Yeltsin immediately calls together his Cabinet and tells them, 'I have two horrendous announcements to make. First, God really does exist. Second, tomorrow He will destroy the earth.'

Clinton calls an emergency session of Congress and tells them, 'I have good news and bad news. The good news is that God does exist, and the bad news is that He will destroy the earth tomorrow.'

Bill Gates goes back to Microsoft headquarters and tells his people, 'I have two fantastic announcements! First, I am one of the three most important people on earth, and secondly, the Y2K problem has been solved!'

Politicians

A British doctor says, 'Medicine in my country is so advanced that we can take a kidney out of one man, put it in another man, and have him looking for work in six weeks.'

A German doctor says, 'That's nothing, we can take a lung out of one person, put it in another man, and have him looking for work in four weeks.'

A Russian doctor says, 'In my country medicine is so advanced, we can take half a heart out of one person, put it in another man, and have both of them looking for work in two weeks.'

The American doctor, not to be outdone, says, 'You guys are way behind. We just took a man with no brain out of Texas, put him in the White House, and almost immediately millions began looking for work.'

Howard and Costello go Bush

John Howard called Peter Costello into his office one day and said, 'Peter, my boy, I have a great idea! We are going to go all out to win the country voters.'

'Good idea, PM! How will we go about it?' said Costello.

'Well,' said Howard, 'we'll get ourselves one of those Driza-Bone coats, some RM Williams boots, a stick and an Akubra hat — oh and a blue cattle dog. Then we'll really look the part. We'll go to a typical old outback country pub and we'll show them that we are really at home there.'

'Right, PM,' said Costello.

Days later, all kitted out and with the requisite blue heeler they set off from Canberra in a westerly direction.

Eventually they arrived at just the place they were looking for and found a typical outback pub. They walked in with the dog and up to the bar.

'G'day, mate,' said Howard to the bartender, 'two middies of your best beer.'

'Good afternoon, Prime Minister,' said the bartender, 'two middies of our best coming up.'

Howard and Costello stood leaning on the bar, drinking their beer and chatting, nodding now and again to those who came into the bar for a drink. The dog lay quietly at their feet.

All of a sudden, the door from the adjacent bar opened and in came a grizzled old stockman, complete with stockwhip. He walked up to the cattle dog, lifted its tail with the whip and looked underneath, shrugged his shoulders and walked back to the other bar.

A few moments later, in came another old stockman with his whip. He walked up to the dog, lifted its tail, looked underneath, scratched his head and went back to the other bar. Over the course of the next hour or so, another four or five stockmen came in, lifted the dog's tail and went away looking puzzled.

Eventually, Howard and Costello could stand it no longer and called the barman over.

'Tell me,' said Howard, 'why did all those old stockmen come in and look under the dog's tail like that? Is it an old outback custom?'

'Struth no!' said the barman. 'It's just that someone went in and told them that there was a dog in this bar with two arseholes!'

Air crash

An aeroplane was about to crash; there were five passengers on board but only four parachutes.

The first passenger said, 'I'm Kobe Bryant, the best NBA basketball player, the Lakers need me, I can't afford to die ...' So he took the first pack and left the plane.

The second passenger, Hillary Clinton, said, 'I am the wife of the former president of the United States, I am the most ambitious woman in the world, I am also a New York Senator and a potential future president.' She just took the second parachute and jumped out of the plane.

The third passenger, John Howard, said, 'I am the Prime Minister of Australia, I have a great responsibility being the leader of a great nation. And above all I'm the most intelligent prime minister in Australian history — Australia's people won't let me die.' So he put on the pack next to him and jumped out of the plane.

The fourth passenger, the Pope, said to the fifth passenger, a 10-year-old school boy, 'I am old and frail and I don't have many years left. As a Christian I will sacrifice my life and let you have the last parachute.'

The boy said, 'It's OK, there's a parachute left for you. Australia's most intelligent prime minister has taken my school backpack.'

Why did the chicken cross the road?

JOHN HOWARD: The chick never crossed the road. And it was not forcibly removed from its mother! Anyway, that's a matter for the states and is of no interest to us. The United Nations should butt out.

KIM BEAZLEY: There *was* a chicken and it *did* cross the road. This is a deliberate act by the government to hide the fact that chickens continue to cross Australian roads.

NATASHA STOTT-DESPOJA: What if it was not a chicken but a bantam? Minority sectors of our community shouldn't be discriminated against based purely on the size of their legs.

EVELYN SCOTT: To demonstrate a commitment to reconciliation with Indigenous chickens.

PETER COSTELLO: Accordingly to documentation submitted to the Live Foods Processing Authority, the chicken in question was uncooked at the time of its journey and therefore will not incur a GST charge. However, if that chicken actually crossed the road for profit, regardless of its raw/cooked status, the road crossing would be considered by the ATO to be a service for which GST will be imposed.

PAULINE HANSON: Please explain.

JOH BJELKE-PETERSEN: It was a Queensland free range chicken and has the right to cross roads. In fact I was feeding the chooks at the time it crossed. It was a long way down the track, but Flo saw it too. Anyhow, it doesn't concern you. Don't you worry about that!

ROBERT DE NIRO: Are you telling me the chicken crossed that road? Is that what you're telling me?

MARTIN LUTHER KING, JR: I envision a world where all chickens, be they black or white or brown or red or speckled, will be free to cross roads without having their motives called into question.

GRANDPA: In my day, we didn't ask why the chicken crossed the road. Someone told us that the chicken crossed, and that was good enough for us.

REV FRED NILE: Because the chicken is gay! Isn't it obvious? Can't you people see the plain truth in front of your face? The chicken was going to the 'other side'. That's what they call it — the 'other side'. Yes, my friends.

CAPTAIN JAMES T. KIRK: To boldly go where no chicken has gone before.

FOX MULDER: You saw it cross the road with your own eyes. How many more chickens have to cross before you believe it's true?

HANSIE CRONJE: What if I could guarantee that it won't get to the other side?

FREUD: The fact that you are at all concerned that the chicken crossed the road reveals your underlying sexual insecurity. How do you feel about your mother?

THE CIA: Who told you about the chicken? Did you see the chicken? There was no chicken. Please step into the car.

EINSTEIN: Did the chicken really cross the road or did the road move beneath the chicken?

BILL CLINTON: I did not cross the road with *that* chicken!

Fifty dollars

Every morning, Bill Clinton would take a jog near his home in NY State and on each run, he happened to jog past a hooker standing on the same street corner, day after day.

Apprehensive, he would brace himself as he approached her for what was most certainly about to follow.

'Fifty dollars!' she would shout from the kerb.

'No. Five dollars!' fired back Clinton.

This ritual between the ex-president and the hooker continued for several days. He'd run by. She'd holler, 'Fifty dollars,' and he'd yell back, 'Five dollars!'

One day, Hillary decided that she wanted to accompany her husband on his jog. As the jogging couple neared the now infamous street corner, Bill suddenly realised the pro would bark her $50 offer for all to hear (including Hillary) and he would have to come up with a very good explanation for his wife.

As they jogged into the turn that would take them past the hooker, Bill was overcome with anxiety on how to handle the situation.

Sure enough there she was — standing where she always did.

Bill tried to evade the streetwalker's eyes as she looked up at the jogging executives. Then from the sidewalk, she yelled to Bill: 'See what you get for five bucks?'

Terrorism

A journalist assigned to the Jerusalem bureau has an apartment overlooking the Western Wall. Every day she looks out and sees an old bearded Jewish man praying vigorously. Certain that he would be a good interview, she goes to the wall and introduces herself.

'You come every day to the Wall. Sir, how long have you done that, and what are you praying for?'

'I have come here to pray every day for 25 years. In the morning I pray for world peace and for the brotherhood of man. I go home to have a cup of tea, and I come back and pray for the eradication of illness and disease.

And, very, very important, I pray for peace and understanding between the Israelis and Palestinians.'

'How does it make you feel to come here every day for 25 years and pray for these wonderful things?'

'Like I'm talking to a fucking brick wall.'

A public service announcement

Australians are asked to assist in identifying any terrorists amongst us.

Since the Taliban cannot stand nudity and consider it a sin to see a naked woman apart from your wife, this Saturday afternoon at 2 p.m. Eastern Standard Time all Australian women are asked to walk out of their house completely naked to help weed out any neighbourhood terrorists. Circling your block for one hour is recommended for this anti-terrorist effort. All men are to position themselves in lawn chairs in front of their house to prove they think it's OK to see other women in the nude. And since the Taliban also does not approve of alcohol, an Esky containing a cold slab is to be at your side as further proof of your anti-Taliban sentiment. Australia appreciates your efforts to root out terrorists and applauds your participation. Come on, all Aussie men, get out there and support the girls as they weed out the terrorists hiding in *your* neighbourhood!

A Texan in a Stetson

Three men are sitting on a bench. One's a Texan wearing a Stetson, one's a Muslim wearing a turban, and the last an Apache with an eagle feather woven into his hair.

The Indian is rather glum and says, 'Once my people were many, but now we are few.'

The Muslim puffs up and says, 'Once my people were few, but now we are many millions.'

The Texan adjusts his hat, finishes rolling a smoke, leans back and drawls, 'That's 'cause we ain't played cowboys and Muslims yet.'

New government emblem

The government announced today that it is changing its emblem to a condom because it more clearly reflects the government's political stance: a condom stands up to inflation, halts production, destroys the next generation, protects a bunch of pricks, and gives you a sense of security while it's actually screwing you.

Globalisation

Q: How to define globalisation?

A: Princess Diana's death.

Q: How come?

A: An English princess with an Egyptian boyfriend crashes in a French tunnel, driving a German car with a Dutch engine, driven by a Belgian who was pissed on Scottish whisky, followed closely by an Italian paparazzi, on Japanese motorcycles, treated by an American doctor, using Brazilian medicine. And this is sent to you via an Australian using technology stolen from the Taiwanese.

A European news bulletin

The European Commission has just announced an agreement whereby English will be the official language of the EU rather than German, which was the other possibility. As part of the negotiations, Her Majesty's government conceded that English spelling had some room for improvement and has accepted a five-year phase-in plan that would be known as 'EuroEnglish'.

In the first year, 's' will replace the soft 'c'. Sertainly, this will make the sivil servants jump with joy. The hard 'c' will be dropped in favour of the 'k'. This should klear up konfusion and keyboards kan have one less letter.

There will be growing publik enthusiasm in the sekond year, when the troublesome 'ph' will be replased with the 'f'. This will make words like 'fotograf' 20 per cent shorter.

In the third year, publik akseptanse of the new spelling kan be expekted to reach the stage where more komplikated changes are possible. Governments will enkourage the removal of double letters, which have always ben a deterent to akurate speling. Also, al wil agre that the horible mes of the silent 'e's in the language is disgraseful, and they should go away.

By the fourth yar, peopl wil be reseptiv to steps such as replasing 'th' with 'z' and the 'w' with 'v'.

During the fifz yar, ze unesesary 'o' kan be dropd from vords containing 'ou' and similar changes vud of kors be aplid to ozer kombinations of leters.

After ze fifz yar, ve vil hav a realy sensibl vriten styl. Zer vil be no mor trubls or difikultis and evryvun vil find it easy tu understand each ozer.

Ze drem of a united urop vil finali kum tru. Und after ze fifz yar, ve vil al be speking German like zey vunted in ze forst plas.

Food shortages

The UN conducted a worldwide survey last month. The only question asked was: 'Would you please give your honest opinion about solutions to the food shortage in the rest of the world?' Unfortunately, the survey was a massive failure.

In Eastern Europe they didn't know what 'honest' meant.

In Western Europe they didn't know what 'shortage' meant.

In China they didn't know what 'opinion' meant.

In the Middle East they didn't know what 'solution' meant.

And in the US they didn't know what 'the rest of the world' meant.

11 THEM, NOT US

Racial jokes have travelled down through history and, more often than not, are also told by the cultures being targeted. Jewish jokes, for example, are certainly told by Jews to Jews; however, they're not usually told to non-Jews by Jews. This is an area of humour that deserves considerable study and it is fascinating to track such jokes as they move from group to group. A Jewish joke can be adapted and reappear as an Albanian joke etc, for this is the very nature of joke-telling. It is usually a 'no-holds-barred' area and everyone is a possible target. Under the mask of humour, our society allows infinite aggressions, by everyone and against everyone. Of course, there are degrees of racism and one hopes that the distribution of racist jokes, spoken or via e-mail, are nothing more than an unconscious revisiting of stereotypes. We feel more secure if we can show our superiority. One line of thought is that the telling or passing on of these jokes, usually to an unwilling audience, betrays a hidden hostility and signals the joke-teller's victory by being, theoretically at least, the one person who does not laugh.

Some jokes can, of course, be shockingly cruel and also offensive, and whilst these cannot be condoned they are a fact of life. Some groups are more sensitive than others, and joke relating, either verbally or via e-mail, deserves some censoring. The e-mail, being once removed, is more anonymous and therefore these jokes are transmitted without a face-to-face response (which could be a punch in the face!). In circulating jokes that focus on particular ethnic groups one needs to tread a careful path. I believe these jokes are not necessarily distributed to attack minorities; however, it is clear that they are used to perpetuate conceived ideas as racial slurs: Jews as financially crafty, Scots as thrifty, Irish as dumb, English as dirty, Muslims as terrorists, French as arrogant, Americans as loud and Australians, well, we cop it all ways, especially in retaliation from the Poms whom we have taunted for years, particularly as sporting competitors.

Many of the racial-related jokes are what Australians call 'put downs', where one tries to belittle a person's standing. In America, for example, Polish immigrants were once a target for jokes like:

Q: Why are there so few Polish suicides?
A: Well, have you ever tried to jump out of a basement?

This joke immediately assumes that all Polish people are poor, live in basements, and are therefore easy targets for 'put-down' humour. To study this particular joke one would need to look at the 20th century history of New York when hundreds of thousands of Poles sought refugee status in America. After detention at Ellis Island they would eventually find cheap accommodation in the lower-income areas of New York, often in basements. As they opened businesses, entered the workforce etc, they came into competition with the other minority groups of the city, especially the Italians and Irish, who had been there for many years.

Ignorance always results in suspicion and as the New York Poles assimilated, the jokes started to disappear, although stereotypes tend to stick around in certain environments and population pockets.

Irish jokes are also widely circulated despite protestations from the Celts; however, many of these jokes received their first public outing on early television by Irish American artists including Bing Crosby. Hal Roach, a very popular Irish comedian, made a career out of lampooning the Irish, as did Dave Allen, who hosted one of Australia's longest-running television variety shows.

New Zealanders come in for a bit of good-natured fun in several jokes, and Aussies, never one to let our own people get off without a nudge, get stuck into Tasmanians through the traditional 'Black Bob' stories.

Australia has often been referred to as a 'melting pot' of many streams of immigration. I prefer to look at it as a giant bush stew, with fascinating ingredients from all over the world. New ethnic groups, be they European, Asian or, as of late, Middle Eastern, are always met with suspicion — are they going to take our jobs, our women, and so forth. These expressed fears usually result in jokes that allow us, in some ways, to let off a bit of steam and to share our unconscious fears. Laughter will definitely break down barriers. It has in the past and will in the future.

Irish sausages

Paddy goes into a shop and asks for Irish sausages.

The assistant looks at him and asks, 'Are you Irish?'

Paddy says, 'If I asked you for Italian sausages, would you ask me if I was Italian? Or, if I asked for German Bratwurst, would you ask me if I was German? Or, if I asked you for a kosher hot dog, would you ask me if I was Jewish? Or, if I asked you for a taco, would you ask me if I was Mexican? Would ya, ay? Would ya?'

The assistant says, 'Well, no.'

'And if I asked you for some Bourbon whisky, would you ask me if I was American? What about Danish bacon; would you ask me if I was Danish?'

'Well, I probably wouldn't.'

With indignation, the man says, 'Well, all right then, why did you ask me if I'm Irish — just because I asked for Irish sausages?'

The assistant replies, 'Because you're in Bunnings hardware.'

British red shirts

A long time ago, Britain and France were at war and during one battle the French captured an English major. At the French headquarters, a general began to question him. The French general asked, 'Why do you English officers all wear red coats? Don't you know the red material makes you easier targets for us to shoot at?'

In his quiet English way, the major informed the general that the reason English officers wear red coats is so that if they are shot, the blood won't show and the men they are leading won't panic.

This little-known historical fact clearly explains why, from that day until now, all French army officers have worn brown pants.

Asian-Australian

Here are some phrases to help build race relations:
1) That's not right: Sum Ting Wong
2) Are you harbouring a fugitive? Hu Yu Hai Ding
3) See me ASAP: Kum Hia Nao
4) Stupid man: Dum Fuk
5) Small horse: Tai Ni Po Ni

6) Did you go to the beach? Wai Yu So Tan?

7) I bumped into a coffee table: Ai Bang Mai Fa Kin Ni

8) I think you need a facelift: Chin Tu Fat

9) It's very dark in here: Wao So Dim

10) I thought you were on a diet: Wai Yu Mun Ching

11) This is a tow-away zone: No Pah King

12) Staying out of sight: Lei Ying Lo

13) He's cleaning his automobile: Wa Shing Ka

14) Your body odour is offensive: Yu Stin Ki Pu

15) Great: Fa Kin Su Pah

Crocodile pool party

A rich man living in Darwin decided he wanted to throw a party and invited all of his mates and neighbours, including Jimmy Goh, the only Aborigine in his neighbourhood.

He held the party around the pool in the backyard of his mansion.

Everyone was having a good time drinking, dancing, flirting, and eating prawns and oysters.

At the height of the party, the host said, 'I have a 15-foot crocodile in my pool and I'll give a million dollars to anyone who has the balls to jump in.'

The words were barely out of his mouth when there was a loud splash and everyone turned around and saw Jimmy in the pool!

Jimmy was fighting the crocodile and giving it a real beating! He was jabbing the croc in the eyes with his thumbs, throwing punches, head butts, chokeholds, biting the croc on the tail and, finally, flipping the croc through the air like some kind of Judo instructor. The water was churning and splashing everywhere. Both Jimmy and the croc were screaming and raising hell.

Finally Jimmy strangled the croc and let it float to the top like a goldfish. Jimmy then slowly climbed out of the pool.

Everybody was just staring at him in disbelief.

Finally the host said, 'Well, Jimmy, I reckon I owe you a million dollars.'

'Nah, you're right, I don't want it,' said Jimmy.

The rich man said, 'Jimmy, I have to give you something. You won the bet. How about half a million bucks then?'

'No thanks. I don't want it,' answered Jimmy.

The host said, 'Come on, I insist on giving you something. That was absolutely amazing. How about a new Porsche and a Rolex and some stock options?'

Again Jimmy said no.

Confused, the rich man asked, 'Well, Jimmy, then what do you want?'

Jimmy said, 'I want the name of the bastard who pushed me in the pool.'

Still the one

An Italian–American family was considering putting their grandfather in a nursing home. All the Catholic facilities were completely full so they had to put him in a Jewish home. After a few weeks in the Jewish facility, they came to visit Grandpa.

'How do you like it here?' asks the grandson.

'It's wonderful! Everyone here is so courteous and respectful,' said Grandpa.

'We're so happy for you. We were worried that this was the wrong place for you.'

'Let me tell you about how wonderfully they treat the residents here,' Grandpa said with a big smile.

'There's a musician here — he's 85 years old. He hasn't played the violin in 20 years and everyone still calls him "Maestro"! And there's a physician here — 90 years old. He hasn't been practising medicine for 25 years and everyone still calls him "Doctor"! Also a federal judge retired for over 30 years is still addressed as "Your Honour".

'And me, I haven't had sex for 30 years and they still call me "the fucking Italian"!'

Marital relations

A New Zealand man walks into his bedroom with a sheep under his arm and says: 'Darling, this is the pig I have sex with when you have a headache.'

His wife turns in bed and replies: 'I think you'll find that's a sheep, you idiot.'

The man says: 'I think you'll find I wasn't talking to you.'

National superiority

A Greek and an Italian are sitting down one day debating who has the superior culture.

The Greek says, 'We have the Parthenon.'

The Italian says, 'We have the Coliseum.'

The Greek says, 'We had great mathematicians.'

The Italian says, 'We had the Roman Empire,' and so on and so on.

Then the Greek says, 'We invented sex.'

The Italian says, 'That is true, but it was the Italians who introduced it to women.'

Taki the Greek

Taki the Greek's 21-year-old, unmarried daughter tells her parents she thinks she is expecting. Very worried, they go to the chemist to buy a pregnancy kit. The test result shows that the girl is indeed pregnant.

Shouting, cursing and crying, Taki says, 'Who dat pig what did you like dis? I want to know!'

The girl picks up the phone and makes a call.

Half an hour later a Ferrari stops in front of Taki's house. A mature and distinguished man with grey hair, impeccably dressed in a very expensive suit, steps out of the car and enters the house.

He sits in the living room with Taki, the mother and the girl and says to them, 'Good morning, your daughter has informed me of the problem. I can't marry her because of my personal family situation, but I'll take responsibility.

'If a girl is born, I will bequeath her two retail stores, a townhouse, a beach villa and a million-dollar bank account. If a boy is born, my legacy will be a couple of factories and a two-million-dollar bank account. If it is twins, a factory and one million dollars each. However, if there is a miscarriage, I am unsure. What do you suggest I do?'

At this point, Taki, who has remained silent, places a hand firmly on the man's shoulder and tells him, 'Den you try agin!'

Coloured?

Dear white fella,

Couple things you should know.

When I born, I black

When I grow up, I black
When I go in sun, I black
When I cold, I black
When I scared, I black
When I sick, I black
And when I die, I still black.
You white fella,
When you born, you pink
When you grow up, you white
When you go in sun, you red
When you cold, you blue
When you scared, you yellow
When you sick, you green
And when you die, you grey.
And you have the balls to call me coloured?

Arab news

A story is told of a Jewish man who was riding on the subway reading an Arab newspaper. A friend of his, who happened to be riding in the same subway car, noticed this strange phenomenon. Very upset, he approached the newspaper reader. 'Moshe, have you lost your mind? Why are you reading an Arab newspaper?'

Moshe replied, 'I used to read the Jewish newspaper, but what did I find? Jews being persecuted, Israel being attacked, Jews disappearing through assimilation and intermarriage, Jews living in poverty. So I switched to the Arab newspaper. Now what do I find? Jews own all the banks, Jews control the media, Jews are all rich and powerful, and Jews rule the world. The news is so much better!'

Ain't it grand!

An Irishman goes to the doctor with rectal problems. 'Dactor, it's me ahrse. I'd loik ya ta teyhk a look, if ya woot.'

So the doctor gets him to drop his pants and takes a look. 'Incredible!' he says. 'There is a $20 note lodged up there.'

Tentatively he eases the 20 out of the man's bottom, and then a $10 note appears.

'This is amazing!' exclaims the doctor. 'What do you want me to do?'

'Well fur gadness sake teyhk it out, man!' shrieks the patient.

The doctor pulls out the tenner and another 20 appears, and another and another and another, etc … Finally the last note comes out and no more appear.

'Ah, Dactor, tank ya koindly, dat's moch batter. How moch is dare den?'

The doctor counts the pile of cash. '$1,990 exactly.'

'Ah, dat'd be roit. I knew I wasn't feeling two grand.'

Shopping for olives

McQuillan walked into a bar and ordered martini after martini, each time removing the olives and placing them in a jar.

When the jar was filled with olives and all the drinks consumed, the Irishman picked up the jar and started to leave.

'S'cuse me,' said a customer, who was puzzled over what McQuillan had done, 'what was that all about?'

'Nothin',' said the Irishman, 'my wife just sent me out for a jar of olives!'

I've lost me luggage

An Irishman arrived at Mascot airport and wandered around the terminal with tears streaming down his cheeks. An airline employee asked him if he was already homesick.

'No,' replied the Irishman, 'I've lost all me luggage!'

'How'd that happen?'

'The cork fell out!' said the Irishman.

Irish last request

Mary Clancy goes up to Father O'Grady's after his Sunday morning service, and she's in tears.

He says, 'So what's bothering you, Mary my dear?'

She says, 'Oh, Father, I've got terrible news. My husband passed away last night.'

The priest says, 'Oh, Mary, that's terrible. Tell me, did he have any last requests?'

She says, 'That he did, Father.'

The priest says, 'What did he ask, Mary?'

She says, 'He said, "Please, Mary, put down that damn gun!"'

Where are the Australians?

A Somali man arrives in Sydney as a new immigrant. He stops the first person he sees walking down the street and says, 'Thank you, Mr Australian, for letting me in this country!'

But the passer-by says, 'You are mistaken. I am from Ireland.'

The man goes on and encounters another passer-by. 'Thank you for having such a beautiful country here in Australia.'

The person says, 'I no Australian, I Vietnamese.'

The new arrival walks further, and the next person he sees he stops, shakes his hand and says, 'Thank you for the wonderful Australia.'

That person puts up his hand and says, 'I am from Iraq. I am not an Australian.'

He finally sees a nice lady and asks suspiciously, 'Are you an Australian?'

She says, 'No, I am from New Zealand.'

So he is puzzled, and asks her, 'Where are all the Australians?'

The New Zealand lady looks at her watch, shrugs, and says, 'Probably at work.'

The two Arabs and the American

Two Arabs boarded a flight out of London. One took a window seat and the other sat next to him in the middle seat. Just before takeoff, an American sat down in the aisle seat.

After takeoff, the American kicked his shoes off, wiggled his toes and was settling in when the Arab in the window seat said, 'I need to get up and get a Coke.'

'Don't get up,' said the American, 'I'm in the aisle seat, I'll get it for you.'

As soon as he left, one of the Arabs picked up the American's shoe and spat in it.

When he returned with the Coke, the other Arab said, 'That looks good, I'd really like one too.'

Again, the American obligingly went to fetch it.

While he was gone the other Arab picked up his other shoe and spat in it.

When the American returned, they all sat back and enjoyed the flight, the two Arabs laughing, drinking their Cokes and smirking.

As the plane was landing, the American slipped his feet into his shoes and knew immediately what had happened.

'Why does it have to be this way?' he asked. 'How long must this go on? This fighting between our nations, this hatred, this animosity — this spitting in shoes and pissing in Cokes?'

Proper English – lost in translation

In a Bangkok temple: 'IT IS FORBIDDEN TO ENTER A WOMAN, EVEN A FOREIGNER, IF DRESSED AS A MAN.'

Cocktail lounge, Norway: 'LADIES ARE REQUESTED NOT TO HAVE CHILDREN IN THE BAR.'

At a Budapest zoo: 'PLEASE DO NOT FEED THE ANIMALS. IF YOU HAVE ANY SUITABLE FOOD, GIVE IT TO THE GUARD ON DUTY.'

Doctor's office, Rome: 'SPECIALIST IN WOMEN AND OTHER DISEASES.'

Hotel, Acapulco: 'THE MANAGER HAS PERSONALLY PASSED ALL THE WATER SERVED HERE.'

Dry cleaners, Bangkok: 'DROP YOUR TROUSERS HERE FOR THE BEST RESULTS.'

In a Nairobi restaurant: 'CUSTOMERS WHO FIND OUR WAITRESSES RUDE OUGHT TO SEE THE MANAGER.'

On the grounds of a private school: 'NO TRESPASSING WITHOUT PERMISSION.'

In a Sydney restaurant: 'OPEN SEVEN DAYS A WEEK AND WEEKENDS.'

A sign seen on an automatic restroom hand dryer: 'DO NOT ACTIVATE WITH WET HANDS.'

In a Pumwani maternity ward: 'NO CHILDREN ALLOWED.'

In a cemetery: 'PERSONS ARE PROHIBITED FROM PICKING FLOWERS FROM ANY BUT THEIR OWN GRAVES.'

Tokyo hotel's rules and regulations: 'GUESTS ARE REQUESTED NOT TO SMOKE OR DO OTHER DISGUSTING BEHAVIOURS IN BED.'

On the menu of a Swiss restaurant: 'OUR WINES LEAVE YOU NOTHING TO HOPE FOR.'

In a Tokyo bar: 'SPECIAL COCKTAILS FOR THE LADIES WITH NUTS.'

Hotel brochure, Italy: 'THIS HOTEL IS RENOWNED FOR ITS PEACE AND SOLITUDE. IN FACT, CROWDS FROM ALL OVER THE WORLD FLOCK HERE TO ENJOY ITS SOLITUDE.'

Hotel lobby, Bucharest: 'THE LIFT IS BEING FIXED FOR THE NEXT DAY. DURING THAT TIME WE REGRET THAT YOU WILL BE UNBEARABLE.'

Hotel elevator, Paris: 'PLEASE LEAVE YOUR VALUES AT THE FRONT DESK.'

Hotel, Yugoslavia: 'THE FLATTENING OF UNDERWEAR WITH PLEASURE IS THE JOB OF THE CHAMBERMAID.'

Hotel, Japan: 'YOU ARE INVITED TO TAKE ADVANTAGE OF THE CHAMBERMAID.'

In the lobby of a Moscow hotel across from a Russian Orthodox monastery: 'YOU ARE WELCOME TO VISIT THE CEMETERY WHERE FAMOUS RUSSIAN AND SOVIET COMPOSERS, ARTISTS, AND WRITERS ARE BURIED DAILY EXCEPT THURSDAY.'

Taken from a menu, Poland: 'SALAD A FIRM'S OWN MAKE; LIMPID RED BEET SOUP WITH CHEESY DUMPLINGS IN THE FORM OF A FINGER; ROASTED DUCK LET LOOSE; BEEF RASHERS BEATEN IN THE COUNTRY PEOPLE'S FASHION.'

Supermarket, Hong Kong: 'FOR YOUR CONVENIENCE, WE RECOMMEND COURTEOUS, EFFICIENT SELF-SERVICE.'

From the *Soviet Weekly*: 'THERE WILL BE A MOSCOW EXHIBITION OF ARTS BY 15,000 SOVIET REPUBLIC PAINTERS AND SCULPTORS. THESE WERE EXECUTED OVER THE PAST TWO YEARS.'

In an East African newspaper: 'A NEW SWIMMING POOL IS RAPIDLY TAKING SHAPE SINCE THE CONTRACTORS HAVE THROWN IN THE BULK OF THEIR WORKERS.'

Hotel, Vienna: 'IN CASE OF FIRE, DO YOUR UTMOST TO ALARM THE HOTEL PORTER.'

A sign posted in Germany's Black Forest: 'IT IS STRICTLY FORBIDDEN ON OUR BLACK FOREST CAMPING SITE THAT PEOPLE OF DIFFERENT SEX, FOR INSTANCE, MEN AND WOMEN, LIVE TOGETHER IN ONE TENT UNLESS THEY ARE MARRIED WITH EACH OTHER FOR THIS PURPOSE.'

Hotel, Zurich: 'BECAUSE OF THE IMPROPRIETY OF ENTERTAINING GUESTS OF THE OPPOSITE SEX IN THE BEDROOM, IT IS SUGGESTED THAT THE LOBBY BE USED FOR THIS PURPOSE.'

An advertisement by a Hong Kong dentist: 'TEETH EXTRACTED BY THE LATEST METHODISTS.'

Tourist agency, Czechoslovakia: 'TAKE ONE OF OUR HORSE-DRIVEN CITY TOURS. WE GUARANTEE NO MISCARRIAGES.'

Advertisement for donkey rides, Thailand: 'WOULD YOU LIKE TO RIDE ON YOUR OWN ASS?'

In the window of a Swedish furrier: 'FUR COATS MADE FOR LADIES FROM THEIR OWN SKIN.'

The box of a clockwork toy made in Hong Kong: 'GUARANTEED TO WORK THROUGHOUT ITS USEFUL LIFE.'

In a Swiss mountain inn: 'SPECIAL TODAY — NO ICE-CREAM.'

Airline ticket office, Copenhagen: 'WE TAKE YOUR BAGS AND SEND THEM IN ALL DIRECTIONS.'

On the door of a Moscow hotel room: 'IF THIS IS YOUR FIRST VISIT TO THE USSR, YOU ARE WELCOME TO IT.'

A laundry in Rome: 'LADIES, LEAVE YOUR CLOTHES HERE AND SPEND THE AFTERNOON HAVING A GOOD TIME.'

Pakistani shoes

A married couple was on holiday in Pakistan. They were touring around the marketplace looking at the goods and such, when they passed this small sandal shop. From inside they heard a gentleman with a Pakistani accent say, 'You're foreigners! Come in! Come into my humble shop.'

So the married couple walked in. The Pakistani man said to them, 'I have some special sandals I think you would be interested in. Dey make you wild at sex, like a great desert camel.'

Well, the wife was really interested in buying the sandals after hearing what the man claimed, but her husband felt he really didn't need them, being the sex god he was.

The husband asked the man, 'How could sandals make you into a sex freak?'

The Pakistani man replied, 'Just try dem on, sahib.'

With that, after much badgering from his wife, he finally agreed to try them on. As soon as he slipped them onto his feet, he got this wild look in his eyes; something his wife hadn't seen in many years … raw sexual power.

In a blink of an eye, the husband grabbed the Pakistani man, bent him violently over a table, yanked down his pants, ripped down his own pants, and grabbed a firm hold of the Pakistani's thighs.

The Pakistani began screaming: *'You have dem on the wrong feet … You have dem on the wrong feet!'*

Tongue-tied

A fleeing Taliban, desperate for water, was plodding through the Afghanistan desert when he saw something far off in the distance. Hoping to find water, he walked towards the object, only to find a little old Jewish man sitting at a card table with neckties laid out on it.

The Arab said, 'My thirst is killing me. Please, do you have water?'

The Jew replied, 'I have no water. Would you like to buy a tie? They are only $150. This one goes very nicely with your robes.'

The Arab shouted, *'Idiot!* I do not need your overpriced tie. I need water!'

'All right,' said the Jew. 'It does not matter that you do not want to buy a tie. I will show you have not offended me. If you walk over that hill to the east about four miles, you will find a lovely restaurant. Go! Walk that way! The restaurant has all the water you need!'

The Arab staggered away towards the hill and disappeared. Eight hours later he came crawling back to the Jewish man's table.

The Jew said, 'I told you the restaurant with the water is about four miles over the hill. Could you not find it?'

'I found it,' rasped the Arab, 'but your brother wouldn't let me in without a tie.'

Kiwi culture

Fifty thousand Kiwis meet in Eden Park for a 'Kiwis Are Not Stupid' Convention.

Prime Minister Helen Clark says, 'We are all here today to prove to the world thet Kiwis are not stupid. Ken I hev a volunteer?'

The All Black Carlos Spencer gingerly works his way through the crowd and steps up to the stage.

Helen asks him, 'What uz fufteen plus fufteen?'

After 15 or 20 seconds Carlos says, 'Eighteen!'

Obviously everyone is a little disappointed. Then all 50,000 Kiwis start chanting, '*Guv hum another chance! Guv hum another chance!*'

Helen says, 'Well sunce we've gone to the trouble of gitting 50,000 of you un one place end we have the worldwide priss end global broadcast media here, I thunk we ken guv hum another chance.'

So she asks, 'What uz sivven plus sivven?'

After nearly 30 seconds he eventually says, 'Ninety!'

Helen, quite perplexed, looks down and just lets out a dejected sigh — everyone is disheartened. Carlos starts crying and the 50,000 Kiwis begin to yell and wave their hands, shouting, '*Guv hum another chance! Guv hum another chance!*'

Helen, unsure whether or not she is doing more harm than good eventually says, 'OK! OK! Just one more chance ... What uz two plus two?'

Carlos closes his eyes, and after a whole minute eventually says, 'Four!'

Throughout the stadium pandemonium breaks out as all 50,000 Kiwis jump to their feet, wave their arms, stamp their feet and scream ...

'*Guv hum another chance! Guv hum another chance!*'

Italians

Five Germans in an Audi Quattro arrive at the Italian border. The Italian customs officer stops them and tells them, 'It'sa illegala to putta five people in a Quattro.'

'Vot do you mean it's illegal?' asks the German driver.

'*Quattro* meansa four,' replies the Italian official.

'Quattro is just ze name of ze fokken automobile,' the German says unbelievingly. 'Look at ze dam papers: ze car is designed to karry five persons.'

'You canta pulla thata one on me!' replies the Italian customs officer. '*Quattro* meansa four. You have five-a people ina your car and you are thereforea breaking the law.'

The German driver replies angrily, 'You idiot! Call your zupervisor over. I vant to speak to someone viz more intelligence!'

'Sorry,' responds the Italian officer, 'he can'ta come. He'sa busy witha two guys in a Fiat Uno.'

NZ thesaurus for Aussies

Amejen: visualise

Beard: a place to sleep

Beers: large savage animals found in US forests

Beggage chucken: place to leave your suitcase at the airport

Brudge: structure spanning a stream

Bug hut: popular recording

Bun button: been bitten by insect

Chully bun: Esky

Cuds: children

Cuttin: baby cat

Day-old chuck: very young poultry

Duffy cult: not easy

Ear New Zulland: national airline

Ear roebucks: exercise at the gym

Ear: mix of nitrogen and oxygen

Earplane: large flying machine

Ever cardeau: avocado

Fear hear: blonde

Fitter cheney: type of pasta

Fush: marine creatures

Guess: vapour

Iggs ecktly: Precisely

Inner me: enemy

Jumbo: pet name for someone called Jim

Jungle Bills: Christmas carol

Ken's: Cairns

Kiri Pecker: famous Australian businessman

Kittle crusps: potato chips

Leather: foam produced from soap

Lift: departed

McKennock: person who fixes cars

Mere: Mayor

Mess kara: eye make-up

Milburn: capital of Victoria

Min: male of the species

Munce: usually served on toast

Munner stroney: soup

Nin tin dough: computer game

One doze: well-known computer program

Peck: to fill a suitcase

Pigs: for hanging out washing with

Pissed aside: chemical which kills insects

Pits: domestic animals

Pug: large pink animal with a curly tail

Sex: one less than sivven

Sivven Sucks Sivven: large Boeing aircraft

Sivven Four Sivven: larger Boeing aircraft

Sucks peck: Half a dozen beers

Tin: one more than nine

Veerjun: mythical New Zealand maiden

You've been on the drink again!

An Irishman had been drinking at a pub all night. The bartender finally said that the bar was closing. So the Irishman stood up to leave and fell flat on his face. He tried to stand one more time; same result. He figured he'd crawl outside and get some fresh air and maybe that would sober him up.

Once outside, he stood up and fell on his face again. So he decided to crawl the four blocks home.

When he arrived at the door he stood up and fell flat on his face. He crawled through the door and into his bedroom. When he reached his bed he tried one more time to stand up. This time he managed to pull himself upright, but he quickly fell right into the bed and was sound asleep as soon as his head hit the pillow.

His wife standing over him shouting awakened him the next morning. *'You've been drinking!'*

Putting on an innocent look, and intent on bluffing it out he said, 'What makes you say that?'

'The pub just called — you left your wheelchair there again.'

Terrible fire in New Zealand

Helen Clark, Prime Minister of New Zulland, is rudely awoken at 4 a.m. by the telephone.

'Hillen, its the hilth munister here. Sorry to bother you at this hour but there is an emergency! I've just received word thet the Durex fectory en Auckland has burned to the ground. It is istimated thet the entire New Zulland supply of condoms will be gone by the ind of the week.'

'Shut!' the prime minister says. 'The economy wull niver be able to cope with all those unwanted babies — wi'll be ruined! We're going to hef to shup some in from abroad ... Brutain?'

'No chence! The Poms will have a field day on thus one!'

'What about Australia?'

'Maybe — but we don't want them to know thet we are stuck. You call John Howard — tell hum we need one moollion condoms; 10 enches long and eight enches thuck! That way they'll know how bug the Kiwis really are!'

Helen calls John, who agrees to help the Kiwis out in their hour of need.

Three days later a van arrives in Auckland — full of boxes.

A delighted Hillen rushes out to open the boxes. She finds condoms; 10 unches long; eight unches thuck, all coloured green and gold. She then notices in small writing on each and every one: MADE IN AUSTRALIA — SIZE: MEDIUM.

Sheep

A Kiwi man buys several sheep, hoping to breed them for wool.

After several weeks, he notices that none of the sheep are getting pregnant, and phones a vet for help. The vet tells him that he should try artificial insemination.

The farmer doesn't have the slightest idea what this means but, not wanting to display his ignorance, only asks the vet how he will know when the sheep are pregnant.

The vet tells him that they will stop standing around and instead will lie down and wallow in grass when they are pregnant.

The man hangs up and gives it some thought. He comes to the conclusion that artificial insemination means he has to impregnate the sheep himself.

So, he loads the sheep into his Land Rover, drives them out into the woods, has sex with them all, brings them back, and goes to bed.

Next morning, he wakes and looks out at the sheep.

Seeing that they are all still standing around, he deduces that the first try didn't take, and loads them in the Land Rover again.

He drives them out to the woods, bangs each sheep twice for good measure, brings them back, and goes to bed exhausted.

Next morning, he wakes to find the sheep still just standing round.

'Try again,' he tells himself, and proceeds to load them up, and drive them out to the woods. He spends all day shagging the sheep and upon returning home, falls listlessly into bed. The next morning, he cannot even raise himself from the bed to look out of the window.

He asks his wife to look, and tell him if the sheep are lying in the grass.

'No,' she says, 'they're all in the Land Rover, and one of them is beeping the horn.'

Car park

Moshe is driving in Jerusalem. He's late for a meeting. He's looking for a place to park. He can't find one. In desperation he looks towards heaven and says, 'God, if you find me a parking space, I promise I'll eat only kosher, respect the Shabbat and all holidays and go to shul regularly.'

Miraculously a space opens up in front of him. He turns his face towards heaven again and says, 'Never mind, I just found one.'

The captain and the camel

A new army captain is assigned to an outfit in a remote Iraqi desert post.

During his first inspection of the outfit, he notices a camel hitched up behind the mess tent. He asks the sergeant why the camel is kept there.

The nervous sergeant says, 'Well, sir, as you know, there are 250 men here on the post and no women. And, sir, sometimes the men have "urges". That's why we have the camel.'

The captain says, 'I can't say that I condone this, but I understand about urges, so the camel can stay.'

About a month later, the captain starts having his own urges. Crazy with passion, he asks the sergeant to bring the camel to his tent.

Putting a ladder behind the camel, the captain stands on the ladder, pulls his pants down and has wild, insane sex with the camel.

When he's done, he asks the sergeant, 'Is that how the men do it?'

'No, not really, sir … They usually just ride the camel into town where the girls are.'

Home Office security memo

Re: Towel Heads

Recently we received a warning about the use of the above politically incorrect term. Please note: we all need to be more sensitive in our choice of words.

We have been informed that the terrorists who hate our guts, our religion, our freedom and our way of life in general — and want to kill all of us for the greater glory — do not like to be called 'Towel Heads'.

This is because the item they wear on their heads is not a towel but actually a small, folded sheet. Therefore, from this point forward you should only refer to them as 'Sheet Heads'.

Thank you for your support and compliance on this delicate matter.

Russian Roulette

An African leader makes an official trip to Russia. At the end of the trip, the Russian leader tells the African that in Russia they have a custom performed at farewells called 'Russian Roulette' to demonstrate one's courage.

The Russian then whips out a revolver, loads one chamber, gives the cylinder a spin, puts the gun to his head and pulls the trigger ... *click* ... empty chamber.

He hands the revolver to his African guest, and says, 'Your turn.'

Not to be outdone, the African repeats the ritual ... *click* ... empty.

The next year, the Russian visits the African country. At the end of the trip, the African tells his Russian peer that he was very impressed with 'Russian Roulette' and that he has spent the last year devising an African ritual to demonstrate one's courage. The African then disappears through a door only to reappear a few minutes later smiling, and says, 'Your turn.'

The African escorts the Russian through the door. In the room are six of the most beautiful naked women he has ever seen. The African explains that he is to choose one of the women, who will perform oral sex on him. Absolutely dumbfounded, the Russian asks, 'What kind of test of courage is this?'

The African calmly answers, 'One of them is a cannibal.'

Pierre goes down

Pierre, a brave French fighter pilot, takes his girlfriend, Marie, out for a pleasant little picnic by the River Seine. It's a beautiful day and love is in the air. Marie leans over to Pierre and says, 'Pierre, kiss me!'

Pierre grabs a bottle of Merlot and splashes it on Marie's lips. 'What are you doing, Pierre?' says the startled Marie.

'I am Pierre, the fighter pilot! When I have red meat, I have red wine!'

She smiles and they start kissing. Things began to heat up a little and Marie says, 'Pierre, kiss me lower.'

Our hero tears her blouse open, grabs a bottle of Chardonnay and pours it on her breasts. 'Pierre! What are you doing now?' asks the bewildered Marie.

'I am Pierre, the fighter pilot! When I have white meat, I have white wine!'

She giggles and they resume their passionate interlude, and things really steam up. Marie leans close to his ear and whispers, 'Pierre, kiss me much lower!'

Pierre rips off her underwear, grabs a bottle of Cognac and pours it on her lap. He then strikes a match and lights the Cognac.

Marie shrieks and dives into the River Seine. Standing waist deep, she throws her arms into the air and screams furiously, '*Pierre, what the hell do you think you are doing?*'

Our hero stands and says defiantly, 'I am Pierre, the fighter pilot! If I go down, I go down in flames!'

Wisdom

Virginity like a bubble: one prick and it's gone.

Passionate kiss like a spider's web: soon lead to undoing of fly.

Man who run in front of car get tyred.

Man who run behind car get exhausted.

Man with hand in pocket feel cocky all day.

Foolish man give wife grand piano; wise man give wife upright organ.

Man who walk through airport turnstile sideways going to Bangkok.

Man with one chopstick go hungry.

Man who scratch arse should not bite fingernails.

Man who eat many prunes get good run for money.

Baseball is wrong — man with four balls cannot walk.

Panties not best thing on earth but next to best thing on earth.

War doesn't determine who right, war determine who left.

Wife who put husband in doghouse soon find him in cathouse.

Man who fight with wife all day get no piece at night.

Man who drive like hell bound to get there.

Man who stand on toilet is high on pot.

Man who fart in church sit in own pew.

It take many nails to build a crib but one screw to fill it.

The Hussein family history

Now that Saddam, Uday and Qusay have been eliminated, many of the lesser-known family members are coming to the attention of authorities. Among the brothers and sisters:

Ballay, the dancing sister

Beaujolay, the wine merchant

Beray, the half-French commando brother

Bidday, the toilet maker

Bouquay, the florist
Bufay, the 200 kilogram sister
Cabriolay, the convertible manufacturer
Chardonnay, Beaujolay's sister
Chevrolay, the large car manufacturer
Decoray, the shampoo merchant
Dushay, the clean sister
Ebay, the Internet czar
Ecksray, the radiologist
Guday, the half-Australian brother
Gudlay, the prostitute
Gulay, the singer/entertainer
Huray, the sports fanatic
Lattay, the coffee shop owner
Ojay, the stalker/murderer
Ollay, the half-Mexican sister
Ontray, who specialises in hors d'oeuvres
Phayray, the zoo worker in the gorilla house
Puray, the blender factory owner
Pusay, the 'loose' 22-year-old
Regay, the half-Jamaican brother
Sapheway, the grocery store owner
Sashay, the gay brother
Sooflay, the restaurateur
Sorbay, the dessert manufacturer
Tupay, the one with bad hair
Valay, the parking attendant

Dinky-di

Two families move from Saudi Arabia to Australia.

When they arrive, the fathers make each other a rather large bet — in a year's time, whichever family has become more Australian will win.

A year later when they meet again, the first guy says, 'My son's playing cricket, I went to McDonald's for breakfast, and I'm on my way to pick up some grog for the rugby tonight. How about you?'

The second guy says, 'Bugger you, towelhead!'

New Zealand earthquake

A major earthquake measuring 9.1 on the Richter scale has hit New Zealand this morning. Some 350,000 New Zealanders are missing, and over 100,000 have been reported injured. The country is totally ruined and the government doesn't know where to start with providing help. The rest of the world is in shock.

Canada is sending troops to assist the clean-up.

The USA is sending food, medical aid and money.

France has pledged doctors, nurses and medical supplies.

Russia is sending tents and warm clothing.

Australia is sending 350,000 replacement Kiwis.

Irish coffee

An elderly Irish woman goes to the doctor and asks his help to revive her husband's sex drive.

'What about trying Viagra?' asks the doctor.

'Not a chance,' says Mrs Murphy. 'He won't even take an aspirin for a headache.'

'No problem,' replies the doctor. 'Drop it into his coffee; he won't even taste it. Try it and then call me in a week to let me know how it worked out.'

A week later, Mrs Murphy calls the doctor and he inquires as to how things went.

'Oh, faith and bejaysus and begorrah, it was terrible, just terrible, Doctor.'

'What happened?' asks the doctor.

'Well, I did as you advised and slipped it in his coffee. The effect was immediate. He jumped straight up, with a gleam in his eye and with his pants bulging fiercely! He swept the cutlery off the table, at the same time ripping my clothes off and then proceeded to make wild, mad, passionate love to me on the tabletop! It was terrible!'

'What was terrible?' said the doctor. 'Was the sex not good?'

'Oh no, Doctor, the sex was the best I've had in 25 years, but I'll never be able to show me face in Starbucks again.'

Foreign names

A good-looking man walks into an agent's office in Hollywood and says, 'I want to be a movie star.' Tall, handsome and with experience on Broadway, he has all the right credentials.

The agent asks, 'What's your name?'

The guy says, 'My name is Penis Van Lesbian.'

The agent says, 'Sir, I hate to tell you, but in order to get into Hollywood, you are going to have to change your name.'

'I will *not* change my name! The Van Lesbian name is centuries old, I will not disrespect my grandfather by changing my name. Not ever.'

The agent says, 'Sir, I have worked in Hollywood for years … you will *not* succeed with a name like Penis Van Lesbian! I'm telling you, you will *have to* change your name, or I will not be able to represent you.'

'So be it! I guess we will not do business together,' the guy says, and leaves the agent's office.

Five years later, the agent opens an envelope sent to his office. Inside the envelope is a letter and a cheque for $50,000.

The agent is awestruck … who would possibly send him $50,000?

He reads the letter enclosed:

Dear sir,

Five years ago, I came into your office wanting to become an actor in Hollywood. You told me I needed to change my name. Determined to make it with my God-given birth name, I refused. You told me I would never make it in Hollywood with a name like Penis Van Lesbian. After I left your office, I thought about what you said and decided you were right. I had to change my name. I had too much pride to return to your office, so I signed with another agent. I would never have made it without changing my name, so the enclosed cheque is a token of my appreciation.

Thank you for your advice.
Dick Van Dyke

Two Italians on a bus

A bus stops and two Italian men get on.

They sit down and engage in an animated conversation.

The lady sitting behind them ignores them at first, but her attention is galvanised when she hears one of the men say the following:

'Emma come first. Den I come. Den two asses come together. I come once-a-more. Two asses, they come together again. I come again and pee twice. Then I come one lasta time.'

'You foul-mouthed sex-obsessed swine,' retorts the lady indignantly.

'Hey, coola down, lady,' says the man. 'Who talkin' abouta sexa? I'm a justa tellin' my frienda how to spella "Mississippi".'

Spanish flavour

An Australian touring Spain stopped at a local restaurant following a day of exhaustive sightseeing. While sipping his sangria, he noticed a sizzling, scrumptious-looking platter being served at the next table. Not only did it look good, the smell was wonderful.

He asked the waiter, 'What is that you just served?'

The waiter replied, 'Ah, senor, those are bulls' testicles from the bullfight this morning. A local delicacy!'

The Australian, though momentarily daunted, said, 'What the hell, I'm on holidays! Bring me a plate of that.'

The waiter replied, 'I am so sorry, senor. There is only one serving per day because there is only one bullfight each morning. If you come early tomorrow and place your order, we will be sure to save you this delicacy!'

The next morning, the Aussie returned, placed his order, and then that evening he was served the one and only special delicacy of the day.

After a few bites, and inspecting the contents of his platter, he called to the waiter and said, 'These are delicious, but they are much, much smaller than the ones I saw you serve yesterday.'

The waiter shrugged his shoulders and replied, 'Si, senor. Sometimes the bull wins.'

Bob the builder

Bob the builder was going through a house he had just built, accompanied by the woman who owned it. She was telling him what colour to paint each room.

They went into the first room and she said, 'I want this room to be painted a light blue.'

Bob went to the front door and yelled, '*Green side up!*'

When he went back into the house, she told him that the next room was to be bright red.

Bob again went to the front door and yelled, '*Green side up!*'

When he went back into the house, she told him that the next room was to be painted tan.

Bob again went to the front door and yelled, '*Green side up!*'

When he came back, the lady was pretty curious, so she asked him, 'I keep telling you colours, but you go out the front and yell "Green side up"; what is that for?'

Bob said, 'Oh, don't worry about that. I've got a couple of Kiwis laying the turf out front.'

The daughters

An Englishman, Irishman and Scotsman were talking about their teenage daughters.

The Englishman says, 'I was cleaning my daughter's room the other day and I found a packet of cigarettes. I was really shocked — I didn't even know she smoked.'

The Scotsman says, 'That's nothing. I was cleaning my daughter's room the other day when I came across a half full bottle of vodka. I was really shocked as I didn't even know she drank.'

With that the Irishman says, 'Both of you have got nothing to worry about. I was cleaning my daughter's room the other day when I found a packet of condoms. I was really shocked. I didn't even know she had a willy.'

Not so silly

An old man lived alone in Ireland. He wanted to plant his potato garden but it was very hard work. His only son, who would have helped him, was in Long Kesh Prison.

The old man wrote a letter to his son and mentioned his predicament.

Shortly, he received this reply: 'For heaven's sake, Dad, don't dig up that garden; that's where I buried the guns!'

At four o'clock the next morning, a dozen British soldiers showed up and dug up the entire garden, without finding any guns.

Confused, the old man wrote another note to his son, telling him what had happened, and asking him what to do next.

His son's reply was: 'Now plant your potatoes, Dad. This is the best I can do for you at this time.'

Some club

A hunter walking through the jungle was surprised to find a pigmy standing beside a very large, dead beast. Amazed, he asked, 'Did you kill that animal?'

The pigmy answered, 'Yes.'

The hunter then asked, 'How could a little bloke like you kill a beast as huge as that?'

Said the pigmy, 'I killed it with my club.'

Even more astonished, the hunter gasped and then asked, 'How big is your club?'

The pigmy replied, 'There are about 60 of us.'

Wiremu

Wiremu, a New Zealander, landed at Heathrow to watch the All Blacks and was not feeling well, so he decided to see a doctor. 'Hey, Doc, I don't feel so good, ay,' said Wiremu.

The doctor gave him a thorough examination and informed Wiremu that he had prostate problems, and that the only cure was testicular removal.

'No way, Doc,' replied Wiremu. 'I'm gitting a sicond opinion, ay!'

The second Pommy doctor gave Wiremu the same diagnosis and also advised him that testicular removal was the only cure. Not surprisingly, Wiremu refused the treatment. Wiremu was devastated but, with only hours to go before the All Blacks' opening game, he found an expat Kiwi doctor and decided to get one last opinion from someone he could trust.

The Kiwi doctor examined him and said, 'Wiremu, you huv prostate suckness, ay.'

'What's the cure thin, Doc, ay?' asked Wiremu, hoping for a different answer.

'Wull, Wiremu,' said the Kiwi doctor, 'wi're gonna huv to cut off your balls.'

'Phew, thunk Gud for thut!' said Wiremu. 'Those Pommy bastards wanted to take my Test tickets off me.'

Black Bob and his Tasmanian family

Did you hear about the time Black Bob's cousin passed away and left his entire estate in trust for his beloved widow? The only catch was that she couldn't touch it till she turned 14.

A Tasmanian policeman pulls over Black Bob's ute and says to Black Bob, 'Got any ID?'

Bob says, ''Bout what?'

Two Tasmanians are walking towards each other, and one is carrying a sack. When they meet, one recognises the other and says, 'Hey, Black Bob, watcha got in the bag?'

'Jes' some lambs.'

'If I guesses how many they is, kin I have one?'

'Hey, if ya guesses right, I'll give you both of 'em.'

'OK. Ummmmmmmm … five?'

Black Bob came home and found his house on fire. He rushed next door, phoned the fire brigade and shouted, 'Hurry over here — muh house is on fahr.'

'OK,' replied the fireman. 'How do we get there?'

'Gees, don't you fellers still have those big red trucks?'

Why do Black Bob and his family go to R-rated movies in groups of 18 or more?

Because they heard 17 and under aren't admitted.

Know why they raised the minimum drinking age in Tasmania to 32?

They wanted to keep alcohol out of the high schools.

Where was the toothbrush invented?

Tasmania. If it were invented anywhere else, it would have been called a teethbrush.

Did you hear about the $3 million Tasmanian state lottery?

The winner gets $3 a year for a million years.

Why do most murderers want to move to Tasmania?

Because everyone has the same DNA.

A new law was recently passed in Tasmania so that when a couple gets divorced they're still brother and sister.

After having their 11th child, Black Bob and his wife decided that was enough, as they could not afford a larger bed. So Bob went to his doctor/veterinarian and told him that he and his wife/cousin didn't want to have any more children.

The doctor told him that there was a procedure called a vasectomy that could fix the problem but that it was expensive. A less costly alternative, said the doctor, was to go home, get a firecracker, light it, put it in a beer can, then hold the can up to his ear and count to 10.

Black Bob said to the doctor, 'I may not be the smartest man in the world, but I don't see how putting a firecracker in a beer can next to my ear is going to help me.'

'Trust me,' said the doctor.

So Bob went home, lit a firecracker and put it in a beer can. He held the can up to his ear and began to count, '1, 2, 3, 4, 5,' at which point he paused, placed the beer can between his legs, and resumed counting on his other hand. This procedure also works in New Zealand.

12 DOWN ON THE FUNNY FARM

'Man bites dog' must be one of the earliest animal-related jokes. It wasn't even that funny compared with the howlers you will find in this section. Animals in humour receive miraculous powers, especially the power to talk, drink alcohol and, possibly not surprisingly, think like humans. No doubt there's a little bit of animal in all of us and the jokes help us recognise our own silliness. The prevailing jokes in Down On The Funny Farm are about 'man's best friend' — dogs — who seems to get into all sorts of mischief. There are also yarns about Northern Territory crocodiles, horse whisperers, fowl play, royal corgis, rodeo bulls, and extremely bad behaviour by ducks, donkeys and feisty felines. There's a revealing 'dog's diary' and a list of their 10 main complaints about humans. Talking parrots are also very popular in folklore and especially parrots who dob in wayward wives or husbands.

I've always liked the old bush yarns about dogs, like the story of Dad and Dave pushing their way through the bush. Dave suddenly stops and whispers to Dad, 'Hey, Dad, look at that dingo.' Dad looks through the undergrowth and sees the dingo busily licking his knackers. Dave whispers, 'Yer know, Dad, I've always wanted to do that.' To which Dad responds, 'Well, Dave, he looks dangerous. I'd suggest yer pat him first.'

Reasons men are more likely to have two dogs rather than two wives

1. The later you are, the more excited your dogs are to see you.
2. Dogs will forgive you for playing with other dogs.
3. If a dog is beautiful, other dogs don't hate it.
4. Dogs don't notice if you call them by another dog's name.
5. Dogs like it if you leave a lot of things on the floor.
6. A dog's parents never visit.
7. Dogs do not hate their bodies.
8. Dogs agree that you have to raise your voice to get your point across.
9. Dogs like to do their snooping outside, rather than in your wallet or desk.
10. Dogs seldom outlive you.
11. Dogs can't talk.
12. You never have to wait for a dog; they're ready to go 24 hours a day.
13. Dogs find you amusing when you're drunk.
14. Dogs like to go hunting and fishing.
15. Another man will seldom steal your dog.
16. A dog will not wake you up at night to ask, 'If I died, would you get another dog?'
17. If a dog has babies, you can put an advertisement in the paper and give them away.
18. A dog will let you put a studded collar on it without calling you a pervert.
19. A dog won't hold out on you to get a new car.
20. If a dog smells another dog on you, they don't get mad, they just think it's interesting.
21. On a car trip, your dog never insists on running the heater.
22. Dogs don't let magazine articles guide their lives.
23. When your dog gets old, you can have it put to sleep.
24. Dogs like to ride in the back of a pickup truck.
25. Dogs are not allowed in shops or fancy restaurants; and, last but not least:
26. If a dog leaves, it won't take half of your stuff.

Dead duck

A woman brought a very limp duck into a veterinary surgeon's consulting room. As he laid her pet on the table, the vet pulled out his stethoscope and listened to the bird's chest.

After a moment or two, the vet shook his head sadly and said, 'I am so sorry, there is nothing I can do here. Your duck has passed away.'

The distressed owner wailed, 'Are you sure?'

'Yes, I am sure. The duck is dead,' he replied.

'How can you be so sure?' she protested. 'I mean you haven't done any testing on him or anything. He might just be in a coma or something.'

The vet rolled his eyes, turned around and left the room, and returned a few moments later with a black labrador dog.

As the duck's owner looked on in amazement, the dog stood on his hind legs, put his front paws on the examination table and sniffed the duck from top to bottom. He then looked at the vet with sad eyes and shook his head.

The vet patted the dog, took him out, and returned a few moments later with a cat. The cat jumped up on the table and also sniffed delicately at the bird from head to foot. The cat sat back on her haunches, shook her head, meowed softly and strolled out of the room.

The vet looked at the woman and said, 'I'm sorry, but as I said, this is most definitely a 100 per cent certifiably dead duck.'

Then the vet turned to his computer terminal, hit a few keys and produced a bill, which he handed to the woman.

The duck's owner, still in shock, took the bill. 'Two hundred and fifty dollars!' she cried. 'Two hundred and fifty dollars just to tell me my duck is dead!'

The vet shrugged. 'I'm sorry. If you'd taken my word for it, the bill would have been $15, but with the lab report and the CAT scan, it's now $250.'

Why are you here?

Three labrador retrievers, one brown, one yellow and one black, were sitting in the waiting room at the vet's when they struck up a conversation. The black lab turned to the brown and said, 'So why are you here?'

The brown lab replied, 'I'm a pisser. I piss on everything ... the sofa, the curtains, the cat, the kids. But the final straw was last night when I pissed in the middle of my owner's bed.'

The black lab said, 'So what is the vet going to do?'

'Gonna cut my nuts off,' came the reply from the brown lab. 'They reckon it'll calm me down.'

The black lab then turned to the yellow lab and asked, 'Why are you here?'

The yellow lab said, 'I'm a digger. I dig under fences, dig up flowers and trees. I dig just for the hell of it and when I'm inside I dig up the carpets. But I went over the line last night when I dug a great big hole in my owner's couch.'

'So what are they going to do to you?' the black lab inquired.

'Looks like I'm losing my nuts too,' the dejected yellow lab said.

The yellow lab then turned to the black lab and asked, 'Why are you here?'

'I'm a humper,' the black lab said. 'I'll hump anything. I'll hump the cat, a pillow, the table, post-boxes, whatever. I want to hump everything I see. Yesterday, my owner had just got out of the shower and was bending down to dry her toes, and I just couldn't help myself. I hopped on her back and started humping away.'

The yellow and brown labs exchanged a sad glance and said, 'So, nuts off for you too, huh?'

The black lab said, 'No, I'm here to get my nails clipped.'

All you need to know about donkeys

Q: What do you call a donkey with one leg?

A: Wonky Donkey.

Q: What do you call a donkey with one leg and one eye?

A: Winky wonky donkey.

Q: What do you call a miniature donkey with one leg and one eye?

A: Dinky winky wonky donkey.

Q: What do you call a miniature donkey with one leg and one eye, makin' love?

A: Bonky dinky winky wonky donkey.

Q: What do you call a miniature donkey with one leg and one eye, makin' love while farting?

A: Stinky bonky dinky winky wonky donkey.

Q: What do you call a miniature donkey with one leg and one eye, makin' love while farting, and wearing blue suede shoes?

A: Honky tonky stinky bonky dinky winky wonky donkey.

Q: What do you call a miniature donkey with one leg and one eye, makin' love while farting, wearing blue suede shoes and playing piano?

A: Plinky plonky honky tonky stinky bonky dinky winky wonky donkey.

Q: What do you call a miniature donkey with one leg and one eye, makin' love while farting, wearing blue suede shoes, playing piano and driving a bus?

A: Fuckin' talented!

Woof

A cattle dog went to Australia Post, took out a blank form and wrote: 'Woof. Woof. Woof. Woof. Woof. Woof. Woof. Woof. Woof.'

The clerk examined the paper and politely told the dog: 'There are only nine words here. You could send another Woof for the same price.'

'But,' the dog replied, 'that would make no sense at all.'

Dead easy

A city boy, Rodney, moved to the country and bought a donkey from an old farmer for $100. The farmer agreed to deliver the donkey the next day.

The next day the farmer drove up and said, 'Sorry, son, but I have some bad news. The donkey died.'

Rodney replied, 'Well then, just give me my money back.'

The farmer said, 'Can't do that. I went and spent it already.'

Rodney said, 'OK then, at least give me the donkey.'

The farmer asked, 'What ya gonna do with him?'

Rodney: 'I'm going to raffle him off.'

Farmer: 'You can't raffle off a dead donkey!'

Rodney: 'Sure I can. Watch me. I just won't tell anybody he is dead.'

A month later the farmer met up with Rodney and asked, 'What happened with that dead donkey?'

Rodney: 'I raffled him off. I sold 500 tickets at $2 a piece and made a profit of $998.'

Farmer: 'Didn't anyone complain?'

Rodney: 'Just the guy who won. So I gave him his $2 back.'

Turtle talk

A turtle was walking down an alley in Kings Cross when a gang of snails mugged him. A police detective came to investigate and asked the turtle if he could explain what happened. The turtle looked at the detective with a confused expression on his face and replied, 'I don't know — it all happened so fast.'

Bully for you

A man took his wife to the rodeo and one of the exhibits featured breeding bulls. They went up to the first pen and there was a sign that said: THIS BULL MATED 50 TIMES LAST YEAR.

The wife poked her husband in the ribs and said, 'He mated 50 times last year.'

They walked a little further and saw another pen with a sign that said: THIS BULL MATED 120 TIMES LAST YEAR. The wife hit her husband and said, 'That's more than twice a week! You could learn a lot from him.'

They walked further and a third pen had a bull with a sign saying: THIS BULL MATED 365 TIMES LAST YEAR. The wife got really excited and said, 'That's once a day; you could *really* learn something from this one.'

The husband looked at his wife and said, 'Go up and ask him if it was with the same cow every time.'

Dog walker

A little girl asks her mum, 'Mum, may I take the dog for a walk around the block?'

Her mum replies, 'No, because she is in heat.'

'What does that mean?' asked the child.

'Go and ask your father. I think he is in the garage.'

The little girl goes out to the garage and says, 'Dad, may I take Belle for a walk around the block? I asked Mum, but she said the dog was in heat, and to come and ask you.'

Dad said, 'Bring Belle over here.'

He took a rag, soaked it with petrol, and scrubbed the dog's backside to disguise the scent, and said, 'OK, you can go now, but keep Belle on the leash, and only go one time round the block.'

The little girl left and returned a few minutes later with no dog. Surprised, Dad asked, 'Where's Belle?'

The little girl said, 'She ran out of petrol about halfway around the block — so another dog is pushing her home.'

A dog's life

On the first day God created the dog.

God said, 'Sit all day by the door of your house and bark at anyone who comes in or walks past. I will give you a life span of 20 years.'

The dog said, 'That's too long to be barking. Give me 10 years and I'll give you back the other 10.' God agreed.

On the second day God created the monkey. God said, 'Entertain people, do monkey tricks, make them laugh. I'll give you a 20-year life span.'

The monkey said, 'How boring — monkey tricks for 20 years? I don't think so. Dog gave you back 10, so that's what I'll do too, OK?' And God agreed.

On the third day God created the cow. God said, 'You must go to the field with the farmer all day long and suffer under the sun, have calves and give milk to support the farmer. I will give you a life span of 60 years.'

The cow said, 'That's kind of a tough life you want me to live for 60 years. Let me have 20 and I'll give back the other 40.' And God agreed again.

On the fourth day God created man. God said, 'Eat, sleep, play, marry and enjoy your life. I'll give you 20 years.'

Man said, 'What? Only 20 years! Tell you what, I'll take my 20, and the 40 the cow gave back and the 10 the monkey gave back and the 10 the dog gave back — that makes 80, OK?'

'OK,' said God. 'You've got a deal.'

So that is why for the first 20 years we eat, sleep, play, and enjoy ourselves; for the next 40 years we slave in the sun to support our family; for the next 10 years we do monkey tricks to entertain the grandchildren; and for the last 10 years we sit on the front verandah and bark at everyone.

At Taronga Park

A bloke starts his new job as a keeper at the zoo and is given three tasks.

First is to clear the exotic fish pool of weeds. As he does this a huge fish jumps out and bites him.

To show who is boss, he beats it to death with a shovel.

Realising the director won't be pleased, he disposes of the fish by feeding it to the lions, as lions will eat anything.

Moving on to the second job of clearing out the chimp house, he is attacked by the chimps, who pelt him with coconuts. He swipes at two chimps with a shovel, killing them both. What can he do? 'Feed them to the lions,' he says to himself, because lions eat anything. He hurls the corpses into the lion enclosure.

He moves on to the last job, which is to collect honey from the South American bees. As soon as he starts, the bees attack him. He grabs the shovel and smashes the bees to a pulp. By now he knows what to do and throws them into the lion's cage because lions eat anything.

Later that day a new lion arrives at the zoo. He wanders up to another lion and says, 'What's the food like here?'

The lion says: 'Absolutely brilliant. Today we had fish and chimps with mushy bees.'

The top 10 dog complaints about humans

1. Blaming your farts on me … not funny … not funny at all!
2. Yelling at me for barking … *I'm a fuckin' dog, you idiot!*
3. Taking me for a walk, then not letting me check stuff out. Exactly whose walk is this anyway?
4. Any trick that involves balancing food on my nose … stop it!
5. Any haircut that involves bows or ribbons. Now you know why we chew your stuff up when you're not home.
6. The sleight of hand, fake fetch throw. You fooled a dog!
   Whoooo hoooooooo! What a proud moment for the top of the food chain!

7. Taking me to the vet for 'the big snip', then acting surprised when I freak out every time we go back!
8. Getting upset when I sniff the crotches of your guests. Sorry, but I haven't quite mastered that handshake thing yet.
9. Dog sweaters. Hello? Haven't you noticed the fur?
10. How you act disgusted when I lick myself. Look, we both know the truth — you're just jealous.

Up Darwin way

Two crocodiles were sitting at the side of a river near Darwin, waiting for the tourist buses. The smaller croc turned to the bigger one and said, 'I can't understand how you can be so much bigger than me. We're the same age, we were the same size as kids. I just don't get it.'

'Well,' said the big crocodile, 'what you been eatin', boy?'

'Politicians, same as you,' replied the small croc.

'Hmm, well, where do you catch 'em?'

'Down at t'other side of the river, near the parkin' lot by Government House.'

'Same here. Hmm. How do you catch 'em?'

'Well, I crawl up under one of them Lexus cars and wait for someone to unlock the door. Then I jump out, grab 'em on the leg, shake the shit out of 'em, and eat 'em!'

'Ah!' said the big croc. 'I think I see your problem. You ain't gettin' any real nourishment. See, by the time you get done shakin' the shit out of a politician, there ain't nothin' left but lips and a briefcase!'

Service fee

A Croweater farmer got in his pickup, drove to a neighbouring farm and knocked at the farmhouse door. A young boy of about 12 opened the door.

'Is yer dad home?' the farmer asked.

'No, he ain't,' the boy replied. 'He went into town.'

'Well,' said the farmer, 'is yer mum here?'

'No, she ain't here neither. She went into town with Dad.'

'How about your brother, Howard? Is he here?'

'He went with Mum and Dad.'

The farmer stood there for a few minutes, shifting from one foot to the other and mumbling to himself.

'Is there anything I can do fer ya?' the boy asked politely. 'I know where all the tools are, if you want to borrow anything, or maybe I could take a message fer Dad.'

'Well,' said the farmer uncomfortably, 'I really wanted to talk to yer dad. It's about your brother Howard getting my daughter Betsy pregnant.'

The boy considered for a moment. 'You would have to talk to Dad about that,' he finally conceded. 'If it helps you any, I know that Dad charges $50 for the bull and $25 for the hog, but I really don't know how much he gets fer Howard.'

Bee-lieve it

Two bees met in a field. One said to the other, 'How are things going?'

'Really bad,' said the second bee. 'The weather has been cold, wet and damp, and there aren't any flowers, so I can't make honey.'

'No problem,' said the first bee. 'Just fly down five blocks and turn left. Keep going until you see all the cars. There's a Bar Mitzvah going on and there are all kinds of fresh flowers and fresh fruit.'

'Thanks for the tip,' said the second bee, and flew away.

A few hours later the two bees ran into each other again. The first bee asked, 'How'd it go?'

'Great!' said the second bee. 'It was everything you said it would be. There was plenty of fruit and, oh, such huge floral arrangements on every table.'

'Uh, what's that thing on your head?' asked the first bee.

'That's my yarmulke,' said the second bee. 'I didn't want them to think I was a WASP.'

Little Nancy and the parakeet

Little Nancy was in her family's garden filling in a hole when her neighbour peered over the fence. Interested in what the rosy-faced youngster was doing, he asked, 'What are you up to there, Nancy?'

'My parakeet died,' replied little Nancy tearfully without looking up, 'and I've just buried him.'

The neighbour chuckled and said condescendingly, 'That's a really big hole for a parakeet, isn't it?'

Little Nancy patted down the last heap of earth, then replied, 'That's because he's inside your fucking cat.'

Whales ahoy!

A male whale and a female whale were swimming off the coast of Japan when they noticed a whaling ship. The male whale recognised it as the same ship that had harpooned his father many years earlier. He said to the female whale, 'Let's both swim under the ship and blow out of our air holes at the same time and it should cause the ship to turn over and sink.'

They tried it and, sure enough, the ship turned over and quickly sank. Soon, however, the whales realised the sailors had jumped overboard and were swimming to the safety of shore. The male was enraged that they were going to get away and told the female, 'Let's swim after them and gobble them up before they reach the shore.'

At this point, he realised the female was becoming reluctant to follow him. 'Look,' she said, 'I went along with the blow job, but I absolutely refuse to swallow the seamen.'

A moral tale

An old man, a boy and a donkey were going to town.

The boy rode on the donkey and the old man walked. As they went along they passed some people who remarked it was a shame the old man was walking while the boy was riding. The man and boy thought maybe the critics were right, so they changed positions. Later, they passed some people who remarked, 'What a shame, he makes that little boy walk.' They then decided they both would walk. Soon they passed some more people who thought they were stupid to walk when they had a decent donkey to ride. So, they both rode the donkey.

Then they passed some people who shamed them by saying how awful to put such a load on a poor donkey. The boy and man said they were probably right, so they decided to carry the donkey. As they crossed the bridge, they lost their grip on the animal and it fell into the river and drowned.

The moral of the story? If you try to please everybody, you might as well kiss your ass goodbye.

Jesus is watching you

A burglar broke into a house one night. He shone his flashlight around, looking for valuables, and when he picked up a CD player to place in his sack, a strange, disembodied voice echoed from the dark, saying, 'Jesus is watching you.'

He nearly jumped out of his skin, clicked his flashlight off, and froze.

When he heard nothing, he shook his head and promised himself a holiday after the next big score. Then he clicked the light on and began searching for more valuables. Just as he pulled the stereo out so he could disconnect the wires, clear as a bell he heard, 'Jesus is watching you.'

Freaked out, he shone his light around frantically, looking for the source of the voice. Finally, in the corner of the room, his flashlight beam came to rest on a parrot.

'Did you say that?' he hissed at the parrot.

'Yep,' the parrot confessed, and then squawked, 'I'm just trying to warn you.'

The burglar relaxed. 'Warn me, huh? Who in the world are you?'

'Moses,' replied the bird.

'Moses?' the burglar laughed. 'What kind of people would name a bird "Moses"?'

'The same kind of people that would name a Rottweiler "Jesus".'

Talking parrots

A lady approaches her priest and tells him, 'Father, I have a problem. I have two female talking parrots, but they only know how to say one thing.'

'What do they say?' the priest inquired.

'They only know how to say, "Hi, we're prostitutes. Want to have some fun?"'

'That's terrible,' the priest exclaimed, 'but I have a solution to your problem. Bring your two female parrots over to my house and I will put them with my two male talking parrots that I taught to pray and read the Bible. My parrots will teach your parrots to stop saying that terrible phrase and your female parrots will learn to praise and worship.'

'Thank you!' the woman responded.

The next day the woman brought her female parrots to the priest's house. His two male parrots were holding rosary beads and praying in their cage. The lady put her two female parrots in with the male parrots, and the female parrots said, 'Hi, we're prostitutes. Want to have some fun?'

One male parrot looked over at the other male parrot and exclaimed, 'Quick! Put the beads away. Our prayers have been answered!'

A man and his dog

A man and his dog were walking along a road. The man was enjoying the scenery when it suddenly occurred to him that he was dead.

He remembered dying, and that the dog walking beside him had been dead for years. He wondered where the road was leading them.

After a while, they came to a high, white stone wall along one side of the road. It looked like fine marble. It stood at the top of a long hill and was broken by a tall arch that glowed in the sunlight. Standing before it he saw a magnificent gate that looked like mother-of-pearl, and the street that led to the gate looked like pure gold.

He and the dog walked towards the gate, and as he got closer, he saw a man at a desk to one side. When he was close enough, he called out, 'Excuse me, where are we?'

'This is heaven, sir,' the man answered.

'Wow! Would you happen to have some water?' the traveller asked.

'Of course, sir, come right in, and I'll have some ice water brought right up.' The man gestured, and the gate began to open.

'Can my friend come in, too?' the traveller asked, indicating his dog.

'I'm sorry, sir, but we don't accept pets.'

The man thought a moment and then turned back towards the road and continued the way he had been going with his dog.

After another long walk, and at the top of another long hill, he came to a dirt road, which led through a farm gate that looked as if it had never been closed.

There was no fence. As he approached the gate, he saw a man inside, leaning against a tree and reading a book. 'Excuse me!' he called to the reader. 'Do you have any water?'

'Yeah, sure, there's a pump over there.' The man pointed to a place that couldn't be seen from outside the gate. 'Come on in.'

'How about my friend here?' the traveller gestured to the dog.

'There should be a bowl by the pump.'

They went through the gate, and sure enough, there was an old-fashioned hand pump with a bowl beside it.

The traveller filled the bowl and took a long drink himself, then he gave some to the dog. When they were full, he and the dog walked back towards the man who was standing by the tree waiting for them.

'What do you call this place?' the traveller asked.

'This is heaven,' the man answered.

'Well, that's confusing,' the traveller said. 'The man down the road said that was heaven, too.'

'Oh, you mean the place with the gold street and pearly gates? Nope. That's hell.'

'Doesn't it make you mad for them to use your name like that?'

'No. I can see how you might think so, but we're just happy that they screen out the folks who'd leave their best friends behind.'

Hold on!

Jack was lonely and decided life would be more fun if he had a pet. So he went to the pet store and told the owner he wanted to buy an unusual pet. After some discussion, he finally bought a centipede, which came in a little white box to use for his house.

He took the box back home, found a good location for it, and decided he would start off by taking his new pet to the pub to have a drink.

So he asked the centipede in the box, 'Would you like to go to Frank's with me and have a beer?'

But there was no answer from his new pet. This bothered him a bit, but he waited a few minutes and then asked him again, 'How about going to the pub and having a drink with me?'

But again, there was no answer. So he waited a few minutes more, thinking about the situation.

He decided to ask him one more time, this time putting his face up against the centipede's house and shouting, 'Hey in there! Would you like to go to Frank's place and have a drink with me?'

A little voice came out of the box: 'I heard you the first time! I'm putting on my shoes.'

The lion tamer

A circus owner runs an advertisement for a lion tamer and two people show up. One is a good-looking older man in his mid-60s, and the other is a gorgeous blonde in her mid-20s.

The circus owner tells them, 'I'm not going to sugar coat it. This is one ferocious lion. He ate my last tamer so you guys better be good or you're history. Here's your equipment — chair, whip and a gun. Who wants to start?'

The girl says, 'I will.' She walks past the chair, the whip and the gun and steps right into the lion's cage. The lion starts to snarl and pant and begins to charge her. When the lion is about halfway there, she throws open her coat revealing her beautiful naked body. The lion stops dead in his tracks, sheepishly crawls up to her and starts licking her feet and ankles. He continues to lick and kiss her entire body for several minutes and then rests his head at her feet.

The circus owner's mouth is on the floor. He says, 'I've never seen a display like that in my life.' He then turns to the older man and asks, 'Can you top that?'

The older man replies, 'No problem. Just get that lion out of the way.'

The horse whisperer

A fellow calls his mate, a horse breeder, and says he's sending a friend over to look at a horse.

His friend asks, 'How will I recognise him?'

'That's easy — he's a very small person with a speech impediment.'

So the midget shows up, and the guy asks him if he's looking for a male or female horse.

'A female horth.'

So he shows him a prized filly.

'Nith lookin' horth. Can I thee her eyeth?'

So the bloke picks up the little fellow and he gives the horse's eyes the once over.

'Nith eyeth; can I thee her earzth?'

So he picks the little fella up again, and shows him the horse's ears.

'Nith earzth; can I see her mouf?'

The breeder is getting pretty ticked off by this point, but he picks him up again and shows him the horse's mouth.

'Nice mouf; can I see her twat?'

Mad as hell at this point, the breeder grabs the midget under his arms and rams his head as far as he can up the horse's arse, pulls him out, and slams him on the ground.

The midget gets up, wiping his eyes, sputtering and coughing. 'Perhapth I thould rephrase that — can I thee her wun awound a widdle bit?'

The Great Lobster Ball

Duncan the humble crab and Katie the lobster princess were madly, deeply and passionately in love. For months they enjoyed an idyllic relationship until one day Katie scuttled over to Duncan in tears.

'We can't see each other any more,' she sobbed.

'Why?' gasped Duncan.

'Daddy says that crabs are too common,' she wailed. 'He claims you are a mere crab, and a poor one at that, and crabs are the lowest class of crustacean … and that no daughter of his will marry someone who can only walk sideways.'

Duncan was shattered, and scuttled sidewards away into the darkness to drink himself into a filthy state of aquatic oblivion.

That night, the Great Lobster Ball was taking place. Lobsters came from far and wide, for dancing and merry-making, but the lobster princess refused to join in, choosing instead to sit by her father's side, inconsolable.

Suddenly the doors burst open, and Duncan strode in. The lobsters all stopped their dancing, the princess gasped and King Lobster rose from his throne. Slowly, painstakingly, Duncan made his way across the floor. All could see that he was walking, not sideways, but *forwards*, one claw after another!

Step by step he made his approach towards the throne, until he finally looked King Lobster in the eye. There was a deadly hush for quite a while.

Finally, Duncan spoke: 'Shit! I'm pissed.'

Odd couple

A man goes into a pub with an emu and a pussycat.

He orders a beer, the emu orders a whisky and the cat says, 'I'd like a gin cocktail and I'm not paying for it.'

The same scenario occurs every night, always with the pussycat saying, 'I'd like a drink but I'm not paying for it.'

Finally the barman asks, 'What's going on here?'

The man replies, 'Well, it's the usual story. I was out in the shed and found an old bottle. I rubbed it and out came a genie who offered me a couple of wishes and I said I'd like a bird with long legs and a tight pussy. So look what I'm stuck with.'

Croak

A woman went into a store to buy her husband a pet for his birthday. After looking around, she found that all the pets were very expensive. She told the clerk she wanted to buy a pet, but she didn't want to spend a fortune.

'Well,' said the clerk, 'I have a very large bullfrog. They say it's been trained to give blow jobs!'

'Blow jobs!' the woman replied.

'It hasn't been proven but we've sold 30 of them this month,' he said.

The woman thought it would be a great gag gift, and what if it was true: no more blow jobs for her!

She bought the frog. When she explained the frog's ability to her husband, he was extremely sceptical and laughed it off. However, the woman went to bed happy, thinking she may never need to perform this less-than-riveting act again.

In the middle of the night, she was awakened by the noise of pots and pans flying everywhere, making raucous banging and crashing sounds. She ran downstairs to the kitchen, only to find her husband and the frog reading cookbooks.

'What are you two doing at this hour?' she asked.

The husband replied, 'If I can teach this frog to cook, you're gone!'

For dog and cat lovers

Adam and Eve said, 'Lord, when we were in the garden, you walked with us every day. Now we do not see you any more. We are lonesome here, and it is difficult for us to remember how much you love us.'

And God said, 'No problem! I will create a companion for you who will be with you forever and who will be a reflection of my love for you, so that you will love me even when you cannot see me.

Regardless of how selfish or childish or unlovable you may be, this new companion will accept you as you are and will love you as I do, in spite of yourselves.'

And God created a new animal to be a companion for Adam and Eve. And it was a good animal, and God was pleased. And the new animal was pleased to be with Adam and Eve and he wagged his tail.

And Adam said, 'Lord, I have already named all the animals in the kingdom and I cannot think of a name for this new animal.'

And God said, 'No problem. Because I have created this new animal to be a reflection of my love for you, his name will be a reflection of my own name, and you will call him Dog.'

And Dog lived with Adam and Eve and was a companion to them and loved them. And they were comforted. And God was pleased. And Dog was content and wagged his tail.

After a while, it came to pass that an angel came to the Lord and said, 'Lord, Adam and Eve have become filled with pride. They strut and preen like peacocks and they believe they are worthy of adoration. Dog has indeed taught them that they are loved, but perhaps too well.'

And God said, 'No problem! I will create for them a new companion who will be with them forever and who will see them as they are. The companion will remind them of their limitations, so they will know that they are not always worthy of adoration.'

And God created Cat to be a companion to Adam and Eve.

And Cat would not obey them. And when Adam and Eve gazed into Cat's eyes, they were reminded that they were not the supreme beings. And Adam and Eve learnt humility. And they were greatly improved. And God was pleased.

And Dog was happy. And Cat didn't care one way or the other.

How many dogs does it take to change a light bulb?

Golden Retriever: 'The sun is shining, the day is young, we've got our whole lives ahead of us and you're inside worrying about a stupid burned-out bulb.'

Border Collie: 'Just one. And then I'll replace any wiring that's not up to code and repaint the wall, where you scuffed it in the dark, before moving on to the plumbing.'

Dachshund: 'You know I can't reach that stupid lamp!'

Rottweiler: 'Make me.'

Boxer: 'Who cares? I can play with my squeaky toy in the dark.'

Lab: 'Oh, me, me! Pleeeeeeeeeeeze let me change the light bulb! Can I? Can I? Huh? Huh? Huh? Can I? Pleeeeeeeze, please, please, please pick me!'

German Shepherd: 'I'll change it as soon as I've led everyone from the dark room, made sure no one was hurt, checked to make sure I haven't missed any, and made one more perimeter patrol to see that no one has tried to take advantage of the dark situation.'

Jack Russell: 'I'll just pop it in while I'm bouncing off the walls and furniture.'

Old English Sheepdog: 'Light bulb? I don't see a light bulb, I don't see a lamp. Where am I? Where are you?'

Cocker Spaniel: 'Why change it? If I pee on the carpet in the dark I won't get caught till you step in it.'

Chihuahua: 'Yo quiero Taco Bulb.'

Pointer: 'I see it, there it is, there it is … right there.'

Greyhound: 'It isn't moving, so who cares?'

Blue Heeler: 'First, let me put all the light bulbs in a little circle.'

Poodle: 'I'll just blow in the Border Collie's ear and he'll do it. By the time he finishes rewiring the house, my nails will be dry.'

Tall one

A man walks into a restaurant with a full-grown emu behind him, and as he sits, the waitress comes over and asks for their order.

The man says, 'I'll have a hamburger, fries and a Coke, please,' and turns to the emu. 'What's yours?'

'I'll have the same,' says the emu.

A short time later the waitress returns with the order. 'That will be $6.40, please,' she says, and the man reaches into his pocket and pulls out exact change for payment.

The next day, the man and the emu come again and the man says, 'I'll have a hamburger, fries and a Coke, please,' and the emu says, 'I'll have the same.' Once again the man reaches into his pocket and pays with exact change.

This becomes a routine until late one evening the two enter again.

'The usual?' asks the waitress.

'No, this is Friday night, so I will have a steak, baked potato and salad,' says the man. 'Same for me,' says the emu.

A short time later the waitress comes with the order and says, 'That will be $12.62.' Once again the man pulls exact change out of his pocket and places it on the table.

The waitress can't hold back her curiosity any longer. 'Excuse me, sir. How do you manage to always come up with the exact change out of your pocket every time?'

'Well,' says the man, 'several years ago I was cleaning the attic and I found an old lamp. When I rubbed it a genie appeared and offered me two wishes. My first wish was that if I ever had to pay for anything, I'd just put my hand in my pocket, and the right amount of money would always be there.'

'That's brilliant!' says the waitress. 'Most people would wish for a million dollars or something, but you'll always be as rich as you want for as long as you live!'

'That's right! Whether it's a litre of milk or a Rolls-Royce, the exact money is always there,' says the man.

The waitress asks, 'One other thing, sir — what's with the emu?'

The man sighs and answers, 'My second wish was for a tall chick with long legs who agrees with everything I say!'

In there somewhere

A man was helping one of his cows give birth, when he noticed his 11-year-old son standing wide-eyed at the fence, soaking in the whole event. The man thought, 'Great … he's 11 and now I'm gonna have to start explaining the birds and bees. No need to jump the gun — I'll just let him ask, and I'll answer.'

After everything was over, the man walked over to his son and said, 'Well, son, do you have any questions?'

'Just one, Dad,' gasped the still wide-eyed lad.

Just as the father was preparing his birds and bees story, his son asked: 'How fast was that calf going when he hit that cow?'

On safari

A wealthy old lady decides to go on a photo safari in Africa. She takes her beloved pet dachshund along for company. One day, the dachshund starts chasing butterflies and before long he discovers that he is lost. So, wandering about, he notices a leopard heading rapidly in his direction with the obvious intention of having him for lunch. The dachshund thinks, 'OK, I'm in deep trouble now!' Then he sees some bones on the ground close by, and immediately settles down to chew on them, with his back to the approaching cat. Just as the leopard is about to leap, the dachshund exclaims loudly, 'Boy, that was one delicious leopard. I wonder if there are any more around here.'

Hearing this, the leopard halts his attack in mid-stride, a look of terror comes over him, and he slinks away into the trees. 'Whew,' says the leopard. 'That was close. That dachshund nearly had me.'

Meanwhile, a monkey — who had been watching the whole scene from a nearby tree — figures he can put this knowledge to good use and trade it for protection from the leopard. So, off he goes. But the dachshund sees him heading after the leopard with great speed, and realises that something must be up. The monkey soon catches up with the leopard, spills the beans and strikes a deal for himself with the leopard.

The leopard is furious at being made a fool of and says, 'Here, monkey, hop on my back and see what's going to happen to that conniving canine.'

Now the dachshund sees the leopard coming with the monkey on his back, and thinks, 'What am I going to do now?' But instead of running, he coolly sits down with his back to his attackers, pretending he hasn't seen them yet, and just when they get close enough to hear, he says, 'Where's that damn monkey? I sent him off half an hour ago to bring me another leopard!'

Moral: if you can't dazzle them with brilliance, baffle them with bullshit.

Royal corgis

Prince Charles drove over one of the Queen's corgis and flattened it. Trying to revive it, he accidentally kicked a discarded gin bottle, from which a genie flew out.

The genie shook itself and offered, 'Phew, thanks, I've been stuck in that old bottle for a while. For that you can have one wish.'

Prince Charles replied, 'Can you bring the corgi back to life or my name will be mud with Mummy.'

Genie: 'Gee, sorry, but I'm only a minor genie and that's too big an ask. Anything else?'

Prince Charles: 'Can you make Camilla as beautiful as Diana was?'

Genie: 'Hmm, let's have another look at that corgi.'

The parrot

Wanda's dishwasher stopped working so she called a repairman.

Since she had to go to work the next day, she told the repairman, 'I'll leave the key under the mat. Fix the dishwasher, leave the bill on the counter, and I'll mail you a cheque. Oh, by the way, don't worry about my bulldog. He won't bother you. But, whatever you do, do *not*, under *any* circumstances, talk to my parrot! *I repeat, do not talk to my parrot!*'

When the repairman arrived at Wanda's apartment the following day, he discovered the biggest, meanest-looking bulldog he had ever seen. But, as she'd said, the dog just lay there on the carpet watching the repairman go about his work.

The parrot, however, drove him nuts the whole time with his incessant yelling, cursing and name-calling. Finally the repairman couldn't contain himself any longer and yelled, 'Shut up, you stupid ugly bird!'

To which the parrot replied, 'Get him, Spike!'

Pet instructions

Dear dogs and cats:

When I say to move, it means go someplace else — not switch positions with each other so there are still two of you in the way.

The dishes with the paw print are yours and contain your food. The other dishes are mine and contain my food. Please note: placing a paw print in the middle of my plate or food does not stake a claim for it becoming your food and dish. Nor do I find that aesthetically pleasing in the slightest.

The stairway is not a racetrack. Beating me to the bottom is not the object. Tripping me doesn't help, because I fall faster than you can run.

I cannot buy anything bigger than a king-size bed. I am very sorry about this. Do not think I will continue to sleep on the couch to ensure your comfort. Look at videos of dogs and cats sleeping. They can actually curl up in a ball. It is not necessary to sleep perpendicular to each other and stretched out to the fullest extent possible. I also know that sticking tails straight out and having tongues hanging out the other end to maximise space used is nothing but sarcasm.

My compact discs are not miniature Frisbees.

For the last time, there is not a secret exit from the bathroom. If by some miracle I beat you there and manage to get the door shut, it is not necessary to claw, whine, and try to turn the knob, or get your paw under the edge and try to pull the door open. I must exit through the same door I entered. In addition, I have been using bathrooms for years; canine attendance is not mandatory.

And finally, the proper order is: 1) kiss me, and then 2) go smell the other dog's butt. I cannot stress this enough. It would be such a simple change for you and contribute enormously to our continuing relationship.

Excerpts from a dog's diary

Day number 180

8.00 a.m. — OH BOY! DOG FOOD! MY FAVOURITE!

9.30 a.m. — OH BOY! A CAR RIDE! MY FAVOURITE!

9.40 a.m. — OH BOY! A WALK! MY FAVOURITE!

10.30 a.m. — OH BOY! A CAR RIDE! MY FAVOURITE!

11.30 a.m. — OH BOY! DOG FOOD! MY FAVOURITE!

12.00 noon — OH BOY! THE KIDS! MY FAVOURITE!

1.00 p.m. — OH BOY! THE GARDEN! MY FAVOURITE!

4.00 p.m. — OH BOY! THE KIDS! MY FAVOURITE!

5.00 p.m. — OH BOY! DOG FOOD! MY FAVOURITE!

5.30 p.m. — OH BOY! MUM! MY FAVOURITE!

Day number 181

8.00 a.m. — OH BOY! DOG FOOD! MY FAVOURITE!

9.30 a.m. — OH BOY! A CAR RIDE! MY FAVOURITE!

9.40 a.m. — OH BOY! A WALK! MY FAVOURITE!

10.30 a.m. — OH BOY! A CAR RIDE! MY FAVOURITE!

11.30 a.m. — OH BOY! DOG FOOD! MY FAVOURITE!

12.00 noon — OH BOY! THE KIDS! MY FAVOURITE!

1.00 p.m. — OH BOY! THE GARDEN! MY FAVOURITE!

4.00 p.m. — OH BOY! THE KIDS! MY FAVOURITE!

5.00 p.m. — OH BOY! DOG FOOD! MY FAVOURITE!

5.30 p.m. — OH BOY! MUM! MY FAVOURITE!

Day number 182

8.00 a.m. — OH BOY! DOG FOOD! MY FAVOURITE!

9.30 a.m. — OH BOY! A CAR RIDE! MY FAVOURITE!

9.40 a.m. — OH BOY! A WALK! MY FAVOURITE!

10.30 a.m. — OH BOY! A CAR RIDE! MY FAVOURITE!

11.30 a.m. — OH BOY! DOG FOOD! MY FAVOURITE!

12.00 noon — OH BOY! THE KIDS! MY FAVOURITE!

1.00 p.m. — OH BOY! THE GARDEN! MY FAVOURITE!

4.00 p.m. — OH BOY! THE KIDS! MY FAVOURITE!

5.00 p.m. — OH BOY! DOG FOOD! MY FAVOURITE!

5.30 p.m. — OH BOY! MUM! MY FAVOURITE!

Excerpts from a cat's diary

Day 752

My captors continue to taunt me with bizarre little dangling objects. They dine lavishly on fresh meat, while I am forced to eat dry cereal. The only thing that keeps me going is the hope of escape, and the mild satisfaction I get from ruining the occasional piece of furniture. Tomorrow I may eat another houseplant.

Day 761

Today my attempt to kill my captors by weaving around their feet while they were walking almost succeeded; must try this at the top of the stairs. In an attempt to disgust and repulse these vile oppressors, I once again induced myself to vomit on their favourite chair; must try this on their bed.

Day 765

Decapitated a mouse and brought them the headless body, in attempt to make them aware of what I am capable of, and to try to strike fear into their hearts. They only cooed and condescended about what a good little cat I was … Hmmm. Not working according to plan.

Day 768

I am finally aware of how sadistic they are. For no good reason I was chosen for the water torture. This time, however, it included a burning foamy chemical called 'shampoo'. What sick minds could invent such a liquid? My only consolation is the piece of thumb still stuck between my teeth.

Day 771

There was some sort of gathering of their accomplices. I was placed in solitary throughout the event. However, I could hear the noise and smell the foul odour of the glass tubes they call 'beer'. More importantly I overheard that my confinement was due to *my* power of 'allergies'. Must learn what this is and how to use it to my advantage.

Day 774

I am convinced the other captives are flunkies and maybe snitches. The dog is routinely released and seems more than happy to return. He is obviously a half-wit. The bird on the other hand has got to be an informant, and speaks with them regularly. I am certain he reports my every move. Due to his current placement in the metal room his safety is assured.

But I can wait; it is only a matter of time …

The parrot's question

A young man named John received a parrot as a gift. Unfortunately, the parrot had a really bad attitude and an even worse vocabulary. All of its behaviour was rough and rowdy, and every word out of the bird's mouth was rude, obnoxious and laced with profanity.

John tried and tried to change the bird's attitude. He consistently would say only polite words and play soft music and did anything else he could think of to try to 'clean up' the bird's vocabulary and behaviour.

Finally, one day John was totally fed up and he yelled at the parrot. The parrot yelled back. John shook the parrot and the parrot got angrier and even ruder. John, in desperation, threw up his hand, grabbed the bird and shoved him into the freezer. For a few minutes the parrot squawked and kicked and screamed. Then suddenly there was total quiet. Not a peep was heard for over a minute. Fearing that he'd hurt the parrot, John quickly opened the door to the freezer.

The parrot calmly stepped out onto John's outstretched arms and said in an amazingly civilised tone, 'I believe I may have offended you with my rude language and actions. I'm sincerely remorseful for my inappropriate transgressions and I fully intend to do everything I can to correct my rude and unforgivable behaviour.'

John was stunned at the change in the bird's attitude. As he was about to ask the parrot what had caused such a dramatic change in his behaviour, the bird continued, 'May I ask what the turkey did?'

Guilt

Doctor Bob had slept with one of his patients and had felt guilty all day long. No matter how much he tried to forget about it, he couldn't. The guilt and sense of betrayal were overwhelming. But every once in a while he'd hear that soothing voice within, trying to reassure him: 'Bob, don't worry about it. You aren't the first doctor to sleep with one of their patients … and you won't be the last. Just let it go.'

But invariably another voice would bring him back to reality: 'Bob, you're a vet.'

Put him down

A man takes his Rottweiler to the vet and says, 'My dog's cross-eyed. Is there anything you can do for him?'

'Well,' says the vet, 'let's have a look at him.'

So he picks the dog up and examines his eyes, then checks his teeth. Finally, he says, 'I'm going to have to put him down.'

'What? Because he's cross-eyed?'

'No, because he's really heavy.'

The three bears

Baby Bear goes downstairs and sits in his small chair at the table. He looks into his small bowl. It is empty. 'Who's been eating my porridge?' he squeaks.

Papa Bear arrives at the big table and sits in his big chair. He looks into his big bowl, and it is also empty. 'Who's been eating my porridge?' he roars.

Momma Bear puts her head through the serving hatch from the kitchen and yells, 'For goodness sake, how many times do we have to go through this with you idiots? It was Momma Bear who got up first, it was Momma Bear who woke everyone in the house, it was Momma Bear who made the coffee, it was Momma Bear who unloaded the dishwasher, and put everything away, it was Momma Bear who went out in the cold early morning air to fetch the newspaper, it was Momma Bear who set the table, it was Momma Bear who put the frigging cat out, cleaned the litter box, and filled the cat's water and food dish, and, now that you've decided to drag your sorry bear-carcasses downstairs and grace Momma Bear's kitchen with your grumpy presence, listen good, 'cause I'm only going to say this one more time. *I haven't made the fucking porridge yet!*'

Inner strength

If you can start the day without caffeine or pep pills,
If you can be cheerful, ignoring aches and pains,
If you can resist complaining and boring people with your troubles,
If you can eat the same food every day and be grateful for it,
If you can understand when loved ones are too busy to give you time,
If you can overlook when people take things out on you when, through no
    fault of yours, something goes wrong,
If you can take criticism and blame without resentment,
If you can face the world without lies and deceit,
If you can conquer tension without medical help,
If you can relax without liquor,
If you can sleep without the aid of drugs,
If you can do all these things …
Then you are probably the family dog!

Talking dog

This bloke sees a sign in front of a house: 'Talking Dog for Sale'. He rings the bell and the owner tells him the dog is in the backyard. The guy goes into the backyard and sees a mutt sitting there.

'You talk?' he asks.

'Yep,' the dog replies.

Our man can't resist asking, 'So, what's your story?'

The mutt looks up and says: 'Well, I discovered this when I was pretty young and I wanted to help the government, so I told ASIO about my gift, and in no time they had me jetting from country to country, sitting in rooms with spies and world leaders, 'cause no one figured a dog would be eavesdropping. I was one of their most valuable spies eight years running. The jetting around really tired me out, and I knew I wasn't getting any younger and I wanted to settle down. So I signed up for a job at the airport to do some undercover security work, mostly wandering near suspicious characters and listening in. I uncovered some incredible dealings there and was awarded a batch of medals. Had a wife, a mess of puppies, and now I'm just retired.'

The bloke is amazed. He goes back in and asks the owner what he wants for the dog. The owner says, 'Ten dollars.'

Our friend says he'll buy him but asks the owner, 'This dog is amazing. Why on earth are you selling him?'

The owner replies, 'Because he's a liar and can't keep his mouth shut.'

Turtle picnic

Three turtles, Joe, Steve and Raymond, decide to go on a picnic.

So Joe packs the picnic basket with biscuits, bottled drinks and sandwiches. The trouble is that the picnic site is 10 kilometres away so the turtles take 10 whole days to get there. By the time they do arrive, everyone's exhausted.

Joe takes the stuff out of the basket. He takes out the drinks and says, 'All right, Steve, gimme the bottle opener.'

'I didn't bring the bottle opener,' Steve says. 'I thought you packed it.'

Joe gets worried. He turns to Raymond. 'Raymond, do you have the bottle opener?'

Naturally, Raymond doesn't have it, so the turtles are stuck 10 kilometres away from home without drinks. Joe and Steve beg Raymond to turn back home and retrieve it, but Raymond flatly refuses, knowing that they'll eat everything by the time he gets back. After about two hours, the turtles manage to convince Raymond to go, swearing on their great-grand-turtles' graves that they won't touch the food. So, Raymond sets off down the road, slow and steadily.

Twenty days pass, but no Raymond. Joe and Steve are hungry and puzzled, but a promise is a promise. Another day passes, and still no Raymond, but a promise is a promise.

After three more days pass without Raymond in sight, Steve starts getting restless. '*I need food!*' he says, with a hint of dementia in his voice.

'*No!*' Joe retorts. 'We promised.'

Five more days pass. Joe realises that Raymond probably skipped out to the cafe down the road, so the two turtles weakly lift the lid, get a sandwich, and open their mouths to eat. But suddenly, right at that instant, Raymond pops out from behind a rock, and says: 'I knew it! I'm not fucking going back for the bloody bottle opener.'

Fowl play

Jake was in the fertilised egg business. He had several hundred young layers, called pullets, and eight or 10 roosters, whose job was to fertilise the eggs.

Jake kept records, and any rooster that didn't perform well went into the soup pot and was replaced. That took an awful lot of Jake's time, so he got a set of tiny bells and attached them to his roosters. Each bell had a different tone so that he could tell, from a distance, which rooster was performing. Now he could sit on the porch and fill out an efficiency report simply by listening to the bells.

Jake's favourite rooster was old Brewster. A very fine specimen he was, too. But on this particular morning, Jake noticed that Brewster's bell had not rung at all! So he went to investigate.

The other roosters were chasing pullets, bells a-ringing! The pullets, hearing the roosters coming, would run for cover. But, to Jake's amazement, Brewster had his bell in his beak, so it couldn't ring. He'd sneak up on a pullet, do his job and walk on to the next one.

Jake was so proud of Brewster that he entered him in the county show.

Brewster was an overnight sensation.

The judges not only awarded him the No Bell Piece Prize but also the Pullet Surprise.

Seeking companionship

The following advertisement appeared in a rural newspaper.

Single black female seeks male companionship, ethnicity unimportant.

I am a very good-looking girl who loves to play. I love long walks in the woods, riding in ute, hunting, camping, and fishing trips, cosy winter nights lying by the fire. Candlelight dinners will have me eating out of your hand. Rub me the right way and watch me respond. I'll be at the front door when you get home from work, wearing only what nature gave me.

Kiss me and I'm yours.
Call xxx-xxxx and ask for Daisy.

Over 10,000 men found themselves talking to the local Humane Society about an eight-week-old black labrador retriever.

Men are so easy!

How much can a koala bear?

A koala and a hooker go back to her place and they get undressed. The koala goes down on the hooker for three hours straight. She has multiple orgasms! After three hours he stops, gets up and puts on his little koala clothes.

The woman is hanging back, huffing and puffing from exhaustion. 'Oh, God, that was great! Now I need my money.'

The koala just looks at her and shrugs.

Then the hooker says, 'No, I need my money. I'm a hooker and this is how I make a living.'

The koala just looks at her and continues to put on his clothes. Then the hooker gets up and runs to the bookshelf, grabs a dictionary and thumbs through it to 'hooker'. She hands the dictionary to the koala, and it reads:

HOOKER: Person who has sex for money.

Then the koala turns the page to 'koala' and walks out the door.

KOALA: Eats bushes and leaves.

Raw prawns

Far away in the warm waters of the Gulf of Carpentaria, two prawns were swimming around in the sea — one called Justin and the other called Christian. The prawns were constantly being harassed and threatened by sharks that patrolled the area. Finally, one day Justin said to Christian, 'I'm bored and frustrated at being a prawn. I wish I was a shark, then I wouldn't have any worries about being eaten …'

As Justin had his mind firmly on becoming a predator, a mysterious cod appeared and said, 'Your wish is granted,' and lo and behold, Justin turned into a shark. Horrified, Christian immediately swam away, afraid of being eaten by his old mate.

Time went on and Justin found himself becoming bored and lonely as a shark. All his old mates simply swam away whenever he came close to them. Justin didn't realise that his new menacing appearance was the cause of his sad plight. While out swimming alone one day he saw the mysterious cod again and couldn't believe his luck. Justin figured that the fish could change him back into a prawn. He begged the cod to change him back and instantly he was turned back into a prawn.

With tears of joy in his tiny little eyes, Justin swam back to his friends and bought them all a cocktail. (The punch line does not involve a prawn cocktail — it's much worse.) Looking around the gathering at the reef, he searched for his old pal. 'Where's Christian?' he asked.

'He's at home, distraught that his best friend changed sides to the enemy and became a shark,' came the reply.

Eager to put things right again and end the mutual pain and torture, he set off to Christian's house. As he opened the coral gate the memories came flooding back. He banged on the door and shouted, 'It's me, Justin, your old friend — come out and see me again.'

Christian replied, 'No way, man, you'll eat me. You're a shark, the enemy, and I'll not be tricked.'

Justin cried back, 'No, I'm not. That was the old me. I've changed … I've found Cod. I'm a prawn again, Christian.'

Go, Colin, go

Colin the rooster cost a lot of money, but the farmer decides he'd be worth it, so he buys him. The farmer takes Colin home and sets him down in the barnyard, first giving the rooster a pep talk. 'I want you to pace yourself now. You've got a lot of chickens to service here, and you cost me a lot of money. Consequently, I'll need you to do a good job. So, take your time and have some fun,' the farmer says, with a chuckle.

Colin seems to understand, so the farmer points towards the hen house and Colin takes off like a shot. WHAM! Colin nails every hen three or four times, and the farmer is really shocked. Then the farmer hears a commotion in the duck pen; sure enough, Colin is in there too. Later, the farmer sees Colin after a flock of geese down by the lake. Once again — WHAM! He gets all the geese. By sunset he sees Colin out in the fields chasing quail and pheasants. The farmer is distraught and worried that his expensive rooster won't even last 24 hours. Sure enough, the farmer goes to bed and wakes up the next day, to find Colin on his back, stone-cold still in the middle of the yard, vultures circling overhead. The farmer, saddened by the loss of such a colourful and expensive animal, shakes his head and says, 'Oh, Colin, I told you to pace yourself. I tried to get you to slow down — now look what you've done to yourself.'

Colin opens one eye, nods towards the vultures circling in the sky and says, 'Shhh, they're getting closer.'

Mission impossible

There is a space shuttle mission to the moon with two monkeys and a woman on board. The control centre in the US calls: 'Monkey number 1, Monkey number 1 to the television screen.'

The first monkey sits down and is told to release the pressure in compartment one, increase the temperature in engine four and to release oxygen to the reactors. So the monkey does the pressure, temperature, and releases the oxygen.

A few moments later the control centre calls again: 'Monkey number 2, Monkey number 2 to the television screen.'

The second monkey sits down and is told to add carbon dioxide to room four, to stop the fuel injection to engine three, to add nitrogen to the fuel compartment and to analyse the solar radiation. So the monkey does the carbon dioxide, the fuel injection, the nitrogen and the analysis of solar radiation.

A little later on, headquarters calls again: 'Woman, please, woman, approach the screen.'

The woman sits down and just as she is about to be told what to do, she says: 'I know, I know! Feed the monkeys, and don't touch anything.'

Crocodiles

A man walks into a hotel bar with a pet crocodile by his side. He puts the croc up on the bar. He turns to the astonished patrons. 'I'll make you a deal. I will open this crocodile's mouth and place my genitals inside. Then the croc will close his mouth for one minute. He will then open his mouth and I will remove my parts unscathed. In return for witnessing this spectacle, each of you will buy me a drink.'

The crowd murmured their approval. The man stood up on the bar, dropped his trousers, and placed his privates in the croc's open mouth. The croc closed his mouth as the crowd gasped.

After a minute, the man grabbed a beer bottle and rapped the crocodile hard on the top of its head. The beast opened his mouth and the man removed his genitals unscathed as promised. The crowd cheered and the first of his free drinks was delivered. The man stood up again and made another offer. 'I'll pay anyone $100 who's willing to give it a try.'

A hush fell over the crowd. After a while, a hand went up in the back of the bar. A blonde woman timidly spoke up. 'I'll try, but you have to promise not to hit me on the head with the beer bottle.'

Animal farm

A woman went to her boyfriend's parents' house for dinner. This was to be her first time meeting the family, and she was very nervous.

They all sat down and began eating a fine meal. The woman was beginning to feel a little discomfort, thanks to her nervousness and the broccoli casserole. The gas pains were making her eyes water. Left with no other choice, she decided to relieve herself a bit and let out a dainty fart. It wasn't loud, but everyone at the table heard the *poof.* Before she even had a chance to be embarrassed, her boyfriend's father looked over at the dog which had been snoozing at the woman's feet and said in a rather stern voice, 'Skippy!'

The woman thought, 'This is great!' and a big smile came across her face. A few minutes later, she was beginning to feel the gas pain again. This time, she didn't even hesitate. She let a much louder and longer fart rip.

The father again looked at the dog and yelled, 'Dammit, Skippy!'

Once again the woman smiled and thought, 'Yes!' A few minutes later, the woman had to let another one rip. This time, she didn't even think about it. She let rip a fart that rivalled a train whistle blowing.

Once again, the father looked at the dog with disgust and yelled, 'Dammit, Skippy, get away from her before she shits on you!'

The magician

A magician worked on a cruise ship in the Caribbean.

Since the audience was different each week, the magician allowed himself to do the same tricks over and over again. There was only one problem: the captain's parrot saw the shows each week, and began to understand how the magician did every trick.

Once he understood, he started shouting out in the middle of the show, 'Look, it's not the same hat!' 'Look, he's hiding the flowers under the table!' 'Hey, why are all the cards the ace of spades?'

The magician was furious, but couldn't do anything about it. It was the captain's parrot, after all.

One day the ship had an accident and sank. The magician found himself on a piece of wood in the middle of the sea with, as fate would have it, the parrot. They stared at each other with hatred, but did not utter a word.

This went on for the whole day, and then another.

Finally, on the third day, the parrot couldn't hold back any longer: 'OK, I give up. Where's the fucking ship?'

Bird brained

Two Irishmen walk into a pet shop. Right away they go to the bird section and Mick says to Paddy, 'Dat's dem.'

The shopkeeper comes over and asks if he can help. 'Yeah, we'll take four of dem dere budgies in dat cage op dere,' says Mick. 'Put dem in a pepper bag.'

The shopkeeper does as asked, and the two pay for the birds and leave. They get into Mick's van and drive until they reach a cliff with a 200-metre drop. 'Dis looks loike a grand place,' says Mick. He then takes the two birds out of the bag, places them on his shoulders and jumps off the cliff. Paddy watches as his mate drops off the edge and goes straight down for a few seconds, followed by a *splat*.

As Paddy looks over the edge of the cliff he shakes his head and says, 'Fock dat — dis budgie jumping is too fockin' dangerous for me …'

A few minutes later, Shamus approaches. He too has been to the pet shop and he's carrying the familiar 'pepper bag'. He then pulls a parrot out of the bag and Paddy notices that in the other hand Shamus is carrying a gun.

'Watch this, Paddy,' he says, as he launches himself over the edge of the cliff. Paddy watches as halfway down Shamus takes the gun and blows the parrot's head off. Shamus continues to plummet until there is another *splat* and he joins Mick at the bottom of the cliff.

Paddy shakes his head and says, 'An' oim never troyin' that parrotshooting noider …'

After a few minutes, Sean strolls up. He too has been to the pet shop and walks up with his 'pepper bag'. Instead of a parrot he pulls a chicken out of the bag and launches himself off the cliff with the usual result.

Once more Paddy shakes his head. 'Fock me, Sean. First der was Mick wit his budgie jumping, den Shamus parrotshooting — and now you, fockin' hengliding.'

A day at the zoo

It's a beautiful warm spring morning and a man and his wife are spending the day at the zoo. She's wearing a cute loose-fitting red sleeveless dress with thin straps. He's wearing his normal jeans and T-shirt.

As they walk through the ape exhibit, they pass in front of a very large hairy gorilla. Noticing the girl, the gorilla goes crazy. He jumps up on the bars and, holding his penis with one hand, he grunts and pounds his chest with his free hand.

The husband, noticing the gorilla's excitement, thinks this is funny. He asks his wife to tease the poor fellow some more. The husband suggests she pucker her lips, wiggle her bottom at him and play along to stir the gorilla up. She does and the gorilla gets more excited, making whooping noises that would wake the dead.

Then the husband suggests that she let one of her straps fall to show a little more skin. She does and Mr Gorilla is about to tear down the bars.

'Now try lifting your dress up your thighs and sort of fan it at him,' he says. This drives the gorilla crazy and now he's doing back flips.

Then the husband grabs his wife by the hair, rips open the door to the cage, slings her in with the gorilla and slams the cage door shut. 'Now tell him you have a headache.'

Cheap deal

A bloke is browsing in a pet shop and sees a parrot sitting on a little perch. It doesn't have any feet or legs. The guy says aloud: 'Jeesh. I wonder what happened to this bird.'

The parrot says, 'I was born this way. I'm a defective parrot.'

'Holy shit,' the bloke replies. 'You actually understood and answered me!'

'I understood every word,' says the parrot. 'I happen to be a highly intelligent, thoroughly educated bird.'

'Oh yeah?' the bloke asks. 'Then answer this — how do you hang on to your perch without any feet?'

'Well,' the parrot says, 'this is very embarrassing, but since you asked, I wrap my cock around this wooden bar like a little hook. You can't see it because of my feathers.'

'Wow,' says the guy, 'you really can understand and speak English, can't you!'

'Actually, I speak both Spanish and English and I can converse with reasonable competence on almost any topic: politics, religion, sport, physics, philosophy. I'm especially good at ornithology. You really ought to buy me. I'd be a great companion.'

The bloke looks at the $400 price tag and says, 'Sorry, but I just can't afford that.'

'Pssssssst,' says the parrot, 'I'm defective, so the truth is, nobody wants me 'cause I don't have any feet. You can probably get me for $75 — just make the owner an offer!'

The bloke offers $75 and walks out with the parrot. Weeks go by. The parrot is sensational company. He has a great sense of humour, he's interesting, he's a great pal, he understands everything, he sympathises, and he's insightful. The bloke is delighted. One day he comes home from work and the parrot goes 'Pssssssssssssst' and motions him over with one wing.

'I don't know if I should tell you this or not, but it's about your wife and the postman.'

'What are you talking about?' asks the bloke.

'When the postman delivered today, your wife greeted him at the door in a sheer black nightie and kissed him passionately.'

'*What?*' the bloke asks incredulously. '*Then* what happened?'

'Well, then the postman came into the house and lifted up her nightie and began petting her all over,' reports the parrot.

'My God!' the bloke exclaims. 'Then what?'

'Then he lifted up the nightie, got down on his knees and began to lick her all over, starting with her breasts and slowly going down …'

'WELL?' demanded the frantic bloke. 'THEN WHAT HAPPENED?'

'Who knows! I got a hard-on and fell off my perch!'

Duck off

A duck walks into a pub and says to the barman, 'Got any bread?'

Barman says, 'No.'

Duck says, 'Got any bread?'

Barman says, 'No.'

Duck says, 'Got any bread?'

Barman says, 'No, we have no bread.'

Duck says, 'Got any bread?'

Barman says, 'No, we haven't got any fucking bread.'

Duck says, 'Got any bread?'

Barman says, 'No, are you deaf, we haven't got any fucking bread. Ask me again and I'll nail your fucking beak to the bar, you irritating bastard bird!'

Duck says, 'Got any nails?'

Barman says, 'No.'

Duck says, 'Got any bread?'

13 THE GODS MUST BE CRAZY

We live in a world exploding with religion. There are the old religions like Judaism, Catholicism, Taoism, Hinduism and Islam, not forgetting the hundreds of African and South American sect religions and the Pan religions founded on animal and territorial worship. Then there are some not so old brands like the Calvinists, Lutherans, Anglicans and Methodists. Then come the parade of new religions led by the Mormons, Christian Scientists, Amish, Quakers, Shakers and hundreds of Asian and Indian religions. Religion seems to attract fervent ratbags, some who even hand around deadly rattlesnakes in praise of the Lord. Who is to say which religion is right — and we all accept that whenever two tribes go to war their gods give them the thumbs-up. The world is still fighting in the name of religion, be it the Christian right or in the name of Allah. Then comes the increasing history of sexual predators who work for the Lord. It is small wonder organised religion is losing the plot *and* its traditional power base. Also small wonder jokes about clergy increase in popularity as we take them down a notch. One needs to realise that the clergy in most cultures used to have an incredibly strong hold over the population at large. Sometimes the combination of Church and State made them unbelievably powerful and, of course, the target of anonymous social humour. An offbeat popular film about a small African tribe summed religion up very succinctly — *The Gods Must Be Crazy*.

Nearly every brand of tambourine-thumper and halo-chaser is represented in this section, including the ubiquitous stories that commence with: 'A priest, pastor and a rabbi walk into . . .' There are jokes about strange Bible lessons, Sunday schools gone wrong, sozzled priests, mad mullahs and naughty nuns. There are also some wacky creation stories and a series that asks, 'How many Christians does it take to change a light bulb?'

Jokes often have more than one theme. The first joke in this section manages to be about God and also a collection of cultural stereotypes, insulting Arabs, blacks, Mexicans, French and Jews — all in one joke.

How Moses got the 10 Commandments

God went to the Arabs and said, 'I have Commandments for you that will make your lives better.'

The Arabs asked, 'What are Commandments?'

And the Lord said, 'They are rules for living.'

'Can you give us an example?'

'Thou shall not kill.'

'Not kill? We're not interested.'

He went to the blacks and said, 'I have Commandments.'

The blacks wanted an example, and the Lord said, 'Honour thy father and mother.'

'Father? We don't know who our fathers are.'

Then He went to the Mexicans and said, 'I have Commandments.'

The Mexicans also wanted an example, and the Lord said, 'Thou shall not steal.'

'Not steal? We're not interested.'

Then He went to the French and said, 'I have Commandments.'

The French too wanted an example and the Lord said, 'Thou shall not commit adultery.'

'Not commit adultery? We're not interested.'

Finally, He went to the Jews and said, 'I have Commandments.'

'Commandments?' they said. 'How much are they?'

'They're free.'

'We'll take 10.'

Water to wine

A priest is stopped for speeding in Goulburn.

The policeman smells alcohol on the priest's breath and then sees an empty wine bottle on the floor of the car. He says, 'Sir, have you been drinking?'

'Just water,' says the priest.

The policeman says, 'Then why do I smell wine?'

The priest looks at the bottle and says, 'Good Lord! He's done it again!'

The brothel

Two Irishmen were sitting in a Melbourne pub having a beer and watching the brothel across the street.

They saw a Baptist minister walk into the brothel, and one of them said, 'Aye, 'tis a shame to see a man of the cloth goin' bad.'

Then they saw a rabbi enter the brothel, and the other Irishman said, 'Aye, 'tis a shame to see that the Jews are fallin' victim to temptation as well.'

Then they see a Catholic priest enter the brothel, and one of the Irishmen said, 'What a terrible pity … one of the girls must be dying.'

Bless 'em all

The Pope was finishing his sermon. He ended it with the Latin phrase *Tutti Homini* (Blessed be mankind).

A women's rights group approached the Pope the next day. They pointed out that the Pope blessed all mankind, but not womankind.

The next day, after his sermon, the Pope concluded by saying, '*Tutti Homini, et Tutti Femini.*'

A gay-rights group approached the Pope the next day. They asked if he could also bless gay people.

The next day, the Pope concluded his sermon with, '*Tutti Homini, Tutti Femini, et Tutti Frutti.*'

Fanny green

O'Sullivan enters a confessional and says to the Irish priest, 'Father, it has been one month since my last confession. I've had sex with Fanny Green every week for the last month.'

The priest tells the sinner, 'You are forgiven. Go out and say three Hail Marys.'

Soon, O'Donnell enters the confessional. 'Father, it has been two months since my last confession. I have had sex with Fanny Green twice a week for the last two months.'

This time the priest asks, 'Who is this Fanny Green?'

'A new woman in the neighbourhood,' O'Donnell replies.

'Very well,' says the priest. 'Go and say 10 Hail Marys.'

The next morning in church, the priest is preparing to deliver his sermon when a gorgeous, tall woman enters the church. All the men's eyes fall upon her as she slowly sashays up the aisle and sits down in front of the altar.

Her dress is green and very short, with matching shiny emerald green shoes. The priest and altar boy gasp as the woman sits down with her legs slightly spread apart, Sharon Stone-style. The priest turns to little Ritchie, an altar boy, and whispering, asks, 'Is that Fanny Green?'

Ritchie replies, 'No, Father, I think it's just the reflection off her shoes.'

Holiday time

A man, his wife and mother-in-law went on vacation to Jerusalem.

While they were there the mother-in-law passed away. The undertaker told them, 'You can have her shipped home for $5000, or you can bury her here in the Holy Land for $350.'

The man thought about it and told him he would have her shipped home.

The undertaker asked, 'Why would you spend $5000 to ship your mother-in-law home, when it would be wonderful to be buried here and you would spend only $350?'

The man replied, 'Long ago a man died here, was buried here, and three days later he rose from the dead. I just can't take that chance.'

Next of kin

Father O'Malley rose from his bed. It was a fine spring day in his new Northern Territory mission parish. He walked to the window of his bedroom to get a deep breath of the beautiful day outside. He then noticed there was a billygoat lying dead in the middle of his front lawn. He promptly called the local police station. The conversation went like this:

'Good morning. This is Sergeant Flaherty. How might I help you?'

'This is Father O'Malley at St Brigid's. There's a billygoat lying dead on my front lawn. Would ye be so kind as to send a couple o' yer lads to take care of the matter?'

Sergeant Flaherty, considering himself to be quite a wit, replied with a smirk, 'Well now, Father, it was always my impression that you people took care of last rites!'

There was dead silence on the line for a long moment. Father O'Malley then replied: 'Aye, that's certainly true, but we are also obliged to notify the next of kin.'

Confession

A nun is sitting with her Mother Superior chatting. 'I used some horrible language this week and feel absolutely terrible about it.'

'When did you use this awful language?' asks the Mother Superior.

'Well, I was golfing and hit an incredible drive that looked like it was going to go over 280 yards, but it struck a phone line that is hanging over the fairway and fell straight to the ground after going only about 100 yards.'

'Is that when you swore?'

'No, Mother,' says the nun. 'After that a possum ran out of the bushes and grabbed my ball in its mouth and began to run away.'

'Is that when you swore?' asks the Mother Superior again.

'Well, no,' says the nun. 'You see, as the possum was running, an eagle came down out of the sky, grabbed the possum in his talons and began to fly away!'

'Is that when you swore?' asks the amazed Mother Superior.

'No, not yet. As the eagle carried the possum away in its claws, it flew near the green and the possum dropped my ball.'

'Did you swear then?' asks Mother Superior, becoming impatient.

'No, because the ball fell on a big rock, bounced over the sand trap, rolled onto the green and stopped about six inches from the hole.'

The two nuns were silent for a moment. Then the Mother Superior sighs and says, 'You missed the fucking putt, didn't you?'

Family matters

A Jewish girl brings her fiancé home to meet her parents.

After dinner, her mother tells her father to find out about the young man. He invites the fiancé to his study for schnapps. 'So what are your plans?' the father asks the fiancé.

'I am a Torah scholar,' he replies.

'A Torah scholar,' the father says. 'Admirable, but what will you do to provide a nice house for my daughter to live in, as she's accustomed to?'

'I will study,' the young man replies, 'and God will provide for us.'

'And how will you buy her a beautiful engagement ring, such as she deserves?' asks the father.

'I will concentrate on my studies,' the young man replies. 'God will provide for us.'

'And children?' asks the father. 'How will you support children?'

'Don't worry, sir, God will provide,' replies the fiancé.

The conversation proceeds like this, and each time the father questions, the fiancé insists that God will provide.

Later, the mother asks, 'How did it go?'

The father answers, 'He has no job and no plans, but the good news is he thinks I'm God.'

Save the Pope

Interesting Year 1981: Prince Charles got married, Liverpool crowned soccer champions of Europe, Australia lost the Ashes, and the Pope died.

Interesting Year 2005: Prince Charles got married, Liverpool crowned soccer champions of Europe, Australia lost the Ashes, and the Pope died.

Lesson learnt? The next time Charles gets married, someone had better warn the Pope.

Santa's legacy

One particular Christmas a long time ago, Santa was getting ready for his annual trip ... But there were problems everywhere. Four of his elves got sick, and the trainee elves did not produce the toys as fast as the regular ones. Santa was beginning to feel the pressure of being behind schedule.

Then, Mrs Claus told him that her mother was coming to visit. This stressed Santa even more. Then when he went to harness the reindeer, he found three of them were about to give birth and two had jumped the fence and were out, heaven knows where. More stress. Then when he began to load the sleigh one of the boards cracked and the toy bag fell to the ground and scattered the toys.

Frustrated, Santa went back to the house for a cup of coffee and a shot of whisky. When he went to the cupboard he discovered the elves had drunk the whisky and there was nothing to drink. In his frustration, he accidentally dropped the coffee pot and it broke into hundreds of little pieces all over the kitchen floor. He went to get the broom and found that mice had eaten the straw it was made from.

Just then the doorbell rang and Santa cursed his way to the door. He opened the door and there was a little angel with a great big Christmas tree. The angel said, very cheerfully, 'Merry Christmas, Santa. Isn't it just a lovely day? I have a beautiful tree for you. Isn't it just a lovely tree? Where would you like me to stick it?'

Thus began the tradition of the little angel on top of the Christmas tree.

A priest, a minister and a rabbi

A priest, a minister and a rabbi used to meet weekly to discuss problems affecting their congregations. One day they decided that they ought to try to spread 'the Word' to animals as well as to humans.

At their meeting a week later, the priest turned up with his arm heavily bandaged. 'I tried reading the Psalms to a wolf at the zoo,' he explained. 'I thought the soothing verses would calm him down, but he just went wild and bit me.'

The next week the minister arrived even more heavily bandaged. 'I went to the zoo to tell the lion about how to live in peace with other animals, but I guess he must have been hungry because he tried to eat me.'

The third week the rabbi didn't show, but sent a message for his colleagues to meet him at the hospital, where they found him swathed in bandages and with his arms and legs in traction. 'I discovered one thing, fellows,' he said. 'Never try to circumcise a gorilla.'

Here's a Bible lesson – spelling included

Children in a Catholic primary school were asked questions about the Old and New Testaments. The following statements about the Bible were written by the children and have not been corrected. Incorrect spelling has been intentionally left in.

1. In the first book of the bible, Guinness's, God got tired of creating the world so he took the Sabbath off.
2. Adam and Eve were created from an apple tree. Noah's wife was Joan of Ark. Noah built an ark and the animals came on in pears.
3. Lot's wife was a pillar of salt during the day, but a ball of fire during the night.
4. The Jews were a proud people and throughout history they had trouble with unsympathetic genitals.
5. Sampson was a strongman who let himself be led astray by a jezebel like Delilah.

6. Samson slayed the philistines with the axe of the apostles.
7. Moses led the Jews to the red sea where they made unleavened bread, which is bread without any ingredients.
8. The Egyptians were all drowned in the dessert. Afterwards, Moses went up to Mount Cyanide to get the Ten Commandments.
9. The first commandments was when Eve told Adam to eat the apple.
10. The seventh commandment is thou shalt not admit adultery.
11. Moses died before he ever reached Canada. Then Joshua led the Hebrews in the battle of Geritol.
12. The greatest miracle in the bible is when Joshua told his son to stand still and he obeyed him.
13. David was a Hebrew king who was skilled at playing the liar. He fought the Finkelsteins, a race of people who lived in biblical times.
14. Solomon, one of David's sons, had 300 wives and 700 porcupines.
15. When Mary heard she was the mother of Jesus, she sang the Magna Carta.
16. When the three wise guys from the east side arrived they found Jesus in the manager.
17. Jesus was born because Mary had an immaculate contraption.
18. St John the blacksmith dumped water on his head.
19. Jesus enunciated the golden rule, which says to do unto others before they do one to you. He also explained a man doth not live by sweat alone.
20. It was a miracle when Jesus rose from the dead and managed to get the tombstone off the entrance.
21. The people who followed the lord were called the 12 decibels.
22. The Epistels were the wives of the apostles.
23. One of the Oppossums was St Matthew who was also a taximan.
24. St Paul cavorted to christianity, He preached holy acrimony which is another name for marriage.
25. Christians have only one spouse. This is called monotony.

Tell all

Girl: 'Father, I have sinned, I called a man a bastard.'
Priest: 'Why did you call the man a bastard?'
Girl: 'Because he kissed me on the lips.'

Priest: 'What? Like this?'

Girl: 'Yes, Father.'

Priest: 'That's no reason to call a man a bastard!'

Girl: 'He also touched me on my breasts!'

Priest: 'What? Like this?'

Girl: 'Yes, Father.'

Priest: 'That's no reason to call a man a bastard!'

Girl: 'He put his hands up my dress.'

Priest: 'What? Like this?'

Girl: 'Yes, Father.'

Priest: 'That's no reason to call a man a bastard!'

Girl: 'He touched me on my private parts.'

Priest: 'What? Like this?'

Girl: 'Yes, Father.'

Priest: 'That's no reason to call a man a bastard!'

Girl: 'He had sex with me.'

Priest: 'What? Like this?'

Girl: 'Yes, Father.'

Priest: 'That's no reason to call a man a bastard!'

Girl: 'He had AIDS!'

Priest: '*That bastard!*'

What causes arthritis?

A drunk man who smelt like beer sat down on a subway seat next to a priest. The man's tie was stained, his face was plastered with red lipstick, and a half empty bottle of gin was sticking out of his torn coat pocket. He opened his newspaper and began reading. After a few minutes the man turned to the priest and asked, 'Say, Father, what causes arthritis?'

The priest replied, 'My son, it's caused by loose living, being with cheap, wicked women, too much alcohol, a contempt for your fellow man, sleeping around with prostitutes and lack of bath.'

The drunk muttered in response, 'Well, I'll be damned,' then returned to his paper.

The priest, thinking about what he had said, nudged the man and apologised. 'I'm very sorry. I didn't mean to come on so strong. How long have you had arthritis?'

The drunk answered, 'I don't have it, Father. I was just reading here that the Pope does.'

Schmuck

A rabbi was opening his mail one morning. Taking a single sheet of paper from an envelope he found written on it only one word: 'shmuck'. At the next Friday night service, the rabbi announced, 'I have known many people who have written letters and forgot to sign their names, but this week I received a letter from someone who signed his name ... and forgot to write a letter.'

The good son

Four Catholic women are having coffee together, discussing how important their children are.

The first one tells her friends, 'My son is a priest. When he walks into a room, everyone calls him "Father".'

The second Catholic woman chirps, 'Well, my son is a bishop. Whenever he walks into a room, people say "Your Grace".'

The third Catholic woman says smugly, 'Well, not to put you down, but my son is a cardinal. Whenever he walks into a room, people say "Your Eminence".'

The fourth Catholic woman sips her coffee in silence.

The first three women give her this subtle 'Well ... ?'

She replies, 'My son is a gorgeous, six foot two, hard-bodied, well-hung, male stripper. Whenever he walks into a room, women say "My God ..."'

Sunday school

Little Margaret was not the best student in Sunday school. Usually she slept through the class. One day her teacher, a nun, called on her while she was napping: 'Tell me, Margaret, who created the universe?'

When Margaret didn't stir, little Johnny, an altruistic boy seated in the chair behind her, took a pin and jabbed her in the rear. 'God Almighty!' shouted Margaret, the nun said 'Very good' and Margaret fell back asleep.

A while later the nun asked Margaret, 'Who is our Lord and Saviour?' But Margaret didn't even stir from her slumber. Once again, little Johnny came to the rescue and stuck her again. 'Jesus Christ!' shouted Margaret and the nun said 'Very good'. Margaret fell back asleep.

Then the nun asked Margaret a third question. 'What did Eve say to Adam after she had her 23rd child?' Again Johnny came to the rescue. This time Margaret jumped up and shouted, 'If you stick that damn thing in me one more time, I'll break it in half!'

The nun fainted.

God loves blondes

A blonde finds herself in serious financial trouble. Her business has gone bust and she's in dire fiscal straits. She's so desperate that she decides to ask God for help. She begins to pray, 'God, please help me. I've lost my business and if I don't get some money soon, I'm going to lose my car as well. Please let me win the lotto.'

Lotto night comes, and somebody else wins it. She again prays, 'God, please let me win the lotto! I've lost my business and my car and I'm probably going to lose my house as well.'

Lotto night comes and she still has no luck.

Once again, she prays, 'My God, why have you forsaken me? I've lost my business, my car and my house, and my children are starving. I don't often ask you for help, and I have always been a good servant to you. *Please* let me win the lotto just this one time so I can get my life back in order.'

Suddenly there is a blinding flash of light and the heavens open.

The blonde is overwhelmed by the voice of God himself. 'Sweetheart, work with me on this … buy a ticket!'

Poser

A college class was told they had to write a short story in as few words as possible. The instructions were that the short story had to contain the following three things: (a) Religion, (b) Sexuality and (c) Mystery.

Below is the only A+ contribution in the entire class.

'Good God! I'm pregnant! I wonder who did it?'

Holy soap!

Two priests are off to the bathroom late one night. They undress and step into the showers before they realise there is no soap.

Father John says he has soap in his room and goes to get it, not bothering to dress. He grabs two bars of soap, one in each hand, and heads back. He is halfway down the hall when he sees three nuns heading his way. Having no place to hide, he stands against the wall and freezes like he's a statue.

The nuns stop and comment on how lifelike he looks. The first nun suddenly reaches out and pulls on his manhood. Startled, he drops a bar of soap. 'Oh look,' says the first nun, 'it's a soap dispenser.' To test her theory the second nun also pulls on his manhood. Sure enough, he drops the second bar of soap.

Now the third nun decides to have a go. She pulls once, then twice and three times but nothing happens. So she gives several more tugs, then yells: 'Holy Mary, Mother of God — hand lotion too!'

Osama in heaven

After his death, Osama bin Laden went to heaven and came face to face with George Washington, who proceeded to slap him across the face and yell at him, 'How dare you try to destroy the nation I helped conceive!'

Patrick Henry approached and punched Osama in the nose and shouted, 'You wanted to end our liberties but you failed.'

James Madison entered, kicked Osama in the stomach and said, 'This is why I allowed our government to provide for the common defence!'

Thomas Jefferson came in and proceeded to beat Osama many times with a long cane and said, 'It was evil men like you that provided me the inspiration to pen the Declaration of Independence!'

These beatings and thrashings continued as John Rudolph, James Monroe and 66 other early Americans came in and unleashed their anger on the Muslim terrorist leader.

As Osama lay bleeding and writhing in unbearable pain an angel appeared. Bin Laden said to the angel, 'This is not what you promised me.' The angel replied, 'I told you … there would be 72 Virginians waiting for you in heaven. What did you think I said?'

The popular young rabbi

This is a story about a popular young rabbi, who on Sabbath eve announces to his congregation that he will not renew his contract. He explains that he is moving on to a larger congregation that will pay him more. There is a hush. No one wants him to leave.

Sol Epstein, who owns several car dealerships, stands up and proclaims, 'If the rabbi stays, I will provide him with a new Cadillac every year and his wife with a Honda mini-van to transport their children!' The congregation sighs in appreciation, and applauds.

Sam Goldstein, the entrepreneur and investor, stands and says, 'If the rabbi will stay on here, I'll personally double his salary, and also establish a foundation to guarantee the college educations of his children!' More sighs and loud applause.

Sadie Goldfarb, age 70, stands and announces with a smile, 'If the rabbi stays, I'll give him sex!'

There is total silence.

The rabbi, blushing, asks her, 'Mrs Goldfarb, whatever possessed you to say that?'

Sadie answers, 'I just asked my husband how we could help, and he said, "Screw the rabbi."'

Passing on

Upon hearing that her elderly grandfather had just passed away, Katie went straight to her grandparents' house to visit her 95-year-old grandmother and comfort her. When she asked how her grandfather had died, her grandmother replied, 'He had a heart attack while we were making love on Sunday morning.'

Horrified, Katie told her grandmother that two people nearly 100 years old having s-e-x would surely be asking for trouble.

'Oh no, my dear,' replied her granny. 'Many years ago, realising our advanced age, we figured out the best time to do it was when the church bells would start to ring. It was just the right rhythm. Nice and slow and even. Nothing too strenuous — simply in on the *ding* and out on the *dong*.'

She paused to wipe away a tear, and continued, 'He'd still be alive if the ice-cream truck hadn't come along.'

The preacher's salary

There was a preacher whose wife was expecting a baby so he went to the congregation and asked for a raise. After much consideration and discussion, they passed a rule that whenever the preacher's family expanded, so would his pay cheque.

After six children, this started to get expensive and the congregation decided to hold another meeting to discuss the preacher's salary.

There was much yelling and bickering about how much the clergyman's additional children were costing the church.

Finally, the preacher got up and spoke to the crowd. 'Children are a gift from God,' he said. Silence fell on the congregation.

In the back of the room, a little old lady stood up and in her frail voice said, 'Rain is also a gift from God but when we get too much, we wear rubbers.'

The Garden of Eden

After three weeks in the Garden of Eden, God came to visit Eve.

'So, how is everything going?' inquired God.

'It is all so beautiful, God,' she replied. 'The sunrises and sunsets are breathtaking, the smells, the sights, everything is wonderful, but I have just one problem. It is these breasts you have given me. The middle one pushes the other two out and I am constantly knocking them with my arms, catching them on branches and snagging them on bushes. They are a real pain,' reported Eve.

She went on to tell God that since many other parts of her body came in pairs, such as her limbs, eyes, ears, etc, she felt that having only two breasts might leave her body more 'symmetrically balanced', as she put it.

'That is a fair point,' replied God, 'but it was my first shot at this, you know. I gave the animals six breasts, so I figured that you needed only half of those, but I see that you are right. I will fix it up right away.' God reached down, removed the middle breast and tossed it into the bushes.

Three weeks passed and God once again visited Eve in the Garden of Eden.

'Well, Eve, how is my favourite creation?'

'Just fantastic,' she replied, 'but for one oversight on your part. You see all the animals are paired off. The ewe has a ram and the cow has her bull. All the animals have a mate except me. I feel so alone.'

God thought for a moment and said, 'You know, Eve, you are right. How could I have overlooked this? You do need a mate and I will immediately create a man from a part of you. Now let's see … where did I put the useless boob?'

(Now doesn't *that* make more sense than that crap about the rib?)

All in a driver's work

The Pope's driver meets Benedict XVI at the airport.

After getting the Pope's entire luggage loaded into the limo (and he doesn't travel light), the driver notices that the Pope is still standing on the kerb.

'Excuse me, Your Holiness,' says the driver. 'Would you please take your seat so we can leave?'

'Well, to tell you the truth,' says the Pope, 'they never let me drive at the Vatican, and I'd really like to drive today.'

'I'm sorry but I cannot let you do that. I'd lose my job! And supposing something should happen?' protests the driver, wishing that he'd never gone to work that morning.

'There might be something extra in it for you,' says the Pope.

Reluctantly, the driver gets in the back as the Pope climbs in behind the wheel.

The driver quickly regrets his decision when, after exiting the airport, the Pontiff floors it, accelerating the limo to 160 kilometres an hour.

'Please slow down, Your Holiness!' pleads the worried driver, but the Pope keeps the pedal to the metal until they hear sirens.

'Oh, dear God, I'm going to lose my licence,' moans the driver.

The Pope pulls over and rolls down the window as the cop approaches, but the cop takes one look at him, goes back to his motorcycle, and gets on the two-way radio.

'I need to talk to the chief,' he says to the dispatcher.

The chief gets on the radio and the cop tells him that he's stopped a limo going 160.

'So bust him,' says the chief.

'I don't think we want to do that — he's really important,' says the cop.

The chief exclaims, 'All the more reason!'

'No, I mean really important,' says the cop.

The chief then asks, 'Who you got there, the mayor?'

Cop: 'Bigger.'

Chief: 'Governor?'

Cop: 'Bigger.'

'Well,' says the chief, 'who is it?'

Cop: 'I think it's God!'

Chief: 'What makes you think it's God?'

Cop: 'He's got the bloody Pope as a chauffeur!'

Candles

Mrs Donovan was walking down O'Connell Street, Dublin, when she met up with Father Rafferty.

The father said, 'Aren't ye Mrs Donovan, and didn't I marry ye and yer husband two years ago?'

She replied, 'Aye, that ye did, Father.'

The father asked, 'And are there any wee ones yet?'

She replied, 'No, not yet, Father.'

The father said, 'Well now, I'm going to Rome next week and I'll light a candle for ye and yer husband.'

She replied, 'Oh, thank ye, Father.'

They parted ways and some years later they met again. The priest asked, 'Well now, Mrs Donovan, how are ye these days?'

She replied, 'Oh, very well, Father.'

The father asked, 'And tell me, have ye any wee ones yet?'

She replied, 'Oh yes, Father, three sets of twins and four singles — 10 in all.'

The father said, 'Glory be! That's wonderful! How is yer loving husband doing?'

She replied, 'He's gone to Rome to blow out yer fekking candle.'

A lift

A priest was driving along and saw a nun on the side of the road. He stopped and offered her a lift which she accepted. She got in and crossed her legs, forcing her gown to open and reveal a lovely thigh. The priest had a look and nearly had an accident. After controlling the car, he stealthfully slid his hand up her leg.

The nun looked at him and immediately said, 'Father, remember Psalm 129?'

The priest was flustered and apologised profusely. He forced himself to remove his hand. However, he was unable to remove his eyes from her leg. Further on while changing gear, he let his hand slide up her leg again.

The nun once again said, 'Father, remember Psalm 129?'

Once again the priest apologised. 'Sorry, sister, but the flesh is weak.'

Arriving at the convent, the nun got out, gave him a meaningful glance and went on her way. On his arrival at the church, the priest rushed to retrieve a Bible and looked up Psalm 129. It said, 'Go forth and seek, further up, you will find glory.'

Donation

Father O'Malley answers the phone:

'Hello, is this Father O'Malley?'

'It is.'

'This is the Australian Taxation Office. Can you help us?'

'I'll try.'

'Do you know a Ted Hoolihan?'

'I do.'

'Is he a member of your congregation?'

'He is.'

'Did he donate $10,000 to the church?'

'He will.'

Confession

An elderly man walks into a confessional. The following conversation ensues:

Man: 'I am 92 years old, have a wonderful wife of 70 years, many children, grandchildren, and great grandchildren. Yesterday, I picked up two college girls, hitchhiking; we went to a motel, where I had sex with each of them three times.'

Priest: 'Are you sorry for your sins?'

Man: 'What sins?'

Priest: 'What kind of a Catholic are you?'

Man: 'I'm Jewish.'

Priest: 'Then why are you telling me all this?'

Man: 'I'm telling everybody.'

Baptising the drinker

A man is stumbling through the woods, totally drunk, when he comes upon a preacher baptising people in the river. He proceeds to walk into the water and subsequently bumps into the preacher. The preacher turns around and is almost overcome by the smell of alcohol, whereupon he asks the drunk, 'Are you ready to find Jesus?'

The drunk answers, 'Yes, I am.'

So the preacher grabs him and dunks him in the water. He pulls him up and asks the drunk, 'Brother, have you found Jesus?'

The drunk replies, 'No, I haven't found Jesus.'

The preacher, shocked at the answer, dunks him into the water again for a little longer. He pulls him out and asks again, 'Have you found Jesus, my brother?'

The drunk again answers, 'No, I haven't found Jesus.'

By this time the preacher is at his wits' end and dunks the drunk in the water again — but this time holds him down for about 30 seconds and when he begins kicking his arms and legs he pulls him up.

The preacher again asks the drunk, 'For the love of God, have you found Jesus?'

The drunk wipes his eyes, catches his breath and says to the preacher, 'Are you sure this is where he fell in?'

Desert capers

A nun and a priest go into the desert on a camel. The camel dies and now the nun and the priest are stranded.

The priest says to the nun, 'Well, since we are going to die, you should know that I have never seen a woman's body.'

So the nun removes her clothes and the priest is excited to see her naked.

Then the nun says to the priest, 'I have never seen a man's body before, either.'

Happily the priest obliges and gets undressed.

The nun sees the priest's erect penis. Embarrassed, she asks, 'What is that?'

The priest says to her, 'I've heard that if I stick it in you, it will bring the gift of life.'

The nun looks at the priest and says, 'So what are you waiting for? Stick it in the camel and let's get the hell out of here!'

Bless me, Father

'Bless me, Father, for I have sinned. I have been with a loose woman.'

'Is that you, little Tommy Shaughnessy?' asks the priest.

'Yes, Father, it is.'

'And who was the woman you were with?'

'I won't be tellin' you, Father. I don't want to ruin her reputation.'

'Well, Tommy, I'm sure to find out sooner or later, so you may as well tell me now. Was it Brenda O'Malley?'

'I cannot say.'

'Was it Patricia Kelly?'

'I'll never tell.'

'Was it Liz Shannon?'

'I'm sorry, but I can't name her.'

'Was it Cathy Morgan?'

'My lips are sealed.'

'Was it Fiona McDonald, then?'

'Please, Father, I cannot tell you.'

The priest sighs in frustration. 'You're a steadfast lad, Tommy Shaughnessy, and I admire that. But you've sinned, and you must atone. You cannot attend church for three months — be off with you now.'

Tommy walks back to his pew.

His friend Sean slides over and whispers, 'What'd you get?'

'Three months' vacation and five good leads,' says Tommy.

Is sex work or play?

A man wonders if having sex on the Sabbath is a sin because he is not sure if sex is work or play. So he goes to a priest and asks for his opinion on this question. After consulting the Bible, the priest says, 'My son, after an exhaustive search, I am positive that sex is work and is therefore not permitted on Sundays.'

The man thinks: 'What does a priest know about sex?' So he goes to a minister, who after all is a married man and experienced in this matter.

He queries the minister and receives the same reply: 'Sex is work and therefore not for the Sabbath!'

Not pleased with the reply, he seeks out a rabbi, a man of thousands of years of tradition and knowledge. The rabbi ponders the question, then states, 'My son, sex is definitely play.'

The man replies, 'Rabbi, how can you be so sure when so many others tell me sex is work?'

The rabbi softly speaks, 'My son, if sex was work, my wife would have the maid do it.'

The lift-off

An Amish boy and his father were in a shopping mall for the first time.

They were amazed by almost everything they saw, but especially by two shiny, silver walls that could move apart and then slide back together again.

The boy asked, 'What is this, Father?'

The father (never having seen an elevator) responded, 'Son, I have never seen anything like this in my life — I don't know what it is.'

While the boy and his father were watching with amazement, a fat old lady in a wheelchair moved up to the walls and pressed a button. The walls opened and the lady rolled between them into a small room. The walls closed and the boy and his father watched the small circular numbers above the walls light up sequentially. They continued to watch until it reached the last number and then the numbers began to light in the reverse order. Finally the walls opened up again and a gorgeous 24-year-old blonde stepped out.

The father said quietly to his son: 'Son, go get your mother.'

New at the monastery

A new young monk arrives at the monastery.

He is assigned to help the other monks in copying, by hand, the old canons and laws of the church. He notices, however, that all of the monks are copying from copies, not from the original manuscript.

So, the new monk goes to the abbot to question this, pointing out that if someone made even a small error in the first copy, it would never be picked up. In fact, that error would be continued in all of the subsequent copies.

The abbot says, 'We have been copying from the copies for centuries, but you make a good point, my son.' So, he goes down into the dark caves underneath the monastery where the original manuscript is held in a locked vault that hasn't been opened for hundreds of years.

Hours go by and nobody sees the old abbot.

Eventually the young monk gets worried and goes downstairs to look for him. He sees him banging his head against the wall. His forehead is all bloody and bruised and he is crying uncontrollably.

The young monk asks the abbot, 'What's wrong, Father?'

In a choking voice, the abbot replies, 'The word is "celebrate", not "celibate"!'

Female prayer

Before I lay me down to sleep,
I pray for a man who's not a creep.
One who's handsome, smart and strong.
One who loves to listen long.
One who thinks before he speaks,
When he says he'll call, he won't wait weeks.
I pray that he is gainfully employed.
When I spend his cash, he won't be annoyed.
Pulls out my chair and opens my door.
Massages my back and begs to do more.
Oh! Send me a man who'll make love to my mind,
Knows what to answer to 'How big is my behind?'
I pray that this man will love me no end,
And never attempt to hit on my friend.
Amen

Male prayer

I pray for a nymphomaniac with huge boobs who also owns a liquor store and a boat. Amen.

The atheist and the bear

An atheist was taking a walk through the woods. 'What majestic trees! What powerful rivers! What beautiful animals!' he said to himself.

As he was walking alongside the river he heard a loud rustling in the bushes behind him. He turned to look and saw a seven-foot grizzly bear charging towards him.

He turned and ran as fast as he could. He looked back over his shoulder and saw that the bear was closing in on him. He looked over his shoulder again, and the bear was even closer.

He tripped and fell on the ground. He rolled over to pick himself up but saw the bear right on top of him, reaching for him with his left paw and raising his right paw to strike him.

At that instant the atheist cried out: 'Oh, my God!'

Time stopped. The bear froze. The forest was silent.

As a bright light shone upon the man, a voice came out of the sky: 'You deny my existence for all of these years, teach others I don't exist, and even credit creation to a cosmic accident. Do you expect me to help you out of this predicament? Am I to count you as a believer?'

The atheist looked directly into the light. 'It would be hypocritical of me to suddenly ask you to treat me as a Christian now, but perhaps could you make the *bear* a Christian?'

'Very well,' said the voice.

The bright light went out. The sounds of the forest resumed. And then the bear dropped his right paw, brought both paws together, bowed his head and spoke: 'Lord, bless this food, which I am about to receive from thy bounty through Christ our Lord. Amen.'

He's in the closet

A woman sneaks her lover into her home one day, while she is supposed to be at work. Her nine-year-old son comes home unexpectedly, sees them and hides in the bedroom closet to watch.

When the woman's husband also comes home she puts her lover in the closet, not realising that the little boy is in there already.

The little boy says, 'Dark in here.'

The man says, 'Yes, it is.'

Boy: 'I have a baseball.'

Man: 'That's nice.'

Boy: 'Want to buy it?'

Man: 'No, thanks.'

Boy: 'My dad's outside.'

Man: 'OK, how much?'

Boy: '$250.'

In the next few weeks, it happens again that the boy and the lover are in the closet together.

Boy: 'Dark in here.'

Man: 'Yes, it is.'

Boy: 'I have a baseball glove.'

The lover, remembering the last time, asks the boy: 'How much?'

Boy: '$750.'

Man: 'Fine.'

A few days later, the father says to the boy, 'Grab your glove, let's go outside and have a game of catch.'

The boy says, 'I can't. I sold my baseball and my glove.'

The father asks, 'How much did you sell them for?'

The boy says, '$1000.'

The father says, 'That's terrible to overcharge your friends like that … that is way more than those two things cost. I'm going to take you to church and make you confess.'

They go to the church and the father makes the little boy sit in the confession booth and he closes the door.

The boy says, 'Dark in here.'

The priest says, 'Don't start that shit.'

The Wild West

Back in the Wild West, a westbound wagon train was lost and very low on food. No other people had been seen for days.

Unexpectedly, they saw an old Jewish man sitting beneath a tree.

The leader rushed up to him and said, 'We're lost. Is there some place up ahead where we can get food?'

'Vell,' the old Jewish man said, 'I vould definitely *not* go over dat hill. Somevun told me you'd run into a big bacon tree.'

'A bacon tree?' asked the wagon train leader.

'Yah, yah, ah bacon tree. Trust me. For nutting vud I lie.'

The leader went back and told his people what the Jewish man had told him.

'So why did he say not to go there?' some pioneers asked.

'Oh, you know the Jewish folks — they don't eat bacon.'

So the wagon train went up the hill and down the other side.

About an hour later the leader of the wagon train returned to where the old Jewish man was sitting and enjoying his drink.

The wagon train leader was dishevelled and wounded. He started shouting, 'You fool! You sent us to our deaths! We followed your instructions, but there was no bacon tree. Just hundreds of Indians — they killed everyone but me.'

The Jewish man held up his hand and said, 'Oy, vait a minute, vait a minute.' He got out an English–Yiddish dictionary and began thumbing through it. 'Oh, mine Gott, I made myself ah big mistake. It vuz not a bacon tree. I meant to say it vuz a ham bush!'

Papal decree

A few centuries ago, the Pope decided that all the Jews had to leave Rome. Naturally, there was a big uproar from the Jewish community, who had been there for centuries. Because of the uproar, the Pope decided to make a deal. He would have a religious debate with one member of the Jewish community. If the Jew won, the Jews could stay. If the Pope won, then the Jews had to leave.

Having no alternative, and no volunteers, the Jews had no choice but to pick a middle-aged man called Moshe to represent them.

Moshe asked for one additional requirement for the debate, namely that there would be no talking, because he said that this would make the debate more interesting.

The Pope readily agreed, confident of his position.

The great day came and Moshe and the Pope sat opposite each other for a full minute, before the Pope raised his hand and showed three fingers.

Moshe looked back at him and raised one finger.

The Pope waved his fingers in a circle around his head.

Moshe pointed to the ground where he sat.

The Pope produced a wafer and a glass of wine.

Moshe pulled out an apple.

Whereupon the Pope got up, and said, 'I give up. This man is too good. The Jews can stay.'

There was uproar among the cardinals, who as one were demanding to know what happened.

The Pope said, 'First I held up three fingers to represent the Holy Trinity. He responded by holding up one finger to remind me that there was only one God. I then waved my fingers around to show him that God was all around us. He pointed to the ground to show that God was right here with us. I produced the blood and the body of Christ, to show him that God absolves us of our sins. He produced the apple to remind me of original sin. So how could I argue with this man? He had an answer for everything.'

Meanwhile in the Jewish community, the crowd around Moshe demanded to know what had happened.

'Well,' Moshe said, 'first he said that we had three days to get out of Rome. I told him that not one of us was leaving. Then he told me that the whole city would be cleared of Jews. I let him know that we were staying.'

A woman then asked, 'And then?'

'I don't know, exactly,' said Moshe. 'He took out his lunch and I took out mine.'

The priest and the rabbi

A priest and a rabbi are sitting next to each other on an airplane.

After a while, the priest turns to the rabbi and asks, 'Is it still a requirement of your faith that you not eat pork?'

The rabbi responds, 'Yes, that is still one of our beliefs.'

The priest then asks, 'Have you ever eaten pork?'

To which the rabbi replies, 'Yes, on one occasion I did succumb to temptation and ate a ham sandwich.'

The priest nods in understanding and goes on with his reading.

A while later, the rabbi speaks up and asks the priest, 'Father, is it still a requirement of your church that you remain celibate?'

The priest replies, 'Yes, that is still very much a part of our faith.'

The rabbi then asks him, 'Father, have you ever fallen to the temptations of the flesh?'

The priest replies, 'Yes, Rabbi, on one occasion I was weak and broke with my faith.'

The rabbi nods understandingly. He is silent for about five minutes and then says, 'Beats the hell out of a ham sandwich, doesn't it?'

The Creation stories

Version 1: What everyone knows

Adam was walking around the Garden of Eden feeling very lonely, so God asked him, 'What is wrong with you?' Adam said he didn't have anyone to talk to. God said that he was going to make Adam a companion and that it would be a woman. He said, 'This person will gather food for you, cook for you; when you discover clothing, she'll wash it for you. She will always agree with every decision you make. She will bear your children and never ask you to get up in the middle of the night to take care of them. She will not nag you, and will always be the first to admit she was wrong when you've had a disagreement. She will never have a headache, and will freely give you love and passion whenever you need it.'

Adam asked God, 'What will a woman like this cost?'

God replied, 'Your right arm, right leg and right testicle.'

Adam: 'What can I get for a rib?'

The rest is history.

Version 2: The untold story

One day in the Garden of Eden, Eve calls out to God, 'Lord, I have a problem!'

'What's the problem, Eve?'

'Lord, I know you've created me and have provided this beautiful garden and all of these wonderful animals, and that hilarious comedic snake, but I'm just not happy.'

'Why is that, Eve?' comes the reply from above.

'Lord, I am lonely. And I'm sick to death of apples.'

'Well, Eve, in that case, I have a solution. I shall create a man for you.'

'What's a "man", Lord?'

'This man will be a flawed creature, with many bad traits. He'll lie, cheat, and be vainglorious; all in all, he'll give you a hard time. But he'll be bigger, faster, and will like to hunt and kill things. He will look silly aroused, but since you've been complaining, I'll create him in such a way that he will satisfy your, ah, physical needs. He'll be witless and will revel in childish things like fighting and kicking a ball about. He won't be too smart, so he'll also need your advice to think properly.'

'Sounds great,' says Eve, with an ironically raised eyebrow. 'What's the catch, Lord?'

'Yeah, well … you can have him on one condition.'

'What's that, Lord?'

'As I said, he'll be proud, arrogant and self-admiring. You'll have to let him believe that I made him first. So, just remember, it's our secret … woman-to-woman!'

Was Jesus a woman?

There were three good arguments that Jesus was black:

1. He called everyone brother.
2. He liked Gospel.
3. He couldn't get a fair trial.

But then there were three equally good arguments that Jesus was Jewish:

1. He went into his father's business.
2. He lived at home until he was 33.
3. He was sure his mother was a virgin and his mother was sure he was God.

But then there were three equally good arguments that Jesus was Italian:

1. He talked with his hands.
2. He had wine with every meal.
3. He used olive oil.

But then there were three equally good arguments that Jesus was from Nimbin:

1. He never cut his hair.
2. He walked around barefoot all the time.
3. He started a new religion.

But then there were three equally good arguments that Jesus was Irish:

1. He never got married.
2. He was always telling stories.
3. He loved green pastures.

But the most compelling evidence of all — three proofs that Jesus was a woman:

1. He fed a crowd at a moment's notice when there was no food.
2. He kept trying to get a message across to a bunch of men who just didn't get it.
3. And even when he was dead, he had to get up because there was more work to do.

A single word

A minister decided to do something a little different one Sunday morning. He said, 'Today, in church, I am going to say a single word and you are going to help me preach. Whatever single word I say, I want you to sing whatever hymn comes to your mind.'

The pastor shouted out, 'Cross.'

Immediately the congregation started singing in unison 'The Old Rugged Cross'.

The pastor hollered out, 'Grace.'

The congregation began to sing 'Amazing Grace, how sweet the sound …'.

The pastor said, 'Power.'

The congregation sang 'There is Power in the Blood'.

The pastor said, 'Sex.'

The congregation fell in total silence. Everyone was in shock. They all nervously began to look around at each other, afraid to say anything. Then all of a sudden, from the back of the church, a little 87-year-old grandmother stood up and began to sing 'Precious Memories'.

God's voice mail

Most of us have now learnt to live with voice mail as a necessary part of our lives. Have you ever wondered what it would be like if God decided to install voice mail? Imagine praying and hearing the following:

Thank you for calling heaven.
For English press 1
For Spanish press 2
For all other languages, press 3

Please select one of the following options:

Press 1 for request

Press 2 for thanksgiving

Press 3 for complaints

Press 4 for all others

I am sorry, all our angels and saints are busy helping other sinners right now. However, your prayer is important to us and we will answer it in the order it was received. Please stay on the line.

If you would like to speak to:

God, press 1

Jesus, press 2

Holy Spirit, press 3

To find a loved one who has been assigned to heaven, press 5, then enter his or her passport number followed by the hash sign.

(If you receive a negative response, please hang up and dial area code 666)

For reservations to heaven, please enter JOHN followed by the numbers 3 16.

For answers to nagging questions about dinosaurs, life and other planets, please wait until you arrive in heaven for the specifics.

If you are calling after hours and need emergency assistance, please contact your local pastor.

Thank you and have a heavenly day.

Cock fights

The priest in a small Tasmanian village was very fond of the chickens he kept in the hen house, out the back of the parish manse. He had a cock rooster and about 10 hens. One Saturday night the cock rooster was missing and as that was the time he suspected cock fights occurred in the village he decided to do something about it at church the next morning. At Mass, he asked the congregation, 'Has anybody got a cock?' All the men stood up. 'No, no,' he said. 'That wasn't what I meant. Has anybody seen a cock?' All the women stood up.

'No! No!' he said. 'That wasn't what I meant. Has anybody seen a cock that doesn't belong to them?' Half the women stood up.

'No! No!' he said. 'That wasn't what I meant either. Has anybody seen my cock?' All the choirboys stood up.

Parting words

A dying man gathered his lawyer, doctor and clergyman at his bedside and handed each of them an envelope containing $25,000 in cash. He made them each promise that after his death and during his repose, they would place the three envelopes in his coffin. He told them that he wanted to have enough money to enjoy the next life.

A week later the man died. At the wake, the lawyer, doctor and clergyman each concealed an envelope in the coffin and bid their old client and friend farewell. By chance, these three met several months later. Soon the clergyman, feeling guilty, blurted out a confession, saying that there was only $10,000 in the envelope he placed in the coffin. He felt, rather than waste all the money, he would send it to a mission in South America. He asked for their forgiveness.

The doctor, moved by the gentle clergyman's sincerity, confessed that he too had kept some of the money for a worthy medical charity. The envelope, he admitted, had only $8000 in it. He said he too could not bring himself to waste the money so frivolously when it could be used to benefit others.

By this time the lawyer was seething with self-righteous outrage. He expressed his deep disappointment in the felonious behaviour of two of his oldest and most trusted friends. 'I am the only one who kept his promise to our dying friend. I want you both to know that the envelope I placed in the coffin contained the full amount. Indeed, my envelope contained my personal cheque for the entire $25,000.'

Noah knew all

Everything you need to know about life, you can learn from the story of Noah and his ark.

One: Don't miss the boat.
Two: Remember that we are all in the same boat.
Three: Plan ahead. It wasn't raining when Noah built the ark.
Four: Stay fit. When you're 600 years old, someone may ask you to do something really big.
Five: Don't listen to critics; just get on with the job that needs to be done.
Six: Build your future on high ground.
Seven: For safety's sake, travel in pairs.

Eight: Speed isn't always an advantage. The snails were on board with the cheetahs.

Nine: When you're stressed, float for a while.

Ten: Remember, amateurs built the ark — the *Titanic* was built by professionals.

Is that Jesus?

An Australian, an Irishman and an Englishman are sitting in a bar. There is only one other person in the bar, a man. The three men keep looking at this other man, for he seems terribly familiar. They stare and stare, wondering where they have seen him before, when suddenly the Irishman cries out, 'My God, I know who that man is. It's Jesus!'

The others look again and, sure enough, it is Jesus himself, sitting alone at a table.

The Irishman calls out, 'Hey! You! Are you Jesus?'

The man looks over at him, smiles a small smile, and nods his head. 'Yes, I am Jesus,' he says.

The Irishman calls the bartender over and says to him, 'I'd like you to give Jesus over there a pint of Guinness from me.'

So the bartender pours Jesus a Guinness and takes it over to his table.

Jesus looks over, raises his glass, smiles thank you and drinks.

The Englishman then calls out, 'Err, excuse me, sir, but would you be Jesus?'

Jesus smiles and says, 'Yes, I am Jesus.'

The Englishman beckons the bartender and tells him to send over a pint of Newcastle Brown Ale for Jesus, which the bartender duly does.

As before, Jesus accepts the drink and smiles over at the men.

Then the Australian calls out, 'Oi, you! D'ya reckon you're Jesus, or what?'

Jesus nods and says, 'Yes, I am Jesus.'

The Australian is mighty impressed and has the bartender send over a pint of VB for Jesus, which he accepts with pleasure.

Some time later, after finishing the drinks, Jesus leaves his seat and approaches the three men.

He reaches for the hand of the Irishman and shakes it, thanking him for the Guinness.

When he lets go, the Irishman gives a cry of amazement. 'Oh, God, the arthritis is gone,' he says. 'The arthritis I've had for years is gone. It's a miracle!'

Jesus then shakes the hand of the Englishman, thanking him for the Newcastle Brown Ale.

Upon letting go, the Englishman's eyes widen in shock. 'By Jove,' he exclaims, 'the migraine I've had for over 40 years is completely gone. It's a miracle!'

Jesus then approaches the Australian, who has a terrified look on his face. 'Piss off, mate. I'm on worker's comp.'

Vodka courage

A new priest at his first Mass was so nervous he could hardly speak. After Mass he asked the monsignor how he had done. The monsignor replied, 'When I am worried about getting nervous on the pulpit, I put a glass of vodka next to the water glass. If I start to get nervous, I take a sip.'

So, next Sunday he took the monsignor's advice. At the beginning of the sermon, he got nervous and took a drink. He proceeded to talk up a storm. Upon his return to his office after Mass, he found the following note on the door:

1. Sip the vodka, don't gulp.
2. There are 10 commandments, not 12.
3. There are 12 disciples, not 10.
4. Jesus was consecrated, not constipated.
5. Jacob wagered his donkey, he did not bet his ass.
6. We do not refer to Jesus Christ as the late JC.
7. The Father, Son, and Holy Ghost are not referred to as Daddy, Junior and the Spook.
8. David slew Goliath; he did not kick the shit out of him.
9. When David was hit by a rock and was knocked off his donkey, don't say he was stoned off his ass.
10. We do not refer to the cross as the 'Big T'.
11. When Jesus broke the bread at the Last Supper he said, 'Take this and eat it, for it is my body.' He did not say, 'Eat me.'
12. The Virgin Mary is not called 'Mary with the Cherry'.

13. The recommended grace before a meal is not: Rub-A-Dub-Dub, thanks for the grub, yeah, God.
14. Next Sunday there will be a taffy-pulling contest at St Peter's, not a peter-pulling contest at St Taffy's.

Church bulletins

These are (allegedly) actual clippings from church newspapers. A little proofreading would have saved a fair bit of embarrassment.

Announcement in the church bulletin for a National Prayer and Fasting Conference: 'The cost for attending the Prayer and Fasting Conference includes meals.'

'Ladies, don't forget the rummage sale. It's a chance to get rid of those things not worth keeping round the house. Don't forget your husbands.'

'The peacemaking meeting scheduled for today has been cancelled due to a conflict.'

'Don't let worry kill you — let the Church help.'

'Irving Benson and Jessie Carter were married on October 24 in the church; so ends a friendship that began in their school days.'

'At the evening service tonight, the sermon topic will be: "What is Hell?" Come early and listen to our choir practice.'

'Scouts are saving aluminium cans, bottles, and other items to be recycled. Proceeds will be used to cripple children.'

'The Lutheran men's group will meet at 6 p.m. Steak, mashed potatoes, green beans, bread and dessert will be served for a nominal feel.'

'For those of you who have children and don't know it, we have a nursery downstairs.'

'Please place your donation in the envelope along with the deceased persons you want remembered.'

'Attend and you will hear an excellent speaker and heave a healthy lunch.'

'The church will host an evening of fine dining, superb entertainment, and gracious hostility.'

'Potluck supper Sunday at 5 p.m. — prayer and medication to follow.'

'The ladies of the Church have cast off clothing of every kind. They may be seen in the basement on Friday afternoon.'

'Low Self-Esteem Support Group will meet Thursday at 7 p.m. Please use the back door.'

'Weight Watchers will meet at 7 p.m. at the First Presbyterian Church. Please use large double door at the side entrance.'

'The eighth-graders will be presenting Shakespeare's *Hamlet* in the Church basement Friday at 7 p.m. The congregation is invited to attend this tragedy.'

On a church door: 'This is the gate of Heaven. Enter ye all by this door. (This door is kept locked because of the draft. Please use side entrance.)'

Clergy

Two priests are in a Vatican bathroom using the urinals. One of them looks at the other one's penis and notices there's a Nicoderm patch on it. He turns to the other priest and says, 'I believe you're supposed to put that patch on your arm or shoulder, not your penis.'

The other one replies, 'It's working just fine. I'm down to two butts a day.'

Quasimodo

After Quasimodo's death, the bishop of the Cathedral of Notre Dame sent word through the streets of Paris that a new bell ringer was needed. The bishop decided that he would conduct the interviews personally and went up into the belfry to begin the screening process. After observing several applicants demonstrate their skill, he had decided to call it a day. Just then, an armless man approached him and announced that he was there to apply for the bell ringer's job.

The bishop was incredulous. 'You have no arms!'

'No matter,' said the man. 'Observe!'

And he began striking the bells with his face, producing a beautiful melody on the carillon. The bishop listened in astonishment, convinced he had finally found a replacement for Quasimodo. But suddenly, rushing forward to strike a bell, the armless man tripped and plunged headlong out of the belfry window to his death in the street below. The stunned bishop rushed to his side. When he reached the street, a crowd had gathered around the fallen figure, drawn by the beautiful music they had heard only moments before. As they silently parted to let the bishop through, one of them asked, 'Bishop, who was this man?'

'I don't know his name,' the bishop sadly replied, 'but his face rings a bell.'

The following day, despite the sadness that weighed heavily on his heart due to the unfortunate death of the armless campanologist, the bishop continued his interviews for the bell ringer of Notre Dame.

The first man to approach him said, 'Your Excellency, I am the brother of the poor armless wretch that fell to his death from this very belfry yesterday. I pray that you honour his life by allowing me to replace him in this duty.'

The bishop agreed to give the man an audition, and, as the armless man's brother stooped to pick up a mallet to strike the first bell, he groaned, clutched at his chest, twirled around, and died on the spot.

Two monks, hearing the bishop's cries of grief at this second tragedy, rushed up the stairs to his side.

'What has happened? Who is the man?' the first monk asked breathlessly.

'I don't know his name,' sighed the distraught bishop, 'but he's a dead ringer for his brother.'

Little Sisters of St Francis

A man is driving down a deserted stretch of highway when he notices a sign out of the corner of his eye. It reads:

SISTERS OF ST FRANCIS

HOUSE OF PROSTITUTION

10 MILES

He thinks it is a figment of his imagination and drives on without a second thought. Soon he sees another sign, which says:

SISTERS OF ST FRANCIS

HOUSE OF PROSTITUTION

5 MILES

He begins to realise that these signs are for real. Then he drives past a third sign saying:

SISTERS OF ST FRANCIS

HOUSE OF PROSTITUTION

NEXT RIGHT

His curiosity gets the best of him and he pulls into the drive. On the far side of the parking lot is a stone building with a small sign next to the door reading:

He climbs the steps and rings the bell. The door is answered by a nun in a long black habit who asks, 'What may we do for you, my son?'

He answers, 'I saw your signs along the highway, and was interested in possibly doing business.'

'Very well, my son. Please follow me.' He is led through many winding passages and is soon quite disoriented. The nun stops at a closed door and tells the man, 'Please knock on this door.' He does as he is told and another nun in a long habit, holding a tin cup, answers the door. This nun instructs, 'Please place $100 in the cup, then go through the large wooden door at the end of this hallway.' He gets $100 out of his wallet and places it in the second nun's cup, then trots eagerly down the hall and slips through the door, pulling it shut behind him.

As the door locks behind him, he finds himself back in the parking lot, facing another small sign:

GO IN PEACE. THE SISTERS OF ST FRANCIS HAVE JUST SCREWED YOU. SERVES YOU RIGHT — YOU HAVE PAID THE WAGES OF SIN!!

Taxi service

A cabbie picks up a nun. She gets into the cab, and the cab driver won't stop staring at her. She asks him why he is staring. He replies, 'I have a question to ask you, but I don't want to offend you.'

She answers, 'My son, you cannot offend me. When you're as old as I am and have been a nun as long as I have, you get a chance to see and hear just about everything. I'm sure that there's nothing you could say or ask that I would find offensive.'

'Well, I've always had a fantasy to have a nun kiss me.'

She responds, 'Well, let's see what we can do about that. Firstly, you have to be single, and secondly, you must be Catholic.'

The cab driver is very excited and says, 'Yes, I am single; and I'm Catholic too!'

'All right,' the nun says, 'pull into the next alley.'

He does and the nun fulfils his fantasy with a kiss that would make you blush. But when they get back on the road, the cab driver starts crying.

'My dear child,' says the nun, 'why are you crying?'

'Forgive me, Sister, but I have sinned. I lied. I must confess, I'm married and I'm Jewish.'

The nun says, 'That's OK. My name is Kevin and I'm on my way to a Halloween party.'

One climax

An older Jewish man married a younger woman. After several months, the young bride complained that she had never climaxed during sex and, by birthright, all Jewish women are entitled to at least one climax during sex. So they went to see the rabbi.

The rabbi told them to get a young, strong, handsome, virile man to wave a towel while they were having sex. This, said the rabbi, would cause the woman to climax.

So the couple tried it. After several attempts, still no climax. So they went back to the rabbi.

The rabbi said for the bride to change partners and have sex with the virile, handsome guy while her husband waved the towel.

They tried it that night and the woman went into wild, screaming, ear-splitting climaxes, one after another.

When this was over, the husband smugly looked down at the young man and said: 'You see, schmuck, that's how you have to wave the towel!'

Business as usual

Two beggars were sitting side by side on a street in Mexico City. One had a crucifix in front of him, the other one the Star of David. Many people went by and looked at both beggars, but put money only into the hat of the beggar sitting behind the crucifix.

A priest came by, stopped and watched throngs of people giving money to the beggar behind the crucifix, but none gave to the beggar behind the Star of David.

Finally, the priest went over to the beggar behind the Star of David and said, 'My poor fellow, don't you understand? This is a Catholic country. People aren't going to give you money if you sit there with a Star of David in front of you, especially when you're sitting beside a beggar who has a crucifix. In fact, they would probably give to him just out of spite.'

The beggar behind the Star of David listened to the priest, turned to the beggar with the crucifix and said, 'Moshe, look who's trying to teach the Ginsberg brothers about marketing.'

The troublesome possums

There were five houses of worship in a small South Australian town: the Presbyterian church, the Baptist church, the Methodist church, the Catholic church, and the Jewish synagogue. Each was overrun with pesky possums.

One day, the Presbyterian church called a meeting to decide what to do about the possums. After much prayer and consideration they determined that the possums were predestined to be there and they shouldn't interfere with God's divine will.

In the Baptist church the possums had taken up habitation in the baptistery. The deacons met and decided to put a cover on the baptistery and drown the possums in it. The possums escaped somehow and there were twice as many there the next week.

The Methodist church got together and decided that they were not in a position to harm any of God's creation. So, they humanely trapped the possums and set them free a few miles outside of town. Three days later, the possums, being possums, were back.

But the Catholic church came up with the best and most effective solution. They baptised the possums and registered them as members of the church. Now they only see them at Christmas and Easter.

Not much was heard about the Jewish synagogue except that they had taken one possum and had a short service with him called circumcision and they haven't seen a possum on the property since.

Mixed religion

Although born to a Catholic family, Chester had always wanted to be Jewish. As a senior in college, he decided to take the plunge and go through the formal conversion process. He studied Judaism all semester. Finally, he felt he was ready to take the test and complete the conversion. On the appointed day, he arrived at the rabbi's office, ready to begin. The rabbi said, 'I'm sorry, but before I give you the test, I must discuss my fee — it's $5000.'

'Five thousand dollars!' exclaimed Chester. 'That's a lot of money. How about $500?'

'Congratulations, you pass,' said the rabbi.

A talk with the Almighty

A man takes it easy, lying on the grass and looking up at the clouds. As he identifies the different shapes, he begins to talk with God.

'God,' he asks, 'how long is a million years?'

God answers, 'In my frame of reference, it's about a minute.'

The man asks, 'God, how much is a million dollars?'

God answers, 'To me, it's a penny.'

The man thinks about this for a brief period, and then asks, 'God, can I have a penny?'

God answers, 'In a minute.'

14 DRUNK AS A SKUNK AND FULL AS A GOOG

There was a time in Australia's history, around the goldrush era, when the population of a town was measured by the number of drinking establishments in the area, be it wayside shanty tent, grog shop or pub. Ballarat, in 1873, for example, had nearly 500 drinking establishments — one for every 60 people, including children. We worked hard and played harder, consuming all manner of alcoholic drinks, including Dutch gin, rum, ale and champagne. Being a male-dominated society, hard boozing was considered par for the course. If you believe the media, times haven't changed too much, and evidence points to young Australians as being at the top of the ladder for binge drinking. Maybe our determined hard drinking is closely related to our reputation as a 'sports crazy' nation.

Much of our bush tradition, be it song, poetry or yarn-telling, is intrinsically linked to drink. Certainly, many of today's most popular jokes centre on hotel life, the effects of booze and how 'the devil made me do it'.

In Australia we 'drink like a fish', 'get on the booze', get 'shickered', 'stonkered', or 'full as a goog', we get 'pissed as a fart' and 'pie-eyed'. We're a colourful lot of 'booze artists'.

Talking clock

A drunk was proudly showing off his new apartment to a couple of his friends late one night. When they entered the bedroom, they saw a big brass gong next to the bed.

'What's that big brass gong doing in your bedroom?' one of the guests asked.

'It's not a gong. It's a talking clock,' the drunk replied.

'A talking clock? Seriously?' asked his astonished friend.

'Yup,' replied the drunk.

'How's it work?' the friend asked, squinting at it.

'Watch,' the drunk replied. He picked up the mallet, gave it an ear-shattering pound, and stepped back. The three friends stood looking at one another for a moment.

Suddenly, someone on the other side of the wall screamed, 'You arsehole, it's three o'clock in the morning!'

Now this is drunk!

A drunk walks out of a bar with a key in his hand and he is stumbling back and forth. A cop on the beat sees him and approaches. 'Can I help you, sir?'

'Yessh! Ssssomebody ssstole my carrr,' the man replies.

The cop asks, 'Where was your car the last time you saw it?'

'It wasss on the end of thisshh key,' the man replies.

About that time the cop looks down and sees the man's willy is hanging out of his fly for all the world to see.

He asks the man, 'Sir, are you aware that you are exposing yourself?'

Momentarily confused, the drunk looks down at his crotch and, without missing a beat, blurts out: 'I'll be damned, my girlfriend's gone too!'

Wise investment

In 2001 if you had bought $1000 of One.Tel stock, it would now be worth about $9 to you as an unsecured creditor if you were lucky.

In 2002 if you had bought HIH stock, you would have about $6.50 left of the original $1000.

In 2003 if you had gone overseas and bought Enron you would have less than $5 left.

But, if you had purchased $1000 worth of beer only one year ago, drank all the beer, then turned in the cans for the aluminium recycling price, you would have $24.

Based on the above, the best investment advice is to drink heavily and recycle.

Biker bar

A drunken man walks into a biker bar, sits down at the bar and orders a drink. Looking around, he sees three men sitting at a corner table.

He gets up, staggers to the table, leans over, looks the biggest, meanest biker in the face and says: 'I went by your grandma's house today and I saw her in the hallway buck-naked. Man, she is a fine-looking woman!'

The biker looks at him and doesn't say a word. His mates are confused, because he is one bad biker and would fight at the drop of a hat.

The drunk leans on the table again and says: 'I got it on with your grandma and she is good — the best I ever had!'

The biker's mates are starting to get really mad but the biker still says nothing.

The drunk leans on the table one more time and says, 'I'll tell you something else, boy, your grandma liked it!'

At this point the biker stands up, takes the drunk by the shoulders, looks him square in the eyes and says, 'Grandpa ... go home, you're drunk.'

AMA warning

Due to increasing products liability litigation, beer manufacturers have accepted the Australian Medical Association's suggestion that the following warning labels be placed immediately on all beer containers:

WARNING: Consumption of alcohol may make you think you are whispering when you are not.

WARNING: Consumption of alcohol is a major factor in dancing like a wanker.

WARNING: Consumption of alcohol may cause you to tell the same boring story over and over again until your friends want to smash your head in.

WARNING: Consumption of alcohol may cause you to thay shings like thish.

WARNING: Consumption of alcohol may lead you to believe that ex-lovers are really dying for you to telephone them at four in the morning.

WARNING: Consumption of alcohol may leave you wondering what the hell happened to your trousers.

WARNING: Consumption of alcohol may make you think you can logically converse with members of the opposite sex without spitting.

WARNING: Consumption of alcohol may make you think you have mystical Kung Fu powers.

WARNING: Consumption of alcohol may cause you to roll over in the morning and see something really scary (whose name and/or species you can't remember).

WARNING: Consumption of alcohol is the leading cause of inexplicable rug burns on the forehead.

WARNING: Consumption of alcohol may create the illusion that you are tougher, more attractive, and smarter than some really, really big guy called Bruno.

WARNING: Consumption of alcohol may lead you to believe you are invisible.

WARNING: Consumption of alcohol may lead you to think people are laughing with you.

WARNING: Consumption of alcohol may cause a flux in the time-space continuum, whereby small (and sometimes large) gaps of time may seem to literally disappear.

WARNING: Consumption of alcohol may actually cause pregnancy.

Things that are difficult to say when you're drunk

a)   Innovative
b)   Preliminary
c)   Proliferation
d)   Cinnamon

Things that are *very* difficult to say when you're drunk

a)   Specificity
b)   British Constitution
c)   Passive-aggressive disorder
d)   Transubstantiate

Things that are *downright impossible* to say when you're drunk

a) Thanks, but I don't want to sleep with you.

b) Nope, no more booze for me.

c) Sorry, but you're not really my type.

d) No kebab for me, thank you.

e) Good evening, officer, isn't it lovely out tonight?

f) I'm not interested in fighting you.

g) Oh, I just couldn't — no one wants to hear me sing.

h) Thank you, but I won't make any attempt to dance — I have zero coordination.

i) Where is the nearest toilet? I refuse to vomit in the street.

In the supermarket

A woman was shopping at her local supermarket where she selected:

- a 2 litre bottle of skim milk,
- a carton of free-range eggs,
- a litre of orange juice,
- a head of cos lettuce,
- a 2 kilogram can of coffee,
- and a 1 kilogram package of streaky bacon.

As she was unloading her items on the conveyor belt to check out, a drunk standing behind her watched as she placed the items in front the cashier. While the cashier was ringing up her purchases, the drunk calmly stated, 'You must be single.'

The woman was a bit startled by this proclamation, but she was intrigued by the drunk's intuition, since she was indeed single. She looked at her six items on the belt and saw nothing particularly unusual about her selections that could have tipped him off about her marital status.

Curiosity getting the better of her, she said, 'Well, you know what, you're absolutely correct. But how on earth did you know that?'

The drunk replied, ''Cause you're ugly.'

Cuddly

A woman meets a gorgeous man in a bar. They talk, they connect and they end up leaving together. They get back to his apartment and she notices that his bedroom is completely packed with sweet cuddly teddy bears. Hundreds of cute small bears on a shelf all the way along the floor, cuddly medium-sized ones on a shelf a little higher, and huge enormous bears on the top shelf along the wall. The woman is surprised that this guy would have a collection of teddy bears, especially one that's so extensive, but she decides not to mention this to him, and actually is quite impressed by his sensitive side. She turns to him, they kiss, and then they rip each other's clothes off.

After an intense night of passion with this sensitive guy, when they are lying there together in the afterglow, the woman rolls over and asks, smiling, 'Well, how was it?'

The guy says: 'Help yourself to any prize from the bottom shelf.'

Who'll buy me a drink?

A large woman, wearing a sleeveless sundress, walked into a bar.

She raised her right arm, revealing a huge, hairy armpit as she pointed to all the people sitting at the bar and asked, 'What man here will buy a lady a drink?'

The bar went silent as the patrons tried to ignore her. But down at the end of the bar, a glassy-eyed drunk slammed his hand down on the counter and bellowed, 'Give the ballerina a drink!'

The bartender poured the drink and the woman chugged it down.

She turned to the patrons and again pointed around at all of them, revealing the same hairy armpit, and asked, 'What man here will buy a lady a drink?'

Once again, the same little drunk slapped his money down on the bar and said, 'Give the ballerina another drink!'

The bartender approached the drunk and said, 'I say, old chap, it's your business if you want to buy the lady a drink, but why do you keep calling her the ballerina?'

The drunk replied, 'Any woman who can lift her leg that high has to be a ballerina!'

A good pub

An Australian, an Englishman and a Scotsman were sitting in a bar. The view was fantastic, the beer excellent, and the food exceptional. 'Y'know,' said the Scotsman, 'I still prefer the pubs back home. Why, in Glasgow there's a little bar called The Thistle. Now the landlord there goes out of his way for the locals so much that when you buy four drinks he will buy the fifth drink for you.'

'Well,' said the Englishman, 'at my local, The Red Lion, the barman there will buy you your third drink after you buy the first two.'

'Ahhh that's nothin',' said the Aussie. 'Back home in Dubbo there's Ryan's. Now the moment you set foot in the place they'll buy you a drink, then another, all the drinks you like. Then when you've had enough drinks they'll take you upstairs and see that you get laid. All on the house.'

The Englishman and Scotsman immediately pour scorn on the Australian's claims, but he swears every word is true.

'Well,' said the Englishman, 'did this actually happen to you?'

'Not me myself, personally, no,' said the Aussie. 'But it did happen to me sister.'

That's me!

Late one night a police patrol officer was doing his rounds when he spotted a very drunk man trying to get into a house. Upon approaching the man, the officer asked, 'Is this your house, sir?'

In a very drunk reply the man said, 'It sure is and I can prove it.'

Once inside, the drunk said, 'See that lounge suite? It's my suite.' Then walking to the bedrooms, he said, 'See those two boys in bed? They're my boys.' And approaching the main bedroom, he said, 'See that woman in bed? That's my wife.' And in closing he said, 'See that man next to her? *That's me!*'

16 reasons why alcohol should be served at work

1. It's an incentive to show up.
2. It leads to more honest communications.
3. It reduces complaints about low pay.
4. Employees tell management what they think, not what they want to hear.
5. It encourages car-pooling.
6. It increases job satisfaction because if you have a bad job, you don't care.
7. It eliminates vacations because people would rather come to work.

8. It makes fellow employees look better.
9. It makes the cafeteria food taste better.
10. Bosses are more likely to hand out raises when they are wasted.
11. Salary negotiations are a lot more profitable.
12. Employees work later since there's no longer a need to relax at the bar.
13. It makes everyone more open with his or her ideas.
14. It eliminates the need for employees to get drunk on their lunch break.
15. Employees no longer need coffee to sober up.
16. Sitting 'bare arse' on the copy machine will no longer be seen as gross.

A message for the manager

A very attractive lady goes up to a bar in a quiet pub near Woop Woop. She gestures alluringly to the bartender who comes over immediately. When he arrives, she seductively signals that he should bring his face closer to hers. When he does she begins to gently caress his full beard. 'Are you the manager?' she asks, softly stroking his face with both hands.

'Actually, no,' the man replies.

'Can you get him for me? I need to speak to him,' she says, running her hands beyond his beard and into his hair.

'I'm afraid I can't,' breathes the bartender. 'Is there anything I can do?'

'Yes, there is. I need you to give him a message,' she continues, running her forefinger across the bartender's lips and slyly popping a couple of her fingers into his mouth and allowing him to suck them gently.

'What should I tell him?' the bartender manages to ask.

'Tell him,' she whispers, 'there is no toilet paper, soap, or paper towels in the ladies room.'

Date-rape drug alert

Police are warning all men who frequent clubs and pubs or who attend parties to be alert and stay cautious when offered a drink by any woman.

A new date-rape drug on the market called 'beer' is being used by many females to target unsuspecting males. The drug is generally found in liquid form and is now available almost anywhere.

It comes in bottles, cans, from taps and in large 'kegs'. 'Beer' is used by female sexual predators at parties and bars to persuade their male victims to go home and have sex with them. Typically, a woman needs only to persuade a guy to consume a few units of 'beer' and then simply ask him home for no-strings attached sex. Men are rendered helpless by this approach.

After several 'beers' men will often succumb to desires to perform sexual acts on horrific-looking women to whom they would never normally be attracted.

After drinking 'beer', men often awaken with only hazy memories of what happened to them the night before, often with just a vague feeling that something bad occurred.

At other times these unfortunate men are swindled out of their life's savings in a familiar scam known as 'a relationship'.

It has been reported that in extreme cases, the female may even be shrewd enough to entrap the unsuspecting male into a long-term form of servitude and punishment referred to as 'marriage'. Apparently, men are much more susceptible to this scam after 'beer' is administered and sex is offered by the predatory female.

Please! Forward this warning to every male you know.

However, if you fall victim to this insidious 'beer', and the predatory women administering it, there are male support groups with venues across Australia where you can discuss the details of your shocking encounter in an open and frank manner with similarly affected, like-minded guys. For the support group nearest you, just look up 'Golf Courses' in the Yellow Pages.

Rocks: a meaning for life

A philosophy professor stood before his class with some items in front of him. When the class began, wordlessly he picked up a large empty mayonnaise jar and proceeded to fill it with rocks about 5 centimetres in diameter. He then asked the students if the jar was full. They agreed that it was.

So the professor then picked up a box of pebbles and poured them into the jar. He shook the jar lightly. The pebbles, of course, rolled into the open areas between the rocks. He then asked the students again if the jar was full. They agreed it was.

The students laughed. The professor picked up a box of sand and poured it into the jar. Of course, the sand filled up everything else.

'Now,' said the professor, 'I want you to recognise that this is your life. The rocks are the important things — your family, your partner, your health, and your children — things that if everything else was lost and only they remained, your life would still be full. The pebbles are the other things that matter, like your job, your house, and your car. The sand is everything else. The small stuff.

'If you put the sand into the jar first, there is no room for the pebbles or the rocks. The same goes for your life. If you spend all your time and energy on the small stuff, you will never have room for the things that are important to you. Pay attention to the things that are critical to your happiness. Play with your children. Take time to get medical check-ups. Take your partner out dancing. There will always be time to go to work, clean the house, give a dinner party and fix the garbage disposal.

'Take care of the rocks first — the things that really matter. Set your priorities. The rest is just sand.'

But then a student took the jar that the other students and the professor agreed was full, and proceeded to pour in a glass of beer. Of course, the beer filled the remaining spaces within the jar, making the jar truly full. Which shows that no matter how full your life is, there is always room for a beer.

Christmas cake recipe

Ingredients
* 1 cup of water
* 1 tsp baking soda
* 1 cup of sugar
* 1 tsp salt
* 1 cup of brown sugar
* lemon juice
* 4 large eggs
* nuts
* 1 bottle Absolut vodka
* 2 cups of dried fruit

Preparation
1. Sample the vodka to check quality.
2. Take a large bowl, check the vodka again.
3. To be sure it is of the highest quality, pour one level cup and drink.
4. Repeat.

5. Turn on the electric mixer.
6. Beat one cup of butter in a large fluffy bowl.
7. Add one teaspoon of sugar.
8. Beat again.
9. At this point it's best to make sure the vodka is shtill OK.
10. Try another cup … just in case.
11. Turn off the mixerer.
12. Break 2 leggs and add to the bowl and chuck in the cup of dried fruit.
13. Pick fruit off floooooor.
14. Mix on the turner.
15. If the fried druit gets stuck in the beaterers pry it loose with a drewscriver.
16. Sample the vodka to check for tonsisticity.
17. Next, sift two cups of salt. Or something. Who giveshz a shit.
18. Check the vodka.
19. Now shift the lemon juice and strain your nuts.
20. Add one table.
21. Add a spoon of sugar, or somefink. Whatever you can find.
22. Greash the oven.
23. Turn the cake tin 360 degrees and try not to fall over.
24. Don't forget to beat off the turner.
25. Finally, throw the bowl through the window, finish the vodka and kick the cat.

Cherry Mistmas!

Police inspection

Recently a routine Sunshine Coast police patrol parked outside a local neighbourhood tavern. Late in the evening the officer noticed a man leaving the bar so intoxicated that he could barely walk. The man stumbled around the car park for a few minutes, with the officer quietly observing.

After what seemed an eternity, and trying his keys on five vehicles, the man managed to find his car, which he fell into.

He was there for a few minutes as a number of other patrons left the bar and drove off. Finally he started the car, switched the wipers on and off (it was a fine dry night), flicked the indicators on and off, tooted the horn and then switched on the lights. He moved the car forward a few centimetres, reversed a little and then remained stationary for a few more minutes as more patrons left in their vehicles.

At last he pulled out of the car park and started to drive slowly down the road.

The police officer, having patiently waited all this time, now started up the patrol car, put on the flashing lights, promptly pulled the man over and carried out a Breathalyser test.

To his amazement the Breathalyser indicated no evidence of the man having consumed alcohol at all. Dumbfounded, the officer said, 'I'll have to ask you to accompany me to the police station. This Breathalyser equipment must be broken.'

'I doubt it,' said the man. 'Tonight I'm the designated decoy.'

Ethel and her wheelchair

Ethel is a bit of a demon in her wheelchair, and loves to charge around the nursing home, taking corners on one wheel and getting up to maximum speed on the long corridors. Because she and her fellow residents are one sandwich short of a picnic, they all tolerate each other, some of the men actually joining in.

One day, Ethel was speeding up one corridor when a door opened and Mad Mike stepped out of his room with his arm outstretched. '*Stop!*' he said in a firm voice. 'Have you got a licence for that thing?' Ethel fished around in her handbag and pulled out a Kit Kat wrapper and held it up to him. 'OK,' he said, and away Ethel sped down the hall.

As she took the corner near the TV lounge on one wheel, Weird William popped out in front of her and shouted, '*STOP!* Have you got proof of insurance?' Ethel dug into her handbag, pulled out a beer coaster and held it up to him. William nodded and said, 'Carry on, ma'am.'

As Ethel neared the final corridor before the front door, Bonkers Brian stepped out in front of her, stark naked, holding a very sizeable (for his age) erection in his hand. 'Oh, no!' said Ethel. 'Not the Breathalyser again!'

Magic Bitter

A woman walks into a pub and sees a really good-looking bloke sitting at the bar. She goes over and asks him what he is drinking.

He says, 'Magic Bitter.'

She thinks he's a bit of a nutter, so she continues walking around the pub. After realising that there is no one else worth talking to, she goes back to the man sitting at the bar. She says, 'That isn't really Magic Bitter, is it?'

He says, 'Yes. I'll show you.' So he takes a gulp of the bitter, jumps out the window, flies around the building three times, and comes back in the window.

She can't believe it. She says to him, 'I bet you can't do that again.'

So he takes another drink of the bitter, jumps out the window, flies around the building three times, and comes back in the window.

She is amazed. She says she wants a Magic Bitter too.

So the bloke says to the bartender, 'Give her a pint of what I'm having.'

She gets her pint, takes a gulp, jumps out the window, plummets 30 storeys, breaks every bone in her body and dies.

The bartender looks up at the bloke and says, 'Superman, you're such a wanker when you're pissed.'

20 reasons when you should call it a night

1. You have absolutely no idea where your bag or wallet is.
2. You truly believe that dancing with your arms overhead and wiggling your bottom while yelling 'She Bangs She Bangs' is the hottest dance.
3. You've suddenly decided that you want to fight someone and you honestly believe that you could do it too.
4. In your last trip to the toilet you realised you now look more like Edna Everage than the goddess you were just four hours ago.
5. You drop your 3 a.m. kebab on the floor, pick it up and carry on eating it.
6. You start crying and telling everyone you see that you love them sooooo.
7. There are less than three hours before you're due to start work.
8. You've found a deeper/spiritual side to the geek sitting next to you.
9. The man you're flirting with used to be your biology teacher.
10. The urge to take off articles of clothing becomes strangely overwhelming.

11. Your eyes just don't seem to want to stay open on their own so you decide to keep them half closed and think it looks exotic.

12. You seem to think that it's a really good idea to get your mates to push you down the street in a shopping trolley.

13. You yell at the bartender, who (you think) cheated you by giving you just lemonade, but that's just because you can no longer taste the vodka.

14. You think you're in bed, but the pillow feels strangely like the kitchen floor.

15. You start every conversation with a booming, 'DON'T take this the WRONG WAY but …'

16. You fail to notice that the toilet lid's down when you sit on it.

17. Your hugs begin to resemble wrestling takedown moves.

18. You're soooo tired you just sit on the floor (wherever you happen to be standing).

19. You begin leaving the buttons open on your fly to cut down on the time you're in the bathroom away from your drink.

20. You take your shoes off because you really believe it's their fault that you're having problems walking straight.

15 MEDICAL MARVELS

M edicine, like the modern office, continues to change at a staggering pace. Once-frightening operations are now done as day procedures, computers track our every breath and heartbeat, blood is analysed to reveal its innermost secrets, and it's said that you can still get a pizza delivery quicker than an ambulance.

We have a fascination with the medical profession that has been fuelled by countless medical television dramas, including the latest hit, *Grey's Anatomy*, where the sex lives of doctors and nurses are detailed with never-ending monotony.

Sickness is never funny, especially to the sick; however, this has not stopped the flow of humour about hospitals, emergency medical situations, medical workers or individuals who face the knife. We are fascinated because we secretly fear being the patient. Laughing at medicine allows us to steady ourselves in case we eventually face the same fate. Mind you, some of the jokes in this category would see you in rather awkward situations best avoided as they tackle vasectomies, pill poppers, out-of-control patients on Viagra, mental instability and the strange language of doctors.

Medical procedures

When a panel of doctors was asked to vote on adding a new wing to its hospital, the allergists voted to scratch it and the dermatologists advised no rash moves. The gastroenterologists had a gut feeling about it, but the neurologists thought the administration had a lot of nerve, and the obstetricians stated they were all labouring under a misconception.

The ophthalmologists considered the idea short-sighted, the pathologists yelled, 'Over my dead body!' while the paediatricians said, 'Grow up!'

The psychiatrists thought the whole idea was madness, the surgeons decided to wash their hands of the whole thing, and the radiologists could see right through it! The internists thought it was a bitter pill to swallow. The plastic surgeons said, 'This puts a whole new face on the matter.' The podiatrists thought it was a step forward, but the urologists felt the scheme wouldn't hold water. The anaesthesiologists thought the whole idea was a gas, and the cardiologists didn't have the heart to say no.

And in the end, the proctologists left the decision up to some arsehole who didn't give a shit!

Check-up time

An old man goes to the doctor for his yearly physical, his elderly wife tagging along. When the doctor enters the examination room, he tells the old man, 'I need a urine sample, a stool sample and a sperm sample.'

The old man, being hard of hearing, looks at his wife and yells: *'What? What did he say? What's he want?'*

His wife yells back, 'Just give him your underwear.'

Bird flu symptoms

The Australian Medical Association has released a list of symptoms of bird flu. If you experience any of the following, please seek medical attention immediately:

1. High fever
2. Congestion
3. Nausea
4. Fatigue

5. Aching in the joints
6. An irresistible urge to shit on someone's windscreen

A visit to the asylum

During a visit to the mental asylum, a visitor asked the director what defined whether or not a patient should be institutionalised.

'Well,' said the director, 'we fill up a bathtub, then we offer the patient a teaspoon, a teacup and a bucket and ask them to empty the bathtub.'

'Oh, I understand,' said the visitor. 'A normal person would use the bucket because it's bigger than the spoon or the teacup.'

'No,' said the director, 'a normal person would pull out the plug. Do you want a room with or without a view?'

Viagra

An elderly gentleman went to the local drug store and asked the pharmacist for the little blue Viagra pill.

The pharmacist asked, 'How many?' The man replied, 'Just a few, maybe a half dozen. I cut each one into four pieces.'

The pharmacist said, 'That's too small a dose. That won't get you through sex.'

The old fellow said, 'Oh, I'm past 90 years old and I don't even think about sex much any more. I just want it to stick out far enough so I don't pee on my new golf shoes.'

The Scot and the dentist

A Scotsman asks the dentist the cost for a tooth extraction.

'Eighty-five dollars for an extraction,' was the dentist's reply.

'Eighty-five dollars! Huv ye no' got anythin' cheaper?'

'That's the normal charge,' said the dentist.

'Whit aboot if ye didnae use any anaesthetic?'

'That's unusual, sir, but I could do it and knock $15 off.'

'Whit aboot if ye used one of your dentist trainees and still without an anaesthetic?'

'I can't guarantee their professionalism and it'll be painful. But the price could drop to $40.'

'How aboot if ye make it a trainin' session, and 'ave yer student do the work?'

'It'll be good for the students,' mulled the dentist. 'I'll charge you $5. But it will be very painful and traumatic.'

'Och, now yer talkin', laddie! It's a deal,' said the Scotsman. 'Can ye confirm an appointment for the wife next Tuesday then?'

Medical benefits

A wealthy hospital benefactor was being shown around the hospital when, during her tour, she passed a room where a male patient was masturbating furiously.

'Oh my *God*!' screamed the woman. 'That's disgraceful! Why is he doing that?'

The doctor who was leading the tour calmly explained, 'I'm very sorry that you were exposed to that, but this man has a serious condition where his testicles rapidly fill with semen, and if he doesn't do that at least five times a day, he'll be in extreme pain and his testicles could easily rupture.'

'Oh well, in that case, I guess it's OK,' commented the woman.

In the very next room, a male patient was lying in bed and it was obvious that a female therapist was performing oral sex on him.

Again the woman screamed, 'Oh my *God*! How can *that* be justified?'

Again the doctor spoke very calmly. 'Same condition, better health plan.'

Double dose of Viagra

A man went to the doctor's office to get a double dose of Viagra. The doctor told him that he couldn't allow him a double dose.

'Why not?' asked the man.

'Because it's not safe,' replied the doctor.

'But I need it really bad,' said the man.

'Well, why do you need it so badly?' asked the doctor.

The man said, 'My girlfriend is coming into town on Friday, my ex-wife will be here on Saturday and my wife is coming home on Sunday! Can't you see? I must have a double dose!'

The doctor finally relented, saying, 'OK, I'll give it to you but you must come in on Monday morning so I can check to see if there are any side effects.'

On Monday the man dragged himself in with his arm in a sling.

The doctor asked, 'What happened to you?'

The man said, 'No one showed up …'

Love letter

I shall seek and find you.

I shall take you to bed and have my way with you.

I will make you ache, shake, and sweat until you moan and groan.
I will make you beg for mercy, beg me to stop.

I will exhaust you to the point that you will be relieved when I finish with you. And you will be weak for days.

All my love,
The Flu

Twenty-four hours to live

A man returns from the doctor and tells his wife that the doctor has told him he has only 24 hours to live. Given this prognosis, he asks his wife for sex. Naturally, she agrees, and they make love.

About six hours later, the husband goes to his wife and says, 'Honey, you know I now have only 18 hours to live. Could we please do it one more time?' Of course, the wife agrees and they do it again.

Later, as the man gets into bed, he looks at his watch and realises he now has only eight hours left. He touches his wife's shoulder and asks, 'Honey, please … just one more time before I die?'

She says, 'Of course, dear,' and they make love for the third time.

After this session, the wife rolls over and falls asleep. The man, however, worried about his impending death, tosses and turns until he's down to four more hours. He taps his wife, who groans as he whispers, 'Honey, I have only four more hours. Do you think we could …?'

At this point the wife sits up and says, 'Listen, I have to get up in the morning … You don't!'

Weighing machine

Allen took his blind date to Luna Park at St Kilda Beach.

'What would you like to do first?' asked Allen.

'I want to get weighed,' said Sandra.

They ambled over to the weight guesser. He guessed 120 pounds. She got on the scale; it read 117 and she won a prize.

Next, the couple went on the ferris wheel. When the ride was over, Allen again asked Sandra what she would like to do.

'I want to get weighed,' she said.

Back to the weight guesser they went. Since they had been there before, he guessed her correct weight, and Allen lost his dollar.

The couple walked around the carnival and again he asked where to next.

'I want to get weighed,' she responded.

By this time, Allen figured she was really weird and took her home early, dropping her off with a handshake.

Her roommate, Laura, asked her about the blind date: 'How did it go?'

Sandra responded, 'Oh, Waura, it was wousy.'

The redhead

A young redhead goes into the doctor's office and says that her body hurts wherever she touches it.

'Impossible,' says the doctor. 'Show me.'

She takes her finger, pushes her elbow and screams in agony. She then pushes her knee and screams, and pushes her ankle and screams. Everywhere she touches makes her scream.

The doctor says, 'You're not really a redhead, are you?'

'No,' she says, 'I'm actually a blonde.'

'I thought so,' the doctor says. 'Your finger is broken.'

Dental work

A guy and a girl meet at a bar. They get along so well that they decide to go to the girl's place. A few drinks later, the guy takes off his shirt and then washes his hands. He then takes off his trousers and washes his hands again.

The girl has been watching him and says, 'You must be a dentist.'

The guy, surprised, says, 'Yes … how did you figure that out?'

'Easy,' she replies. 'You keep washing your hands.'

One thing leads to another and they make love.

After they are done, the girl says, 'You must be a really good dentist.'

The guy, now with a boosted ego, says, 'Well yes, I'm a good dentist. How did you figure that out?'

'I didn't feel a thing!'

Eye nerve fact

Did you know that in the human body there is a nerve that connects the eyeball to the anus? It is called the anal optic nerve.

It is responsible for giving people a shitty outlook on life. If you don't believe it, pull a hair from your arse, and see if it doesn't bring a tear to your eye.

Baby's first examination

A woman and a baby were in the doctor's examining room waiting for the doctor to come in for the baby's first examination.

The doctor arrived, examined the baby, checked his weight, and being a little concerned, asked if the baby was breast-fed or bottle-fed.

'Breast-fed,' she replied.

'Well, strip down to your waist,' the doctor ordered.

She did. He pinched her nipples, then pressed, kneaded, and rubbed both breasts for a while in a detailed examination.

Motioning to her to get dressed, he said, 'No wonder this baby is underweight. You don't have any milk.'

'I know,' she said, 'I'm his grandma, but I'm glad I came.'

Big Maccas

A woman decides to have a facelift for her birthday She spends $5000 and feels pretty good about the results. On her way home, she stops at a newsagent to buy a paper. Before leaving, she says to the shop assistant, 'I hope you don't mind my asking, but how old do you think I am?'

'About 32,' comes the reply.

'I'm exactly 47,' the woman says happily.

A little while later she goes into McDonald's and asks the counter girl the very same question.

The girl replies, 'I guess about 29.'

'Nope, I'm 47.'

Now, she's feeling really good about herself. She stops at a chemist on her way down the street. She goes up to the counter to get some mints and asks the pharmacist this burning question.

The pharmacist responds, 'Oh, I'd say 30.'

Again she proudly responds, 'I am 47, but thank you.'

While waiting for the bus to go home, she asks an old man the same question.

He replies, 'Lady, I'm 78 and my eyesight is going. Although, when I was young, there was a sure way to tell how old a woman was. It sounds very forward, but it requires you to let me put my hands under your bra. Then I can tell you exactly how old you are.'

They wait in silence on the empty street until curiosity gets the best of her. She finally blurts out, 'What the heck — go ahead.'

He slips both of his hands under her blouse and under her bra and begins to feel around very slowly and carefully.

After a couple of minutes of this, she says, 'OK, OK … how old am I?'

He completes one last squeeze of her breasts, removes his hands, and says, 'Madam, you are 47.'

Stunned and amazed, the woman says, 'That was incredible — how could you tell?'

The old man replies, 'Promise you won't get mad?'

'No, I won't get mad,' she says.

He replies, 'I was behind you in line at McDonald's.'

Easy solution

Patient: 'Doctor, I've got a strawberry stuck up my bum.'

Doctor: 'I've got some cream for that!'

Medical quickies

Doctor: 'Do you suffer from stress?'

Patient: 'No, but I think I'm a carrier.'

Patient: 'Well, Doc, how do I stand?'

Doctor: 'I don't know, it's a damned miracle.'

After a careful examination, the doctor came out of the consulting room and spoke to the patient's wife. 'I'm afraid I don't like the look of your husband.'

Wife: 'Neither do I, but he's nice to the kids.'

The doctor checked the patient over and with a puzzled look said to him, 'I can't work it out. I think it must be due to drinking.'

Patient: 'I understand, Doc. I'll come back when you're sober.'

Old Bill was in for his annual check-up. After the examination, the doctor tactfully said: 'Well, old fella, I think it's time to take it easy and cut back on half your sex life.'

Old Bill replied: 'Which half? Talking about it or thinking about it?'

Medical language

Artery: The study of paintings

Bacteria: Back door to cafeteria

Barium: What doctors do when patients die

Benign: What you be, after you be eight

Caesarean Section: A neighbourhood in Rome

Catscan: Searching for Kitty

Cauterise: Made eye contact with her

Colic: A sheep dog

Coma: A punctuation mark

Dilate: To live long

Enema: Not a friend

Fester: Quicker than someone else

Fibula: A small lie

Impotent: Distinguished, well known

Labour Pain: Getting hurt at work

Medical Staff: A doctor's cane

Morbid: A higher offer

Nitrates: Cheaper than day rates

Node: I knew it

Outpatient: A person who has fainted

Pelvis: Second cousin to Elvis

Post Operative: A letter carrier

Recovery Room: Place to do upholstery

Rectum: Nearly killed him

Secretion: Hiding something

Seizure: Roman emperor

Tablet: A small table

Terminal Illness: Getting sick at the airport

Tumour: One plus one more

Two Condoms: To be sure, to be sure

Urine: Opposite of 'you're out'

Reporting off

Hung Chow calls into work and says, 'Hey, boss, I not come work today. I really sick. I got headache, stomach ache, and my legs hurt. I not come work.'

The boss says, 'You know, Hung Chow, I really need you today. When I feel like that I go to my wife and tell her to give me sex. That makes me feel better and I can go to work. You should try that.'

Two hours later Hung Chow calls again: 'Boss, I do what you say, and I feel great! I be at work real soon. You got nice house.'

Smack him again

Due to a power outage at the time, only one paramedic responded to the call. The house was very, very dark, so the paramedic asked Katelyn, a three-year-old girl, to hold a flashlight high over her mummy so he could see while he helped deliver the baby. Very diligently, Katelyn did as she was asked. Mum pushed and pushed, and after a little while the baby was born.

The paramedic lifted him by his little feet and spanked him on his bottom. The baby began to cry. The paramedic then thanked Katelyn for her help and asked the wide-eyed three-year-old what she thought about what she had just witnessed. Katelyn quickly responded, 'He shouldn't have crawled in there in the first place. Smack him again!'

Good work

A gynaecologist had a burning desire to change careers and become a mechanic. So he found out from the local tech college what was involved, signed up for evening classes, attended diligently, and learnt all he could.

When the time for the practical exam approached, the gynaecologist prepared carefully for weeks, and completed the exam with tremendous skill.

When the results came back, he was surprised to find that he had obtained a mark of 150 per cent.

Fearing an error, he called the instructor, saying, 'I don't want to appear ungrateful for such an outstanding result, but I wondered if there had been an error which needed adjusting.'

The instructor said, 'During the exam, you took the engine apart perfectly, which was worth 50 per cent of the total mark. You put the engine back together again perfectly, which is also worth 50 per cent of the mark. I gave you an extra 50 per cent because you did all of it through the muffler.'

Five surgeons

Five surgeons are discussing who makes the best patients to operate on.

The first surgeon says, 'I like to see accountants on my operating table, because when you open them up, everything inside is numbered.'

The second responds, 'Yeah, but you should try electricians! Everything inside them is colour coded.'

The third surgeon says, 'No, I really think librarians are the best; everything inside them is in alphabetical order.'

The fourth surgeon chimes in: 'You know, I like construction workers … those guys always understand when you have a few parts left over at the end, and when the job takes longer than you said it would.'

But the fifth surgeon shut them all up when he observed: 'I think you're all wrong. Politicians are the easiest to operate on. There's no guts, no heart, no balls, no brains and no spine, and the head and the arse are interchangeable.'

Sunburn

A man falls asleep on the beach for several hours and gets severe sunburn. He goes to the hospital and is promptly admitted after being diagnosed with second-degree burns. He is already starting to blister and is in obvious agony.

The doctor prescribes continuous intravenous feeding with saline and electrolytes, a sedative, and a Viagra pill every four hours.

The nurse, rather astounded, says, 'What good will Viagra do him?'

The doctor replies, 'It'll keep the sheets off his legs.'

Hello, and welcome to the Mental Health Hotline ...

If you are 'Obsessive-Compulsive', please press 1, repeatedly.

If you are 'Co-Dependent', please ask someone to press 2, for you.

If you have 'Multiple Personalities', please press 3, 4, and 5.

If you are 'Paranoid', we know who you are and what you want. Stay on the line, so we can trace your call.

If you are 'Delusional', please press 7 and your call will be transferred to the mother ship.

If you are 'Schizophrenic', listen carefully and a small voice will tell you which number to press.

If you are a 'Manic-Depressive', it doesn't matter which number you press, no one will answer.

If you are 'Dyslexic', press 9696969696969696.

If you have a 'Nervous Disorder', please fidget with the hash key, until a representative comes on the line.

If you have 'Amnesia', press 8 and state your name, address, telephone number, date of birth, social security number, and your mother's maiden name.

If you have 'Bi-Polar Disorder', please leave a message after the beep, or before the beep or after the beep. Please wait for the beep.

If you have 'Short-Term Memory Loss', please press 9. If you have 'Short-Term Memory Loss', please press 9. If you have 'Short-Term Memory Loss', please press 9.

If you have 'Low Self-Esteem', please hang up. All operators are too busy to talk to you.

If you are 'Blonde' don't press any buttons. You'll just screw it up.

Something to eat?

A woman asks her husband if he'd like some breakfast. 'Would you like bacon and eggs, perhaps? A slice of toast and maybe some grapefruit and coffee?'

He declines. 'It's this Viagra,' he says. 'It's really taken the edge off my appetite.'

At lunchtime, she asks if he would like something. 'A bowl of homemade soup, homemade muffins or a cheese sandwich?' she inquires.

He declines. 'The Viagra,' he says, 'really trashes my desire for food.'

Come dinner time, she asks if he wants anything to eat. 'Would you like a steak and apple pie? Maybe a microwave pizza or a tasty stir-fry that would only take a couple of minutes?'

He declines. 'No, still not hungry.'

'Well,' she says, 'would you mind letting me up? I'm starving!'

Medical lesson

First-year students at Med School were receiving their first anatomy class with a real dead human body. They all gathered around the surgery table with the body covered with a white sheet.

The professor began the lecture by telling them: 'It is necessary to possess two important qualities as a doctor: the first is that you not be disgusted by anything involving the human body.'

To illustrate, he pulled back the sheet, stuck his finger in the anus of the corpse, withdrew it, and stuck it in his mouth.

'Go ahead and do the same thing,' he told his students.

The students freaked out, hesitated for several minutes, but eventually took turns sticking a finger in the butt of the dead body and sucking on it.

When everyone finished, the professor looked at them and said, 'The second most important quality is observation. I stuck in my middle finger and sucked on my index finger. Now learn to pay attention.'

Script

A woman walks into a pharmacy and tells the pharmacist she wants to buy some arsenic. The pharmacist says, 'What do you want with arsenic?'

She says, 'I want to kill my husband because he cheats on me by having sex with another woman.'

The pharmacist says, 'I can't sell you arsenic so you can kill your husband, even if he is having sex with another woman.'

So she reaches into her pocket and pulls out a photo of her husband having sex with the pharmacist's wife.

The pharmacist says, 'Oh, I didn't realise you had a prescription.'

Health warning

For those of you who watch what you eat, here's the final word on nutrition and health. It's a relief to know the truth after all those conflicting medical studies.

1. The Japanese eat very little fat and suffer fewer heart attacks than the British, Americans or Australians.
2. The Mexicans eat a lot of fat and suffer fewer heart attacks than the British, Americans or Australians.
3. The Japanese drink very little red wine and suffer fewer heart attacks than the British, Americans or Australians.
4. The Italians drink excessive amounts of red wine and suffer fewer heart attacks than the British, Americans or Australians.
5. The Germans drink a lot of beers and eat lots of sausages and fats and suffer fewer heart attacks than the British, Americans or Australians.

Conclusion: Eat and drink what you like. Speaking English is apparently what kills you.

Thought for today

There is more money being spent on breast implants and Viagra than on Alzheimer's research.

This means that by 2020, there should be a large elderly population with perky boobs and huge erections and absolutely no recollection of what to do with them.

Are you a doctor?

A dad walks into a market with his young son. The kid is holding a 20-cent piece. Suddenly, the boy starts choking, going blue in the face. The dad realises the boy has swallowed the coin and starts panicking, shouting for help.

A well-dressed, attractive, but serious-looking woman in a blue business suit is sitting at a coffee bar in the market reading her newspaper and sipping a cup of coffee. At the sound of the commotion, she looks up, puts her coffee cup down on the saucer, neatly folds the newspaper and places it on the counter, gets up from her seat and makes her way, unhurried, across the market.

Reaching the boy, the woman carefully takes hold of the boy's testicles and starts to squeeze, gently at first and then ever more firmly. After a few seconds the boy convulses violently and coughs up the coin, which the woman deftly catches in her free hand. Releasing the boy, the woman hands the coin to the father and walks back to her seat in the coffee bar without saying a word.

As soon as he is sure that his son has suffered no lasting ill effects, the father rushes over to the woman and starts thanking her, saying, 'I've never seen anybody do anything like that before, and it was fantastic. Are you a doctor?'

'No,' the woman replies. 'Divorce lawyer.'

Punk patient

A nurse was on duty in the Emergency room, when a young woman with purple hair styled into a punk rocker mohawk, sporting a variety of tattoos and wearing strange clothes, entered. It was very quickly determined that the patient had acute appendicitis, so she was scheduled for immediate surgery. When she was completely disrobed on the operating table, the staff noticed that her pubic hair had been dyed green, and above it there was a tattoo that read, 'Keep off the grass.' Once the surgery was completed, the surgeon wrote a short note on the patient's dressing, which said, 'Sorry, had to mow the lawn.'

Anatomy lesson

A medical student was at the morgue one day after classes, getting a little practice in before the final exams. He went over to a table where a body was lying face down. He removed the sheet covering the body and to his surprise he found a cork in the corpse's rectum. Figuring this was fairly unusual he pulled the cork out, and to his surprise, music began playing — a country music song.

The student was amazed, and placed the cork back in the rectum. The music stopped. Totally freaked out, the student called the medical examiner over to the corpse.

'Look at this. This is really something!' the student told the examiner as he pulled the cork back out and the country music song started again.

'So what?' the medical examiner replied, obviously unimpressed with the student's discovery.

'But isn't that the most amazing thing you've ever seen?' asked the student.

'Are you kidding?' replied the examiner. 'Any arsehole can sing country music.'

16 RIPER! NOT OLDER!

In traditional societies where the majority of people live in a communal setting, be it an African village or under an Inuit igloo, there are usually rigid rules pertaining to most aspects of life. Rites of passage like circumcision, marriage, birth etc are celebrated and make an important statement of that achievement. Life from the cradle to the grave is respected and, in some cultures, the elderly are revered as carriers of wisdom. In Western society, however, our elderly are usually not revered and in most countries they are increasingly viewed as an inconvenience. The system is geared to encourage early departure from the workforce, the elderly are seldom consulted for knowledge, they reputedly drain public funding, and especially medical resources — the list is endless and, as one grows older, more depressing.

Humour ridicules the elderly and countless jokes concentrate on premature aging and memory loss. Sexual dysfunction is also high on the list despite the reality that it doesn't necessarily diminish that rapidly. Living long and well is the best revenge!

Old is when ...

- Your sweetie says, 'Let's go upstairs and make love,' and you answer, 'Pick one, I can't do both!'
- Your friends compliment you on your new crocodile shoes, and you're barefoot.
- A sexy babe catches your eye and your pacemaker opens the garage door.
- Going bra-less pulls all the wrinkles out of your face.
- You don't care where your spouse goes, just as long as you don't have to go along.
- You are cautioned to slow down by the doctor instead of by the police.
- 'Getting a little action' means you don't need to take any fibre today.
- 'Getting lucky' means you find your car in the parking lot.
- An 'all-nighter' means not getting up to pee.

Great truths that adults have learnt

1. Raising teenagers is like nailing jelly to a tree.
2. Wrinkles don't hurt.
3. Families are like fudge — mostly sweet, with a few nuts.
4. Today's mighty oak is just yesterday's nut that held its ground.
5. Laughing is good exercise. It's like jogging on the inside.
6. Middle age is when you choose your cereal for the fibre, not the toy.

Great truths about growing old

1. Growing old is mandatory; growing up is optional.
2. Forget the health food. I need all the preservatives I can get.
3. When you fall down, you wonder what else you can do while you're down there.
4. You're getting old when you get the same sensation from a rocking chair that you once got from a roller coaster.
5. It's frustrating when you know all the answers but nobody bothers to ask you the questions.
6. Time may be a great healer, but it's a lousy beautician.
7. Wisdom comes with age, but sometimes age comes alone.

The four stages of life

1. You believe in Santa Claus.
2. You don't believe in Santa Claus.
3. You are Santa Claus.
4. You look like Santa Claus.

Accident case

A middle-aged woman had a heart attack and was taken to the Brisbane hospital. While on the operating table she had a near-death experience. Seeing God, she asked, 'Is my time up?'

God said, 'No, you have another 43 years, two months and eight days to live.'

Upon recovery, the woman decided to stay in the hospital and have a facelift, liposuction, and a tummy tuck. She even had someone come in and change her hair colour. Since she had so much more time to live, she figured she might as well make the most of it.

After her last operation, she was released from the hospital. While crossing the street on her way home, she was killed by an ambulance.

Arriving in front of God, she demanded, 'I thought you said I had another 40 years? Why didn't you pull me from out of the path of the ambulance?'

God replied: 'I didn't recognise you.'

The Amazing Claude

It was variety night at the Woolloomooloo seniors centre and the Amazing Claude was topping the bill. People came from miles around to see the famed hypnotist do his stuff.

As Claude went to the front of the meeting room, he announced, 'Unlike most hypnotists who invite two or three people up here to be put into a trance, I intend to hypnotise each and every member of the audience.'

The excitement was electric as the Amazing Claude withdrew a beautiful antique pocket watch from his coat. 'I want you each to keep your eye on this antique watch. It's a very special watch. It's been in my family for six generations.'

He began to swing the watch gently back and forth while quietly chanting, 'Watch the watch, watch the watch, and watch the watch ...'

The crowd became mesmerised as the watch swayed back and forth, light gleaming off its polished surface. Hundreds of pairs of eyes followed the swaying watch until suddenly it slipped from the hypnotist's fingers and fell to the floor, breaking into a hundred pieces.

'Shit!' said the hypnotist.

It took three weeks to clean up the seniors centre.

Romantic memories

An elderly couple was lying in bed one night. The husband was falling asleep but the wife felt romantic and wanted to talk. She said, 'You used to hold my hand when we were courting.' Wearily, he reached across, held her hand for a second and tried to get back to sleep. A few moments later she said, 'Then you used to kiss me.' Mildly irritated, he reached across, gave her a peck on the cheek and settled down to sleep. Thirty seconds later she said, 'Then you used to bite my neck.' Angrily, he threw back the bed covers and got out of bed.

'Where are you going?' she asked.

'To get my teeth!'

Lifetime friends

Two elderly ladies had been friends for many decades. Over the years they had shared all kinds of activities and adventures. Lately, their activities had been limited to meeting a few times a week to play cards.

One day they were playing cards when one looked at the other and said, 'Now don't get mad at me … I know we've been friends for a long time, but I just can't think of your name! I've thought and thought, but I can't remember it. Please tell me what your name is.'

Her friend glared at her for at least three minutes with a dazed look. Finally she said, 'How soon do you need to know?'

Reading test

This was developed as an age test by a research and development department at Harvard University. Take your time and see if you can read each line aloud without a mistake. The average person over 50 years of age can't do it! (To those of you under 50 — don't laugh too loud, because you will get there.)

1. This is this cat
2. This is is cat
3. This is how cat
4. This is to cat
5. This is keep cat
6. This is an cat
7. This is old cat
8. This is fart cat
9. This is busy cat
10. This is for cat
11. This is forty cat
12. This is seconds cat

Now go back and read the third word in each line from the top down.

For all the good it did me

Two elderly women were eating at a restaurant one morning.

Ethel noticed something funny about Mabel's ear and she said, 'Mabel, did you know you've got a suppository in your left ear?'

Mabel answered, 'I have a suppository?' She pulled it out and stared at it. Then she said, 'Ethel, I'm glad you saw this thing. Now I think I know where my hearing aid is.'

Death notice

When the husband finally died, his wife put the usual death notice in the newspaper, but added that he died of gonorrhoea. No sooner were the papers delivered than a good friend of the family phoned and complained bitterly, 'You know very well that he died of diarrhoea, not gonorrhoea.'

Replied the widow, 'I nursed him night and day so of course I know he died of diarrhoea, but I thought it would be better for posterity to remember him as a great lover rather than the big shit he always was.'

25 signs you have grown up

1. Your houseplants are alive, and you can't smoke any of them.
2. Having sex in a twin bed is out of the question.
3. You keep more food than beer in the fridge.

4. Six a.m. is when you get up, not when you go to bed.
5. You hear your favourite song in an elevator.
6. You watch the Weather Channel.
7. Your friends marry and divorce instead of 'hook up' and 'break up'.
8. You go from 130 days of vacation time to 28.
9. Jeans and a sweater no longer qualify as 'dressed up'.
10. You're the one calling the police because those %&@# kids next door won't turn down the stereo.
11. Older relatives feel comfortable telling sex jokes around you.
12. You don't know what time McDonald's closes any more.
13. Your car insurance goes down and your car payments go up.
14. You feed your dog Science Diet instead of takeaway leftovers.
15. Sleeping on the couch makes your back hurt.
16. You take naps.
17. Dinner and a movie is the whole date instead of the beginning of one.
18. Eating a basket of chicken wings at 3 a.m. would severely upset, rather than settle, your stomach.
19. You go to the chemist for ibuprofen and antacid, not condoms and pregnancy tests.
20. A $4 bottle of wine is no longer 'pretty good shit'.
21. You actually eat breakfast food at breakfast time.
22. 'I just can't drink the way I used to' replaces 'I'm never going to drink that much again.'
23. Ninety per cent of the time you spend in front of a computer is for real work.
24. You have drinks at home to save money before going to dinner.
25. When you find out your friend is pregnant you congratulate them instead of asking, 'Oh shit, what the hell happened?'

Stroke victims

Three senior ladies named Patsy, Betty and Nellie were sitting on a park bench having a quiet conversation, when a flasher approached from across the park.

The flasher came up to the ladies, stood right in front of them and opened his trench coat. Both Betty and Nellie had a stroke.

But Patsy, being older and feebler, couldn't reach that far.

Bless her heart.

Knock knock

Three sisters aged 92, 94 and 96 lived in a house together.

One night the 96-year-old prepared a bath. She put her foot in, paused, and yelled to the other sisters, 'Was I getting in or out of the bath?'

The 94-year-old yelled back, 'I don't know. I'll come up and see.' She started up the stairs and paused. 'Was I going up the stairs or down?'

The 92-year-old was sitting at the kitchen table having tea, listening to her sisters. She shook her head and said, 'I sure hope I never get that forgetful.' She knocked on wood for good measure, then yelled, 'I'll come up and help both of you as soon as I see who's at the door.'

Perks of being over 50

1.   Kidnappers are not very interested in you.
2.   In a hostage situation you are likely to be released first.
3.   No one expects you to run — anywhere.
4.   People call at 9 p.m. and ask, 'Did I wake you?'
5.   People no longer view you as a hypochondriac.
6.   There is nothing left to learn the hard way.
7.   Things you buy now won't wear out.
8.   You can eat dinner at 4 p.m.
9.   You can live without sex but not your glasses.
10. You enjoy hearing about other people's operations.
11. You get into heated arguments about pension plans.
12. You no longer think of speed limits as a challenge.
13. You stop trying to hold your stomach in no matter who walks into the room.
14. Your eyes won't get much worse.
15. Your investment in health insurance is finally beginning to pay off.
16. Your joints are more accurate meteorologists than the national weather service.
17. Your secrets are safe with your friends because they can't remember them either.
18. Your supply of brain cells is finally down to a manageable size.
19. You can't remember who sent you this list.
20. And you notice these are all in Big Print for your convenience.

What age is best?

'Sixty is the worst age to be,' said the 60-year-old man. 'You always feel like you have to pee and most of the time you stand there and nothing comes out.'

'Ah, that's nothing,' said the 70-year-old. 'When you're 70, you don't have a bowel movement any more. You take laxatives, eat bran, and sit on the toilet all day and nothing comes out!'

'Actually,' said the 80-year-old, '80 is the worst age of all.'

'Do you have trouble peeing, too?' asked the 60-year-old.

'No, not really. I pee every morning at six. I pee like a racehorse on a flat rock; no problem at all.'

'So, do you have a problem with your bowel movement?'

'No, I have one every morning at 6.30.'

With great exasperation, the 60-year-old said, 'Let me get this straight. You pee every morning at six and poop every morning at 6.30. So what's so bad about being 80?'

'I don't wake up until seven.'

A day with AAADD

Recently, I was diagnosed with AAADD — Age Activated Attention Deficit Disorder. This is how it manifests:

I decide to water my garden. As I turn on the hose in the driveway, I look over at my car and decide my car needs washing.

As I start towards the garage, I notice that there is mail on the porch table that I brought up from the mailbox earlier. I decide to go through the mail before I wash the car.

I lay my car keys down on the table, put the junk mail into the garbage can under the table, and notice that the can is full.

So, I decide to put the bills back on the table and take out the garbage first. But then I think, since I'm going to be near the mailbox when I take out the garbage anyway, I may as well pay the bills first.

I take my chequebook off the table, and see that there is only one cheque left. My extra cheques are in my desk in the study, so I go inside the house to my desk, where I find the can of beer that I had been drinking. I'm going to look for my cheques, but first I need to push the beer aside so that I don't accidentally knock it over. I see that the beer is getting warm, and I decide I should put it in the refrigerator to keep it cold.

As I head towards the kitchen with the beer, a vase of flowers on the counter catches my eye — they need to be watered. I set the beer down on the counter and I discover my reading glasses that I've been searching for all morning. I decide I better put them back on my desk, but first I'm going to water the flowers.

I set the glasses back down on the counter, fill a container with water and suddenly I spot the TV remote. Someone left it on the kitchen table. I realise that tonight, when I go to watch TV, I will be looking for the remote, so I decide to put it back in the den where it belongs, but first I'll water the flowers. I pour some water in the flowers, but quite a bit of it spills on the floor. So, I set the remote back down on the table, get some towels and wipe up the spill.

Then I head down the hall trying to remember what I was planning to do.

At the end of the day: the car isn't washed, the bills aren't paid, there is a warm can of beer sitting on the counter, the flowers don't have enough water, there is still only one cheque in my chequebook, I can't find the remote, I can't find my glasses, and I don't remember what I did with the car keys. Then when I try to figure out why nothing got done today, I'm really baffled because I know I was busy all day long, and I'm really tired.

To all the kids

To all the kids who survived the 1930s, '40s, '50s, '60s and '70s! First, we survived being born to mothers who smoked and/or drank while they were pregnant. They took aspirin, ate blue-cheese dressing as well as tuna from a can, and didn't get tested for diabetes. Then after that trauma, we were put to sleep on our tummies in baby cribs covered with brightly coloured lead-based paints. We had no childproof lids on medicine bottles, special locks on doors or cabinets, and when we rode our bikes, we had no helmets; not to mention the risks we took hitchhiking.

As infants and children, we would ride in cars with no car seats, booster seats, seat belts or air bags. Riding in the back of a ute on a warm day was always a special treat. We drank water from the garden hose and *not* from a bottle. We shared one soft drink with four friends, from one bottle and no one actually died from this. We ate cakes, white bread and real butter, and drank lemonade made with sugar, but we weren't overweight because we were always outside playing! We would leave home in the morning and play all day, as long as we were back when the streetlights came on. No one was able to reach us all day. And we were okey-dokey. We would spend hours building our go-carts out of scraps and then ride down the hill, only to find out we forgot the brakes. After running into the bushes a few times, we learnt to solve the problem.

We did not have PlayStations, Nintendos, Xboxes, no video games at all, no cable TV, no video movies or DVDs, no surround-sound or CDs, no mobile phones, no personal computers, no Internet or chat rooms — we had friends, and we went outside and found them!

We fell out of trees, got cut, trod on bindi-eyes, broke bones and teeth and there were no lawsuits from these accidents. We ate worms and mud pies made from dirt, and the worms did not live in us forever. We were given BB guns for our 10th birthdays, made up games with sticks and tennis balls and, although we were told it would happen, we did not poke out very many eyes. We rode bikes or walked to a friend's house and knocked on the door or rang the bell, or just walked in and talked to them! Junior football had tryouts and not everyone made the team. Those who didn't had to learn to deal with disappointment. Imagine that! The idea of a parent bailing us out if we broke the law was unheard of. They actually sided with the law!

These generations have produced some of the best risk-takers, problem solvers and inventors ever! The past 50 years have been an explosion of innovation and new ideas. We had freedom, failure, success and responsibility, and we learnt how to deal with it all! If you are one of them — *congratulations*!

Ed Zachary Disease

An elderly woman was distraught at the fact that she had not had a date or any sex in quite some time. She was afraid she might have something wrong with her, so she decided to seek the medical expertise of a sex therapist. Her doctor recommended that she see the well-known Chinese therapist, Dr Ho. So she went to see him. Upon entering the examination room, Dr Ho said, 'OK, take off all your crose.'

The woman did as she was told. 'Now, get down and craw reery, reery fass to odderside of room.'

Again, the woman did as she was instructed.

Dr Ho then said, 'OK, now craw reery, reery fass back to me.'

So she did.

Dr Ho shook his head slowly and said, 'Your probrem vewy bad. You haf Ed Zachary Disease. Worse case I ever see. Dat why you not haf sex or dates.'

Worried, the woman asked anxiously, 'Oh, my God, Dr Ho, what is Ed Zachary Disease?'

Dr Ho sighed deeply, and replied: 'Ed Zachary Disease is when your face look ed zachary like your ass.'

Today's sermon

Sunday's sermon was 'Forgive your enemies'. Towards the end of the service, the minister asked, 'How many of you have forgiven your enemies?'

Eighty per cent of the congregation held up their hands.

The minister then repeated his question. Everyone responded this time, except one small elderly lady.

'Mrs Jones? Are you not willing to forgive your enemies?'

'I don't have any,' she replied, smiling sweetly.

'Mrs Jones, that is very unusual. How old are you?'

'Ninety-eight,' she replied.

'Oh, Mrs Jones, would you please come down the front and tell us all how a person can live 98 years and not have an enemy in the world?'

The little sweetheart of a lady tottered down the aisle, faced the congregation, and loudly declared, 'I outlived the bitches.'

Sperm count

An 85-year-old man went to his doctor's office to get a sperm count.

The doctor gave the man a jar and said, 'Take this jar home and bring back a semen sample tomorrow.'

The next day the 85-year-old man reappeared at the doctor's office and gave him the jar, which was as clean and empty as on the previous day.

The doctor asked what happened and the man explained: 'Well, Doc, it's like this. First I tried with my right hand, but nothing. Then I tried with my left hand, but still nothing. Then I asked my wife for help. She tried with her right hand, then her left, still nothing. She tried with her mouth, first with the teeth in, then with her teeth out, and still nothing. We even called up Arleen, the lady next door, and she tried too, first with both hands, then an armpit, and she even tried squeezing it between her knees, but still nothing.'

The doctor was shocked. 'You asked your neighbour?'

The old man replied, 'Yep. And no matter what we tried, we still couldn't get the jar open.'

Up or down?

At the Tuggerawong senior citizens luncheon, an elderly gentleman and an elderly lady struck up a conversation, where they discovered that they both loved to fish. Since both of them were widowed, they decided to go fishing together the next day.

The gentleman picked the lady up, and they headed to the river to his fishing boat and started out on their adventure. They were gliding down the river when they came to a fork, and the gentleman asked the lady, 'Do you want to go up or down?' All of a sudden the lady stripped off her shirt and pants and made passionate love to the man right there in the boat!

When they finished, the man couldn't believe what had just happened, but he had just experienced the best sex that he'd had in years. They fished for a while and continued on down the river when soon they came upon another fork in the river. He asked the lady, 'Up or down?' There she went again, stripped off her clothes, and made wild passionate love to him.

This really impressed the elderly gentleman, so he asked her to go fishing again the next day. She said yes, and there they were the next day, riding in the boat when they came upon the fork in the river, and the elderly gentleman asked, 'Up or down?' The woman replied, 'Down.' A little puzzled and disappointed, the gentleman guided the boat down the river when he came upon another fork in the river and he asked the lady, 'Up or down?' She replied, 'Up.'

This really confused the gentleman, so he asked, 'What's the deal? Yesterday, every time I asked you if you wanted to go up or down, you made mad passionate love to me. Now today, nothing!'

She replied, 'Well, yesterday I wasn't wearing my hearing aid and I thought the choices were "fuck or drown".'

Why God invented menopause

With all the new technology regarding fertility, a 75-year-old woman was able to give birth to a baby recently. When she was discharged from the hospital and went home, her relatives came to visit.

'May we see the new baby?' one asked.

'Not yet,' said the mother. 'I'll make coffee and we can chat for a while first.'

Thirty minutes had passed, and another relative asked, 'May we see the new baby now?'

'No, not yet,' said the mother.

After another few minutes had elapsed, they asked again, 'May we see the baby now?'

'No, not yet,' replied the mother.

Growing very impatient, they asked, 'Well, when can we see the baby?'

'When it cries!' she told them.

'When it cries?' they demanded. 'Why do we have to wait until it *cries*?'

'*Because*, I forgot where I put it ...'

Electrifying sex

An elderly couple is enjoying an anniversary dinner together in a small hotel lounge. The husband leans over and asks his wife, 'Do you remember the first time we had sex together over 50 years ago? We went behind this tavern where you leant against the fence and I made love to you.'

'Yes,' she says, 'I remember it well.'

'OK,' he says, 'how about taking a stroll round there again and we can do it for old time's sake?'

'Oooh, Henry, you devil, that sounds like a good idea,' she answered.

A police officer is sitting in the next booth listening to all this, and having a chuckle to himself. He thinks, 'I've got to see these two old-timers having sex against a fence. I'll just keep an eye on them so there's no trouble.'

He follows them. They walk haltingly along, leaning on each other for support, aided by walking sticks. Finally they get to the back of the tavern and make their way to the fence. The old lady lifts her skirt, takes her knickers down and the old man drops his trousers. She turns around and as she hangs on to the fence, the old man moves in. Suddenly, they erupt into the most furious sex that the watching policeman has ever seen. They are bucking and jumping like 18-year-olds.

This goes on for about 40 minutes! She's yelling, 'Ohhhh, God!' He's hanging on to her hips for dear life. This is the most athletic sex imaginable. Finally, they both collapse panting on the ground.

The policeman is amazed. He thinks he has learnt something about life that he didn't know. After about half an hour of lying on the ground recovering, the old couple struggle to their feet and put their clothes back on. The policeman, still watching, thinks, 'That was truly amazing. He was going like a train! I've got to ask him what his secret is.'

As the couple passes, he says to them, 'That was something else! You must have been having sex for about 40 minutes. How do you manage it? You must have had a fantastic life together. Is there some sort of secret?'

The old man says, 'Fifty years ago that wasn't an electric fence.'

Age shall not weary them

Billy, age 92, and Mary, age 89, living in Portsea, are all excited about their decision to get married. They go for a stroll to discuss the wedding, and on the way they pass a chemist. Billy suggests they go in and he then addresses the man behind the counter: 'Are you the owner?'

The pharmacist answers, 'Yes.'

Billy: 'We're about to get married. Do you sell heart medication?'

Pharmacist: 'Of course we do.'

Billy: 'How about medicine for circulation?'

Pharmacist: 'All kinds.'

Billy: 'Medicine for rheumatism and scoliosis?'

Pharmacist: 'Definitely.'

Billy: 'How about Viagra?'

Pharmacist: 'Of course.'

Billy: 'Medicine for memory problems, arthritis, jaundice?'

Pharmacist: 'Yes, a large variety. The works.'

Billy: 'What about vitamins, sleeping pills, Geritol, antidotes for Parkinson's disease?'

Pharmacist: 'Absolutely.'

Billy: 'You sell wheelchairs and walkers?'

Pharmacist: 'All speeds and sizes.'

Finally Billy announces: 'Thanks, we'd like to use this store as our bridal registry.'

Sharing

A little old couple walked slowly into the McDonald's in Surfers Paradise one cold winter evening. They looked out of place amid the young families and couples eating there that night.

Some of the customers looked admiringly at them. You could tell what the admirers were thinking. 'Look, there is a couple who has been through a lot together, probably for 60 years or more!'

The little old man walked up to the cash register, placed his order with no hesitation and then paid for their meal. The couple took a table near the back wall and started taking food from the tray.

There was one hamburger, one order of French fries and one drink. The little old man unwrapped the plain hamburger and carefully cut it in half. He placed one half in front of his wife. Then he carefully counted out the French fries, divided them in two piles and neatly placed one pile in front of his wife. He took a sip of the drink, and then his wife took a sip as the man began to eat his few bites. Again, you could tell what people around the old couple were thinking: 'That poor old couple.'

As the old man began eating his French fries, a young man stood up and walked to the old couple's table. He politely offered to buy another meal. The old man replied that they were just fine. They were used to sharing everything.

Then the crowd noticed that the little old lady still hadn't eaten a thing. She just sat there watching her husband eat and occasionally sipped some of the drink.

Again, the young man came over and begged them to let him buy them another meal. This time, the lady explained that, no, they were used to sharing.

As the little old man finished eating and was wiping his face neatly with a napkin, the young man came over again and asked, 'Ma'am, why aren't you eating? You said that you share everything. What is it that you are waiting for?'

She answered, 'I'm waiting for the teeth.'

Swimming hole

An elderly man in Innisfail, North Queensland had owned a large farm for several years. He had a pond out the back, picnic tables, tennis courts, and some stone fruit and mango trees. The pond was properly shaped and fixed up for swimming when it was built. One evening the old farmer decided to go down to the pond, as he hadn't been there for a while, and look it over. He grabbed a 20-litre plastic bucket to bring back some fruit.

As he neared the pond, he heard voices shouting and laughing with glee. As he came closer he saw it was a group of young women skinny-dipping in his pond. He made the women aware of his presence and they all went to the deep end. One of the women shouted to him, 'We're not coming out until you leave!'

The old man frowned. 'I didn't come down here to watch you ladies swim naked or make you get out of the pond.' Holding the bucket up he said, 'I'm here to feed the crocodile.'

Moral: Old men can still think fast.

The flower show

Two old ladies were sitting on a park bench outside the Geelong Town Hall, where a flower show was in progress. One leant over and said, 'Life is so boring. We never have any fun any more. For $20, I'd take my clothes off and streak through that stupid flower show!'

'You're on!' said the other old lady, holding up a $20 bill.

As fast as she could, the first little old lady fumbled her way out of her clothes and, completely naked, streaked through the front door of the flower show.

Waiting outside, her friend soon heard a huge commotion inside the hall, followed by loud applause.

The naked lady burst out through the door surrounded by a cheering crowd.

'What happened?' gasped her waiting friend.

'I won first prize as Best Dried Arrangement.'

Hand job

Mary and Donald met at the Darlinghurst Nursing Home and struck up a most unusual relationship. Day and night they would sit together with

Mary holding Donald's penis in her hand. This puzzled the staff, as this was all they did, not joining in any of the other activities organised by the home. After a while the staff thought some action had to take place since they always sat there — with Mary holding Donald's dick, not saying or doing anything else. The staff thought the best thing to do was to separate them for a while, and sent Mary home to her relatives, telling them the reason. Of course, Mary was pining for Donald and after a few weeks they sent her back. When she was returned to the nursing home the matron came to greet her and told her that she had some rather upsetting news — that Donald had found a new companion, Ada. Mary was heartbroken, rushed to Donald's room and saw Ada sitting in her place.

Not being able to contain herself, Mary demanded: 'What has Ada got that I haven't?'

'Parkinson's,' was Donald's prompt reply.

A trip to the brothel

An elderly man goes into a brothel and tells the madam he would like a young girl for the night. Surprised, she looks at the ancient man and asks how old he is. 'I'm 90 years old,' he says.

'Ninety!' replies the woman. 'Don't you realise you've had it?'

'Oh, sorry,' says the old man. 'How much do I owe you?'

Lost in the shopping centre

A small boy was lost at the Westfield Shopping Centre.

He approached a uniformed policeman and said, 'I've lost my grandpa.'

The policeman asked, 'What's he like?'

The little boy thought about this and replied, 'Jack Daniel's and women with big tits.'

Control methods

One evening a family brings their frail, elderly mother to a nursing home and leaves her, hoping she will be well cared for.

The next morning, the nurses bathe her, feed her a tasty breakfast, and set her in a chair at a window overlooking a lovely flower garden. She seems OK, but after a while she slowly starts to lean over sideways in her chair. Two attentive nurses immediately rush up to catch her and straighten her up.

Again she seems OK, but after a while she starts to tilt to the other side. The nurses rush back and once more bring her back upright. This goes on all morning.

Later the family arrives to see how the old woman is adjusting to her new home. 'So, Mum, how is it here? Are they treating you all right?' they ask.

'It's pretty nice,' she replies. 'Except they won't let you fart.'

I can hear you

Three retirees, each with hearing loss, were playing golf one fine March day. One remarked to the other, 'Windy, isn't it?'

'No,' the second man replied, 'it's Thursday.'

And the third man chimed in, 'So am I. Let's have a beer.'

Supersex

A little old lady was walking up and down the halls in a nursing home. As she walked, she would flip up the hem of her nightgown and say, 'Supersex.'

She walked up to an elderly man in a wheelchair. Flipping her gown at him, she said, 'Supersex.'

He sat silently for a moment or two and finally answered, 'I'll take the soup.'

Down at the retirement centre

Eighty-year-old Bessie bursts into the recreation room at the retirement home. She holds her clenched fist in the air and announces, 'Anyone who can guess what's in my hand can have sex with me tonight!'

An elderly gentleman in the rear shouts out, 'An elephant?'

Bessie thinks a minute and says, 'Close enough.'

Senior driving

As a senior citizen was driving down the Lane Cove freeway, his car phone rang. Answering, he heard his wife's voice urgently warning him, 'Herman, I just heard on the news that there's a car going the wrong way on the expressway. Please be careful!'

'Hell,' said Herman, 'it's not just one car. It's hundreds of them!'

Punks

An old man was sitting on a bench at the shopping centre when a young man walked up and sat down next to him.

He had long, spiked hair in different colours — green, red, orange, blue and yellow.

The old man just stared at him.

The young man turned to him and said sarcastically, 'What's the matter, old-timer — never done anything wild in your life?'

Without batting an eyelid, the old man replied, 'Got drunk once and rooted a parrot. I was just wondering if you were my lost son.'

Success

At age four, success is … not peeing in your pants.
At age 12, success is … having friends.
At age 16, success is … having a driver's licence.
At age 20, success is … having sex.
At age 35, success is … having money.
At age 50, success is … having money.
At age 60, success is … having sex.
At age 70, success is … having a driver's licence.
At age 75, success is … having friends.
At age 80, success is … not peeing in your pants.

The nudist colony

A 68-year-old man joins an exclusive nudist colony. On his first day there he takes off his clothes and starts to wander around, when a gorgeous petite blonde walks by, and the man immediately gets an erection. The woman notices his erection, comes over to him and says, 'Did you call for me?'

The man replies, 'No, what do you mean?'

She says, 'You must be new here. Let me explain. It's a rule here that if you get an erection it implies you called for me.'

Smiling, she leads him to the side of the swimming pool, lies down on a towel, eagerly pulls him to her and happily lets him have his way with her.

The man continues to explore the colony's facilities. He enters the sauna and as he sits down, he farts. Within seconds a huge, hairy man lumbers out of the steam room towards him. 'Did you call for me?' says the hairy man.

'No, what do you mean?' says the newcomer.

'You must be new,' says the hairy man. 'It's a rule that if you fart, it implies that you called for me.' The huge man easily spins him around, bends him over a bench and has his way with him.

The newcomer staggers back to the colony office, where he is greeted by the smiling, naked receptionist. 'May I help you?' she says.

The man yells, 'Here's my membership card. You can have the key back and you can keep the $500 membership fee.'

'But, sir,' she replies, 'you've only been here for a few hours. You haven't had the chance to see all our facilities.'

The man replies, 'Listen, lady, I'm 68 years old; I only get an erection once a month, but I fart 15 times a day! I'm outta here!'

Hits from the vaults

Some of the artists from the '60s and '70s are revising their hits with new lyrics to accommodate aging baby boomers. This is good news for those feeling a little older and missing those great old tunes … Remember these?

1. Herman's Hermits — Mrs Brown, You've Got A Lovely Walker
2. The Bee Gees — How Can You Mend A Broken Hip?
3. Bobby Darin — Splish, Splash, I Was Havin' A Flash
4. Roberta Flack — The First Time Ever I Forgot Your Face
5. Johnny Nash — I Can't See Clearly Now
6. Paul Simon — Fifty Ways To Lose Your Liver
7. The Commodores — Once, Twice, Three Times To The Bathroom
8. Procol Harum — A Whiter Shade Of Hair
9. Leo Sayer — You Make Me Feel Like Napping
10. The Temptations — Papa's Got A Kidney Stone
11. Abba — Denture Queen
12. Tony Orlando — Knock Three Times On The Ceiling If You Hear Me Fall
13. Helen Reddy — I Am Woman, Hear Me Snore
14. Willie Nelson — On The Commode Again
15. Lesley Gore — It's My Procedure And I'll Cry If I Want To

Guess what?

One day at the rest home, an old man and woman are talking. Out of nowhere the woman says, 'I can guess your age.'

The man doesn't believe her, but tells her to go ahead and try.

'Pull down your pants,' she says.

He doesn't understand but does it anyway. She inspects his rear end for a few minutes and then says, 'You're 84 years old.'

'That's amazing,' the man says. 'How did you know?'

'You told me yesterday.'

Good point

One night, an 87-year-old woman came home from bingo to find her husband in bed with another woman. Angry, she became violent and ended up pushing him off the balcony of their 20th-floor apartment, killing him instantly.

When brought before the court on the charge of murder, she was asked if she had anything to say in her defence. 'Well, Your Honour,' she began coolly, 'I figured that at 92, if he could screw, he could fly.'

Tamworth

An elderly couple, Dave and Bessie, are vacationing in the west of New South Wales. Dave has always wanted a pair of authentic bush boots. Seeing some on sale one day in Tamworth, he buys them, and wears them back to the hotel, walking proudly.

He walks into their room and says to the wife, 'Notice anything different about me?'

Bessie looks him over. 'Nope.'

Dave says excitedly, 'Come on, Bessie, take a good look. Notice anything?'

'Nope.'

Frustrated, Dave storms off into the bathroom, undresses, and walks back into the room, wearing only his boots, saying a little louder this time, 'Notice anything different?'

Bessie looks up and says, 'Dave, what's different? It's hanging down today, it was hanging down yesterday, it'll be hanging down again tomorrow.'

Furious, Dave yells, 'And do you know why it is hanging down, Bessie? It's hanging down because it's looking at my new boots!'

To which Bessie replies, 'Shoulda bought a hat, Dave. You shoulda bought a hat.'

New rooster

A farmer goes out one day and buys a brand new stud rooster for his chicken coop.

The new rooster struts over to the old rooster and says, 'OK, old fart, time for you to retire.'

The old rooster replies, 'Come on, surely you cannot handle *all* of these chickens. Look what it has done to me. Can't you just let me have the two old hens over in the corner?'

The young rooster says, 'Beat it. You are washed up and I am taking over.'

The old rooster says, 'I tell you what, young stud. I will race you around the farmhouse. Whoever wins gets the exclusive domain over the entire chicken coop.'

The young rooster laughs. 'You know you don't stand a chance, old man. So, just to be fair I will give you a head start.'

The old rooster takes off running. About 15 seconds later the young rooster takes off after him. They round the front porch of the farmhouse and the young rooster has closed the gap. He is already only a few centimetres behind the old rooster and gaining fast.

The farmer, meanwhile, is sitting in his usual spot on the front porch when he sees the roosters running by. He grabs his shotgun and — *boom* — he blows the young rooster to bits.

The farmer sadly shakes his head and says, 'Dammit ... third gay rooster I've bought this month.'

Moral of this story: Don't mess with the old farts — age and treachery will always overcome youth and skill!

Nice tan

The young man stood in front of the mirror admiring his well-built and tanned body, when he realised that his penis was the only part of his body not tanned. Determined to rectify the situation, he made his way to Bondi

Beach. Once there, he proceeded to bury himself completely, except for his penis; this he left poking out of the sand.

Strolling down the beach were two little old ladies. They came across the penis poking out of the sand. One little old lady, using her cane, knocked the penis from side to side, saying, 'There is no justice in the world today.'

The other little old lady asked, 'What do you mean?'

The first little old lady said, 'Look at that. When I was 20, I was curious about it. When I was 30, I enjoyed it. When I was 40, I asked for it. When I was 50, I paid for it. When I was 60, I prayed for it. When I was 70, I forgot about it.

'And now that I'm 80, the darn things are growing wild and I'm too old to squat.'

Remembering men

Three old ladies were sitting side by side in their retirement home, reminiscing about cooking and food prices.

The first lady recalled shopping at the greengrocers, and demonstrated with her hands the length and thickness of a cucumber she could buy for a penny.

The second old lady nodded, adding that onions not only used to be cheaper but much bigger also, and demonstrated the size of two big onions she remembered she could buy for a penny apiece.

The third old lady remarked, 'I can't hear a word you two are saying, but I remember the fellow you're talking about.'

Senility prayer

God grant me the senility to forget the people I never liked anyway, the good fortune to run into the ones I do like, and the eyesight to tell the difference.

Mildred

Aging Mildred was a 93-year-old woman who was getting more and more despondent over the recent death of her husband, Earl. She decided that she would just kill herself and join him in death. Thinking that it would be best to get it over with quickly, she took out Earl's old army pistol and made the decision to shoot herself in the heart, since it was so badly broken anyway.

Not wanting to miss the vital organ and become a vegetable and burden anyone, she called her doctor's office to inquire as to exactly where the heart would be on a woman. The doctor said, 'Your heart would be just below your left breast.'

Later that night, Mildred was admitted to the local hospital with a gunshot wound to her knee.

Sea sick

An elderly couple was on a cruise and it was really stormy. They were standing on the back of the ship watching the moon, when a wave came up and washed the old woman overboard. They searched for days and couldn't find her, so the captain sent the old man back to shore with the promise that he would notify him as soon as they found something. Three weeks went by and finally the old man got a fax from the ship. It read: 'Sir, sorry to inform you that we found your wife dead at the bottom of the ocean. We hauled her up to the deck. Attached to her butt was an oyster and in it was a pearl worth $50,000. Please advise.'

The old man faxed back: 'Send me the pearl and re-bait the trap.'

Pity

When I went to lunch today, I noticed an old lady sitting on a park bench sobbing her eyes out. I stopped and asked her what was wrong.

She said, 'I have a 22-year-old husband at home. He makes love to me every morning and then gets up and makes me pancakes, sausage, fresh fruit and freshly ground coffee.'

I said, 'Well, then why are you crying?'

She said, 'He makes me homemade soup for lunch and my favourite brownies and then makes love to me for half the afternoon.'

I said, 'Well, why are you crying?'

She said, 'For dinner he makes me a gourmet meal with wine and my favourite dessert and then makes love to me until 2.00 a.m.'

I said, 'Well, why in the world would you be crying?'

She said, 'I can't remember where I live!'

Sean Connery

Sean Connery is interviewed by Michael Parkinson, and brags that despite his 72 years of age, he can still have sex three times a night. Lulu, the Scottish pop singer, who is also a guest, looks intrigued.

After the show, Lulu says, 'Sean, if Ah'm no bein' too forward, Ah'd love tae hae sex wi an aulder man. Let's go back tae mah place.'

So they go back to her place and have great sex.

Afterwards, Sean says, 'If you think that was good, let me shleep for half an hour, and we can have even better shex. But while I'm shleeping, hold my baws in your left hand and my wullie in your right hand.'

Lulu looks a bit perplexed, but says, 'OK.'

Sean sleeps for half an hour, awakens, and they have even better sex. Then he says, 'Lulu, that was wonderful. But if you let me shleep for an hour, we can have the besht shex yet. But again, hold my baws in your left hand, and my wullie in your right hand.'

Lulu is now used to the routine and complies. The results are mind blowing.

Once it's all over, and the cigarettes are lit, Lulu asks, 'Sean, tell me, dis mah haudin yer baws in mah left hand and yer wullie in mah right stimulate ye while ye're sleepin'?'

Sean replies, 'No, but the lasht time I shlept wi' a Glashwegian, she shtole my wallet.'

Mannequins

A little boy goes shopping with his mum at Myer and is waiting outside the changing room for her to come out. While waiting, the little lad gets bored and as his mum comes she out sees him sliding his hand up a mannequin's skirt.

'Get your hand out of there!' she shouts. 'Don't you know that women have teeth down there?'

The little boy quickly snatches his hand away and thanks his lucky stars he didn't get bitten. For the next 10 years, this little boy grows up believing all women have teeth between their legs.

When he's 16, he gets a girlfriend. One night, while her parents are out, she invites him over. After an hour she says, 'You know you can go a little further if you want.'

'What do you mean?' he asks.

'Well, why don't you put your hand down my pants?' she says.

'Hell no,' he cries, 'you've got teeth down there.'

'Don't be ridiculous,' she responds, 'there are no teeth down there.'

'Yes there are,' he says, 'my mum told me.'

'No, there aren't,' she insists.

'Here, have a look for yourself.' She whips off her panties, throws her legs behind her head, and says, 'Look, I don't have any teeth down there!'

The boy takes a good long look and replies, 'Well, with the condition of those gums, I'm not surprised.'

The old man

A woman walked up to a little old man rocking in a chair on his porch.

'I couldn't help noticing how happy you look,' she said. 'What's your secret for a long happy life?'

'I smoke three packs of cigarettes a day,' he said. 'I also do a gram of charlie a day, a joint every night, a case of whisky a week, eat junk food, never exercise, and do recreational pills on the weekend.'

'That's amazing,' said the woman. 'How old are you?'

'Twenty-six.'

Inheritance

An old man on his deathbed summons all three of his sons to his bedside. When they arrive, he looks all of them over and says, 'I bet you are all looking forward to the inheritance when I die.' He looks at his eldest son and says, 'You, you were never good as a son. All you were ever interested in was gardening; you even married a girl called Rose. Now get out of here.'

He looks at his middle son and says, 'You, you were never good as a son either. All you were ever interested in was money; you even married a girl called Penny. Now get the hell out of here.'

His youngest son looks at his wife and says, 'Let's get out of here, Fanny; we're not going to stand here and get insulted like that.'

Scotch and water

A lady goes to the bar on a cruise ship and orders a Scotch with two drops of water. As the bartender gives her the drink she says, 'I'm on this cruise to celebrate my 80th birthday and it's today.'

The bartender says, 'Well, since it's your birthday, I'll buy you a drink. In fact, this one is on me.'

As the woman finishes her drink, the woman to her right says, 'I would like to buy you a drink, too.'

The old woman says, 'Thank you. Bartender, I want a Scotch with two drops of water.'

'Coming up,' says the bartender.

As she finishes that drink, the man to her left says, 'I would like to buy you one, too.'

The old woman says, 'Thank you. Bartender, I want another Scotch with two drops of water.'

'Coming right up,' the bartender says. As he gives her the drink, he says, 'Ma'am, I'm dying of curiosity. Why the Scotch with only two drops of water?'

The old woman replies, 'Sonny, when you're my age, you've learnt how to hold your liquor. Holding your water, however, is a whole other issue.'

17 DEATH, WHERE IS THY STING?

Nothing is as final as death. We all succumb to a final parting and it is therefore not surprising that we create and circulate humour about dying, death and the afterlife, be it there or not. You will find here jokes about knocking on heaven's gate, wacky wills, conniving relatives ('where there's a will there's a relative'), and how hell and heaven work. Remember: he who laughs last laughs best!

At the Pearly Gates

A man appeared before St Peter at the Pearly Gates.

'Have you ever done anything of particular merit?' St Peter asked.

'Well, I can think of one thing,' the man offered. 'On a trip to the Black Hills out near Canberra, I came upon a gang of high-testosterone bikers who were threatening a young woman. I directed them to leave her alone, but they wouldn't listen. So, I approached the largest and most heavily tattooed biker and smacked him on the head, kicked his bike over, and ripped out his nose ring and threw it on the ground. I yelled, "Now, back off! Or you'll answer to me!"'

St Peter was impressed. 'When did this happen?'

'Just a couple of minutes ago.'

Fatal accident

On their way to get married, a young couple are involved in a fatal car accident. The couple find themselves sitting outside the Pearly Gates waiting for St Peter to process them into heaven.

While waiting, they begin to wonder: could they possibly get married in heaven? When St Peter shows up, they ask him.

St Peter says, 'I don't know. This is the first time anyone has asked. Let me go and find out.' And he leaves.

The couple sit and wait for an answer — for a couple of months. While they wait, they discuss that *if* they are allowed to get married in heaven, *should* they get married, what with the eternal aspect of it all. 'What if it doesn't work?' they wonder. 'Are we stuck together *forever*?'

After yet another month, St Peter finally returns, looking somewhat bedraggled. 'Yes,' he informs the couple, 'you *can* get married in heaven.'

'Great!' say the couple. 'But we were just wondering, what if things don't work out? Could we also get a divorce in heaven?'

St Peter, red-faced with anger, slams his clipboard onto the ground.

'What's wrong?' ask the frightened couple.

'*Oh, come on!*' St Peter shouts. 'It took me three months to find a priest up here! Do you have *any* idea how long it'll take me to find a lawyer?'

Ducks

Three women die together in an accident and go to heaven.

When they get there, St Peter says, 'We only have one rule here in heaven: don't step on the ducks!'

So they enter heaven, and sure enough, there are ducks all over the place. It is almost impossible not to step on a duck, and although they try their best to avoid them, the first woman accidentally steps on one.

Along comes St Peter with the ugliest man she ever saw. St Peter chains them together and says, 'Your punishment for stepping on a duck is to spend eternity chained to this ugly man!'

The next day, the second woman accidentally steps on a duck and along comes St Peter, who doesn't miss a thing. With him is another extremely ugly man. He chains them together with the same admonishment as for the first woman.

The third woman has observed all this and, not wanting to be chained for all eternity to an ugly man, is very, *very* careful where she steps.

She manages to go months without stepping on any ducks, and one day St Peter comes up to her with the most handsome man she has ever laid eyes on — very tall, long eyelashes, muscular, and thin.

St Peter chains them together without saying a word.

The happy woman says, 'I wonder what I did to deserve being chained to you for all of eternity?'

The guy says, 'I don't know about you, but I stepped on a duck!'

Death, where is thy sting?

Three dead bodies turn up at the mortuary, all with very big smiles on their faces. The coroner calls the police to tell them his results after the examination.

'First body: Frenchman, 60, died of heart failure whilst making love to his girlfriend. Hence the enormous smile.

'Second body: Scotsman, 25, won a thousand pounds on the lottery, spent it all on whisky. Died of alcohol poisoning, hence the smile.'

The inspector asks, 'What of the third body?'

'Ah,' says the coroner, 'this is the most unusual one. Paddy from Belfast, 30, struck by lightning.'

'Why is he smiling then?' inquires the inspector.

'We suspect he thought he was having his picture taken.'

I smell the cheese scones

An elderly Queensland farmer lay dying in his bed. While suffering the agonies of impending death, he suddenly smelt the aroma of his favourite cheese scones wafting up the stairs. He gathered his remaining strength, and lifted himself from the bed. Leaning against the wall, he slowly made his way out of the bedroom, and with even greater effort, gripping the railing with both hands, he crawled downstairs. With laboured breath, he leant against the doorframe, gazing into the kitchen. Were it not for death's agony, he would have thought himself already in heaven, for here, spread out upon waxed paper on the kitchen table, were dozens of his favourite cheese scones.

Was it heaven? Or was it one final act of heroic love from his devoted wife of 60 years, seeing to it that he left this world a happy man?

Mustering one great final effort, he threw himself towards the table, landing on his knees in a rumpled posture. His parched lips parted, he could almost taste the cheese scone before it was in his mouth, seemingly bringing him back to life.

The aged and withered hand trembled on its way to the nearest scone at the edge of the table, when his wife suddenly smacked his hand with a spatula.

'Get off!' she screamed. 'They're for the funeral!'

Some band

Jerry Garcia dies. He wakes up and finds himself on a stage where a number of instruments are set up. A door offstage opens, and in walk Jimi Hendrix, Jim Morrison, Brian Jones, John Lennon, Otis Redding, and Buddy Holly.

Each musician picks up his favourite instrument and begins tuning up.

Jerry Garcia walks up to Jimi and says, 'Man, so this is what heaven is like.'

Jimi looks at him and says, 'Heaven? You think this is heaven?'

At that moment, Karen Carpenter walks in, takes her seat behind the drums, and calls out, 'OK, guys, "Close to You". One, two, three, four.'

Harley-Davidson

The co-founder of the Harley-Davidson motorcycle company, Arthur Davidson, died and went to heaven. At the gates, St Peter told Arthur, 'Since you've been such a good man and your motorcycles changed the world, your reward is that you can hang out with anyone you want in heaven.'

Arthur thought about it for a minute and then said, 'I want to hang out with God.'

St Peter took Arthur to the Throne Room, and introduced him to God.

God recognised Arthur and commented, 'OK, so you were the one who invented motorcycles, eh?'

Arthur said, 'Yeah, that's me …'

God commented, 'Well, what's the big deal in inventing something that's pretty unstable, makes noise and pollution, and can't run without a road?'

Arthur was apparently embarrassed but finally spoke, 'Excuse me but aren't you the inventor of *woman*?'

God said, 'Ah, yes.'

'Well,' said Arthur, 'professional-to-professional, you have some major design flaws in your invention:

1. There's too much inconsistency in the front-end protrusion.
2. It chatters constantly at high speeds.
3. Most of the rear ends are too soft and wobble too much.
4. The intake is placed way too close to the exhaust.
5. The maintenance costs are outrageous!'

'Hmm, you may have some good points there,' replied God. 'Hold on.'

God went to his celestial supercomputer, typed in a few words and waited for the results. The computer printed out a slip of paper and God read it. 'Well, it may be true that my invention is flawed,' God said to Arthur, 'but according to these numbers, more men are riding my invention than yours …'

Chatting with St Peter

An old lady dies and goes to heaven. She's chatting it up with St Peter at the Pearly Gates when all of a sudden she hears the most awful, blood-curdling screams.

'Don't worry about that,' says St Peter. 'It's only someone having the holes put into her shoulder blades for wings.'

The old lady looks a little uncomfortable but carries on with the conversation. Ten minutes later, there are more blood-curdling screams.

'Oh, my God!' says the old lady. 'Now what is happening?'

'Not to worry,' says St Peter. 'She's just having her head drilled to fit the halo.'

'I can't do this,' says the old lady. 'I'm going to hell.'

'You can't go there,' says St Peter. 'You'll be raped and sodomised.'

'Maybe so,' says the old lady, 'but I've already got the holes for that.'

Self-improvement

A mild-mannered man was tired of being bossed around by his wife; so he went to a psychiatrist. The psychiatrist said he needed to build his self-esteem, and gave him a book on assertiveness, which he read on the way home.

He had finished the book by the time he reached the house.

The man stormed into his home and walked up to his wife. Pointing a finger in her face, he said, 'From now on, I want you to know that I am the man of this house, and my word is law! I want you to prepare me a gourmet meal tonight, and when I'm finished eating my meal, I expect a sumptuous dessert afterwards. Then, after dinner, you're going to draw me my bath so I can relax. And, when I'm finished with my bath, guess who's going to dress me and comb my hair?'

'The funeral director,' said his wife.

Einstein, Picasso and Bush

Albert Einstein, Pablo Picasso and George W. Bush arrive at the Pearly Gates and introduce themselves. St Peter says, 'You'll have to prove to me that you are who you say you are.'

Einstein takes out a piece of paper and writes $e = mc^2$ and then starts writing the formulas that led him to it.

St Peter says, 'I believe you; come on in.'

Picasso takes out a pencil and paper and starts to draw.

St Peter says, 'I believe you; come on in.'

George W. Bush says to St Peter, 'Who were those guys?'

St Peter says, 'Come on in, George.'

Grieving

A woman had recently lost her husband. She had him cremated and brought his ashes home. Picking up the urn that he was in, she poured him out on the patio table. Then, while tracing her fingers in the ashes, she started talking to him.

'Irving, you know that fur coat you promised me? I bought it with the insurance money!

'Irving, remember that new car you promised me? Well, I also bought it with the insurance money!

'Irving, do you remember that emerald necklace you promised me? I bought it, too, with the insurance money.'

Still tracing her fingers in the ashes, she said, 'Irving, remember that blow job I promised you? Here it comes ...'

Death

Two blondes are in heaven. One blonde says to the other, 'How did you die?'

'I froze to death,' says the second.

'That's awful,' says the first blonde. 'How does it feel to freeze to death?'

'It's very uncomfortable at first,' says the second blonde. 'You get the shakes, and you get pains in all your fingers and toes. But eventually, it's a very calm way to go. You get numb and you kind of drift off, as if you're sleeping. How about you — how did you die?'

'I had a heart attack,' says the first blonde. 'You see, I knew my husband was cheating on me, so one day I showed up at home unexpectedly. I ran up to the bedroom, and found him alone watching TV. I ran to the basement, but no one was hiding there either. I ran to the second floor, but no one was hiding there either. I ran as fast as I could to the attic, and just as I got there, I had a massive heart attack and died.'

The second blonde shakes her head. 'What a pity ... if you had only looked in the freezer, we'd both still be alive.'

Irish cemetery

Three Irishmen, Paddy, Sean and Shamus, are stumbling home from the pub late one night and find themselves on the road that leads past the old graveyard.

'Come have a look over here,' says Paddy. 'It's Michael O'Grady's grave, God bless his soul. He lived to the ripe old age of 87.'

'That's nothing,' says Sean, 'here's one named Patrick O'Toole — it says here that he was 95 when he died.'

Just then, Shamus yells out, 'Good God, here's a fella that's 145!'

'What was his name?' asks Paddy.

Shamus stumbles around a bit, awkwardly lights a match to see what else is written on the stone marker, and exclaims: 'Miles, from Dublin.'

Condolences

Maggie lost her husband almost four years ago and still hasn't gotten out of her mourning stage. Her daughter is constantly calling her and urging her to get back into the world. Finally, Maggie says she'd go out, but she doesn't know anyone. Her daughter immediately replies, 'Mum! I have someone for you to meet.'

Well, they hit it off immediately. They take to one another and after dating for six weeks, he asks her to join him for a weekend in Thredbo. Their first night there, she undresses, as he does. There she stands, nude except for a pair of black lacy panties, he in his birthday suit. Looking at her he asks, 'Why the black panties?'

She replies, 'My breasts you can fondle, my body is yours to explore, but down there I am still in mourning.'

He knows he's not getting lucky that night.

The following evening it's the same scenario: she's standing there with the black panties on, and he is in his birthday suit, except that on his erection he has a black condom. She looks at him and asks, 'What's with this ... a black condom?'

He replies, 'I want to offer my deepest condolences.'

Heavenly banquet

After a long illness, a woman died and arrived at the Gates of Heaven. As she was waiting for St Peter, she peeked through the Pearly Gates. She saw a beautiful banquet table. Sitting around were her parents and many other people she had loved and who had died before her. Then they saw her and began calling greetings to her — 'Hello!' 'How are you? We've been waiting for you!' 'Good to see you!' and so on.

Then St Peter arrived and the woman said to him, 'This looks like such a wonderful place! How do I get in?'

'You have to spell a word,' St Peter told her.

'Which word?' she asked.

'Love.'

The woman correctly spelled 'Love' and St Peter welcomed her into heaven.

Less than a year later, St Peter came to the woman and asked her to watch the Gates of Heaven for him for a few hours. Strange as it seems, while the woman was standing guard, her husband arrived.

'I'm so surprised to see you,' the woman said. 'You were so robust and healthy? How have you been? What happened?'

'Oh, I'd been doing pretty well since you died,' her husband told her. 'I married the beautiful, young, blonde nurse who took care of you while you were ill. And then I won the lottery. I sold that little house that you and I lived in all our lives, and I bought a big mansion. And my new wife and I travelled all around the world. We were on holiday and I went water skiing today. I fell, the ski hit my head, and here I am. I am still in a state of shock, but since I am here, how do I get in?'

'It is simple, you just have to spell a word,' she told him.

'Oh, that sounds easy. Which word?' her husband asked.

'Czechoslovakia,' came the immediate response.

Death sting

A woman's husband dies. He has only $50,000 to his name. After everything is done at the funeral home and cemetery, she tells her closest friend that there is no money left.

The friend says, 'How can that be? You told me he still had $50,000 a few days before he died. How could you be broke?'

The widow says, 'Well, the funeral home cost $8000. And, of course, I made the obligatory donation to the temple, so that was another $2000. The rest went for the memorial stone.'

The friend says, '$40,000 for the memorial stone? My God, how big is the stone?'

Extending her left hand, the widow says, 'Three carats.'

Tap tap tap

A taxi passenger tapped the driver on the shoulder to ask him a question. The driver screamed, lost control of the car, nearly hit a bus, went up on the footpath, and stopped centimetres from a shop window. For a second everything went quiet in the cab, then the driver said, 'Look, mate, don't ever do that again. You scared the daylights out of me!'

The passenger apologised and said, 'I didn't realise that a little tap would scare you so much.'

The driver replied, 'Sorry, it's not really your fault. Today is my first day as a cab driver — I've been driving a hearse for the last 25 years.'

Spooks

The husband dies, and 30 days later the wife makes contact via a medium. 'What's it like over there?' asks the wife.

The husband explains: 'I wake at 5 a.m., have sex until 8 a.m., then eat my breakfast, then I return to having sex until lunchtime. I eat my lunch, then return to having sex until dinner. I eat my dinner, then continue having sex until 3 a.m., when I sleep for two hours; then off I go again.'

'Wow!' said the wife. 'Heaven sounds wonderful.'

'Heaven?' replied the husband. 'I'm a rabbit in Dubbo.'

ABOUT THE AUTHOR

Warren Fahey claims a degree from the School of Hard Knocks and the Dingo University. He is a folklorist, broadcaster, performer of bush songs and the author of several books, including the best-selling *Bush Yarns*.